Shakespeare's Roman Trilogy

Shakespeare's Roman Trilogy

The Twilight of the Ancient World

PAUL A. CANTOR

The University of Chicago Press
Chicago and London

The University of Chicago Press, Chicago 60637
The University of Chicago Press, Ltd., London
© 2017 by The University of Chicago
All rights reserved. Published 2017
Printed in the United States of America

26 25 24 23 22 21 20 19 18 17   1 2 3 4 5

ISBN-13: 978-0-226-46248-6 (cloth)
ISBN-13: 978-0-226-46251-6 (paper)
ISBN-13: 978-0-226-46265-3 (e-book)
DOI: 10.7208/chicago/9780226462653.001.0001

Library of Congress Cataloging-in-Publication Data

Names: Cantor, Paul A. (Paul Arthur), 1945– author.
Title: Shakespeare's Roman trilogy : the twilight of the ancient world / Paul A. Cantor.
Description: Chicago ; London : The University of Chicago Press, 2017. | Includes
    bibliographical references and index.
Identifiers: LCCN 2016049357 | ISBN 9780226462486 (cloth : alk. paper) |
    ISBN 9780226462516 (pbk. : alk. paper) | ISBN 9780226462653 (e-book)
Subjects: LCSH: Shakespeare, William, 1564–1616—Knowledge—Rome. |
    Rome—In literature. | Nietzsche, Friedrich Wilhelm, 1844–1900.
Classification: LCC PR3069.R6 C29 2017 | DDC 822.3/3—dc23 LC record available at
    https://lccn.loc.gov/2016049357

Contents

Introduction: Shakespeare's Rome Revisited

In publishing a second book on Shakespeare's Roman plays, I am confessing to a lifelong fascination with Shakespeare and Rome. My first serious encounter with Shakespeare occurred in junior high school, when we studied *Julius Caesar*. At the time, the play struck me as the most wonderful literary work I had ever read, and it deepened an interest I had already developed in classical antiquity as a result of my childhood love of Greek and Roman mythology. Our class project on the play led me to read whatever I could find about ancient Rome. In my junior year of college, I took a course that dealt with the theory and practice of the Roman Republic. For that course, I wrote a paper on *Coriolanus* entitled "The Rulerless City and the Citiless Man," which eventually provided the basis for my doctoral dissertation, which in turn provided the basis for my first book, *Shakespeare's Rome: Republic and Empire*. The first course I ever gave on my own centered on the Roman plays. I have taught them regularly ever since and have given lectures and seminars on them at a wide variety of institutions while continuing to publish on the subject. My interest in Rome has continued unabated. I have visited the actual city twice and toured Roman ruins all the way from Manchester, England, to Chersonesus in Sevastopol, Ukraine. I make no apologies for returning again and again to the subjects of Shakespeare and Rome. Either one would justify a lifetime of study, and together they have allowed me to combine my interests in literature, history, art, architecture, archaeology, politics, and philosophy. My obsessions with Rome and Shakespeare have fed on each other. The more I have studied Shakespeare's plays, the more I have learned about Rome, and the more I have studied Rome, the more I have been able to find in the Roman plays. This new book on the subject is the result of all these endeavors.

As I bring out a second book on the Roman plays, I wish that I could make a dramatic announcement, repudiating my first book as a youthful indiscretion and claiming to have gotten the subject right only in my maturity. But even after four decades, I am prepared to stand by *Shakespeare's Rome*. To be sure, I have learned a great deal more about the Roman plays in many years' of teaching them, constantly rereading them and puzzling over the details. I wrote this new book to offer fresh insights into *Coriolanus*, *Julius Caesar*, and *Antony and Cleopatra*, especially into the many ways that the three plays fit together. But *Shakespeare's Roman Trilogy* is not meant to replace *Shakespeare's Rome*; it is meant to supplement it. Although the two books inevitably overlap at times, they develop different perspectives on the subject. For example, *Shakespeare's Rome* contains a fuller analysis of the way that the Roman republican regime operates in *Coriolanus* than I offer in *Shakespeare's Roman Trilogy*. I also analyze the character of Coriolanus in greater depth in my earlier book. To anyone who may complain that I do not deal at length with the love of Antony and Cleopatra in this new book, I will point out that two of the six chapters of *Shakespeare's Rome*—"The Liberation of Eros" and "Love and Tyranny"—are devoted to just that topic. These two books are complementary, and at many times in this new one I refer my readers to aspects of the subject I develop more fully in *Shakespeare's Rome*.[1]

Still, *Shakespeare's Roman Trilogy* is designed to be an independent work, and one need not have read *Shakespeare's Rome* to follow its argument. Nevertheless, I should describe the ways in which this new book develops out of, and advances beyond, the old one. In writing my first book, I tried to keep its claims as modest and manageable as possible. *Shakespeare's Rome* is largely devoted to discussing *Coriolanus* and *Antony and Cleopatra* as contrasting portraits of the Roman Republic and the Roman Empire. As a result, I wrote very little about *Julius Caesar* in my first book. I did suggest at the time that *Julius Caesar* provides the lynchpin of a historical trilogy that begins with *Coriolanus* and ends with *Antony and Cleopatra*, a trilogy that portrays the rise and fall of the Roman Republic. In that story, *Julius Caesar* is central. Due to space limitations and other considerations, I did not feel that I could adequately develop my argument about the Roman plays as a trilogy in my first book. Thus, *Shakespeare's Roman Trilogy* fulfills a promise I made four decades ago. In this new book, I give equal time to *Julius Caesar* and integrate my analysis of the play into my discussion of *Coriolanus* and *Antony and Cleopatra*. Rather than treating each play separately, I move back and forth among the three to show how Shakespeare builds on a grand scale, creating what amounts to a trilogy out of the plays.[2]

Another principal development in *Shakespeare's Roman Trilogy* is that I have brought the Nietzschean subtext of *Shakespeare's Rome* out in the open. Early in my work on the Roman plays, I realized that Friedrich Nietzsche's understanding of what he calls the revaluation of values in ancient Rome provides important clues to how to read Shakespeare's works, especially *Antony and Cleopatra*.[3] As I spell out in this book, the buried theme of Shakespeare's Roman plays is the way that the dissolution of the Roman republican regime prepared the way for the rise of Christianity in the Roman Empire. Even today I suspect that many will find this claim far-fetched, and those willing to entertain it may nevertheless rule out the possibility that Nietzsche's idea of the slave revolt in morality could have any bearing on *Antony and Cleopatra*. In the early 1970s, I had even greater doubts about the advisability of openly using Nietzsche's thought as a guide to Shakespeare's. Accordingly, the buried theme of the Roman plays became the buried theme of *Shakespeare's Rome*.

I did not, however, completely conceal my debt to Nietzsche in my first book. Indeed, I thought that the two long quotations from *Beyond Good and Evil* that serve as epigraphs to parts 1 and 2 of *Shakespeare's Rome* would provide clues to the Nietzschean dimension of my argument. But none of the published comments on the book called attention to the Nietzsche epigraphs or to my covert discussion of the importance of Christianity in *Antony and Cleopatra*, largely carried out in the notes.[4] One of my major goals in *Shakespeare's Roman Trilogy* is to make my debt to Nietzsche explicit. I believe that the conjunction of the Renaissance playwright and the German philosopher—however implausible a pair they may seem at first to form— will serve to illuminate the thoughts of both. Nietzsche sheds light on several aspects of Shakespeare's Roman plays, but they in turn can serve to clarify several controversial issues in Nietzsche's philosophy.

I am well aware that conventional scholarship would dictate that I forget about Nietzsche and analyze Shakespeare's work only in its immediate historical context, that is, in light of the understanding of Rome developed by his Elizabethan and Jacobean contemporaries.[5] While recognizing the value of such an approach, I am trying a thought experiment in this book: to see what happens if we expand the intellectual framework in which we view Shakespeare's Roman plays. I regard Shakespeare as one of the most profound thinkers on the subject of ancient Rome. I therefore judge him worthy of being studied in conjunction with other profound thinkers on Rome, including Nietzsche, as well as someone who may have anticipated—and possibly influenced—both, Niccolò Machiavelli.

Chapter 1, "Shakespeare's Tragic City: The Rise and Fall of the Roman Republic," forms the heart of this book. Moving back and forth among *Coriolanus*, *Julius Caesar*, and *Antony and Cleopatra*, I argue that Shakespeare's

Roman trilogy portrays the tragedy of an entire political community, not just that of its individual heroes. Tragically, the Roman Republic is corrupted and eventually destroyed by its very success in the military and political realms. In conquering the Mediterranean world, the Republic transforms into the Empire, and in the process, it reduces its once-proud citizens into the humble subjects of an imperial regime, thereby foreclosing the grand possibilities for martial heroism it originally created. But at the same time, the dissolution of the republican regime opens up new realms of human experience and aspiration, ranging from the erotic possibilities represented by Antony and Cleopatra to novel forms of spiritual yearning that foreshadow the rise of Christianity in the Roman world. *Antony and Cleopatra* portrays an ethical transformation of the Roman aristocracy that prefigures the revaluation of values that Nietzsche associates with Christianity. The changed conditions of the Empire produce a series of paradoxes: defeat becomes victory, weakness becomes strength, and death becomes life. Octavius Caesar eventually comes to speak paradoxically of "noble weakness" (5.2.344) in the kind of inversion of classical values that Nietzsche called the slave revolt in morality.[6]

Thus, in a remarkable act of imaginative archaeology, Shakespeare uncovers in *Coriolanus* what it was like to live in an ancient city with its republican institutions, civic gods, narrow horizons, and a pagan focus on this-worldly existence.[7] In an equally remarkable act of historical imagination, in *Julius Caesar* and *Antony and Cleopatra* Shakespeare dramatizes the death of the ancient city and the emergence of a new form of life on an imperial scale, with much broader horizons, which even encompass visions of the afterlife. The Empire transforms the relation of the individual to the political community in ways that anticipate what we think of as the medieval and modern worlds, with a growing division between religion and politics and an increasing distance between ruler and ruled that is simultaneously alienating and liberating.

I should explain why I am confining my discussion to *Coriolanus, Julius Caesar,* and *Antony and Cleopatra.* Several critics have worked to expand the category of Shakespeare's Roman plays to include *Titus Andronicus* and *Cymbeline,* and some have brought in the poem *The Rape of Lucrece* as a kind of prequel to *Coriolanus.*[8] I have read these critics with profit, I admire their work, and I have no objections to their efforts to expand our knowledge of Shakespeare's understanding of Rome. I still, however, believe that *Coriolanus, Julius Caesar,* and *Antony and Cleopatra* retain a special and separate status among Shakespeare's works about Rome.[9] As the three plays with a common source in Plutarch's *Lives,* they are more securely grounded in historical facts about Rome than the other works.[10] Moreover, as I am trying to show in this book, these three plays are tightly integrated into a trilogy, with a remarkable continuity of themes and elaborate cross-referencing of motifs.[11] For my purposes, *Coriolanus*, *Julius Caesar*, and *Antony and Cleopatra* provide enough material for one book. Having decided to restrict myself to the three plays that I believe form a trilogy, I console myself with the thought that, as far as I can tell, nothing that my colleagues have uncovered in Shakespeare's other Roman works significantly contradicts what I have to say about my chosen three. If anything, *Titus Andronicus* confirms what I argue about Shakespeare's understanding of the corruption and decadence of the Roman Empire. Indeed, it shows the Romans of the late Empire becoming indistinguishable from the barbarians against whom they claim to be defending Rome.

In working on Chapter 2, "'The Roman Caesar with Christ's Soul': Shakespeare and Nietzsche on Rome and Christianity," I read widely in both the works Nietzsche published in his lifetime and his notebooks. I found that his ideas about Rome and Christianity are more complicated than many have supposed—and at times they are even contradictory. Moreover, I discovered that the central issue of chapter 2—what exactly is the mechanism of the slave revolt in morality as Nietzsche understands it?—is a much debated topic in Nietzsche scholarship. I was pleased that, using Shakespeare's Roman plays, I could shed new light on this controversy and in particular highlight the importance of a divided and corrupt class of masters in Nietzsche's full account of how slave morality was able to overcome the aristocracy's seemingly all-powerful domination in the ancient world. Shakespeare shows that what Nietzsche calls the slave revolt actually began among the aristocratic Roman masters, who became slavish under the rule of the Caesars.

I also examine Nietzsche's idea of hybrid forms of master and slave morality and use Shakespeare's plays, especially *Henry V*, *Hamlet*, *Othello*, and *Macbeth*, to illustrate this possibility. In the process, I show how my work on the Roman plays links up with what I have written about other works by Shakespeare, especially in my book on *Hamlet*. Engaging Shakespeare and Nietzsche in dialogue helps to counteract a common and oversimplified view of Nietzsche, that he simply rejected Christianity in the name of classical values. The way that Christianity opens up new depths in the souls of Shakespearean heroes such as Hamlet, Othello, and Macbeth illustrates what Nietzsche means when he says in *The Genealogy of Morals* that only the priests and the slave revolt in morality made man into an interesting animal.

The two chapters that constitute part 1, "Shakespeare, Nietzsche, and the Revaluation of Roman Values," were written especially for this book and form the core of its new contribution to the study of the Roman plays. The four chapters that constitute part 2, "Further Explorations of Shakespeare's Rome," were written earlier and branch off from my main argument in different directions while offering further evidence that the Roman plays form a trilogy and that Shakespeare was rooted in the classical tradition. Chapters 4, 5, and 6 have already been published, although they have been thoroughly revised and expanded for this volume. Chapter 3 was written earliest; it grows out of what was originally intended to be the conclusion of *Shakespeare's Rome*. Forty years ago, it was cut for reasons of length; now it serves to represent the continuity between my two books. Each of these chapters discusses the Roman plays in a different context and thus opens up a fresh perspective on Shakespeare's achievement. At the risk of some repetition, I have tried to keep each chapter self-contained, and, accordingly, they can be read in any order, depending on the reader's particular interests.

Chapter 3, "Beasts and Gods: Titanic Heroes and the Tragedy of Rome," offers another way of viewing the Roman plays as a trilogy. I discuss tyranny as one of the unifying themes of the three plays and analyze the ways in which Coriolanus, Julius Caesar, and Mark Antony all try to achieve mastery over Rome and eventually a kind of universal recognition of their heroic greatness. At the center of the chapter is Aristotle's provocative claim in his *Politics* that a human being without a city is either a beast or a god. In their quest to achieve self-sufficiency and independence from the city, each of Shakespeare's Roman heroes finds that he is entering uncharted and dangerous territory. Wishing to rise above the ordinary human condition, they threaten to sink below it. Accordingly, Shakespeare associates all three heroes with a complex of god and beast imagery that symbolizes the ambivalence and precariousness of their quest to go beyond the ancient city. The titanic striving of the Roman heroes is modeled on the ambitions of Rome itself as a warrior city. In seeking to conquer the entire Mediterranean world and trying to achieve political universality, the Republic undermines the principles that made Rome great in the first place and ends up destroying itself. Like chapter 1, chapter 3 argues that in the Roman plays Shakespeare correlates the tragedies of his individual heroes with the larger tragedy of Rome itself. Finally, this chapter draws out some of the larger implications for understanding Shakespeare's works that follow from regarding the Roman plays as a trilogy.

Since so much of this book is devoted to analyzing Shakespeare's relation to the classical tradition, in chapter 4, "Shakespeare's Parallel Lives: Plutarch and the Roman Plays," I offer a case study in Shakespeare's use of classical sources. It examines the many ways in which Shakespeare drew upon the Greek historian in crafting his Roman plays and suggests how Plutarch's enterprise can help to understand the unity of *Coriolanus*, *Julius Caesar*, and

Antony and Cleopatra as a trilogy. I trace the way that Shakespeare's read-ing in Plutarch's *Lives* may have led him to pair *Coriolanus* with *Antony and Cleopatra* as contrasting portraits of republic and empire and thus as parallel lives in the Plutarchan sense. I have added to the original published version a discussion of the ways that Plutarch may have contributed to Shakespeare's understanding of the ancient Greek concept of the regime (*politeia*)—the idea that a particular form of government shapes a particular way of life. Also new to this version is a discussion of Plutarch's position as a cosmopolitan Greek living in the Roman Empire. His personal dilemma points to the is-sue of city (*polis*) versus empire that I present as a central concern in Shake-speare's Roman plays.

Continuing my discussion of Shakespeare in relation to the ancient world, chapter 5, "Shakespeare and the Mediterranean: The Centrality of the Clas-sical Tradition in the Renaissance," explores the geography of Shakespeare's imagination. I argue for the centrality of the Mediterranean in a map of Shakespeare's imaginative universe. Given the fact that some twenty of his plays have Mediterranean settings, this may not seem to be a controversial claim. But I am trying to counteract a tendency, especially among American critics, to place the Atlantic at the center of Shakespeare's geography. It is un-derstandable that American critics want to link Shakespeare with New World studies, and they have been able to use *The Tempest*, in particular, to raise the issue of colonialism and the Atlantic slave trade. But even *The Tempest* is squarely set in the Mediterranean and draws deeply on classical sources, with its allusions to Virgil and Ovid. The centrality of the Mediterranean in geographic terms in Shakespeare's plays points to the centrality of the classi-cal tradition in historical terms.

One of the larger aims of this book is to reassert the central importance of the classical tradition in understanding Shakespeare, a goal I share with several other scholars.[12] For a variety of reasons, in the past few decades the classical tradition has been losing its importance in American higher educa-tion, while contemporary American cultural concerns have been in the as-cendancy. The result is to mine Shakespeare's plays for what they might tell us about today's political and social issues. As valuable as these studies have been, the unfortunate result is often to lose sight of whole areas of human experience that preoccupied Shakespeare, including his fascination with the distinctive character of the ancient Roman world. As I argue in this book, Shakespeare deliberately turned to Rome to find an alternative to his own world, to portray aspects of human nature that the ancient city developed more fully than any modern community.

One sign of the reorientation of Shakespeare studies is the widespread use of the term "early modern" to replace "Renaissance." This may seem like a mere matter of semantics, but it actually has broad implications. Scholars have been gravitating toward the term "early modern" because it is forward-looking. It suggests that Shakespeare's concerns point ahead to our own—in his plays we can view the beginnings of developments that culminate in our own late modern era. "Renaissance" is clearly a backward-looking term. It refers to "rebirth," and that means the revival of classical antiquity in Shakespeare's Europe. To speak of the "early modern period" is to orient our study of Shakespeare by our contemporary concerns; to use the term "Renaissance" is to view his plays as an attempt to relate the Europe of his day to the ancient world.

The Roman plays are the greatest monument to Shakespeare's fascination with the ancient world and the ways that it differed from the modern. *Coriolanus*, *Julius Caesar*, and *Antony and Cleopatra* may well be the pinnacle of Renaissance efforts to reach deep into antiquity and bring it back to life. Throughout this book I use the term "Renaissance" in recognition of the fact that Shakespeare was a "Renaissance" figure in the traditional meaning of the term. To understand his world, he constantly harked back to classical antiquity, drawing upon its wisdom, its models, and its historical examples. The term "Renaissance" glorifies the period—it suggests that it had its own integrity and that it represents a peak of human achievement. We speak in awe of "Renaissance man," but who can feel inspired by talk about "early modern man"? The term "early modern" diminishes and deglamorizes the period. It suggests that it was merely a stage on the way to full modernity, as if Raphael's paintings represent the faint stirrings of artistic impulses that culminate only in Andy Warhol's. I hope that this book will help to rehabilitate the term "Renaissance" and to restore the importance of the classical tradition in understanding Shakespeare.[13]

Finally, in chapter 6, "*Antony and Cleopatra*: Empire, Globalization, and the Clash of Civilizations," I proceed from my analysis in chapter 5 of the multicultural civilization of the Mediterranean to offer my own way of relating the Roman plays to contemporary concerns. Drawing upon historical studies of the Romanization of the Mediterranean world, I read *Antony and Cleopatra* as a portrait of what is today known as globalization. In dramatizing the clash of civilizations, Shakespeare juxtaposes the Romanizing of Egypt with the Egyptianizing of Rome, thereby showing that what we call globalization is a two-way street. In particular, *Antony and Cleopatra* suggests that the military victor in such conflicts does not necessarily prevail in the cultural competition. In imperialist encounters, the metropolitan center (in this case, Rome) may be altered even more than the colonized periphery (in this case, Egypt). The way Cleopatra seduces Antony away from the traditional Romanness of the Republic symbolizes the larger movement in the play. Rome succumbs to the enticements of a foreign and imperial way of life, including mystery religions out of the East.

The importance of the East in *Antony and Cleopatra* means that another contemporary concern—Orientalism—surfaces in the play, and indeed, Shakespeare engages with a number of the issues that animate postcolonialist criticism today. At a very early stage in the evolution of the British Empire, Shakespeare develops a number of Orientalist stereotypes that were to be deployed at the peak of British imperialism in the nineteenth century. Cleopatra is a good example of the stereotype of the Oriental despot, as well as of the Oriental temptress (a motif that recurs all the way from Dido in Virgil's *Aeneid* to Rider Haggard's *She* in the nineteenth century). In the story of Mark Antony, Shakespeare anticipates the kind of "going native" narrative that later was to feature in the imperialist romances of authors such as Robert Louis Stevenson, Rudyard Kipling, and Joseph Conrad. Having spent much of this book looking backward to classical antiquity, in the final chapter I show that I too can look forward. I relate the apocalyptic mood of *Antony and Cleopatra* to a similar sense of civilization-wide crisis in the modernist poetry of W. B. Yeats (especially the millennial "The Second Coming"), and even show that the Marx-Engels motto for modernity—"all that is solid melts into air"—could just as well describe Shakespeare's portrait of the world of the ancient city dissolving at the turn of an earlier millennium. For all my interest in the classical past, I am also intrigued by the many ways in which Shakespeare's plays anticipate our contemporary concerns.

That is a brief outline of the subjects I take up in this book in my continuing efforts to uncover what Shakespeare has to say about Rome. In *Shakespeare's Rome*, I challenged the widespread opinion that Shakespeare's Roman plays do not reflect any special knowledge of Rome and are not even particularly about Rome. This opinion has a venerable pedigree—it was maintained by Samuel Johnson and Johann Wolfgang von Goethe. They both argue that Shakespeare's Romans are basically English people dressed up in togas. Such skeptics are able to point to anachronisms in the Roman plays that suggest that Shakespeare was ignorant of some details of Roman daily life—for example, Shakespeare's plebeians wear caps, as if they were English tradespeople.[14] But these are trivial details of dress, which have no bearing on the essential character of Shakespeare's Romans. When it comes to a serious issue such as suicide, Shakespeare knew perfectly well how to differentiate his ancient Romans from the modern Christians in his plays. Consider the way he has Horatio signal his eagerness to follow his friend Hamlet into death: "I am more an antique Roman than a Dane" (5.2.341).[15]

Fortunately, the opinion that Shakespeare knew a good deal about ancient Rome also has a venerable pedigree. As early as 1725, Alexander Pope, in his preface to his edition of Shakespeare's plays, writes, "We find him very knowing in the customs, rites, and manners of Antiquity. In *Coriolanus* and *Julius Caesar*, not only the Spirit, but Manners of the *Romans* are exactly drawn; and still a nicer distinction is shown, between the manners of the *Romans* in the time of the former, and of the latter."[16] I like to think of my writings on the Roman plays as working out Pope's suggestion that Shakespeare was aware of the vast differences between the Rome of the early Republic and Rome in the last days of the Republic. The fact that Shakespeare displays such genuine knowledge of ancient Rome is what emboldens me to lift him out of his limited historical moment and discuss him in dialogue with analysts of Rome from Machiavelli to Nietzsche. If Shakespeare had access—in whatever form—to the historical reality of Rome, then his views on the subject can be profitably compared with those of other thinkers, no matter how remote they may be from him in time and space. The important question is not who influenced whom, but: what can we learn by comparing what they all have to say about their common subject, Rome?

Shakespeare in fact fits into a long tradition of thinking about ancient Rome, one that begins in late antiquity and extends through thinkers such as Machiavelli, Montesquieu, Hegel, and Nietzsche down to the present day. Initiated by Roman statesmen, philosophers, and historians themselves, this tradition focuses, as Shakespeare does, on the contrast between the Roman Republic and the Roman Empire and thus views the events surrounding Julius Caesar's assassination as the great turning point in Roman history.[17] This tradition is largely republican in spirit, and indeed, advocates of republican government often turn to Roman history for guidance (as witness the fact that one of the houses of Congress in the United States is called the Senate).[18] This understanding of Roman history views the Empire in political terms as a massive falling off from the Republic. It offers the early Republic as an example of noble politics, in which the common good prevails, uncorrupted by private interests. By contrast, the republican tradition regards the Empire as having been corrupted by its wealth, allowing private interests to prevail over the common good. This tradition generally views the change from Republic to Empire as sudden and abrupt, and draws the contrast between the two regimes as sharply as possible. The republican tradition emphasizes virtue, not happiness. That is, it does not ask whether people are happier under republics than under empires, but whether they are more disposed to practice the civic virtues and contribute to public life. Thus, in this tradition the opulence of the Roman Empire is not an argument in its favor, and the comparative poverty of the Republic is not an argument against it.

Shakespeare's near contemporary, the French political thinker Jean Bodin (1530–1596), encapsulates this understanding of Rome in the republican tradition:

> I hold a commonwealth to be in its prime when it has reached the highest pitch of perfection and of achievement of which it is capable, or, perhaps more accurately, when it is at its least imperfect. This can only be judged after its decline and fall. Rome passed through the stages of monarchy, tyranny, aristocracy, and popular government, but it reached its highest perfection as a popular state, and during that phase of its history it was never so illustrious in arms and in laws as in the time of Papirius Cursor [circa 325 BCE]. . . . Never after that time was military and domestic discipline so well maintained, faith better kept, the rites of religion more piously observed, vice more severely punished; never afterwards could it boast such valiant citizens. If it is objected that it was still poor and confined within the frontiers of Italy, I would answer that one cannot measure excellence by riches, nor perfection by the extent of the conquered territories. The Romans were never more powerful, rich, and mighty than under the emperor Trajan. He crossed the Euphrates and conquered a great part of Arabia Felix, built a bridge over the Danube whose ruins we can still see, and humbled the barbarous and savage people of those times. Nevertheless ambition, avarice, and luxury had so corrupted the Romans that they only retained a shadow of their ancient virtue.[19]

As Bodin makes clear, republican theorists do not care how pleasant it may have been to live under a benevolent Roman emperor. Despotism is still despotism, no matter how benevolent, and in the republican tradition, nothing can compensate for the loss of freedom and virtue.

This understanding of Roman history appears frequently in literature. Two prominent examples occur in famous works, John Milton's *Paradise Regained* and Jonathan Swift's *Gulliver's Travels*. When Satan tempts Jesus in Book IV of *Paradise Regained*, the devil tries to seduce him with the prospect of the imperial throne. But Milton's Jesus rejects the Roman Empire as a swamp of corruption, the antithesis of the glory days of the noble and freedom-loving Republic:

> For him I was not sent, nor yet to free
> That people victor once, now vile and base,
> Deservedly made vassal, who once just,
> Frugal, and mild, and temperate, conquer'd well,

But govern ill the Nations under yoke,
Peeling their Provinces, exhausted all
By lust and rapine; first ambitious grown
Of triumph that insulting vanity;
Then cruel, by their sports to blood inur'd
Of fighting beasts, and men to beasts expos'd,
Luxurious by thir wealth, and greedier still,
And from the daily Scene effeminate.
What wise and valiant man would seek to free
These thus degenerate, by themselves enslav'd,
Or could of inward slaves make outward free?[20]

One can recognize the decadent imperial world of *Antony and Cleopatra* in Milton's diatribe against the Rome of the Caesars, especially the transformation of republican citizens into imperial subjects. Note that for Milton the corruption of imperial Rome is not a gradual process. Already in the time of Jesus (which means the first decades of the Empire), Rome has lost its virtue and sunk into slavish decadence.

Swift suggests something similar in Book III of *Gulliver's Travels*, when Gulliver journeys to Glubbdubdrib and gets to raise up spirits from the past to learn firsthand about famous historical events. He meets a Roman naval commander who fought bravely at the Battle of Actium and led Octavius Caesar's fleet against Mark Antony's. But far from being rewarded with a distinguished post for his military accomplishments, the Roman sees the honor go to an unqualified court favorite and is unjustly charged with "neglect of duty" by Augustus's associates. Gulliver comments: "I was surprized to find Corruption grown so high and so quick in that Empire, by the Force of Luxury so lately introduced."[21] Swift in *Gulliver's Travels*, just as Shakespeare does in *Antony and Cleopatra*, views Rome as having already lost its nobility by the time of the Battle of Actium—that is, just as one-man rule was emerging in the community.[22] I could multiply these examples, but perhaps two writers as diverse as Milton and Swift are enough to suggest that Shakespeare was working in a broad tradition when he portrayed the Roman Empire as already corrupt at the time of its founding in *Antony and Cleopatra*.[23]

I dwell on the long and widespread tradition of sharply contrasting the Republic and the Empire to defend myself against the charge that I am the one oversimplifying this opposition. Whenever one sees a claim such as "The Republic was noble; the Empire was corrupt," the temptation to find counterexamples becomes overwhelming and one seeks for instances of corruption in the Republic and of nobility in the Empire. Both are not hard to find. The Roman Empire could not have lasted as many centuries as it did without some nobility and public spiritedness surviving in its ruling class (particularly in the military). "Good" emperors, such as Trajan, Hadrian, and Marcus Aurelius, balanced the "bad" ones in Roman history, and even the "bad" may not have been quite as bad as pro-republican historians like Tacitus made them out to be.[24] By the same token, not all Romans in the Republic, even in its heyday, were purely noble; some pursued their own ends at the expense of the common good (Coriolanus, after all, became a traitor to his native city).

Having made all these necessary qualifications, one can still reasonably speak of a broad contrast between the Roman Republic and the Roman Empire. These two regimes are ideal types and as such have functioned in political discourse for centuries.[25] Modern historians may wish to question this traditional way of thinking about Roman history and emphasize the continuities between the Republic and the Empire, rather than the differences. But the tradition Shakespeare inherited highlighted the contrast between the Republic and the Empire, and Shakespeare chose to follow this tradition in the Roman plays. In *Julius Caesar*, the death of the Republic strikes the surviving Romans as the death of Rome itself. They see a world coming to an end— "the sun of Rome is set" (5.3.63)—not the dawning of a new day or a smooth transition to a new, imperial regime.

In an important book, *The Roman Revolution*, historian Ronald Syme analyzes the ways in which Augustus Caesar in fact tried to smooth this transition and paper over his abrupt break with the republican regime. Augustus sought to give his new regime as much of the appearance of the old as possible. Accordingly, he retained many of the old republican institutions, such as the Senate and the consulship, but adapted them to the new imperial regime, often filling the old republican positions with his cronies or even assuming the titles himself. Shakespeare ignores this aspect of Roman history and does everything he can to emphasize the discontinuities between the Republic and the Empire. One would be hard pressed to find evidence in *Antony and Cleopatra* that the Senate in fact survived the death of the Republic. As Shakespeare portrays Rome in *Antony and Cleopatra*, it plunges headlong into decadence at the very beginning of the Empire, with barely a reminder of the republican era. Mark Antony, with his tyrannical impulses, tendency to self-dramatization and self-aggrandizement, and sensual indulgence, provides a foretaste of what was soon to come in imperial Rome: his lineal descendants Caligula and Nero.[26]

In short, if in my writings about the Roman plays I have stressed the contrast between the Republic and the Empire, the reason is that Shakespeare does, and he was hardly the only one to do so. The republican political tradi-

tion is founded on rejecting the corruption and decadence of imperial regimes, as we just saw in Milton's *Paradise Regained*. Milton was of course a
great champion of republics in theoretical and practical terms. Shakespeare's
position on republican government is much harder to determine. Most commentators on the subject have assumed that Shakespeare must have supported monarchical government. Indeed, he is often presented as a staunch
and unthinking champion of the Tudor dynasty in England. In recent decades, critics have begun to explore the possibility that Shakespeare's political
position may have been more complex than has traditionally been assumed.
Some have argued that Shakespeare's political thinking may have been subtly
subversive and undermined traditional support for monarchy.[27] In *Shakespeare and Republicanism*, Andrew Hadfield argues that Shakespeare was in
fact in favor of republican government, and he presents solid evidence in
support of this controversial thesis.[28]

Still, it is difficult to read Shakespeare's practical political position out of
his plays. I will confine myself to saying that if we judge simply by the subjects
of his plays, Shakespeare displays an unusual interest in republican government, both in ancient Rome (*Coriolanus* and *Julius Caesar*) and in the modern commercial republic of Venice (*The Merchant of Venice* and *Othello*).[29]
In the absence of any concrete historical evidence, we may never know what
kind of regime Shakespeare believed best for the England of his day. But it
is difficult to read his history plays and view him as an *uncritical* supporter
of monarchy. The plays uncover too many political weaknesses of monarchy, especially the problem of a secure and reliable succession (too often, a
Henry V is followed by a Henry VI). If Shakespeare supported monarchy,
it must have been with reservations and misgivings. He may well have concluded that in the particular circumstances of England in his day, overturning
the monarchy would create more problems than it would solve (as happened
in the 1640s and 1650s with the Puritan Revolution and Oliver Cromwell's
Commonwealth).[30]

But even if Shakespeare accepted monarchy as the most practical solution for England at one particular historical moment, that does not mean
that he thought that monarchy is the best form of government simply, or
that nothing is to be learned from examples of republican government.[31]
Shakespeare's history plays, with their repeated references to Roman precedents, may be suggesting that monarchical government in England might be
profitably modified on republican models. Shakespeare's *Henry IV* plays and
Henry V, for example, suggest that an English king would benefit from learning to take his people into account in his political calculations, as republican
principles would dictate. Shakespeare shows his Prince Hal learning the lan-

guage of his people, so that later as Henry V he can speak with them in their own terms, become their champion, and ultimately enjoy a kind of Roman triumph through London's streets as a reward for his Roman-like popularity as a military victor.[32]

Even if Shakespeare did not view republicanism as a practical possibility for England, I would argue that it still intrigued him as he thought about human potentiality.[33] His interest in a wide variety of human beings led him to an interest in a wide variety of political regimes, including republics. He realized that not all human possibilities are equally available at all times and places, and that means under different regimes.[34] As we shall see in analyzing *Coriolanus*, Shakespeare understood that to observe a hero single-mindedly devoted to political life (undistracted, for example, by Christian concerns for the afterlife), one has to go back to the pagan republics of antiquity. In general, Shakespeare's interest in ancient Rome was rooted in his perception that certain human possibilities were developed more fully in the Roman Republic than in the Christian monarchies of his day. To understand the pure heroic ethos, one must turn to classical antiquity, where it was able to develop unmixed with and undistorted by all the later complexities introduced by Christianity.

Thus, in focusing on the contrast between republic and empire in Shakespeare's Roman plays, one should not be asking the simple question: which regime did Shakespeare prefer? The two regimes encourage and develop different potentialities in human nature, and to understand the full range of humanity, one must examine both. The republic may be preferable in purely political terms, but is politics all that matters in human life? In setting up the contrast between republic and empire in terms of nobility and public spiritedness versus corruption and decadence, I may seem to have been stacking the deck in favor of republics, and that is exactly how the republican political tradition has presented the matter over the centuries. But political excellence is not coextensive with human excellence. There is something to be said for corruption and decadence, especially as they function in the world of *Antony and Cleopatra*. What appears to be corrupt and decadent from the viewpoint of the republican tradition may from another perspective be seen as a form of liberation from the narrow confines of the ancient city—the discovery of a "new heaven, new earth" (1.1.17), as Antony puts it.

On the issue of republic versus empire Shakespeare characteristically appreciates both sides but also raises doubts about both. This ability to see the different sides of any issue is what makes him a great dramatist. The ancient city's republican regime encourages a certain kind of political and military nobility, but at the expense of narrowing its citizens' horizons to a limited

range of this-worldly goals. The Roman Empire's regime may undermine republican virtue, but at the same time it opens up all sorts of new spiritual possibilities. That is why the Roman plays taken as whole pose a Hegelian tragic
choice between antithetical ways of life, each of which embodies a distinct
and defensible vision of human excellence. In general, one of the central
tragic facts in Shakespeare's plays is that political excellence often comes into
conflict with other forms of human excellence.

In sum, although I present the contrast between republic and empire in
the Roman plays in sharp terms, that does not mean that I think that the
choice between these antithetical ways of life is simple and straightforward.
On the contrary, Shakespeare presents this choice as deeply complicated and
deeply tragic, representing a fundamental dilemma in human existence. That
is why I have moved beyond *Shakespeare's Rome* to open up a larger perspective on the Roman plays in this book. What is happening in them, culminating in *Antony and Cleopatra*, takes place on an apocalyptic scale—the dissolution of an entire way of life. We are witnessing not just the death of the
Roman Republic but the end of the ancient city itself and thus of the ancient
world and all that distinguished its way of life from modern alternatives. With
remarkable historical insight, Shakespeare realized that the emergence of the
Roman Empire marked a fundamental alteration of the human condition
and thereby laid the foundations of the modern European world (which is
one reason Shakespeare correlates the rise of the Roman Empire with the rise
of Christianity). In chapter 1, I discuss Shakespeare's Rome in relation to a
wide variety of phenomena characteristic of late antiquity, including Greek
philosophy (especially Stoicism and Epicureanism) and Eastern mystery religions. Drawing upon a broad range of scholarship, I point out that all these
phenomena have been correlated with the dissolution of the classical polis
as a result of the triumph of the Roman Empire. Whatever Shakespeare's
knowledge of these specific phenomena may have been, he grasped the larger
political, cultural, and philosophical significance of this great turning point
in Roman—and world—history.

This, then, is the final respect in which *Shakespeare's Roman Trilogy*
moves beyond *Shakespeare's Rome*. My first book focuses on the contrast between the Roman Republic and the Roman Empire. As I have thought about
this opposition over the years, I have come to realize that "republic" and
"empire" stand for something larger. The Rome of *Coriolanus* represents
more generally the polis or ancient city,[35] and *Julius Caesar* and *Antony and
Cleopatra* dramatize the process by which Roman military conquests around
the Mediterranean eventually destroyed the way of life characteristic of the
ancient world—the civic existence embraced by the Greeks as well as the

Romans (and other ancient peoples, such as the Carthaginians). Shakespeare presents his characters in *Antony and Cleopatra* as literally and figuratively "at sea" as they try to deal with the newly instituted imperial way of life. Cut off from traditional possibilities, they are alternately exhilarated and unnerved by the new options that have opened up to them. No longer given the opportunity—made possible by the small size of the polis—to participate actively and directly in political life, they explore the alternate routes to satisfaction provided by the vastly expanded cosmopolitan world of empire.

Shakespeare was drawn to the subject of ancient Rome because it provided a way of understanding the fundamental choices that had gone into producing his own world—political options that showed signs of once again becoming available in his day. The possibility of civic existence had been revived in Renaissance Italy in modern republics such as Venice and Florence. At the same time, Shakespeare's world offered striking examples of grand empires on a Roman scale: the Ottoman Empire and the Habsburg Empire. Shakespeare's England had its own imperial aspirations, and he explores these possibilities in *Henry V* (with the king's dream of conquering France and even going on to reclaim Constantinople for Christianity from the Turks). In short, in Shakespeare's day, Renaissance Europeans had revived the choice between republic and empire, and he understood that he could explore its complexities and ramifications by turning back to ancient Rome and its classic formulation of the choice. These are large claims for Shakespeare's Roman plays, but I will now turn to validating them in the only way I can—by detailed and close readings of *Coriolanus*, *Julius Caesar*, and *Antony and Cleopatra*. I will analyze the ways the three plays work together to provide a coherent account of the movement from polis to empire in the ancient world, and thus a fundamental change in the human condition that had profound and lasting consequences for Europe and the entire modern world.

PART ONE

Shakespeare, Nietzsche, and the Revaluation of Roman Values

Shakespeare's Tragic City: The Rise and Fall of the Roman Republic

How many wars do we see undertaken in the history of Rome, how much blood shed, how many peoples destroyed, how many great actions, how many triumphs, how much statecraft, how much sobriety, prudence, constancy, and courage! But how did this project for invading all nations end—a project so well planned, carried out and completed—except by satiating the happiness of five or six monsters? What! This senate had brought about the extinction of so many kings only to fall into the meanest enslavement to some of its most contemptible citizens, and to exterminate itself by its own decrees!

MONTESQUIEU, *Greatness of the Romans and Their Decline*

Rome in Shakespeare's Imagination

The subject of Rome looms large in Shakespeare's career. Of his ten tragedies, four are set in the ancient city. What may well be his first comedy, *The Comedy of Errors*, is based on a Roman model, Plautus's *Manaechmi*. Of his two narrative poems, *The Rape of Lucrece* deals with a famous incident in early Roman history, and *Venus and Adonis* is derived from the Roman poet Ovid. Shakespeare's history plays contain reminders that Britain was once a Roman colony, and one of his last plays, *Cymbeline*, seems to be an attempt to relate British history to Roman. The history plays often use ancient Rome as a reference point, as if Shakespeare were trying to apply lessons from Roman politics to his own country's past—and perhaps its present. For example, in the prologue to act 5 of *Henry V*, the chorus compares the king's return to London after his great victory over the French at Agincourt to a Roman triumph:

> The Mayor and all his brethren in best sort,
> Like to the senators of th' antique Rome,
> With the plebeians swarming at their heels,
> Go forth and fetch their conqu'ring Caesar in. (5.Chor.25–28)[1]

Then, in what is clearly a contemporary political reference, the chorus goes on to draw a further parallel to the wished-for triumphal return of an English general from an expedition to Ireland in Shakespeare's own day.[2]

In perhaps the most haunting reference to ancient Rome in Shakespeare's history plays, the young prince Edward in *Richard III*, glimpsing the Tower of London, asks, "Did Julius Caesar build that place?" (3.1.69). The fact that a Roman edifice lasted for centuries in England becomes a lesson for the prince in the possibility of eternal glory: "Methinks the truth should live from age to age / As 'twere retail'd to all posterity" (3.1.76–77). The memory of Caesar's achievement provokes in the English prince hopes of rivaling his great Roman predecessor:[3]

> That Julius Caesar was a famous man;
> With what his valor did enrich his wit,
> His wit set down to make his valor live.
> Death makes no conquest of this conqueror,
> For now he lives in fame though not in life.
> . . . .
> And if I live until I be a man,
> I'll win our ancient right in France again,
> Or die a soldier as I liv'd a king. (3.1.84–88, 91–93)

This is what Rome came to represent in the Renaissance imagination—the pinnacle of earthly glory, specifically the grandeur of military conquest. Many Europeans in Shakespeare's day could share the experience of young Prince Edward—from the Colosseum in Rome itself to Hadrian's Wall in Britain, monuments of Roman greatness stood all over Europe.[4] Any one of Shakespeare's contemporaries who contemplated an imperial future for Britain might well look back to ancient Rome for models of military and political excellence. Edmund Spenser's epic poem, *The Faerie Queene*, first published in 1590, had already presented Britain as the historical successor to Troy and Rome as the third of the world's great imperial powers.

Shakespeare may have hoped that Britain could recapture something of Roman grandeur, but he was also aware of the huge gulf that separated Britain from Rome. The Britain of Shakespeare's day was a monarchy. Ancient Rome, for much of its history, was a republic, and it was the Republic that conquered all its rivals in the Mediterranean world and laid claim to much of the territory that comprised what we know as Rome's empire. To be sure, after Julius Caesar's death, Rome was ruled by emperors for hundreds of years, and some of them added more territory to Rome's dominions. But except for Shakespeare's early—and some would say immature—play, *Titus Andronicus*, he seems to have been interested primarily in the republican era of Rome. Among his three mature Roman plays, he first wrote *Julius Caesar*, which focuses on the change from the Roman Republic to the Roman Empire—the emergence of one-man rule in the city. Several years later, Shakespeare wrote *Antony and Cleopatra*, which continues the story of *Julius Caesar* and portrays the death throes of the Republic, along with the beginnings of the imperial system under Octavius (who became the first "official" emperor, Augustus Caesar). At roughly the same time, Shakespeare wrote *Coriolanus*, which deals with the early days of the Roman Republic, indeed with its founding, if one regards the institution of the tribunate, which gave the plebeians an active role in the Roman regime, as the distinctive feature of the Roman republican constitution. Shakespeare's mature Roman plays appear to form a trilogy, telling the story of the rise and fall of the Roman Republic and highlighting the differences between republican and imperial principles.[5] Taken together, they form one larger tragedy, what might be called the tragedy of the Republic.

The historical disposition of Shakespeare's three mature Roman plays suggests a sustained effort to understand the nature of the republican regime —what made it work to begin with, what made it so successful politically and militarily, and what eventually undermined and destroyed it.[6] *Coriolanus* displays remarkable insight into what differentiates a republic from a monarchy, and what allows it to function effectively in the absence of a single ruler in control. Moreover, *Coriolanus* seems to reflect Shakespeare's admiration for the political energy and military strength a republican constitution generates. The Rome of *Coriolanus* has many faults and comes near to disaster, but in the city's eventual triumph, one can see why a community with this remarkable ability to hold its citizens together and channel their energies into political life was to go on to conquer the Mediterranean world.

By contrast, insofar as *Antony and Cleopatra* portrays the beginnings of the Roman imperial system, it seems to reflect a negative judgment on it in political terms, ultimately validating Cleopatra's pronouncement: "'Tis paltry to be Caesar" (5.2.2). The martial virtues, devotion to the common good, and heroic spirit that characterize the Roman Republic seem to be fast disappearing in the world of *Antony and Cleopatra*. In the figures of Octavius and Antony, Shakespeare correctly identifies the two prototypes of Roman emperors that were to emerge in the next century. Octavius, who in fact became the first Roman emperor, is the cold-blooded and shrewd administrator, the expert manipulator of human beings, the leader who succeeds by managing his subordinates, not by exhibiting heroic virtue himself. Antony, for all his remaining heroism, is the prototype of the decadent emperor, indulging his appetites, ruling tyrannically, and modeling himself on a Hellenistic god-king who expects his subjects to worship him (thus foreshadowing the coming reigns of Caligula and Nero).[7] As rulers, neither Octavius nor Antony seems admirable, and neither displays the concern for the common good that animates the republican Romans in *Coriolanus* and *Julius Caesar* (even though some of them obviously pursue their private good under the guise of public concerns).

In sum, Shakespeare appears to identify Rome as a distinctive form of community with the Republic and to pass a negative judgment on the Empire in specifically political terms. Speech after speech at the end of *Julius Caesar* suggests that, with the deaths of the last defenders of the Republic, the breed of noble Romans is becoming extinct. The play concludes with an almost apocalyptic sense of an era coming to an end. Cassius's death calls forth imagery of the twilight of Roman greatness:

> But Cassius is no more. O setting sun,
> As in the red rays thou dost sink to-night,
> So in his red blood Cassius' day is set!
> The sun of Rome is set. Our day is gone,
> Clouds, dews, and dangers come; our deeds are done! (5.3.60–64)

When Brutus observes the dead bodies of Cassius and Titinius, he laments:

> Are yet two Romans living such as these?
> The last of all the Romans, fare thee well!
> It is impossible that ever Rome
> Shall breed thy fellow. (5.3.98–101)

One might dismiss such speeches as mere rhetoric, but their cumulative effect is to convey a sense that the death of the Republic means the death of Rome itself, the end of everything Rome traditionally stood for, the destruction of the spirit that animated the community for centuries and made it great politically and militarily.[8]

Antony and Cleopatra does little to dispel this negative impression of the Empire. To be sure, in some sense "Rome" survives in the play, and the characters occasionally refer to old Roman ideals.[9] But in light of the corruption of imperial Rome, these speeches sound hollow, and the old Roman ideals no longer guide the actual conduct of the Romans in the play.[10] Shakespeare does everything he can to stress the discontinuity between the Republic and the Empire. He neglects the ways in which many republican institutions actually survived into the imperial era (or were recreated by Octavius). From reading *Antony and Cleopatra*, one would never know, for example, that the Senate still existed in the days of Octavius, or that he preserved such titles as "consul."[11] The plebeians, who play such an active role in Roman politics in both *Coriolanus* and *Julius Caesar*, are barely mentioned in *Antony and Cleopatra*, and not a single one is represented in the cast of characters.[12]

Cleopatra correctly sees that in imperial Roman politics, the plebeians have been reduced to pure spectators (5.2.55–57, 209–11). Far from drawing the energies of its people into public life as the Republic did, the imperial regime restricts participation in politics to the contenders for the position of Caesar and eventually produces one-man rule. As is evident throughout *Antony and Cleopatra*, an empire replaces active citizens with passive subjects.

This is the key issue that distinguishes the republican world of *Coriolanus* from the imperial world of *Antony and Cleopatra*. What defines a republican regime is the fact that its citizens participate in the political life of the community.[13] It need not be *full* participation. The Rome of *Coriolanus* is not a democracy in either the ancient or the modern sense, but the plebeians do have a distinct role to play in the politics of the city. Their share in power is ratified when the patricians grant them the right to the tribunate as a result of their rebellion (itself a sign of their active participation in Roman political life). What evidently interested Shakespeare in the subject of ancient Rome is this distinctively republican way of life, something very different from the kind of politics he knew in Britain.[14]

Shakespeare evidently admired the Roman Republic and its ability to generate a remarkable series of great military and political leaders. At the same time, however, he reveals his republican Romans to be limited in their range of humanity precisely because of their intense focus on political life. For all its political defects, the Roman Empire may bring to light and foster other forms of human excellence, unknown in the republican era. Thus to say that Shakespeare admired the republican Roman way of life is not to say that he endorsed it as the best way of life simply for all humanity, and especially not to say that he was eager to convert Britain into a republic. But perhaps he believed that modern Britain could learn something about military and political excellence by studying the very different principles that governed ancient Rome. His history plays can be interpreted as a warning to British monarchs against trying to govern absolutely, without reference to the common good, and advice to them to try to recreate in monarchical form some elements of the mixed regime of the Roman Republic, to find ways to accommodate the interests of both the nobles and the commons in the British regime.[15]

In his interest in the Roman republican way of life and what it might teach the modern world, Shakespeare was not alone among Renaissance thinkers.[16] As its name suggests, the Renaissance was at its core a revival of classical antiquity. We normally picture the Renaissance in cultural terms, and think of its architecture, painting, sculpture, and literature—areas in which it broke with medieval traditions by returning to classical models and precedents. But as the great historian of the period, Jacob Burckhardt, insisted, the spirit of

the Renaissance as a rebirth of classical antiquity was also evident in its political life.[17] At the very center of the Renaissance—in Italy—a number of cities,
such as Florence and Venice, revived classical republican life and specifically
harked back to ancient Rome for models of political and military excellence.[18]

The great theorist of this revival of republicanism was Niccolò Machiavelli and his most profound thought on the subject took the form of meditations on ancient Roman history, his *Discourses on the First Ten Books of Livy*.
This book was well known in Elizabethan England, and Shakespeare may well
have read it in some form, or at least have become familiar with its contents.[19]
Without claiming that Shakespeare was a follower of Machiavelli, or even
that he completely shared his understanding of ancient Rome, one can see
similarities between his enterprise in the Roman plays and Machiavelli's in
the *Discourses*. In attempting to recreate ancient Rome on the stage, Shakespeare shows himself to be a true Renaissance artist, and, by the same token,
the Roman plays go right to the heart of the central enterprise of Renaissance
culture—to bring the ancient world back to life in all its striking difference
from the modern. And, for Shakespeare, the republicanism of Rome constitutes the core of that difference.

The Republican Regime and Civic Life

Shakespeare's grasp of the details of the functioning of the republican regime
in *Coriolanus* is remarkable.[20] He understands how the various offices and
institutions of ancient Rome drew its citizens into political life and made it
the focus of their existence. The ambitious among the patricians could aspire
to become consul, and lead the city in warfare and other important matters.
Since two consuls were chosen every year and no one could immediately re-
peat as consul, those chosen for the office had an incentive to win victories
for Rome quickly.[21] Moreover, with constant turnover in the office, Rome
was always well supplied with men who had executive experience at the highest level. The aim was to prevent any one man from becoming too important
in the city—indeed, from presenting himself as indispensable—while satisfying the political aspirations of as many ambitious men as possible. The
tribunate was not as powerful an office as the consulship, but Shakespeare
is careful to show that it gave the plebeians their stake in the republican regime, and in particular provided ambitious types among the plebeians—
such as Sicinius and Brutus in *Coriolanus*—with an outlet for their political
impulses.[22] The result of all the republican institutions for participating in
politics is evident in *Coriolanus*—an intense focus among Roman citizens on
public life. The play opens with the famished plebeians crying out for grain,

but the patricians quiet their rebellion by granting them the tribunate. Even the comparatively unpolitical plebeians would evidently rather satisfy their ambition than their hunger. As we would put it, politics is more important to them than economics.

The Rome of *Coriolanus* focuses its citizens so completely on political life that it forms the comprehensive horizon of their existence. There is no world for them outside the city's walls—only an array of foreign enemies to be fought and conquered. Every aspect of their lives comes to have a distinctively Roman inflection, and their individual interests are subordinated to those of the city. The general Cominius eloquently expresses the primacy of the city in the lives of the Romans:

> I have been consul, and can show for Rome
> Her enemies' marks upon me. I do love
> My country's good with a respect more tender,
> More holy and profound, than mine own life,
> My dear wive's estimate, her womb's increase
> And treasure of my loins. (3.3.110–15)

As Cominius reveals, Rome tries to bring all aspects of life within its orbit, including areas often thought to transcend the world of politics or at least to exist independent of it, such as religion and the family. The family in *Coriolanus* is a decidedly Roman institution.[23] Coriolanus's mother, Volumnia, states clearly that she raised her son for the sake of Rome and she would be happy to see him die for the city: "Had I a dozen sons, each in my love alike, and none less dear than thine and my good Martius, I had rather eleven die nobly for their country than one voluptuously surfeit out of action" (1.3.22–25). The Roman character of the family turns out to be the only thing that can save the city once Coriolanus goes over to lead its enemies, the Volsces. Volumnia persuades Coriolanus to give up his march to destroy Rome by convincing him that, as her son, he cannot escape his identity as a Roman. Rome is fortunate that it absorbed what is often regarded as an area reserved to private life into its political orbit.

As for religion, the gods of *Coriolanus* are distinctly city gods, the gods of Rome.[24] The characters in the play, both patricians and plebeians, constantly refer to the gods and call upon their support, assuming without question that the gods take a proprietary interest in Rome. One way the patricians maintain their rule over the plebeians is to convince them that the senators speak for the gods, as Coriolanus claims when he tells the mob at the beginning of the play: "You cry against the noble Senate, who / (Under the gods) keep you in awe" (1.1.186–87). Everyone in Rome believes that the gods follow the politics of the city carefully; like good republicans, even the gods participate in its affairs. In return for being worshiped in the city, the gods in Coriolanus's view must keep Rome safe and its political life running smoothly: "Th' honor'd gods / Keep Rome in safety, and the chairs of justice / Supplied with worthy men!" (3.3.33–35). When the tribune Sicinius, terrified by the prospect of Coriolanus destroying Rome, says, "The gods be good to us!", Menenius rebukes him: "No, in such a case the gods will not be good onto us. When we banish'd [Coriolanus], we respected not them; and he returning to break our necks, they respect not us" (5.4.30–34). Evidently the gods take sides in Roman partisan politics. Wherever we look in *Coriolanus*, religion operates in a Roman context, specifically a political context.

That is one way of saying that the religion of *Coriolanus* is pagan. Because the horizon of the republican Romans is formed by the city, they are restricted to this world, and Shakespeare grasps the larger consequences of this pagan orientation for their way of life. By contrast, Christianity is a transpolitical religion. It does not limit itself to the boundaries of any political unit, and, far from suggesting that politics is the most important thing in human life, it denigrates the whole realm of the political and insists that human beings should be concerned with higher, spiritual matters that take them beyond the borders, not just of their communities, but of this world itself. The paganism of Rome is thus crucial to its goal of focusing its citizens on political life. Its civic religion works to keep the Romans cut off from any aspect of human life that might transcend the political and undermine its centrality in Roman existence.

Above all, any notion of an afterlife is completely absent from *Coriolanus*. The only form of immortality available to the republican Romans is fame, the eternal glory of having done something great for the city and especially of having won a significant victory over one of Rome's enemies.[25] The republican Romans strive so mightily to perform great deeds for their city because they have no other avenue to immortality. This understanding of what distinguished the ancient Romans is at the heart of Machiavelli's analysis in the *Discourses* of why the republican Romans valued their independence and their participation in political life so highly:

> Thinking then whence it can arise that in those ancient times people were more lovers of freedom than in these, I believe it arises from the same cause that makes men less strong now, which I believe is the difference between our education and the ancient, founded on the difference between our religion and the ancient. For our religion, having shown the truth and the true way, makes us esteem less the honor of the world, whereas the Gentiles, esteeming

it very much and having placed the highest good in it, were more ferocious in their actions.[26]

In this important chapter, Machiavelli goes on to develop the contrast between Christianity and paganism, and their differing impacts on conceptions of human excellence:

> The ancient religion did not beatify men if they were not full of worldly glory, as were captains of armies and princes of republics. Our religion has glorified humble and contemplative more than active men. It has then placed the highest good in humility, abjectness, and contempt of things human; the other placed it in greatness of spirit, strength of body, and all other things capable of making men very strong. And if our religion asks that you have strength in yourself, it wishes you to be capable more of suffering than of doing something strong. This mode of life thus seems to have rendered the world weak and given it in prey to criminal men, who can manage it securely, seeing that the collectivity of men, so as to go to paradise, think more of enduring their beatings than of avenging them.[27]

Machiavelli argues that belief in an afterlife, the hope "to go to paradise," weakens people's commitment to this life, especially their resolve to stand up for their dignity and assert themselves. Shakespeare may not have agreed with every claim in this passage, but his portrayal of the way the Romans in *Coriolanus* put a premium on "greatness of spirit" and "strength of body" accords with Machiavelli's analysis.

The Fatal Flaw of the Republic

Like Machiavelli, then, Shakespeare identifies in *Coriolanus* those elements of the republican regime that made Rome so successful in political terms. The distinctive combination of institutions and beliefs in republican Rome—the comprehensive nature of the regime—made the city a breeder of ambitious leaders, above all military heroes. As regimes go, the Roman Republic lasted a remarkably long time—over four and a half centuries—and it conquered every rival it encountered, gradually carving out an empire that spanned the entire Mediterranean world and more. And yet even the Republic did not last forever, and it eventually gave way to the Roman Empire, which embodied the very opposite of republican principles. Machiavelli in fact blamed the Roman Empire for extinguishing the spirit of republicanism: "The Roman Empire, with its arms and its greatness, eliminated all republics and all civil ways of life. And although that empire was dissolved, the cities still have not been able to put themselves back together or reorder themselves for civil life except in very few places of that empire."[28] With so much in its favor, why did the Roman Republic finally fail and yield to its antithesis, an imperial regime?

Shakespeare devotes *Julius Caesar* and *Antony and Cleopatra* to answering this question, but the fatal flaw of the Republic is already evident in *Coriolanus*. The city is potentially too dependent on its great leaders, as we see when Coriolanus almost brings it to its knees single-handedly. If one of the patricians could master his rivals in the political competition in the city, he could take it over completely. The "revolving door" principle of the consulship worked against this result, but eventually Rome's very success as a military power undermined the republican regime. As Rome's empire grew in extent, it took longer and longer for its generals to reach its frontiers, let alone conduct wars there. Finally Rome found it necessary to prolong its generals' commands beyond their one-year term as consuls, so that they could complete their military missions (this process was known as *prorogatio*, or prorogation). Many analysts, including Machiavelli, trace the demise of the Roman Republic to the prolongation of military commands.[29] This development allowed generals to cement their relation to their armies over a long time period and to cultivate the personal loyalty of their troops. Serving under a different commander every year, Roman armies for much of the republican era felt that their loyalty was to Rome, not to a particular general. But after the institution of prorogation, with years of continuous service under a single general, the Roman troops began to think of him, not the city, as their master. As the career of Julius Caesar demonstrates, an ambitious patrician with the support of his troops could become the most powerful force in Rome and even defy the will of the Senate.[30]

Shakespeare dramatizes the precarious situation of the late Roman Republic in the opening scene of *Julius Caesar*. Caesar is celebrating a Roman triumph, not over a foreign enemy but over the sons of Pompey (once his principal political rival in the city). The tribunes Flavius and Marullus berate the plebeians for slavishly worshiping one of the great rulers in the city:

> Wherefore rejoice? What conquest brings he home?
> What tributaries follow him to Rome,
> To grace in captive bonds his chariot-wheels?
> . . . .
> And do you now strew flowers in his way
> That comes in triumph over Pompey's blood. (1.1.32–34, 50–51)

In opposition to the spirit of the Republic, Caesar has done nothing, according to the tribunes, for the public good in Rome, and is merely pursuing his

personal advantage. He has used his armies to defeat his fellow Romans in a
civil war. The way that the plebeians throng to celebrate his victory is thus
ominous for the Republic. In *Coriolanus*, the plebeians maintain a healthy
distaste for the patricians and hold them at arm's length. They are suspicious
of Coriolanus's ambition and grudgingly approve him as consul, only to take
back their vote soon after and banish him from the city. This course of action
almost has disastrous consequences for Rome, but it reflects the legitimate
republican fear of letting any one man play too great a role in the city. The
tribunes Sicinius and Brutus speak in the spirit of the Republic when they
insist that no one man is indispensable in the city, not even the great soldier
Coriolanus:

> Your Coriolanus
> Is not much miss'd but with his friends;
> The commonwealth doth stand, and so would do,
> Were he more angry at it. (4.6.12–15)

But in *Julius Caesar*, one of the patricians has won the personal loyalty
of his armies and now the plebeians are flocking to his cause. The Roman
Republic depended on a balance between the patricians and the plebeians,
with one party checking the power of the other. Once one patrician gets the
plebeians on his side, he upsets the balance of power in Rome and threatens to become the supreme and sole authority in the city.[31] Coriolanus is so
popular after his great victory against the Volsces that everybody in Rome
thinks that he will take over the whole city, with both plebeians and patricians acknowledging his superiority.[32] Fortunately for the survival of the Republic, Coriolanus cannot contain his patrician contempt for the plebeians
and he alienates them just when he could have won them over to his cause.[33]
Courting the plebeians would require theatrics from Coriolanus; Volumnia
asks him to "perform a part" and Cominius promises: "We'll prompt you"
(3.2.106, 109). But Coriolanus will not lower himself to perform in front of
the base plebeians. He rejects the role of actor: "It is a part / That I shall blush
in acting" (2.2.144–45). By contrast, Julius Caesar has no such aristocratic
scruples, and is perfectly willing to play to the crowd.[34] As Casca explains,
"If the tag-rag people did not clap him and hiss him, according as he pleas'd
and displeas'd them, as they use to do the players in the theatre, I am no true
man" (1.2.258–61). Caesar courts the support of the plebeians by whatever
means necessary, including bribing them. Coriolanus was violently opposed
to distributing grain to the plebeians. Caesar used the enormous wealth he
gained in foreign conquests to win the plebeians with gifts of all kinds. He
established the policy that was later to be known in the imperial era as giv-

ing the people "bread and circuses." As Plutarch reports, "To curry favour
with the people, he made great feasts and common sports. For he feasted all
the Romans at one time at two-and-twenty thousand tables, and gave them
the pleasure to see divers sword-players to fight at the sharp, and battles also
by sea."[35]

Mark Antony shows how much he has learned from his master's political strategy in his funeral oration, a masterpiece of Roman theater, catering
to all the baser instincts of his audience.[36] In a graphic illustration of this
point, Shakespeare has Antony literally descend to the level of the plebeians
in order to address them more effectively (3.2.160–63). He seizes the opportunity to turn the plebeians against the conspirators by reminding them of
Caesar's multiple benefactions to Rome. He directs his remarks against the
original charges of Flavius and Marullus: "He hath brought many captives
home to Rome, / Whose ransoms did the general coffers fill" (3.1.89–90).
Antony makes particularly effective use of Caesar's will, stressing his financial generosity to the Romans: "To every Roman citizen he gives, / To every
several man, seventy-five drachmas" (3.2.241–42). Here we learn the price
tag of freedom in the late Republic—the plebeians are willing to sell their
republican birthright for seventy-five drachmas apiece.[37]

In contrast to what happens in *Coriolanus*, the plebeians in *Julius Caesar*
put economics over politics. For the sake of money, they will allow Caesar
and his followers to ride roughshod over republican institutions and traditions. The tribunes Flavius and Marullus are silenced for taking a stand
against Caesar; given the importance of the tribunate to the republican constitution, their suppression amounts to the death of the Republic. In *Coriolanus*, the plebeians accept tribunes in place of a distribution of grain. In
Julius Caesar, the plebeians in effect accept a distribution of money in place
of their tribunes. Shakespeare evidently agrees with the many commentators on Roman history who claim that the Roman Republic was corrupted
by its wealth.[38] As another example of how the Republic was ruined by its
own success, the vast wealth the Roman generals accumulated as a result of
their foreign conquests allowed them to bribe first their armies and then the
plebeians to rally to their personal cause. Often the rich patricians used their
vast wealth to buy important offices in the Republic for themselves or their
followers.[39] Even the plebeians in *Julius Caesar* seem to be wealthier than
they were in *Coriolanus*. They now have a change of clothing; they can put
on their "best apparel" (1.1.8) to welcome Caesar home (one imagines them
clad in rags in *Coriolanus*). They have time off from work ("do you now cull
out a holiday?" [1.1.49]), and as "idle creatures" (1.1.1), they are prepared to
do mischief in the city. Thanks to a pun from a cobbler, we have a hint from

the beginning of the play that there are now "bad soles," or souls, in Rome
(1.1.14).[40] With the new prominence of economic considerations in the late
Republic, a gap has opened up between public and private interests in the
city. The cobbler admits to leading his fellow plebeians around the streets for
his own economic benefit: "to wear out their shoes, to get myself more work"
(1.1.29–30). The corruption of the plebeians is one of the chief factors in the
degeneration of the republican spirit in Rome.

As a result of courting the plebeians' favor, Julius Caesar becomes too
big for Rome. In Cassius's bitter complaints about Caesar's preeminence, we
hear the traditional voice of the Roman Republic. He tells Brutus that his
republican sense of freedom is offended by Caesar's elevated status in the city:

> I had as lief not be, as live to be
> In awe of such a thing as I myself.
> I was born free as Caesar; so were you. (1.2.95–97)

Cassius's conversation with Brutus culminates in a striking image of one man
becoming too big for the city:

> Why, man, he doth bestride the narrow world
> Like a Colossus, and we petty men
> Walk under his huge legs, and peep about
> To find ourselves dishonorable graves. (1.2.135–38)

Cassius thinks back to the traditional republican principle of making sure
that, at any given moment, Rome is well stocked with many great leaders:

> Age, thou art sham'd!
> Rome, thou hast lost the breed of noble bloods!
> When went there by an age since the great flood
> But it was fam'd with more than with one man?
> When could they say, till now, that talk'd of Rome,
> That her wide walls encompass'd but one man?
> Now is it Rome indeed and room enough,
> When there is in it but one only man. (1.2.150–57)

Here again Rome is identified with the Republic. For Cassius, one-man rule
is incompatible with the true spirit of the city, and he is willing to die if need
be to restore the republican constitution.

But unfortunately for Cassius and the cause of the Republic, as Shakespeare shows in *Julius Caesar*, after decades of civil war among contending
patricians, the balance of power in the city has been so upset that the old
regime may no longer be viable. In particular, the plebeians, who traditionally counterbalanced the power of the patricians and acted as a brake on

their ambitions, are now willing to sell their support to the highest bidder. Brutus in his oration at Caesar's funeral tries to appeal to the old republican principle of the common good: "Not that I lov'd Caesar less, but that I lov'd Rome more" (3.2.21–22). But in the era of Caesar, Brutus's attempt to restore the republican elevation of the political over the personal can only backfire. The plebeians are at first impressed by Brutus's arguments but the result is only that they want to transfer their personal loyalty from Caesar to Brutus. The Third Plebeian says of Brutus, "Let him be Caesar" (3.1.51). These four words truly sound the death knell of the Republic.[41] "Caesar" has ceased to be the name of a particular man and has been transformed into a title, indeed, the greatest of all Roman imperial titles. Here, in the central act of the central play in the Roman trilogy, the plebeians, who struggled against patrician power for centuries, are now content to sit back and allow one great noble after another to rule the city, provided he flatters them, courts their favor, and keeps them happy with gifts. In *Coriolanus* and *Julius Caesar*, Shakespeare shows that the plebeians, while never the true leaders in the city, are the key to the functioning of the republican regime. Ironically, in their last act of participation in Roman politics, the plebeians decide the conflict between the republican and imperial parties in Rome by throwing their support to Antony as the representative of Caesarism.[42] After turning their backs on the republican tradition, the plebeians make their final appearance on stage in act 3, scene 3, as a mindless mob and murder an innocent man, mistaking a poet for a conspirator. Ever since the first scene of *Coriolanus*, the unruly plebeians have seemed to be willing to suspend hostilities temporarily and to hear arguments about the common good, but Caesar's funeral proves to be the last moment when they will listen to reason.[43] Antony sets their passions loose and unleashes their most violent impulses. In act 3 of *Julius Caesar*, the plebeians bring the era of widespread participation in politics in Rome to an end, and never again appear individually or collectively on stage in the remainder of the play or in *Antony and Cleopatra*. They have in effect voted themselves out of history.

Empire and the Hellenization of Rome

Antony and Cleopatra explores how the conditions of life in the Roman world have fundamentally altered with the change from a republican to an imperial regime. With all the institutions that worked to encourage participation in politics moribund or altogether vanished, the Romans predictably start to lose their interest in public life and turn to other objects of aspiration and sources of satisfaction. The plebeians have simply disappeared in the play. In *Coriolanus*, however poor and powerless they may be, they manage to bring about a fundamental change in the Roman regime when they force the patricians to grant them the tribunate. In *Julius Caesar*, the plebeians can only sit back and ratify a change in the regime accomplished by patricians like Antony, and in effect they lose their tribunes in the process. In *Antony and Cleopatra* the plebeians have no active role in politics anymore. As for the patricians, in the absence of the multitude of republican offices like consul, the stages of political life to which a public spirited Roman might reasonably aspire are no longer available. Offices like consul did, in fact, survive into the era of the Empire; for a variety of reasons, the emperors often took such titles themselves. Once again, by exaggerating the discontinuities between the Republic and the Empire, Shakespeare created a more negative view of imperial politics than he had to. *Antony and Cleopatra* captures the new circumstances in the Empire, in which only a few prominent men contend for political eminence and the situation fast becomes one of "emperor or nothing." The younger Pompey learns to his dismay that, with a Caesar in place, the only way to become "lord of all the world" (2.7.61) is by means of a crime. The conspirators can cast the assassination of Julius Caesar as a noble deed, done in the name of the Republic and the common good. But in an imperial system, Pompey realizes that if he knowingly allows the pirate Menas to assassinate the triumvirs on his behalf, it will be viewed as a purely self-serving act, an act of "villainy" (2.7.74). Conditions in the Empire have worked to efface the distinction between a soldier and a pirate (2.6.83–96). Pompey correctly observes that political advancement in the Empire will now principally take illegitimate forms (assassination was, in fact, to become a common political tactic in the Roman Empire). The kind of ambition that used to fuel the rivalry for political preeminence in the Republic—long viewed as noble—is now viewed as evil, a form of treachery.

One obvious effect of the demotion of public life in *Antony and Cleopatra* is the promotion of private life. At the center of the play, Antony's one request of Octavius is to be allowed to live "a private man in Athens" (3.12.15).[44] Private life offers new forms of satisfaction, chiefly erotic, and the increasing role that love plays in Antony's existence is related to the decreasing role of traditional politics. The death of the Republic clearly opens up new possibilities for human experience, and Antony is eager to explore them with Cleopatra. The Romans in *Coriolanus* have narrow horizons, bounded by the walls of their city. But in Antony's first words in the play, he talks of going beyond any boundaries, and finding out "new heaven, new earth" (1.1.17).

As much as Shakespeare admired the Roman Republic, he realized that its concentration on developing the political side of its citizens stunted their growth in other ways. Thus, the imperial world of *Antony and Cleopatra* offers a far greater diversity of human types than does the republican world of *Coriolanus*. In *Coriolanus*, Rome's enemies, the Volsces, basically seem no different in their way of life. With their own senators, they have roughly the same form of government and they evidently lead the same kind of martial existence.[45] Their great warrior Aufidius is the mirror image of Coriolanus (1.1.230–33), although the Volsce is clearly not his equal on the battlefield. But in *Antony and Cleopatra*, genuine alternatives to the traditional Roman way of life abound. The intense focus on a single and largely homogeneous political community in *Coriolanus* contrasts sharply with the richly cosmopolitan world of *Antony and Cleopatra*. The Romans of *Coriolanus* never get to see anything remotely as exotic as Cleopatra, and her "infinite variety" (2.2.234) is characteristic of the new world of the Empire.

This is another way in which the Republic's success in conquering the world ultimately worked to destroy it—by undermining the intense concentration on martial virtue that made its victories possible in the first place. Rome's conquest of foreign lands exposed it to more and more alien ways of life, and the Romans found it increasingly difficult to remain loyal to their original regime.[46] Shakespeare shows this process well underway already in *Julius Caesar*. Rome is fast becoming un-Roman—if one takes one's definition of "Roman" from the traditional standards of the Republic in *Coriolanus*. A well-known exchange shows how the Rome of *Julius Caesar* has been transformed:

CASSIUS: Did Cicero say anything?
CASCA: Ay, he spoke Greek.
CASSIUS: To what effect?
CASCA: Nay, and I tell you that, I'll ne'er look you i' th' face again. But those that understood him smil'd at one another, and shook their heads; but, for mine own part, it was Greek to me. (1.2.278–84)

"It was Greek to me" has become proverbial, and this humorous moment is integral to Shakespeare's portrait of Casca as a blunt and gruff character, the one man of the people, as it were, among the conspirators.[47] But this passage has larger implications for understanding the Rome of the play. Why are the leaders of Rome now speaking Greek? They appear to be employing Greek as an esoteric language, a way for the elite to communicate among themselves.

Not wanting to reveal his opinion of Caesar's imperial ambitions to the broad public, Cicero speaks in a foreign language, known only to an intimate circle of his patrician friends.

This passage thus signals a breakdown in public communication in the Rome of *Julius Caesar*. In *Coriolanus* all the Romans—patricians and plebeians—speak a common language, and in particular they debate matters of public importance in words that everyone in the city can understand. But in *Julius Caesar*, Cicero's turn to Greek marks a privatization of public discourse. Rome is now ruled by an elite who speak their own language—or rather, a foreign language—learned on the frontier of the territories conquered by Roman armies. This is what actually happened to Rome as the Republic kept expanding its borders, bringing more and more foreign lands within the Roman orbit. By having Cicero speak Greek, Shakespeare points to a much broader and significant development: the Hellenization of Rome. The Romans conquered the Greeks militarily, but in the ensuing cultural conflict, the Greeks conquered the Romans. That is to say, faced with the great cultural achievements of the Greeks—in architecture, sculpture, literature, and all the other arts—the Romans in effect admitted their inferiority and began to copy Greek models.

The historical Cicero, for example, openly acknowledged the Greeks' cultural superiority and, above all, their priority in time in fields such as literature: "In learning Greece surpassed us and in all branches of literature, and victory was easy where there was no contest. For while with the Greeks the poets are the oldest literary class, seeing that Homer and Hesiod lived before the foundation of Rome and Archilochus lived in the reign of Romulus, poetry came to us at a later date."[48] As latecomers on the cultural scene, the Romans were forced to copy Greek models in all the arts. In writing the *Aeneid*, for example, Virgil sedulously followed epic conventions laid down by Homer in both the *Iliad* and the *Odyssey*. The majority of Greek sculpture is known today only through Roman marble copies of Greek bronze originals.[49] Well-to-do Romans in the first century BCE sent their children to school in Athens, to learn, for example, the art of oratory. In manifold ways, the Romans of Julius Caesar's day had indeed learned to "speak Greek."

As a modern historian of Rome, Ramsey MacMullen, writes:

By Augustus' day the resulting ascendance of the conquered Greeks over the conquerors in all but the public spheres of life was complete. Chefs, secretaries, interior decorators, physicians, were all from the east. . . . What leaders in taste and opinion were agreed on in calling civilization itself, *humanitas*, was to be sought among the Greeks. "Even as we govern over that race of men in

which civilization is to be found," Cicero remarked to his brother Quintus,
... "we should certainly offer to them what we have received from them ...
for we appear to owe them a special debt."[50]

As MacMullen sums up the situation, "The Romans, to no one's surprise,
won out where arms, administration, and practical technology were in question. As to the rest, in familiar words captive Greece took Rome captive."[51]

The peculiar genius of the Romans as a conquering civilization is that
they developed what Rémi Brague has called an "eccentric culture."[52] The
Romans often took their cultural bearings not from the center of the Roman world (the city itself) but from the periphery. Rather than Romanizing
the Greeks, they chose to be Hellenized themselves. To be sure, the Romans
often imposed their customs on the peoples they conquered. We find distinctive Roman street plans in archaeological sites all around the Mediterranean, as well as the aqueducts, roads, forums, baths, and amphitheaters
the Romans brought with them wherever they went. But to a remarkable
degree, the Romans proved willing to adopt cultural practices from the lands
they conquered. They sought out the best they could find and brought it
back to Rome.[53] As Montesquieu writes, "The main reason for the Romans
becoming masters of the world was that, having fought successively against
all peoples, they always gave up their own practices as soon as they found
better ones."[54] For example, in architecture the Romans did make their own
distinctive contributions, above all in their use of concrete and their ability to
construct arches and domes. Yet we still describe their architectural columns
with the Greek terms "Doric," "Ionic," and "Corinthian," a fact that reveals
how openly derivative Roman architecture was from Greek.

Rome was enriched by what Brague calls its "eccentric culture," but, as
his term implies, these developments involved a kind of decentering of Roman civilization as well. As its territories expanded to encompass the whole
Mediterranean world, Rome became culturally less Roman and more Greek.
That is why many Roman patricians objected to the imperial policy of the Republic.[55] They were concerned that Rome's virtue was being undermined by
its encounter with alien ways of life. This attitude is epitomized by a warning
that Cato the Elder (234–149 BCE) gave to his son against falling under the
spell of the seductive Greeks: "I shall speak about those Greek fellows in their
proper place, son Marcus, and point out the result of my enquiries at Athens, and convince you what benefit comes from dipping into their literature,
and not making a close study of it. They are a quite worthless people, and an
intractable one, and you must consider my words prophetic. When that race
gives us its literature it will corrupt all things."[56] In short, the Hellenization

of Rome, evident in *Julius Caesar*, did not go unopposed.[57] Shakespeare was aware of anti-Greek sentiments among the patricians, and has Coriolanus express them forcefully. In his diatribe against the creation of the tribunate, he cannot refrain from comparing Greek institutions unfavorably with Roman:

> They choose their magistrate,
> And such a one as he, who puts his "shall,"
> His popular "shall," against a graver bench
> Than ever frown'd in Greece. (3.1.104–7)

For Coriolanus, the Greeks provide a model of what *not* to do, especially since their cities are pure democracies:

> Whoever gave that counsel, to give forth
> The corn a' th' store-houses gratis, as 'twas us'd
> Sometime in Greece—
> . . . .
> Though there the people had more absolute pow'r,
> I say they nourish'd disobedience, fed
> The ruin of the state. (3.1.113–18)

For Coriolanus, in Greek democracies the rulers are forced to give the people whatever they want.[58] He demands that the aristocratic Roman regime stand fast against what he regards as the mob rule of Greek democracies. To Coriolanus, whatever is Greek is inevitably un-Roman.

One can imagine, then, how Coriolanus would react to Cicero's speaking Greek among his fellow patricians. Like Cato the Elder, Coriolanus would regard this development as a sign of Rome's corruption by foreign influences. One might dismiss Cicero's speaking Greek as an isolated and essentially trivial development, but Shakespeare shows that the Romans of *Julius Caesar* now "speak Greek" in a more significant sense. Philosophy—specifically Greek philosophy—has come to permeate the Rome of *Julius Caesar*. Philosophy of any kind is nowhere to be found in *Coriolanus*; the words *philosophy* or *philosopher* do not appear in the play. The spirit of the early Republic is in fact antiphilosophical.[59] Given the regime's intense focus on political life, it would frown upon its citizens getting lost in speculations about metaphysical issues. The horizons of Rome in the early Republic are narrow, and the Romans seldom refer to anything beyond the city's borders, and in particular they do not take their bearings from heavenly phenomena or speculate about what they might mean or portend.[60]

This situation changes in *Julius Caesar*. In three scenes (1.3, 2.1, and 2.2), Shakespeare shows the Romans reacting to a massive disturbance in nature, a violent storm in the heavens.⁶¹ The Romans now take their bearings not just from the political guideposts in Rome but also from the natural—or perhaps the unnatural—phenomena they observe. Casca asks Cicero: "Are not you mov'd when all the sway of the earth / Shakes like a thing infirm?" (1.3.3–4), and he seems to draw a parallel between "a civil strife in heaven" (1.3.11) and the political turmoil in Rome. But as a traditional Roman, Casca refuses to approach the strange phenomena philosophically and insists on treating them as divine omens:

> When these prodigies
> Do so conjointly meet, let not men say,
> "These are their reasons, they are natural";
> For I believe they are portentous things. (1.3.28–31)

Cassius, by contrast, insists on enquiring like a philosopher into the "true cause" of these extraordinary happenings in the heavens, and on looking into the "natures" of the things (1.3.62–67). He then interprets the portents in a way that strengthens his political resolve to stand up to Caesar's emerging tyranny.⁶²

In act 2, scene 2, Julius Caesar and his entourage react to the same storm in the heavens, as they also try to draw lessons for Rome's political future from these disturbances and separate the natural from the unnatural. In act 2, scene 1, Brutus responds differently to the storm. Taking the disorder in the heavens in his stride, he views the storm more philosophically—as simply providing him the light he needs: "The exhalations whizzing in the air / Give so much light that I may read by them" (2.1.44–45). Yet even Brutus has come to take his bearings from heavenly phenomena, and notes when he is no longer able to do so: "I cannot by the progress of the stars / Give guess how near the day" (2.1.2–3). Later in the same scene, in a very peculiar stage moment, Shakespeare obtrusively cuts away from Brutus and Cassius discussing the conspiracy to yet another attempt by Romans to orient themselves by heavenly phenomena:

DECIUS: Here lies the east; doth not the day break here?
CASCA: No.
CINNA: O, pardon, sir, it doth; and yon grey lines
    That fret the clouds are messengers of the day.
CASCA: You shall confess that you are both deceiv'd.
    Here, as I point my sword, the sun arises,
    Which is a great way growing on the south,
    Weighing the youthful season of the year.

Some two months hence, up higher toward the north
He first presents his fire; and the high east
Stands, as the Capitol, directly here. (2.1.101–11)

At a time when the conspirators are debating how to proceed with the plot against Caesar, it seems very odd that they would pause to worry about determining due east or exactly where the sun will rise.[63] Evidently, in a moment of political crisis, they are trying to line the city up with nature, to determine if the Capitol in Rome is properly aligned with the point where the sun will rise. In the process they reveal the problem with attempting to guide the city by philosophical enquires into nature. The Capitol is fixed in place, while the location where the sun rises keeps changing throughout the year. The fixity of political institutions means that they cannot perfectly line up with natural phenomena, which are continually changing. I do not claim to understand fully this enigmatic exchange, but it seems to suggest something like this: as the conspirators contemplate the assassination of Caesar, they would like to think that they are taking their bearings from nature and that the Roman Capitol provides them with a fixed reference point for their actions. But Shakespeare raises doubts as to whether any such clear guidance from nature is available for political life. Whatever this mysterious passage may mean, the debate over daybreak provides a good measure of the difference between the Rome of *Julius Caesar* and the Rome of *Coriolanus*.[64] In the early days of the Republic, the Romans never stop whatever they are doing and stand around wondering about phenomena they observe in the heavens. Their eyes are too fixed on civic affairs.

Stoics and Epicureans

Shakespeare gives the emergence of philosophy in the world of *Julius Caesar* a specifically Greek inflection.[65] As was historically the case, the spread of philosophy in late republican Rome was a prime example of its Hellenization. All the varieties of philosophy that appear in *Julius Caesar* have Greek origins, as shown by their Greek names. Cicero was eclectic in his philosophy, but he is often designated as an Academic or an Academic Skeptic.[66] The unnamed poet who interrupts the quarrel between Cassius and Brutus in act 4 is called a "cynic" by Cassius (4.3.133). Cassius identifies himself as an Epicurean, and Brutus is recognized as a Stoic.[67] Academic Skeptic, Cynic, Epicurean, Stoic— *Julius Caesar* includes a wide range of the Greek philosophies that were adopted by the Romans, often as a result of studying in the schools of Athens, as, for example, the historical Cicero did. Cicero is the only famous philosopher Shakespeare ever chose to portray in his plays.[68] He has a very small role in *Julius Caesar*; he speaks only nine lines, but in that brief space he registers his distinctive philosophical position when he expresses skepticism about Casca's wild surmises concerning the meaning of the storm in the heavens:

> Indeed, it is a strange-disposed time:
> But men may construe things after their fashion,
> Clean from the purpose of the things themselves. (1.3.33–35)

Unlike the other characters in this scene, Cicero maintains a philosophical calm and equanimity in the face of the turmoil in the heavens. As a true philosopher, he distinguishes between what things really are and what people merely think they are. Note that Cicero, unlike the other characters, makes no reference to the gods in trying to understand the storm. On such matters, he is indeed a skeptic.[69]

The relation of both Cassius and Brutus to philosophy in *Julius Caesar* is especially interesting. Allan Bloom claims, "There is no other Shakespearean play in which the protagonists are explicitly followers of philosophical doctrines. With Brutus and Cassius, Shakespeare shows the impossibility of the direct application of philosophy to political affairs."[70] As a professed Epicurean, Cassius would not accept the old Roman accounts of the gods. Perhaps his Epicurean doubts about traditional myths help to explain his bitterness over the way that Caesar has risen to the status of a god in Rome:

> And this man
> Is now become a god, and Cassius is
> A wretched creature, and must bend his body
> If Caesar carelessly but nod on him. (1.2.115–18)

With the heretical eyes of an Epicurean, Cassius is ever on the lookout for evidence that contradicts Caesar's divine status, such as his all-too-human fever when he was in Spain: "'tis true, this god did shake" (1.2.121).

Cassius's Epicureanism thus serves him well as a conspirator, helping him to call into question the myths on which Caesar's power has come to rest. But Cassius cannot apply his chosen philosophy consistently. Toward the end of the play, after he suffers several setbacks, his Epicureanism begins to weaken:

> You know that I held Epicurus strong,
> And his opinion; now I change my mind,
> And partly credit things that do presage. (5.1.76–78)

This is not an insignificant or inconsequential change in opinion. Losing faith in his Epicureanism, Cassius becomes fatalistic and even defeatist in attitude, and this in turn leads him to commit suicide prematurely and perhaps unnecessarily. The case of Cassius's Epicureanism seems to raise doubts as to whether a philosophical school can provide a sound and dependable guide to political life, especially when Cassius is unable to maintain one philosophical position consistently.

The case of Brutus and philosophy is even more complex. Although the word "Stoic" does not appear in *Julius Caesar*, Brutus's adherence to Stoic doctrine becomes clear in his exchange with Cassius, when they are trying to achieve a reconciliation after their quarrel:

CASSIUS: I did not think you could have been so angry.
BRUTUS: O Cassius, I am sick of many griefs.
CASSIUS: Of your philosophy you make no use,
    If you give place to accidental evils.
BRUTUS: No man bears sorrow better. Portia is dead. (4.3.143–47)

Cassius has been surprised by Brutus's passionate outbursts during their quarrel. As a Stoic, Brutus should not give way to anger, and he should not allow his even temper to be disrupted by "accidental evils."[71] The distinctive Roman attitude toward philosophy becomes clear in this passage. For Cassius, philosophy is something of which a Roman should "make use." In Rome, the theoretical is always subordinated to the practical.

In response to Cassius's challenge, Brutus finally reveals the source of his distemper—his wife Portia has killed herself. Like Cassius, we can sympathize with the way that Brutus allows his grief to overpower his self-control, but there can be no question that in the process he has failed to live up to his Stoic code. Still the question remains: has Brutus failed Stoicism or has Stoicism failed Brutus? Would we think better of Brutus if he showed no emotion at the news of Portia's death?

Shakespeare explores this possibility just moments later in the same scene. Messengers arrive with news from Rome, including the fact that Octavius, Antony, and Lepidus have had Cicero killed. A cat-and-mouse game ensues between Brutus and Messala, who probes to find out if Brutus already knows of his wife's suicide. Feigning ignorance, Brutus provokes this exchange:

BRUTUS: Now as you are a Roman, tell me true.
MESSALA: Then like a Roman bear the truth I tell:
    For certain she is dead, and by strange manner.
BRUTUS: Why, farewell, Portia. We must die, Messala.
    With meditating that she must die once,

I have the patience to endure it now.
MESSALA: Even so great men great losses should endure.
CASSIUS: I have as much of this in art as you,
     But yet my nature could not bear it so. (4.3.187–95)

Here Brutus gets to play the role of the model Roman Stoic in public, in front
of some of his closest associates, on whose good opinion of him he relies. As
a result, he receives a public tribute to the greatness of his Stoic demeanor
from Messala, who is suitably impressed by Brutus's calm reaction to news
of his wife's death. Cassius joins in the tribute to the singularity of Brutus's
Stoicism, even though Cassius knows full well that Brutus is putting on an
act, since only moments before he had heard the news about Portia from
Brutus's own lips. But it is in Cassius's political and military interest to help
maintain his coconspirator's reputation for Stoic self-command, especially
with the army. It is almost as if Cassius is parading Brutus before the military
crowd as the poster child of Roman Stoicism.

     An astute detective on the scene would have noticed the obvious flaw in
Brutus's performance. Despite the fact that Messala reports that Portia died
"by strange manner," Brutus does not bother to enquire into the exact manner
of her death, as any husband newly confronted with the troubling report of
his wife's death would surely do. Brutus's behavior in this scene, while hardly
criminal, is suspicious, and calls his reputation for pure high-mindedness
into question.[72] Everyone in the play looks up to Brutus and acknowledges
his nobility. Shakespeare presents him as the sort of patrician who, for centuries, formed the backbone of the Roman Republic, and he may be its last
genuine champion. But Shakespeare complicates his portrait of Brutus and
reveals his feet of clay. Brutus's nobility, for all its underlying reality, is a bit
of a pose, carefully crafted for public consumption. One is reminded of what
Friedrich Nietzsche says about the Stoic: "He . . . enjoys having an audience
when he shows off his insensitivity."[73]

     What Shakespeare reveals at this moment about Brutus and Stoicism is
so disturbing that many commentators and editors have searched for other
ways to deal with what has come to be known as the problem of the duplicate
revelation of Portia's death.[74] Some critics have tried to turn the problem into
a textual matter. They argue that Shakespeare wrote one version of the revelation of Portia's death first, then later decided on the other option, but failed to
delete the original version in the manuscript that eventually made its way to
the printer. That may be what happened, but it would require a spectacularly
obtuse printer (not to mention subsequent proofreaders) to fail to notice the

glaring contradiction in what is after all a single scene, in which the contradictory accounts are separated by no more than twenty lines. The evidence
we have concerning the status of the text of *Julius Caesar* is not consistent
with this kind of massive error. The play has come down to us in only a
single text, in the First Folio, and editors regard it as one of the better Shakespeare texts available. In their Signet edition, William and Barbara Rosen,
for example, write, "The Folio text contains remarkably few misprints, serious errors in punctuation, or misattribution of speeches."[75] In the Riverside
edition, G. Blakemore Evans writes, "The text as a whole is a good one; in
fact, it has been called the best-printed play in F1 [the First Folio]."[76] These
judgments on the quality of the printing job seem to rule out an error as
egregious as failing to notice that Shakespeare had deleted a passage that contradicts an adjacent passage. Moreover, Evans says, "Use of a manuscript in
Shakespeare's hand is made most unlikely by the absence of characteristically
Shakespearean spellings in the F1 text."[77] So much for the theory that the
duplicate revelation of Portia's death resulted from some confusion in the
manuscript Shakespeare left behind. In fact, because of the unusually detailed
stage directions in the text of *Julius Caesar*, the Rosens and Evans, as well as
many other editors, conclude that the Folio text was set from some version of
the promptbook of Shakespeare's theater company and thus is connected to
actual theatrical productions of the play. If that is the case, the textual theory
would require us to believe that the duplicate revelation of Portia's death was
never noticed by anyone in Shakespeare's company during all their perfor-
mances of *Julius Caesar*.

In short, the textual theory of the duplicate revelation of Portia's death
is not supported by what we know about the text of *Julius Caesar*. We are
probably better off trying to make sense of this moment in *Julius Caesar* as
it has come down to us, rather than reworking the text to fit some precon-
ceived notions about what Shakespeare must have thought of Brutus and of
Stoicism. In act 4, scene 3, neither Brutus nor Stoicism comes off looking
very good, and perhaps that is exactly the effect Shakespeare was trying to
create. These negative impressions are, in fact, consistent with what Shakespeare shows about philosophy elsewhere in *Julius Caesar*. Although Romans
in the late Republic have started to talk about philosophical issues, and several even claim allegiance to specific philosophical schools, philosophy does
not run very deep in the city. For the Romans, philosophy is something to
be made use of. When it suits their political purposes to appear as Stoic or
Epicurean, they do so, but, with the exception of Cicero, they are not genuine
philosophers.

Philosophy and Politics in Rome

Shakespeare returns to this point in act 5, scene 1, the only other place in the play where the word "philosophy" appears. Cassius asks Brutus what he will do if they lose at Philippi, and Brutus replies:

> Even by the rule of that philosophy
> By which I did blame Cato for the death
> Which he did give himself. (5.1.100–2)

Cassius understandably interprets these words to mean that Brutus has no intention of committing suicide if they lose the impending battle. But, without explanation, Brutus immediately reverses himself, showing once again the weakness of his attachment to his philosophical principles:

> No, Cassius, no. Think not, thou noble Roman,
> That ever Brutus will go bound to Rome;
> He bears too great a mind. (5.1.110–12)

Here Shakespeare seems deliberately to muddy a sequence of thought that is quite clear in Plutarch's account. There Brutus says explicitly that, over the years, he has changed his mind about suicide. In his earlier days, he opposed suicide: "Being yet but a young man and not over greatly experienced in the world, I trust (I know not how) a certain rule of philosophy by the which I did greatly blame and reprove Cato for killing himself."[78] But then Plutarch's Brutus makes it clear that he has changed his mind in the present moment: "But being now in the midst of the dangers, I am of a contrary mind."[79] In Shakespeare's reworking of this passage, Brutus's abrupt and unexplained reversal in his opinion of suicide seems to be just one more example of the inconsistency with which the Romans apply their philosophical principles to practical decisions.[80]

Perhaps the underlying problem is revealed when Brutus speaks of "the rule of that philosophy." These practical-minded Romans are looking for philosophy to provide them with rules—formulas that tell them how to act in particular circumstances ("this is how you react to defeat," "this is how you react to a loved one's death").[81] Believing that philosophy can be encapsulated in simple rules, the Romans repeatedly find themselves ambushed by reality. They find that life does not fit into the philosophical formulas they rely on for guidance. Despite his professed Stoicism, Brutus really is moved by his wife's death. But do we think less of Brutus because he fails to measure up to his Stoic principles, or is Shakespeare calling those principles into question? Shakespeare seems to be suggesting that Stoicism is an inadequate guide to life, specifically to political life. By requiring its adherents to suppress perfectly human emotions, Stoicism proves to be unworkable. Unable to live up to their professed Stoic principles, Romans seem to trot them out mostly for show. Like Epicureanism for Cassius, Stoicism for Brutus is more like an ideology than a genuine philosophy. These philosophical schools provide codes to live by for these Romans, in many respects closer to religious beliefs than philosophical principles.[82] Cassius characteristically refers to "Epicurus . . . and his opinion" (5.1.76), as if philosophy were a matter of opinion, not knowledge.

Many interpreters would be surprised at the claim that Shakespeare could be raising doubts about Stoicism in *Julius Caesar*. Some have argued that Shakespeare was influenced by Stoicism.[83] Others have gone so far as to identify Romanness with Stoicism, or at least to claim that Shakespeare presents his Romans as fundamentally Stoic. If that were the case, it would be difficult to explain why Shakespeare has characters stress the uniqueness of Brutus's Stoicism in *Julius Caesar*, and why the play contrasts it with other philosophical schools in Rome, such as Cassius's Epicureanism. The long history of Rome, stretching a millennium from the Republic through the Empire, requires us to be cautious about taking any one phase of Rome's development as typical of the whole. Stoicism was a relatively late development in the long history of Rome. As its name indicates, it was originally a Greek movement and came to Rome only in the latter days of the Republic (the second century BCE) and encountered resistance when it did.[84] Although it did gain a foothold in the late Republic (as the example of Cato the Younger shows), Stoicism flourished chiefly in the era of the Empire.[85] The most famous Roman Stoic, the emperor Marcus Aurelius, lived in the second century CE, long after the events of *Julius Caesar*, and, as important as Marcus Aurelius was in Roman history, we should not put him forward as *the* representative Roman. There are no Stoics in the Rome of *Coriolanus*. "Anger's my meat" (4.2.50), says Volumnia, and, indeed, anger—freely expressed—is the dominant emotion of the play, and, in particular, the daily diet of Coriolanus. For most of the history of the Republic, the Romans did not behave like Stoics. They hardly would have conquered the Mediterranean world if they had been willing to accept their place in the world calmly and not fought to better it.[86] If, as we have seen, Shakespeare largely identified Rome with the Republic, he could not have viewed Rome as fundamentally Stoic.

As the case of Marcus Aurelius suggests, Stoicism is a philosophy more suited to an empire than to a republic. In fact, Stoicism is the perfect philosophy for an imperial system, which wants to develop a class of public officials devoted to their duty but not eager to challenge their superiors. Stoicism acts as a brake on conventional political ambition, and thus works well in the comparatively rigid hierarchy of an empire, but not in a republic filled with ambitious men contending fiercely for honors. As Gordon Braden writes:

> Indeed, Stoicism so clearly fits the situation of the early empire that it becomes the all-but-official creed of the Roman aristocracy in the first and second centuries [CE]. Its origins adumbrate that destiny; the school begins as an answer to but also a continuation of Cynicism, the philosophy whose founder is supposed to have been unimpressed by Alexander the Great. Cynicism can be described as an attempt, in the decline of the poleis, to affirm, as it were, a postpolitical conception of the self. Systematically flouting established standards of public honor and decorum, which have come to seem groundless and fragile, Cynicism appeals to some deeper, inner form of individual identity not dependent on the recognition of others. Early Stoicism attempts to fill out this appeal in a systematic way . . . . Yet the origins of the effort continue to show, and the concern that reasserts itself as the central focus in what Stoic writings we have intact—those of Seneca, Epictetos, and Marcus Aurelius—is the Cynic focus, sophisticated and disciplined, but still recognizable as a commitment to the self's superiority to all public ambitions and intimidations. . . . It is part of the significance of the school to be the pagan world's main answer to what seemed to be its political fate. . . . Stoicism's central strength is its calculus of adaptation to unchangeable realities. Surrendering the world's goods, we find them false and learn how to want what we have instead of striving to have what we want.[87]

Stoicism teaches people to accept their station in life, whether high or low. To be an emperor or slave makes no difference to Stoics in their inner lives—to be good they must simply fulfill the duties of whatever station in life destiny has assigned them.[88] The philosophies characteristic of the Rome of *Julius Caesar*, chiefly Stoicism and Epicureanism, are all products of *late* antiquity. We should not confuse the tight emotional control of the Stoic with the military discipline, toughness, and sheer orneriness of the classical hero. Homer's heroes, for example, are *not* Stoics (they are far too emotional, given to weeping and outbursts of anger). The philosophies of late antiquity, such as Cynicism, Stoicism, and Epicureanism, developed in the Hellenistic period—that is to say, after Alexander the Great in his quest for empire had effectively brought the era of the Greek polis to a close. Stoicism and Epicureanism were both responses to the dissolution of the world of the polis, and the consequent loss of the focus on political life that the polis had provided.

All the philosophical schools either mentioned or alluded to in *Julius Caesar*—Skepticism, Cynicism, Stoicism, Epicureanism—are essentially apolitical philosophies.[89] Cynicism and Skepticism both call into question the value of public life and lead the philosopher—in Diogenes-like fashion—to turn his back on politics.[90] Perhaps the fact that Cicero plays no role in the political action as we have it in *Julius Caesar* can be traced to his skepticism, especially about the Roman gods.[91] Cicero does not allow himself to become excited by the storm in the heavens or to draw political conclusions from the spectacle. Epicureanism calls upon the philosopher to retreat to his garden and to choose the happiness of tranquility, leaving the needless strife of politics behind him.[92] Of all these schools, Stoicism comes closest to providing a political philosophy, but even Stoicism teaches an emotional detachment from politics (since it teaches an emotional detachment from everything).[93] If born emperor, one should perform the duties of the office, but without the kind of obsessive commitment that conventional political ambition generates. Like the Epicurean, the Stoic retreats to a kind of inner life, even when serving in public office.

The philosophical inconsistency of the Romans in *Julius Caesar* is fundamentally rooted in the fact that they are political men who profess apolitical philosophies. If Cassius were a genuine Epicurean, he would simply retire from Roman politics to a country estate (as many patricians in his day did). If Brutus were a genuine Stoic, he would simply accept his honored place in the new Rome of Julius Caesar. Cassius and Brutus betray their lingering republicanism in the fact that, despite their apparent philosophical beliefs, they remain committed to a life of politics and continue to pursue the goal of preeminence in Rome against the one person (Julius Caesar) who has tried to monopolize the honors in the city. A genuine Stoic or an Epicurean should not be obsessed with personal honor the way that Brutus and Cassius are, or be upset with Julius Caesar's good fortune.[94] Their commitment to the politics of the city contravenes their stated philosophical principles.[95]

The emergence of philosophy in the Rome of *Julius Caesar*, especially of Greek philosophy and specifically Stoicism and Epicureanism, is thus a sign of the weakening of the traditional Roman regime, as a Coriolanus or a Cato the Elder would no doubt insist.[96] One might of course point to the development of philosophy in Rome as a sign of progress. The speculations that have emerged in the Rome of *Julius* Caesar about nature, the heavens, and other philosophical issues highlight the limitations of the provincial community Shakespeare portrays in *Coriolanus*. In the early days of the Republic, the Romans have no way of being exposed to a philosophical tradition, especially given their contempt for all things Greek. No Roman patrician is going to send his children to school in Antium, and in any case Antium is no Athens. Besides, if Coriolanus's son is typical, it is not easy to get Roman children to go to any school: "He had rather see the swords and hear a drum than look upon his schoolmaster" (1.3.55–56). The Republic educates its children in warfare, not philosophy.

We can see the logic of an expanding empire working itself out in *Julius Caesar* (even though it was a republic that put together this empire). Encounters on the frontiers of the lands the Romans conquered expand their horizons, and the Hellenization of Rome in *Julius Caesar* is only one example of the way Rome became increasingly cosmopolitan in the later years of the Republic. Stoicism was the first truly cosmopolitan philosophy, presenting the philosopher as a citizen of the world. But this cosmopolitanism, for all its positive aspects, also has negative effects. As Cato the Elder predicted, it worked to undermine traditional Roman virtues—specifically the republican commitment to political pursuits—precisely by offering new alternatives to the customary way of life in the city. All these developments give some sense of the political and cultural trade-offs Shakespeare explores in the Roman plays. The Romans in *Julius Caesar* have gained access to Greek philosophy, which obviously marks an advance beyond the narrow intellectual horizons of the city in *Coriolanus*, but philosophies such as Epicureanism and Stoicism are in many respects un-Roman (in the republican sense), weakening attachment to civic life and commitment to Roman politics. Philosophers themselves have often argued that philosophy is a form of corruption in the political community, or at least a sign of political decline.[97] Montesquieu writes specifically of the impact of Epicureanism on Rome: "I believe the sect of Epicurus, which was introduced at Rome toward the end of the Republic, contributed much toward tainting the heart and mind of the Romans."[98] As Hegel put it, "The owl of Minerva spreads its wings only with the falling of the dusk."[99] As the wisdom of Athena comes to the city in *Julius Caesar*, Shakespeare conveys a strong sense that the sun is setting on Rome.

Imperial Twilight

The transformation of Rome begun in *Julius Caesar* only accelerates in *Antony and Cleopatra*, as the logic of expanding empire plays itself out. The twilight descends; Cleopatra's servant Iras captures the new mood of despair: "the bright day is done, / And we are for the dark" (5.2.193–94). The Hellenizing of Rome in *Julius Caesar* is followed by the Egyptianizing of Rome in *Antony and Cleopatra*, and the new developments in philosophy are succeeded by equally new developments in religion. In *Coriolanus*, religion remains within a well-defined Roman orbit. The gods of the Republic are Roman gods. But in *Antony and Cleopatra*, the Romans are exposed to all sorts of foreign deities, many of them from Egypt. The Republic linked its Roman virtues to worship of the Roman gods; in the imperial era, the commitment to traditional Roman virtues is seriously weakened by the turn to non-Roman deities. In act 2, scene 6, Octavius seeks to make Antony look bad in the eyes of Rome by charging him with behaving like an Oriental despot and whoring after foreign gods in the form of Cleopatra, who "in th' abiliments of the goddess Isis / That day appear'd" (3.6.17–18).[100]

But Antony's behavior in this scene is becoming less an aberration and more the new norm in Rome. Everywhere we look in *Antony and Cleopatra* we see the Egyptianizing of Rome. As a result of conquering Egypt, Rome exposed its citizens to people who had had centuries to develop an imperial way of life. The corruption of Antony by his encounter with forces out of the East is emphasized from the opening lines of the play. More generally, throughout the play characters who ought to represent the traditional Roman virtues display an inordinate fascination with all things Egyptian and a susceptibility to the charms of alien ways of life. It is customary among critics of *Antony and Cleopatra* to talk about a contrast between Rome and Egypt in the play.[101] But, in fact, Shakespeare shows that the differences between the two regimes are breaking down as Rome absorbs more and more customs from the alien lands it conquered. In *Antony and Cleopatra* Rome is no longer the tight-knit, well-defined community of *Coriolanus*. In that play, Shakespeare is careful to locate the action in relation to famous Roman landmarks, such as the Capitol or the Tarpeian Rock.[102] Some scenes in *Antony and Cleopatra* undoubtedly occur within the traditional city limits of Rome, but it would be difficult to specify which, because no Roman monuments or locations are mentioned.[103] And some of the most "Egyptian" scenes occur in Roman settings. One of the motifs critics associate with Egypt in *Antony and Cleopatra* is eating and drinking.[104] Yet the most lavish (and decadent) banquet in the play takes place just off the coast of Italy, near Misenum (a city on the Bay of Naples, which was then the headquarters of the Roman fleet). In act 2, scene 7, Rome is falling apart among just the men who should be trying to put it back together. What might have been a conference to restore the old Rome of the Republic quickly "ripens" into "an Alexandrian feast," and the Romans are soon dancing "the Egyptian bacchanals" (2.7.96–97, 104). In this scene even the normally austere Octavius ends up drunk (2.7.123–24).

Octavius rejects his momentary indulgence in wine: "But I had rather fast from all, four days, / Than drink so much in one" (2.7.102–3), and several other imperial Romans try to resist the new exotic influences abroad in their cosmopolitan world. Even Antony at one point says of Cleopatra: "Would I had never seen her!" (1.2.152). But Antony's follower Enobarbus is quick to point out: "O, sir, you had then left unseen a wonderful piece of work, which not to have been blest withal would have discredited your travel" (1.2.153–55). Enobarbus often speaks for common sense in the play, and his response is appropriate to the new terms of the empire. In a world in which travel to foreign countries has become commonplace, one should make the best of the situation and enjoy what the new lands have to offer. Shakespeare shows compensations in the imperial world of *Antony and Cleopatra* for what has been lost with the death of the Republic. In the imperial era, life becomes more varied and more interesting. Naturally a vast sprawling empire can offer more opportunities to experience different ways of life than a small provincial city such as the Rome of *Coriolanus* ever could. But for all the feeling of new worlds opening up in *Antony and Cleopatra*, a profound sense of loss pervades the play—above all, a sense of loss of purpose in Rome.

Many of the characters in *Antony and Cleopatra* are bewildered by the changed circumstances in the Empire. They have a hard time choosing a course of action in the first place or sticking to it once they have. Like many characters in the play, Enobarbus does not know whether to serve Antony or Octavius. The pirate Menas does not know whether to work for Pompey or against him. Octavia is torn between her brother Octavius and her husband Antony. Obviously what is missing in all these calculations of personal loyalty is the old lodestar of the Republic—the good of Rome. In the Republic, people could look to the common good of the city as a way to resolve their ethical dilemmas, as Volumnia does in her final encounter with her rebellious son. One's loyalty to Rome was supposed to take precedence over all other obligations. But now in the Empire, loyalties have become personal, and it becomes difficult to weigh one against another. A public obligation can clearly take precedence over a private, but how is one to resolve the conflict between two private obligations? In the absence of the city as a focal point of loyalty, allegiances in *Antony and Cleopatra* become ever more shifting and undependable. To his despair, Antony sees his loyal vassals and then whole armies desert him, and he agonizes over the question of whether Cleopatra is faithful to him.

Antony is the ultimate example of a Roman losing his sense of purpose in the play, indeed losing his bearings: "I am so lated in the world that I / Have lost my way for ever" (3.11.3–4). The Rome of *Coriolanus* is a world of sharp boundaries, with cities clearly marked off from one another by walls. The Rome of *Antony and Cleopatra* is a much more fluid world, a world of transformation, of one thing turning into another, a world where nothing seems to be able to hold its shape for very long. Antony senses his followers melting away:

> The hearts
> Than spaniel'd me at heels, to whom I gave
> Their wishes, do discandy, melt their sweets
> On blossoming Caesar. (4.12.20–23)

His horizon consists of shadowy clouds, perpetually changing their shapes, until they disappear:

> That which is now a horse, even with a thought
> The rack dislimns, and makes it indistinct
> As water is in water. (4.14.9–11)

Finally even Antony's sense of his own identity dissolves:

> My good knave, Eros, now thy captain is
> Even such a body. Here I am Antony,
> Yet cannot hold this visible shape. (4.14.12–14)

Coriolanus has nothing but disdain for objects that change their shape and dissolve away; he voices his contempt for the plebeians in images of animal metamorphosis and melting:

> He that trusts to you,
> Where he should find you lions, finds you hares;
> Where foxes, geese. You are no surer, no,
> Than is the coal of fire upon the ice,
> Or hailstone in the sun. (1.1.170–74)

Shakespeare captures the difference between the Republic and the Empire in the imagery of *Coriolanus* and *Antony and Cleopatra*. With their steadfastness of purpose and devotion to duty, his republican Romans live in a world of sharp outlines and firm ground. By contrast, his imperial Romans, who feel acutely that they have lost their way, live in a world of wispy clouds, shifting sands, and swirling currents. The central image of Antony as a soldier in the play is as a man lost at sea, without the firm guideposts from the city that anchored Coriolanus and the other republican Romans in their world.[105]

The Loss of Human Agency in the Empire

The strong sense of purpose that characterizes the republican Romans is of course a consequence of the city's ability to concentrate their energies on political life. In particular, a soldier like Coriolanus has no doubt what his goal in life should be—to win battles. War does a marvelous job of focusing the mind. Even the common servants among the Volsces understand the energizing power of war. They welcome the news of renewed hostilities with Rome, shrewdly comparing peace unfavorably with war (4.5.218–34). They condemn peace for allowing people to go soft and indulge themselves in plea-sures, while they praise war as a tonic for the spirit, a way to rouse people into heroic action. Peace weakens the sense of the common good, whereas war, because it forces people to recognize that they need each other, brings the common good to the fore. In *Coriolanus* Shakespeare shows that ultimately the only thing that can unite the feuding factions in Rome is a common en-emy. The city seems to function best, or at least more harmoniously, when it is at war.

This fact has profound implications for the Rome of *Antony and Cleo-patra*, which has reached the point where it has almost no enemies remain-ing. It may sound promising that "the time of universal peace is near" (4.6.4), but that is an ominous development for a people who have always identified virtue with military discipline. It turns out to be difficult to make the transi-tion from perpetual war to perpetual peace. After centuries of military cam-paigning, the Romans of *Antony and Cleopatra*, like Alexander the Great, are running out of worlds to conquer. In short, the Romans are fast losing what traditionally gave meaning to their lives as Romans—fighting their enemies. As *Julius Caesar* shows, in the absence of external foes, the Romans begin to turn against each other, with disastrous results for the traditional consti-tution of the city. Enobarbus is aware that harmony among the Romans is always contingent upon their having a common enemy. As he tells Octavius, Antony, and Lepidus, "If you borrow one another's love for the instant, you may, when you hear no more words of Pompey, return it again. You shall have time to wrangle in when you have nothing else to do" (2.2.103–6). Having "nothing else to do" is indeed *the* problem in the Roman Empire.

The change in Roman attitudes in *Antony and Cleopatra* is clearly evident in a scene set on the imperial frontier. Act 3, scene 1 seems extraneous to the main action of the play and is often omitted in stage productions, but it actu-ally provides a key to understanding the new order in the Roman Empire.[106] The Roman captain Ventidius enters "as it were in triumph," having just won a great victory over one of Rome's few remaining enemies, the Parthians.[107] But in what seems to be a very un-Roman gesture, Ventidius declines to pur-sue his victory and win more conquests for his country in Media and Meso-potamia. We want to say, "This never would have happened in the days of the Republic."[108] Then commanders were encouraged to pursue the enemies of Rome relentlessly. But Ventidius explains why his policy is actually appropri-ate to the new imperial system. He wishes to downplay the importance of his victory to avoid awakening suspicions about his ambition in his superior, Antony. Ventidius cites an example of a successful commander who offended Antony by his accomplishments on the battlefield:

> Sossius,
> One of my place in Syria, his lieutenant,
> For quick accumulation of renown,
> Which he achiev'd by th' minute, lost his favor. (3.1.17–20)

In the Republic, Ventidius might have won the position of consul for his victory, but in the Empire, he can no longer gain the consulship on the basis of his own merits but must rely on the emperor to grant it to him. Otherwise he would have to challenge his emperor directly for supremacy (as many military commanders ended up doing in the long history of the Empire).[109] Ventidius prefers to appear humble and not strive for more glory:

> I have done enough; a lower place, note well,
> May make too great an act. For learn this, Silius:
> Better to leave undone, than by our deed
> Acquire too high a fame when him we serve's away. (3.1.12–15)

In the Republic, Roman commanders were encouraged to acquire as much fame as possible; in the Empire, with its absentee generals, field officers must rein in their aspirations.

The spectacle of a Roman commander on the frontier hesitating to take advantage of his military superiority because of the new order of command in the Empire reveals how completely politics has changed in the world of *Antony and Cleopatra*. No wonder the imperial Romans no longer know what they should do and have a hard time settling on a course of action. What used to seem good in Rome—to win victories for the city—now seems bad in the era of the Empire. As Ventidius says:

> I could do more to do Antonius good,
> But 'twould offend him; and in his offense
> Should my performance perish. (3.1.25–27)

Many of the characters in *Antony and Cleopatra* experience this unsettling feeling that the very meaning of "good" has been redefined in the Empire— perhaps into the very opposite of what it used to mean in the Republic. Ventidius thinks solely in terms of Antony's good, not the good of Rome. This is the result of the prolongation of military commands, which leaves a soldier like Ventidius attached only to his immediate superior.

The uncertainty generated by the imperial regime and the way that it redirects the Romans away from their traditional goals undermines any sense of human agency in the Empire. The republican Romans of *Coriolanus* are supremely confident—to the point of arrogance—that they know what to do and that they will be able to do it (even when they turn out to be wrong). By contrast, the imperial Romans of *Antony and Cleopatra* have lost faith in themselves and their ability to accomplish what they set out to do. Coriolanus is the most self-confident of the republican Romans, so self-assured that he even believes that he can do without Rome and win his battles in effect single-handedly. But even more ordinary human beings in the play, such as the tribunes or Menenius, generally have faith in themselves and their ability to carry out their plans. Menenius hesitates before setting off to try to persuade Coriolanus to abandon his campaign against Rome, but once he decides to do so, he is convinced that he will prevail with his old friend and is shocked when he does not. As a result of their confidence in themselves, the republican Romans do not become obsessed with the future and show little interest in trying to predict it. They constantly speak of the gods, but they do not waste time wondering what the will of the gods is or what they might have in store for Rome. The Romans in *Coriolanus* seem to assume automatically that the gods will always be on their side. As a result, they act as if they believe that their fate is largely in their own hands; the gods will simply back up any decisions the Romans make.[110]

Shakespeare goes out of his way to emphasize the self-reliance of the republican Romans. He omits from *Coriolanus* all the apparatus by which they customarily sought to predict the future—augury, reading the auspices, paying attention to omens.[111] His source story in Plutarch contains several prominent examples of the Romans turning to the gods or omens for guidance.[112] In Plutarch, for example, the ladies get the inspiration for their mission to Coriolanus in a divine vision.[113] By suppressing details such as this, Shakespeare evidently sought to maintain the sense of republican Rome as a self-contained community, shut off from influences from beyond the borders of the city.

The Romans in *Coriolanus* rarely speak of fortune—they do not think of themselves as the playthings of forces beyond their own control. One of Coriolanus's few references to the power of fortune is characteristic of him as a supremely self-confident man:

> So, now the gates are open; now prove good seconds:
> 'Tis for the followers fortune widens them
> Not for the fliers. (1.4.43–45)

These words are the Roman equivalent of the modern proverb: "God helps those who help themselves." Coriolanus's point is that if his soldiers will have the courage to surge forward, they will win the battle, but if they hesitate or retreat, they will surely lose. He wants his soldiers to rely on their own arms, not on divine aid. Typically, he does not believe that the outcome of the battle is to be left to fate; it is a matter of human will.[114] The Republican faith in human agency receives its classic formulation in Cassius's famous lines in *Julius Caesar*:

> Men at some time are masters of their fates;
> The fault, dear Brutus, is not in our stars,
> But in ourselves, that we are underlings. (1.2.139–41)

Shakespeare understood that the strength of the Republic rested on the confidence of its citizens that their fate was largely in their own hands and that it was up to them and in their power to accomplish great deeds in the world.[115] With that attitude firmly in place, the Romans could conquer the world.

But this attitude is beginning to change in the late days of the Republic as Shakespeare portrays it in *Julius Caesar*. The Romans' faith in themselves has started to weaken and erode. There is now a soothsayer in the city who, claiming to know the future, presumes to give advice to the rulers of the city. He is not a civic official, part of the political order in the Republic, as the Roman priests were. The soothsayer represents a new force that is entirely absent in *Coriolanus*, a source of authority independent of the city. And the soothsayer gives a genuinely prophetic warning to Caesar. To be sure, Caesar dismisses the soothsayer with the contemptuous words, "He is a dreamer" (1.2.24), displaying the old republican contempt for the idea that the future is beyond human control. But later in the play, Caesar is not so sure of himself. Cassius notes the change in him:

> For he is superstitious grown of late,
> Quite from the main opinion he held once
> Of fantasy, of dreams, and ceremonies.
> It may be these apparent prodigies,
> The unaccustom'd terror of this night,
> And the persuasion of his augurers
> May hold him from the Capitol to-day. (2.1.195–201)

Indeed, after a night of terrifying storms, Caesar turns to the Roman augurs, and Shakespeare gives us a glimpse of the way the Romans did, in fact, try to learn about their future: "Go bid the priests do present sacrifice, / And bring me their opinion of success" (2.2.5–6).

Caesar talks to his wife Calphurnia about the unnerving omens they have observed that night. She too has had a change of heart and altered her opinion about omens and ceremonies: "Caesar, I never stood on ceremonies, / Yet now they fright me" (2.2.13–14). Caesar's reaction is mixed:

> What can be avoided
> Whose end is purpos'd by the mighty gods?
> Yet Caesar shall go forth; for these predictions
> Are to the world in general as to Caesar. (2.2.26–29)

Here Caesar begins to express a sense of fatalism different from what we observe among the Romans in *Coriolanus*, but at the same time he tries to remain true to the heroic spirit of the Republic. He ultimately relies on his own will and his determination to do whatever he set out to do. When the augurs report what would seem to be a bad omen—a beast without a heart—Caesar insists on playing the role of a hero and disregarding any warning signs of a bad fate in store for him personally:

> The gods do this in shame of cowardice;
> Caesar should be a beast without a heart
> If he should stay at home to-day for fear. (2.2.41–43)

Caesar displays the remarkable Roman ability to interpret an omen in light of what he has already decided to do and thereby use it to confirm his resolve.[116] The rest of the scene is devoted to more talk about what omens mean, leading up to Decius Brutus's hermeneutic skill in once again reinterpreting what appears to be an ominous omen—Calphurnia's dream of Caesar's statue spouting blood—into a sign of good fortune. Caesar goes to the Senate House despite all the bad omens, displaying a traditional Roman sense of purpose, but he has evidently been shaken by the dire predictions of his fate.[117]

The most interesting transformations in *Julius Caesar* involve Cassius and Brutus. As the champions of the Republic, they must believe in the principle of human agency; indeed, it is the premise of their whole enterprise. They want to make it possible for human beings in Rome once more to be free, and they believe that they have the power to accomplish the task. They think of themselves as the kind of human beings who can change the course of history by the decisions they make and the deeds they perform. But as events drag on and begin to turn against them, Cassius and Brutus develop an unrepublican sense of fatalism. In their last conversation together, Cassius admits that his Epicurean convictions are weakening and that he has changed his opinion about the validity of omens: "I partly credit things that do presage" (5.1.78).

Remember that this is the man who earlier said, "The fault . . . is not in our stars / But in ourselves"—a thought very much in the spirit of Epicurus, who argued that the gods do not exist, or at least that they do not pay attention to human affairs. But now Cassius is starting to have faith in omens.[118] He goes on to speak of a bad omen involving the flights of birds that leaves him "ready to give up the ghost" (5.1.88). In this scene, Brutus speaks of "the providence of some high powers / That govern us below" (5.1.106–7), as if he too were beginning to have doubts about the power of human agency.

Indeed, in an earlier conversation with Cassius, Brutus shows that he has his fatalistic moments:

> There is a tide in the affairs of men,
> Which taken at the flood, leads on to fortune;
> Omitted, all the voyage of their life
> Is bound in shallows and in miseries.
> On such a full sea are we now afloat,
> And we must take the current when it serves,
> Or lose our ventures. (4.3.218–24)

This passage reflects a conflicted attitude toward the issue of human agency. On the one hand, it still expresses a republican sense of determination. Brutus is, after all, urging Cassius that they seize the initiative and go into battle while they still can choose the ground on which they fight. On the other hand, Brutus speaks of a "tide in the affairs of men." His words are suffused with a sense that forces more powerful than he and Cassius are now governing their lives, and the outcome of the battle is out of their hands. The imagery of "tide," "flood," and "sea" suggests that these Romans of the late Republic are more than halfway to the pervasive feeling in *Antony and Cleopatra* of being "at sea," of being adrift in currents that will sweep them to their fate, no matter what they do to try to prevent it.[119]

The sense of fatalism that both Cassius and Brutus display has a profound effect on their conduct. Because they have begun to doubt that their fate is in their hands, they are overeager to accept defeat and especially to commit suicide. Almost as if he had just read his daily horoscope, Cassius has a superstitious conviction that his birthday should be his death day and he kills himself to fulfill a kind of prophecy: "And where I did begin, there shall I end" (5.3.24). Having mistaken a sign of victory for a sign of defeat, he gives up the struggle prematurely. When Titinius says, "Alas, thou hast misconstrued everything!" (5.3.84), perhaps Shakespeare meant us to hear an echo of Cicero's skeptical remark about how "men may construe things after their fashion."[120]

As for Brutus, he is haunted by the ghost of Caesar on the battlefield and that deepens his sense of fatalism:

> The ghost of Caesar hath appear'd to me
> Two several times by night; at Sardis once,
> And this last night here in Philippi fields.
> I know my hour is come. (5.5.17–20)

Brutus's sense that events have spiraled out of his control leads him to commit suicide, and his death seals the fate of the Republic.[121] It is difficult to sort out cause and effect in the change of heart that both Cassius and Brutus undergo. Do they lose faith in human agency because they realize that the Republic is doomed, or is the Republic doomed because they lose faith in human agency? In any event, Shakespeare makes it clear that something has changed in Rome in the waning days of the Republic. No ghosts appear in *Coriolanus*, and even if they did, no apparition could turn Coriolanus away from what he had resolved to do, just as no god can stop Achilles in his rampage at Troy. The Romans of *Coriolanus* are remarkably fixed in their beliefs and their resolve. Their small-town mentality is revealed in their narrow-mindedness, epitomized by Coriolanus's stubbornness in refusing to alter his opinions about the plebeians. By contrast, the Romans of the late Republic in *Julius Caesar* typically waver in their convictions. In the course of the play, Julius Caesar, Calphurnia, Brutus, and Cassius all change their fundamental beliefs (usually in the direction of becoming more superstitious).

Defeat becomes Victory

In a development appropriate to an empire, the fatalism that begins to grip the republican Romans in *Julius Caesar* and that has such grave consequences at the end of the play becomes endemic in the world of *Antony and Cleopatra*. A republic, by allowing its citizens widespread participation in politics, gives concrete meaning to the idea of human agency. By contrast, an empire, by turning its citizens into subjects, denies agency to its people and makes them feel passive. The Rome of *Coriolanus* is a world of classical heroism, a world in which men make history, a world in which one individual can truly make a difference.[122] When Coriolanus fights for the Romans, the Romans win; when he fights for the Volsces, the Volsces win. This one man seems to make the difference between victory and defeat; as he says of his triumph at Corioles, "Alone I did it" (5.6.116). In *Julius Caesar*, Republican Romans like Cassius hope that individuals can still make a difference in the city. The conspirators have faith that they can reverse the tide of Caesarism and restore

the Republic. For their heroic actions, they expect to be remembered in subsequent ages as great men who made history—indeed, they expect to become
the heroes of dramas:

> How many ages hence
> Shall this our lofty scene be acted over
> In states unborn and accents yet unknown! (3.1.111–13)

But in the Rome of *Antony and Cleopatra*, history now seems to be making men rather than men making history. The actions of individuals become
less and less meaningful; they feel that they are swept up in the great currents of history that govern their lives.[123] The Empire has become a vast
machine that rolls on and accomplishes its purposes without the need for
individual human agency, without the need for heroes. Ventidius points out
that the two contenders for emperor are not responsible for their victories
but rely on subordinates to win their battles for them: "Caesar and Antony
have ever won / More in their officer than person" (3.1.16–17).[124] This is the
opposite of Coriolanus's ideal of winning battles single-handedly, or at least
by one's own heroic virtue. Antony is acutely aware of the issue of individual agency and insists that, in contrast to Octavius, he does win battles on
his own:

> He at Philippi kept
> His sword e'en like a dancer, while I strook
> The lean and wrinkled Cassius, and 'twas I
> That the mad Brutus ended. He alone
> Dealt on lieutenantry, and no practice had
> In the brave squares of war. (3.11.35–40)

But Antony is exaggerating the single-handedness of his victory over Cassius
and Brutus. In fact, he did not kill them; they killed themselves. Already in
the late Republic, massed armies decide battles, not individual heroes acting
on their own.

Wishing he were back in a Homeric world in which individual heroes
decide the outcome of a war, Antony challenges Octavius to single combat:

> His coin, ships, legions,
> May be a coward's, whose ministers would prevail
> Under the service of a child as soon
> As i' th' command of Caesar. I dare him therefore
> To lay his gay comparisons apart,
> And answer me declin'd, sword against sword,
> Ourselves alone. (3.13.22–28)

This is the sort of challenge that Coriolanus would issue; Antony talks as if he is dealing with an Aufidius. But even as Antony longs to be a Homeric hero, he recognizes that the nature of warfare has changed in the Empire. What now matters are the military—and financial—resources of the imperial army and navy.[125] Who happens to command these forces at a given moment has become a matter of indifference; the individual character of the military leader is no longer an issue. Enobarbus immediately realizes the futility of Antony's dream of single combat; Octavius has no intention of letting a gladiatorial contest resolve the issues between him and Antony (3.13.29–31).[126] Octavius laughs at Antony's challenge (4.1.3–6). He knows that in the world of empire, Antony's attachment to classical heroism makes him a walking anachronism.[127] In the era of the Empire, efficient administration of organized forces has become the key to military victory.[128]

In the world of *Antony and Cleopatra*, traditional martial heroism is virtually dead. When Octavius speaks of Antony as a heroic Roman, he is talking about his actions in the past, in the waning days of the Republic (1.4.55–71). In an eerie and uncanny scene, Shakespeare shows the archetype of the classical hero departing the world of the Empire: "'Tis the god Hercules, whom Antony loved, / Now leaves him" (4.3.16–17). Shakespeare presents the Empire as a decidedly post-heroic age.[129] Antony struggles to recapture the old-style Roman heroism, but even his efforts are fitful and half-hearted, and, as one army after another deserts him, he learns to his sorrow that in the Empire no one can win a victory single-handedly anymore.

The dwindling sense of human agency leaves the characters in *Antony and Cleopatra* obsessed with predictions about the future. Soothsayers are absent in the Rome of *Coriolanus*; the one soothsayer in *Julius Caesar* sees his timely advice ignored; but in the Rome of *Antony and Cleopatra*, soothsayers have evidently become standard household items.[130] Antony travels with one in his entourage, and, unlike Julius Caesar, he listens carefully to what the prophet says. He does not wait for advice from his soothsayer, but asks him point blank, "Whose fortunes shall rise higher, / Caesar's or mine?" (2.3.16–17). When the soothsayer tells Antony that Octavius Caesar will have greater luck, Antony dismisses him but, in fact, he believes the prophecy: "He hath spoken true" (2.3.34). Antony is convinced that Octavius has fortune on his side:

> The very dice obey him,
> And in our sports my better cunning faints
> Under his chance. (2.3.34–36)

The contest between Antony and Octavius has been reduced to a game—a game of chance. Antony's attitude toward fortune differs radically from Coriolanus's. For the republican Roman, individual heroic virtue makes one's fortune. For the imperial Roman, fate has become a matter of luck, and it will prevail over virtue. This fatalism contributes to Antony's drift toward defeat and despair.[131] His belief in Octavius's superior luck becomes a kind of self-fulfilling prophecy. Convinced that he will eventually be defeated, Antony goes down to defeat.

Cleopatra also has a soothsayer attached to her court, and Shakespeare devotes the first part of act 1, scene 2 to fortune telling. Everyone in Egypt is interested in knowing what his or her future will be; as Alexas says, "We'll know all our fortunes" (1.2.44). Once people lose faith in their ability to make their own future, they become susceptible to prophets who claim to know the future in advance.[132] Cleopatra's soothsayer stresses the difference between actively making history and passively predicting it: "I make not, but foresee" (1.2.15). The Republic of *Coriolanus* generates activity in its citizens; the Empire of *Antony and Cleopatra* produces passivity in its subjects, most evident in Egypt with all its languor and indolence.[133] Faced with circumstances in which larger forces now seem to control their lives, the characters in *Antony and Cleopatra* are tempted to sit back and let the world take its course. They have a strong sense that their best days are behind them. As Cleopatra's soothsayer predicts, "You have seen and prov'd a fairer former fortune / Than that which is to approach" (1.2.33–34).

This prophecy turns out to be true for Cleopatra, Charmian, Iras, Enobarbus, and indeed all the characters in this scene, but, more generally, it accurately describes the situation of the whole Roman world at this point in its history. Its great achievements are largely behind it, and, as Shakespeare views the situation, traditional Roman heroism has no future in the Empire. *Coriolanus* portrays the Roman Republic at its beginning, when it still had great prospects for its future, when it still had all the world to conquer. *Antony and Cleopatra* portrays Rome after the death of the Republic, with no more foreign enemies and no more challenges to face.[134] In act 4, scene 1, Octavius proclaims, "The last of many battles / We mean to fight" (4.1.11–12). Once again, words that might seem hopeful for most communities are ominous for Rome. Rome is on the verge of losing the military challenges that traditionally made it Rome. With his usual clear-sightedness, Enobarbus senses that only one option is left to genuine Romans: "Think, and die" (3.13.1).

Once victory ceases to be the standard Roman mode in the world of *Antony and Cleopatra*, characters start to reconsider its value. In a profound transformation of the Roman ethos, defeat begins to look preferable to victory. In assessing his position vis-à-vis his emperor, Ventidius makes a very peculiar claim:

> Who does i' th' wars more than his captain can
> Becomes his captain's captain; and ambition
> (The soldier's virtue) rather makes choice of loss
> Than gain which darkens him. (3.1.21–24)

This attitude would be incomprehensible to a republican Roman. What Roman captain in the heyday of the Republic would deliberately make "choice of loss," and, even if he did, how would he dare to call this "ambition" or "the soldier's virtue"? The soldier's virtue in the era of the Republic is choice of victory, not loss.[135]

Of course, for tactical or strategic reasons, a soldier of the Republic might have retreated or accepted a temporary defeat.[136] But such a commander would still have aimed at ultimately achieving victory over Rome's enemies, and no Republican soldier would brag about losing a battle and say that he deliberately set out in pursuit of loss as his ambition. The Romans admired soldiers who died in defense of their country, but not because they made "choice of loss." There is something very un-Roman in Ventidius's speech in act 3, scene 1—although only as long as we identify Rome with the Republic. In fact, Ventidius's policy is perfectly appropriate to the new circumstances of the Empire. He is no longer thinking in terms of the common good of Rome. In his changed political circumstances, he has to worry that a victory might anger his emperor, whose attitude toward Ventidius is the only factor that he needs to take into account in the imperial world. That is why Ventidius downplays his military triumph. From the beginning he attributes his victory not to his own virtue but to "Fortune" (3.1.2). He stresses his subordination to Antony even in his moment of personal triumph: "I'll humbly signify what in his name / That magical word of war, we have effected" (3.1.30–31). In the changed circumstances of the Empire, humility has mysteriously become the new "soldier's virtue," since military victors must always give all credit to their superiors.[137] Indeed, Antony makes it clear to his soldiers that they are fighting for him, not for Rome:

> For doughty-handed are you, and have fought
> Not as you serv'd the cause, but as't had been
> Each man's like mine. (4.8.5–7)

The personalizing of loyalty in the Empire turns even warfare into something nonpolitical.

The paradoxical idea that defeat might be preferable to victory is, of course, wholly absent from *Coriolanus*. But it does emerge at the end of *Julius Caesar* in the waning days of the Republic. Faced with a defeat that he now regards as inevitable, Brutus starts redefining the basic terms of Roman republican discourse:

> My heart doth joy that yet in all my life
> I found no man but he was true to me.
> I shall have glory by this losing day
> More than Octavius and Mark Antony
> By this vile conquest shall attain unto. (5.5.34–38)

One can imagine the contempt Coriolanus would feel for this speech. These are the words of a loser, and in a healthy republic, nobody likes a loser. But Brutus is trying to turn republican values on their head. He will attain "glory" by a "losing day," whereas Octavius and Antony will achieve a "conquest" that is "vile." For Brutus, losing becomes glorious and winning becomes vile. Frustrated by his failure to save the Republic and feeling impotent to do anything further on its behalf, Brutus must content himself with a kind of imaginary triumph over his enemies. In his mind, he achieves his revenge on Octavius and Antony by redefining the nature of victory and defeat so that he can ultimately be said to prevail in their contest.

From the standpoint of the Republic's classical heroism, Brutus's claims sound illogical, but his speech is reasonable in the emerging order of the Empire. Brutus is inverting the logic of his funeral oration, where, in true republican fashion, he eloquently places the political over the personal: "Not that I lov'd Caesar less, but that I lov'd Rome more" (3.2.21–22). At the end of the play, he places the personal over the political, as if he wanted his soldiers to say: "Not that I loved Rome less, but that I loved Brutus more." Brutus no longer cares about the good of Rome or the cause of the Republic that he claimed to be championing earlier in the play.[138] The loyalty of his followers becomes the highest good for him, a sentiment appropriate to an empire, not a republic. Brutus correctly sees that he can lose a battle in a way that will win him greater love from his followers. That is how loss becomes gain for him. Of course that logic would never satisfy Coriolanus. In a clear sign of the death of the Republic, at the end of *Julius Caesar* even its champion, Brutus, converts to an imperial ethic in which personal loyalty to a commander is more important than the good of the community.

As we have already seen in the case of Ventidius, Brutus's ideas of the "glory" of a "losing day" and of "vile conquest" become pervasive in the world of *Antony and Cleopatra*. For example, this ethical revaluation allows Cleopatra to present her defeat at the hand of Octavius as, in fact, a triumph over him:

> My desolation does begin to make
> A better life. 'Tis paltry to be Caesar.
> Not being Fortune, he's but Fortune's knave. (5.2.1–3)

Here again is the inversion of classical values typical of *Antony and Cleopatra*;
what looks to the ancient world like "desolation" is really "a better life," and
Caesar's victory will be what Brutus calls a "vile conquest."[139] Having pursued
imperial power all her life, Cleopatra—once she has lost it completely and
forever—decides that it has been worthless all along. When Cleopatra was in
power as a queen, she had no difficulty appreciating the virtue of the powerful. Only when she feels impotent does she come to question the glory of
imperial rule.[140] One could admire her revaluation more if she had reached
this conclusion while still on the throne, but, as it is, one cannot help thinking that her new belief in the vanity of empire results from frustration, envy,
and spite. With all further outlets to action closed to her, she can enjoy only
an imaginary revenge on Octavius. She takes advantage of the fatalism characteristic of the Empire to claim that Octavius deserves no credit for his victory. It was merely a matter of chance that he, rather than she, won the battles.
The denial of human agency works very well to console losers in their defeat.

Enobarbus also participates in the ethos of losing in *Antony and Cleopatra*, this time from the perspective of a follower in the imperial system:

> He that can endure
> To follow with allegiance a fall'n lord
> Does conquer him that did his master conquer,
> And earns a place i' th' story.[141] (3.13.43–46)

Here is yet another way of redefining "conquest" and turning defeat into victory. If allegiance to one's lord has become the highest value in the imperial
world, then Enobarbus can be content to fight on the losing side in the wars
between Antony and Octavius. In these circumstances, losing will become a
badge of honor and a kind of conquest. Enobarbus can prove his virtue by remaining loyal to his master, no matter whether Antony wins or loses. In fact,
Enobarbus suggests that a soldier now displays more virtue when he serves a
losing rather than a winning master. One might serve a winning master out
of purely mercenary motives, simply to benefit from his victory. But remaining true to a loser, at the risk of losing all oneself, demonstrates the deepest
level of loyalty. In the world of *Antony and Cleopatra*, the new imperative for
soldiers has become paradoxically "to follow with allegiance a fall'n lord."
This is the kind of follower Brutus clearly had in mind on his dying day.

And, of course, Enobarbus is also the kind of follower Antony desires.

Antony is the principal champion of the new ethos of losing in the world of the Empire, as well he might be, since he loses more than anyone else in the play. Toward the end, Antony's speeches become full of the kind of paradoxes we have seen to be characteristic of the Roman Empire, inversions of the Republic's values, in which what was traditionally regarded as good is now viewed as bad, and what was regarded as bad becomes viewed as good. As Antony tells his followers:

> Bid that welcome
> Which comes to punish us, and we punish it
> Seeming to bear it lightly. (4.14.136 –38)

This is the perfect philosophy for a loser, someone who wishes to make a virtue out of suffering. Antony sounds like a Stoic in this passage, reacting much the way Brutus claims to do in response to news of Portia's death. One term after another gets redefined in Antony's imperial discourse:

> By sea and land I'll fight; or I will live,
> Or bathe my dying honor in the blood
> Shall make it live again. (4.2.5–7)

Here death paradoxically becomes a new form of life, as Antony thinks in terms of a kind of resurrection of his honor.[142] He manages to erase the normally crucial military distinction between victory and defeat by suggesting that he will triumph in either case.

In this uncanny scene, in which Antony gathers his followers together for one last meal before what he imagines may be his dying day, he even conceives of inverting the traditional roles of master and servant:

> I wish I could be made so many men,
> And all of you clapp'd up together in
> An Antony, that I might do you service
> So good as you have done. (4.2.16 –19)

The emperor Antony wants to serve his followers, perhaps to sacrifice himself for them. One would think that, as a military commander, he would be stressing his qualities as a master at this moment in order to encourage and invigorate his soldiers. In fact, the way he plays upon their personal feelings has just the opposite effect. Even Cleopatra is puzzled by Antony's behavior: "What does he mean?" (4.2.23). As usual, Enobarbus sees clearly what is at stake: "To make his followers weep" (4.2.24).[143]

Antony is pursuing the same policy Brutus speaks of at the end of *Julius*

Caesar—to make the personal devotion of his followers more important than any mere military victory. Enobarbus sees what the consequences for Antony's army will be:

> What mean you, sir,
> To give them this discomfort? Look, they weep,
> And I, an ass, am onion-ey'd. For shame,
> Transform us not to women. (4.2.33–36)

Antony exudes not just fatalism but defeatism in his effort to deepen the loyalty of his troops to him personally and to ensure that, even if he loses the next day's battle, he will win a victory in their hearts. Enobarbus worries that Antony is weakening his troops just when they most need strength. One cannot imagine Coriolanus—or any genuine soldier of the Republic—putting on a performance like this on the eve of an important military confrontation. At the end of the scene, even Antony realizes that he needs to change the mood, but by then it is too late. He has already dispirited his soldiers with all his talk of defeat rather than victory, or a defeat that will somehow constitute a victory. Just as in *Julius Caesar*, prophecies of defeat eventually, if not immediately, become self-fulfilling.

Weakness Becomes Strength

Shakespeare creates a sharp contrast between the republican ethos of victory in *Coriolanus* and the imperial ethos of defeat in *Antony and Cleopatra*, with *Julius Caesar* portraying the transition from the one to the other. In *Coriolanus*, "valor" is held to be the "chiefest virtue" (2.2.84). In *Antony and Cleopatra*, characters keep offering the ability to endure suffering and make the best out of defeat as a higher good than conquering others. In *Coriolanus*, the pagan horizons of the Republic keep its citizens focused on the glory of this world. In the cosmopolitan empire of *Antony and Cleopatra*, new horizons have opened up and the characters question worldly success, while looking to new sources of satisfaction that transcend political borders. All this calls to mind the contrast Machiavelli draws in his *Discourses* between the ancient pagan and the modern Christian worlds. Recall what Machiavelli writes: "Our religion . . . makes us esteem less the honor of the world, whereas the Gentiles, esteeming it very much and having placed the highest good in it, were more ferocious in their actions." He adds that Christianity "has then placed the highest good in humility, abjectness, and contempt of things human," while the pagan Roman religion "placed it in greatness of spirit, strength of body, and all other things capable of making men very strong." Finally, he argues that Christianity makes people "think more of enduring their beatings than avenging them."[144]

Thus, Machiavelli's analysis of the difference between the pagan and the Christian worlds parallels Shakespeare's characterization of the difference between the Republic and the Empire. Equating the Roman Republic with the pagan world sounds reasonable, but the Roman Empire cannot be so easily identified with the Christian world. Still there are intriguing connections between the two. The emergence of the Roman Empire coincided roughly with the beginnings of Christianity. Many analysts have suggested that the Roman Empire, by uniting the whole Mediterranean world, created the preconditions for the spread of Christianity.[145] Obviously there are many differences between the Roman Empire and Christianity. For the early Christians, the Roman Empire was the very embodiment of the paganism they rejected. And for centuries the Roman Empire persecuted Christians with varying degrees of intensity. Yet eventually the emperor Constantine seems to have recognized that Christianity could provide the appropriate religion for a worldwide empire and might, in fact, be the only way to hold it together.[146] As a religion that acknowledges no political boundaries, Christianity is especially suited to a cosmopolitan empire with aspirations to universality. Moreover, as a religion that preaches resignation in the face of suffering, Christianity seems made to order for an empire that wanted to keep its subjects passive and content with their lot, however oppressed and downtrodden they may have been. Perhaps in portraying the beginnings of the Roman Empire, Shakespeare was also looking into the conditions that gave rise to Christianity.

Several signs in *Antony and Cleopatra* suggest that Shakespeare was trying to correlate the rise of the Roman Empire with the rise of Christianity. Most prominent are several mentions of Herod of Jewry, which map Roman chronology onto biblical chronology and remind us of the fact that Jesus was born during the reign of Augustus Caesar.[147] The first mention of Herod is accompanied by talk of a miraculous birth ("Let me have a child at fifty"; 1.2.28) and a reference to "three kings" (1.2.27; see also 2.2.76).[148] Perhaps strangest of all the biblical references is the way that Shakespeare makes Antony quote the Bible by having him refer to the bulls of Basan (3.13.127) of Psalm 22. The opening line of this psalm is: "My God, my God, why hast thou forsaken me?"—words more famously spoken by Jesus on the cross in the Gospel According to St. Matthew (27:46).[149] As Ethel Seaton was the first to note, if one consults the Geneva translation of the New Testament, one finds that lines from the Book of Revelation are spoken by Antony's guards when he first tries to kill himself: "The star is fall'n" and "time is at his period" (4.14.106–7).[150] Several other phrases in the play resonate with the Book of Revelation.

Octavius's "kings o' th' earth" (3.6.68) calls to mind Revelation 17:2 and his "kings of kings" (3.6.13) echoes Revelation 19:16, while Cleopatra's "Lord of lords" (4.8.16) suggests Revelation 17:14 and 19:16 (as well as 1 Timothy 16:15).[151] And, of course, Antony's talk of "new heaven, new earth" (1.1.17) echoes Revelation 21:1. While looking for New Testament parallels, one might view Antony's evening meal with his followers as a version of the Last Supper, complete with one who will soon, Judas-like, betray him (Enobarbus).[152] Antony sounds quite un-Roman in this scene, and remarkably proto-Christian:

> Tend me to-night;
> May be it is the period of your duty;
> Haply you shall not see me more, or if,
> A mangled shadow. Perchance to-morrow
> You'll serve another master. I look on you
> As one that takes his leave. Mine honest friends,
> I turn you not away, but like a master
> Married to your good service, stay till death.
> Tend me to-night two hours, I ask no more. (4.2.24–32)

Antony virtually invites his followers to desert him, but at the same time, he makes sure that, if they do, they will feel guilty about it. When Enobarbus betrays Antony soon after, his treachery makes him feel like Judas: "I am alone the villain of the earth" (4.6.29). Convinced of his own evil character—his "turpitude" (4.6.32)—and in the grip of a bad conscience, Enobarbus experiences an overwhelming sense of guilt that leads him to wish to die (4.6.36–37).[153] A few scenes later, he seems to will his own death, after accusing himself of "foul thoughts," describing his "revolt" as "infamous," and branding himself a "master-leaver and a fugitive" (4.9.18–22).

Any one of these parallels could be rejected as accidental, and some may seem more plausible than others, but the cumulative effect is hard to dismiss. Shakespeare is creating some kind of link between imperial Rome and early Christianity. But one must be very careful in formulating the significance of these parallels. I am not claiming that Shakespeare embraced Machiavelli's critique of Christianity. Nor am I claiming, as some critics have, that *Antony and Cleopatra*, in the spirit of St. Augustine, champions Christian over pagan ethics.[154] I will confine myself to a more limited claim—that Shakespeare saw a broad correlation between the new ethical principles of the Roman Empire and those of Christianity. Both the Roman Empire and Christianity were linked to the same set of conditions in the ancient Mediterranean world—the dissolution of traditional political life and the opening up of new ethical and religious possibilities in the wake of the cosmopolitanism this development produced.[155] The way that Machiavelli presents these developments, he gives an active role to Christianity as an external force that undermines Rome and the whole world of paganism. Shakespeare is looking at something different—a process internal to Roman history. *Antony and Cleopatra* shows that the corruption and decline of the Roman aristocracy weakened Rome's power and thereby prepared the way for Christianity.

Machiavelli inaugurated a long intellectual tradition of trying to understand how Christianity displaced paganism. One of the most important figures in this tradition is Friedrich Nietzsche. His analysis and terminology may be helpful in understanding the contrast Shakespeare draws between the ethos of victory in *Coriolanus* and the ethos of defeat in *Antony and Cleopatra*. Another way of formulating this contrast is to say that *Coriolanus* portrays the world of what Nietzsche calls "master morality," while *Antony and Cleopatra* portrays the world of what he calls "slave morality."[156] Nietzsche develops his theory of the slave revolt in morality in the ancient world in terms of the difference between two pairs of opposites: "good versus bad" in contrast with "good versus evil." The master morality of the ancient Greeks and Romans was, as its name implies, created by an aristocratic elite, nobles like Coriolanus. They defined themselves and everything associated with them as good. They then derived their notion of what is bad from everything that was their opposite, everything that characterized the slaves they ruled. Here "good versus bad" is the equivalent of "noble versus base."[157] As a caste of noble warriors, the masters value triumphing in battle as good, and hence for them goodness consists of strength, courage, toughness, aggressiveness, and all the qualities required to conquer an opponent. In this ethical framework, what is bad is weakness, cowardice, passivity—anything that makes someone willing to suffer an injury rather than inflict one.

According to Nietzsche, Christianity—for him, a religion of slaves— managed to turn master morality on its head, inverting its values. What the masters regard as good, Christianity redefines as evil; what the masters regard as bad, Christianity revalues as good. That is, the pride and aggressiveness of the master become the very definition of sin in the eyes of Christianity, while the meekness and submissiveness of the slave become the definition of virtue in Christian terms. Humiliated by his inability to stand up to his master in open conflict, the slavish Christian is gripped by envy, spite, and a consuming desire for revenge against the ruling class (a complex of emotions Nietzsche labels with the French word *ressentiment*).[158] In Nietzsche's view, the Christian makes a virtue out of necessity. He has to submit to his

master's will, but he makes the best of a bad situation by claiming that he
consciously chooses to do so. He claims to suffer, not because he is too weak
to do anything about it but because he believes that suffering is good for the
soul and therefore makes him a better human being. The master's victories
are stigmatized as hollow; by contrast, what seems to be the slave's defeat
makes him a morally superior person and thus constitutes the truer form of
victory. In Nietzsche's view, that is the way the Christian turns his weakness
into strength and asserts his moral superiority over the masters of the world.
All of Christian morality derives from this logic of inverting the values of the
classical world—"the meek shall inherit the earth," "turn the other cheek,"
and so on. Turning the tables on their masters, Christians succeed in redefining moral terms so that they come to mean the opposite of what they did in
the classical world.

Shakespeare of course could not have read Nietzsche, but, as we have
seen, already during the Renaissance Machiavelli offered a similar analysis
of the difference between the pagan and Christian worlds. As for other Renaissance authors, Rabelais, for example, comes up with an extraordinarily
Nietzschean formulation of the difference between pagans and Christians
in his *Gargantua and Pantagruel* when Grandgousier says, "Such imitations
of the ancient heroes—Hercules, Alexander, Hannibal, Scipio, Caesar, and
so on—is contrary to the teachings of our Gospel. . . . And what the Sara-
cens and Barbarians once dubbed prowess, we now call brigandage and evil-
doing."[159] In several of Shakespeare's plays, he displays knowledge of just this
kind of dual moral perspective—the difference between a classical morality
that applies to noble warriors and a Christian morality that applies to ordinary human beings. In *Richard II*, for example, the Duchess of Gloucester
tells John of Gaunt: "That which in mean men we entitle patience / Is pale
cold cowardice in noble breasts" (1.1.33–34).[160]

Macbeth consistently contrasts the heroic warrior's moral perspective
with an ordinary Christian's. Lady Macbeth, in trying to get her husband to
overcome his Christian moral scruples about murder, reproaches him for
his lack of manly courage, treating his weakness, as Nietzsche would, as a
sickness: "Worthy thane, / You do unbend your noble strength, to think / So
brain-sickly of things" (2.2.41–43). In one of the most poignant moments in
the play, Shakespeare portrays the opposite attitude in Lady Macduff. As an
otherworldly Christian, she is bewildered by the warrior's conception of good
and bad that prevails in the savage world of Scotland:

> I have done no harm. But I remember now
> I am in this earthly world—where to do harm

> Is often laudable, to do good sometime
> Accounted dangerous folly. (4.2.74–77)

Passages such as this show that Shakespeare was aware of the Nietzschean idea that differing definitions of the very nature of "good" are abroad in a world of clashing moralities.[161] Thus, based on ideas readily available in the Renaissance and without knowing Nietzsche's specific terminology or sharing his evaluation of Christianity, Shakespeare may well have developed a similar understanding of the ethical transformation that occurred at the end of the classical era, which he associates with the death of the Roman Republic. In contrast to Machiavelli and Nietzsche, Shakespeare suggests that just before the emergence of Christianity, the Roman Empire was already undergoing an ethical revaluation that anticipated, and perhaps prepared the way for, Christianity and its new morality.

What Nietzsche calls master morality is evident throughout *Coriolanus*, and Coriolanus is its chief spokesman. Shakespeare may well have been attracted to the subject of Coriolanus because it allowed him to explore the world of master morality in a virtually unadulterated form. Despite the fact that the plebeians are free, Coriolanus regards them as "base slaves" (1.5.7), indeed, as worse than slaves: "You souls of geese, / That bear the shapes of men, how have you run / From slaves that apes would beat!" (1.4.34–36). The plebeians are fearful, tame animals ("hares"), not the noble, wild beasts ("lions") the patricians want their soldiers to be (1.1.171).[162] In the terms of master morality, Coriolanus presents the difference between patrician and plebeian as the difference between two species, sometimes the difference between human beings and beasts. He does not view the plebeians as true Romans and fellow citizens:

> I would they were barbarians, as they are,
> Though in Rome litter'd; not Romans, as they are not,
> Though calved i' th' porch o' th' Capitol. (3.1.237–39)

Here Coriolanus combines his animal imagery for the plebeians ("litter'd," "calved") with the idea that they are barbarians—strangers to true Roman nobility.

In his climactic confrontation with the plebeians in act 3, scene 1, Coriolanus does everything he can to stress the gulf that separates them from the patricians. He objects to "mingling them with us, the honor'd number / Who lack not virtue, no, nor power, but that / Which they have given to beggars" (3.1.72–74). Coriolanus's objection to the institution of the tribunate is that it has overturned the traditional, aristocratic hierarchy in Rome:

If you are learn'd,
Be not as common fools; if you are not,
Let them have cushions by you. You are plebeians,
If they be senators. (3.1.99–102)

Coriolanus thus anticipates what Nietzsche calls the revaluation of values in Rome. Because the patricians give the plebeians a role in the Roman regime, they leave themselves vulnerable to a slave revolt that would invert the city's hierarchy. Coriolanus consistently identifies the patricians with everything good and noble in Rome and the plebeians with everything bad and contemptible. The plebeians understand that the patricians get to define what is good in Rome; as the First Citizen says to his fellows: "We are accounted poor citizens, the patricians good" (1.1.15–16). The patricians' sense of their superiority rests on the visible contrast between their wealth and the plebeians' poverty: "The object of our misery, is as an inventory to particularize their abundance" (1.1.20–22).

In the aristocratic order of *Coriolanus*, the hierarchy of the noble over the base generates a whole series of binary oppositions that constitutes the scale of values in the Roman Republic: rich versus poor, clean versus dirty, healthy versus sick, steadfast versus mutable, wise versus foolish, learned versus ignorant, courageous versus cowardly, warlike versus peace loving, and, above all, strong versus weak. The Roman Republic has the ethos of a military aristocracy, and its measure of virtue is basically the warrior's strength. At a crucial juncture, Coriolanus reminds the plebeians: "There's some among you have beheld me fighting; / Come, try upon yourselves what you have seen me" (3.1.223–24). Indeed, Coriolanus offers a simple mathematical measure of human worth when he compares himself to the plebeians: "On fair ground / I could beat forty of them" (3.1.241–42). Before the age of mechanized warfare, a fighting man distinguished himself by his sheer physical presence, often just his unusual size, which could create the impression of a demigod. Ordinary human beings used to stand in awe of such nearly superhuman prodigies of strength. The Volscian servants are relieved to have survived their brief encounter with a man of Coriolanus's impressive physique: "What an arm he has! he turn'd me about with his finger and his thumb as one would set a top" (4.5.152–53). For the Volsces Coriolanus's sheer physical power elevates him above the normal range of humanity: "He is simply the rarest man i' th' world" (4.5.160–61). Once again, strength becomes the mathematical measure of the man, as the Volscians compare Coriolanus to Aufidius: "worth six on him" (4.5.166). Forty times stronger than a Roman plebeian, Coriolanus is still six times stronger than a Volscian noble.[163]

This equation of pure physical strength with goodness is overturned in the Roman Empire. Everywhere one looks in *Antony and Cleopatra*, one finds the proto-Christian idea that weakness is strength, that nobility is to be found in the humble, that the high is to be made level with the low.[164] Octavia, for example, tells Antony: "The Jove of power make me, most weak, most weak, / Your reconciler!" (3.4.29–30). Things are always changing into their opposite in *Antony and Cleopatra*, especially strength into weakness and weakness into strength. Antony claims:

> Now all labor
> Mars what it does; yea, very force entangles
> Itself with strength. (4.14.47–49)

This kind of inversion of values generates all sorts of paradoxes in Antony's speeches:

> Thou strik'st not me, 'tis Caesar thou defeat'st. (4.14.68)
> Come then; for with a wound I must be cur'd. (4.14.78)[165]
> Let him that loves me strike me dead. (4.14.108)

The redefinition of nobility in the play is perhaps most clearly formulated by Cleopatra when the "rural fellow" brings her the means of committing suicide: "What poor an instrument / May do a noble deed! He brings me liberty" (5.2.236–37). Here the "poor" becomes the "noble," and what had traditionally been regarded as the ultimate loss of human agency—death—is reinterpreted as freedom.

With Cleopatra's insistence that "'Tis paltry to be Caesar," she deprecates the whole world of nobility traditionally admired in Rome, the goal of political preeminence. Her vision works to level the high with the low. She points out that the "dung" is "the beggar's nurse and Caesar's" (5.2.7–8); in this skeptical view of human hierarchy, the mighty emperor's origins are as low as the beggar's.[166] When Antony dies, Cleopatra has a vision of the universal leveling of the differences of rank in the Roman world:

> Noblest of men, woo't die?
> Hast thou no care of me? Shall I abide
> In this dull world, which in thy absence is
> No better than a sty? O, see, my women,
> The crown o' th' earth doth melt. My lord!

> O, wither'd is the garland of the war,
> The soldier's pole is fall'n! Young boys and girls
> Are level now with men; the odds is gone,
> And there is nothing left remarkable
> Beneath the visiting moon. (4.15.59–68)

Cleopatra confirms that *Antony and Cleopatra* portrays a post-heroic world. With the death of Antony, the last remnant of the old heroism and nobility has vanished from the earth, and Cleopatra feels herself surrounded by mediocrity. Her lingering aristocratic nature makes her despise what the Roman patricians have become.[167] She sees through the remaining pretensions to nobility in the new imperial system. Perhaps it takes someone of royal lineage to appreciate how little of true nobility is left in the Roman Empire.[168] Cleopatra has reached the point where she is ready to deny even her own nobility; like Antony, she imagines herself reduced to the level of her servants:

> No more but e'en a woman, and commanded
> By such poor passion as the maid that milks
> And does the meanest chares. (4.15.72–74)

With the effacing of the difference between a queen and a milkmaid, slave morality is well on its way to triumphing over master morality in imperial Rome.[169] Antony expresses the same inversion of values when he addresses his servant Eros: "Thrice-nobler than myself!" (4.14.95). The transformation of the meaning of "noble" in imperial Rome is complete when even Octavius Caesar speaks of "noble weakness" (5.2.344).[170]

Shakespeare highlights the contrast between master morality and slave morality in his Roman plays by one striking verbal link between *Coriolanus* and *Antony and Cleopatra* involving the term "good will." Master morality is a morality of deeds; slave morality is a morality of intentions. That is, in master morality only what one can actually accomplish matters, but slave morality praises people who simply mean well, even if their actions are completely ineffectual. Coriolanus speaks for master morality when he says in front of the Roman army: "He that has but effected his good will / Hath overta'en mine act" (1.9.18–19).

Coriolanus admires a good will, but only when it has been "effected," that is, translated into action. The same term, "good will," appears in *Antony and Cleopatra*, but in a very different context and with the opposite inflection. Cleopatra is joking with Mardian, one of the eunuchs in her court. In response to her request that he "play" with her, he offers to do so "as well as I can, madam." With a ribald pun, Cleopatra recognizes that Mardian will not be able to fulfill her needs as a woman, but she makes excuses for him:

"And when good will is show'd, though't come too short, / The actor may plead pardon" (2.5.6–9). This is the very opposite of Coriolanus's conception of "good will." For Cleopatra it is not necessary to translate one's good intentions into actual deeds. It is enough to have meant well.[171] This is a very comforting philosophy, especially for eunuchs. Throughout *Antony and Cleopatra* the emphasis changes from the solid and objective world of deeds characteristic of *Coriolanus*—where people are judged by what they *do*—to a shadowy and subjective world of intentions—of beliefs, loyalties, suspicions, and surmises—inner notions of soul that are difficult to pin down with any certainty and that therefore make it difficult to assess people when one must judge them only by vague notions of intentions that necessarily remain hidden.

Death Becomes Life

What I have been calling the proto-Christian character of the world of *Antony and Cleopatra* surfaces in many intriguing ways. After being largely excluded in *Coriolanus* and *Julius Caesar*, the idea of the afterlife begins to emerge in *Antony and Cleopatra*. The Romans of *Coriolanus* do not orient themselves in this life according to belief in a potentially more rewarding afterlife. In *Julius Caesar*, Shakespeare actually corrected an error in his source in Plutarch, where the English translator whose version he used, Thomas North, mistakenly introduced a notion of an afterlife into Brutus's last conversation with Cassius.[172] But it is characteristic of the new world of *Antony and Cleopatra*—with the vast expansion of its horizons—that the Romans begin to speak of an existence after death, indeed, the kind of afterlife that one might look forward to and even long for.[173] Antony evidently believes that he and Cleopatra will be reunited in another world:

> Where souls do couch on flowers, we'll hand in hand,
> And with our sprightly port make the ghosts gaze.
> Dido and Aeneas shall want troops,
> And all the haunt be ours.[174] (4.14.51–54)

This notion of the afterlife is one of Rome's most significant imports from Egypt.[175] No country in the ancient world was more obsessed with the afterlife than Egypt, and Cleopatra in particular has long been fascinated with death and its aftermath (5.2.354–56).[176] Her comic exchange with the fig seller who brings her the asp turns on the serious issue of mortality versus immortality, and, above all, on what might or might not happen after death: "Those that do die of it [the asp's bite] do seldom or never recover" (5.2.247–48). *Antony*

and Cleopatra presents a world far more mysterious than that of *Coriolanus,*
and the greatest mystery is what lies beyond the grave.

The possibility of an afterlife transforms the traditional Roman notion
of suicide. Shakespeare consistently associates a willingness to commit suicide with the ancient Roman world. Christian characters in Shakespeare feel
prevented from committing suicide because their religion forbids it; Hamlet, wanting to commit suicide, wishes that "the Everlasting had not fix'd /
His canon 'gainst self-slaughter!" (1.2.131–32). When Horatio hopes to follow Hamlet into death voluntarily, he expresses his intention in these terms:
"I am more an antique Roman than a Dane" (5.2.341). Macbeth captures the
contrast between pagan and Christian attitudes toward suicide when he says,
"Why should I play the Roman fool, and die / On mine own sword?" (5.8.1–
2). In *Julius Caesar,* Shakespeare shows that Republican Romans view suicide
as an honorable course of action. Far from regarding it as forbidden to them,
they view suicide as the only way to avoid dishonor. True to the classical heroic ethic, they prefer suicide to the shame of being dragged in triumph by a
conqueror.[177]

This attitude persists into the Roman Empire and affects the decisions
of both Antony and Cleopatra to commit suicide. Antony insists on the Roman character of his suicide; he remains "a Roman, by a Roman / Valiantly
vanquish'd" (4.15.57–58). This is Antony's ultimate ploy to turn defeat into
victory, and, indeed, he presents his suicide as a kind of Stoic self-conquest.[178]
Cleopatra is at her most Roman when she kills herself: "Let's do't after the
high Roman fashion" (4.15.87). And yet, as she contemplates suicide, Cleopatra introduces a decidedly un-Roman note into her deliberations:

> Then is it sin
> To rush into the secret house of death
> Ere death dare come to us? (4.15.80–82)

This is the only moment in all three Roman plays in which anyone regards
suicide as a sin.[179] The difference in the evaluation of suicide results from taking the afterlife into account. If there is no life after death, then suicide cannot
be attractive or desirable—it is at best a way of bringing an end to shame and
pain. But if there is an afterlife, especially one as glamorous as Antony foresees, then suicide becomes a positive temptation, rather than a mere negation
of life, and a religion might need to prohibit it.

At the moment of her suicide Cleopatra eloquently speaks in anticipation
of an afterlife:

> Give me my robe, put on my crown, I have
> Immortal longings in me. Now no more

> The juice of Egypt's grape shall moist this lip.
> Yare, yare, good Iras; quick. Methinks I hear
> Antony call: I see him rouse himself
> To praise my noble act. I hear him mock
> The luck of Caesar, which the gods give men
> To excuse their after wrath. Husband, I come!
> Now to that name my courage prove my title!
> I am fire and air; my other elements
> I give to baser life. (5.2.280–90)

So convinced has Cleopatra become of an afterlife that she feels that she is in a race with her waiting woman Charmian:

> This proves me base.
> If she first meet the curlèd Antony,
> He'll make demand of her, and spend that kiss
> Which is my heaven to have.[180] (5.2.300–3)

The greatest concentration of proto-Christian language in the play appears in Cleopatra's dying speeches. She speaks of "heaven" and "immortal longings;" the once voluptuary queen becomes an ascetic ("Now no more / The juice of Egypt's grape shall moist this lip;" "I am fire and air; my other elements / I give to baser life"); she continues her critique of worldly glory as a matter of mere luck; and finally she carries on the redefinition of what is "noble" and what is "base" in the Roman world.[181]

The introduction of the idea of an afterlife into *Antony and Cleopatra*, together with the transformation of the idea of suicide, highlights how different the Empire is from the Republic.[182] And the fact that these changes seem to result from Rome's encounter with Egypt shows how the Empire's cosmopolitan embrace of the Mediterranean world fundamentally transforms it. As we saw in *Coriolanus*, excluding any idea of an afterlife in the Roman Republic is basic to the city's attempt to form the comprehensive horizon of its citizens. With its capacity for honoring its heroes, the city is the only path to immortality in republican Rome. How could the city claim to be self-contained if its citizens could look forward to a life after death in some heaven far beyond Rome's borders? It is symptomatic of the expansion of the cosmic horizon in *Antony and Cleopatra* that a number of characters in the play begin to think of new paths to immortality, quite independent of Rome. Antony and Cleopatra hope to be immortalized as lovers; the queen proclaims, "Eternity was in our lips and eyes" (1.3.35).[183] In the final words of the play, Octavius is generous enough to grant their wish for immortal fame: "No grave upon the earth shall clip in it / A pair so famous" (5.2.359–60). But this generosity may be joined with policy, a new imperial policy.[184] It is to Octavius's advantage as emperor to promote love as a new source of honor. Diverting his subjects from the traditional Roman path of honor in politics will make his life as emperor much easier and more secure. In honoring Antony and Cleopatra as lovers, Octavius is implicitly criticizing them as political leaders. The fame that they have gained as lovers has come at the expense of their reputations as rulers. Since their personal triumph has taken the form of a love-death, in the paradoxical fashion of the play their victory in romantic terms is at the same time a defeat in political terms.[185] In the end, as Octavius makes clear, their fame is to be found only in a grave.

The Liberation of Eros

Throughout *Antony and Cleopatra*, especially in Octavius's final tribute to the lovers, the gulf between public and private life that is characteristic of an imperial regime opens up. In the politics of empire, satisfaction in public life is restricted to the few who are able to contend for the imperial throne, while new sources of satisfaction become available in private life. As Octavius demonstrates, an emperor has every reason to encourage his subjects to seek satisfaction in private as opposed to public life. Thus, under an imperial regime, romantic love takes on a new importance, becoming a central concern in the lives of the many people for whom politics has ceased to be a viable and satisfying pursuit. In the Republic, private life tends to be absorbed into public life, since the regime takes an interest in every human activity, including love and procreation. As Volumnia explicitly states, she produces and raises children for the sake of Rome, and in the end it proves fortunate for the city that Coriolanus discovers that he cannot separate his identity as a human being from his identity as a Roman citizen. In the Republic, family life is integrated into civic life. Marriage is a Roman institution, and if the emotional restraint of Coriolanus's relationship to Virgilia is any indication, romantic love in *Coriolanus* participates in the austerity of the republican regime. In striking contrast to what happens in most of Shakespeare's plays, love between man and woman is barely visible as a motive of the action in *Coriolanus*. In accord with the epic, heroic spirit of the play, the competitive relationship between man and man occupies center stage. Characteristically, women do not exert influence in the play as objects of romantic devotion; whatever power Volumnia possesses stems from her role as the matriarch of a Roman family.

In *Julius Caesar* romantic love still does not emerge as a principal motive of the dramatic action. Even in the waning days of the Republic, no Roman is seduced away from his duty by feminine wiles. But in the relationships between men and women in *Julius Caesar*, a tension between public and private life starts to surface. The only woman in *Coriolanus* who has any real impact on the action—Volumnia—speaks on behalf of Rome when she confronts her wayward son at the end of the play. By contrast, the two women in *Julius Caesar*, Portia and Calphurnia, while not exactly speaking against Rome, do try to interfere with their husbands' participation in politics and restrain them from their public enterprises. Calphurnia tries to talk Caesar out of going to the Senate; Portia presses Brutus to tell her what is bothering him, knowing full well that it must be a political concern. On the day of the assassination, she imprudently sends Brutus's servant to the Senate House to get news of events, thereby threatening to expose the conspiracy. Although Calphurnia and Portia basically remain within the bounds of a Roman wife's traditional role, they both show signs of chafing against those limits. Portia questions Brutus about the confines of her married life:

> Within the bond of marriage, tell me, Brutus,
> Is it excepted I should know no secrets
> That appertain to you? Am I yourself
> But, as it were, in sort or limitation.
> To keep with you at meals, comfort your bed,
> And talk to you sometimes? Dwell I but in the suburbs
> Of your good pleasure? (2.1.280–86)

Clearly, Portia would like to play a greater role in her husband's political life than Virgilia, for example, can imagine playing in Coriolanus's.[186] Reading *Julius Caesar* in light of Shakespeare's conception of a changing Rome in his trilogy, one senses that something is happening to the Roman household that is correlated with the dissolution of the republican regime.

Portia's reasonable and moderate desire to play a greater role in her husband's public life mutates in *Antony and Cleopatra* into the queen's unbounded desire to share rule with Antony and, indeed, to dominate every aspect of his existence. From being restricted to a very limited role in the days of the Republic, romantic love explodes in the Empire as a newly dominant power in the action, thus driving a wedge between public and private life. The Roman institution of marriage for the sake of the family is no longer able to contain the power of romantic love and channel it toward the good of the city. Instead, love in *Antony and Cleopatra* becomes an end in itself, and occurs outside of and—to Octavia's sorrow—contrary to conventional marriage bonds.[187] Antony and Cleopatra repeatedly offer love as a good higher than conventional political life, and it proves to be a subversive force within the new world of the Roman Empire. Cleopatra knows how to use her erotic powers to control Antony, employing all her feminine charms to win him away from Rome and make him do her bidding, to the point of virtually emasculating him:

> I laugh'd him out of patience; and that night
> I laugh'd him into patience; and the next morn,
> Even the ninth hour, I drank him to his bed;
> Then put my tires and mantles on him, whilst
> I wore his sword Philippan. (2.5.19–23)

To the Romans, Cleopatra appears to be a witch, casting some kind of erotic spell over Antony, as Pompey claims:

> But all the charms of love,
> Salt Cleopatra, soften thy wan'd lip!
> Let witchcraft join with beauty, lust with both! (2.1.20–22)

Given the way that Shakespeare portrays Cleopatra's seductive powers, Antony's attraction to her seems perfectly understandable. Shakespeare emphasizes the erotic hold she exerts on other men in the play. Nevertheless, in the context of the Roman plays as a trilogy, Antony's obsession with Cleopatra must be viewed as the result of an absence as well as a presence. He is indeed enchanted by her charms whenever he is in her presence, but the absence of the traditional Republic in his life is a major factor in his being susceptible to the allure of erotic life. With the dissolution of all the institutions that used to embody the good of Rome, men like Antony become disoriented and disillusioned, and therefore become susceptible to new influences in their lives. One might perform a thought experiment and wonder whether, in the heyday of the Republic, a man like Coriolanus could have been seduced away from his Roman duties by any woman, even one with the sexual allure of Cleopatra. To object that in the early days of the Republic Coriolanus would never have had the opportunity to encounter as exotic a creature as Cleopatra is already to highlight what distinguishes early Rome. With its narrow horizons and self-contained community, republican Rome protects its citizens from foreign influences and keeps them focused on the city's political life.[188] Cleopatra's overwhelming influence on Antony is testimony to the virtues and defects of the imperial regime.

The Tragedy of the Republic

Montesquieu entitled his reflections on Roman history *Considérations sur les causes de la grandeur des Romains et de leur décadence*. Shakespeare also could have called his trilogy of Roman plays a portrait of the grandeur and the decadence of Rome, the political and military grandeur of the Republic and the moral and cultural decadence of the Empire. Alternatively, he might have called the trilogy "The Rise and Fall of the Roman Republic." When read together in historical sequence, *Coriolanus*, *Julius Caesar*, and *Antony and Cleopatra* tell the tragic stories of a series of great Romans, but they also tell a larger and overarching tragic story, the tragedy of the Roman Republic.[189] Like a tragic hero, republican Rome finds that its very greatness leads to its downfall.[190] The Republic is distinguished by its martial virtue and the single-minded devotion of its citizens to fighting on its behalf. But in the process of conquering the Mediterranean world, the Republic undermines the basis of its traditional civic virtues.

Rome's great captains and even its ordinary people are corrupted by the wealth that flows into the city from conquered lands, and devotion to the common good gradually weakens until the city is ripped apart by private factions. At the same time, the city's commitment to its traditional republican way of life is subverted by exposure to the foreign cultures Rome brings within its orbit.[191] As the capital of a vast and diverse Empire, Rome becomes increasingly cosmopolitan, the crossroads for a wide variety of competing visions of life, some of them antithetical to its republican traditions. The Rome of *Antony and Cleopatra* may try to evoke its republican past, but it has become thoroughly Egyptianized and pervaded by imperial styles of life. In Shakespeare's portrayal, the Roman Republic, like a tragic hero, overreaches itself. In its drive to conquer the world, Rome ends up destroying everything it originally stood for. Indeed, by defeating all its rivals among the cities ringing the Mediterranean and yoking them under its dominion, Rome effectively brings the era of the classical polis to an end and eventually undermines even its own civic existence.[192] Perhaps Shakespeare's most original achievement in the Roman plays is to suggest that tragedy is not restricted to individual human beings; a city can lead a tragic existence as well. If we take seriously all the talk about the death of Rome at the end of *Julius Caesar*, we see how grand the plan of Shakespeare's Roman trilogy truly is. Shakespeare is expanding his conception of tragedy to encompass not just individual heroes but an entire political community.[193]

The mention of competing visions of life in Rome points to another way in which Shakespeare's Roman plays can be spoken of as an integrated tragic trilogy. In his *Aesthetics*, Hegel defines tragedy as a situation in which two legitimate but incompatible goods come into conflict, leaving the tragic hero unable to escape doing wrong no matter which course of action he or she chooses.[194] In Hegel's paradigmatic tragedy, Sophocles's *Antigone*, the heroine is charged with the task of interring her brother, Polyneices, who, as a traitor to their native city of Thebes, has been left unburied by order of Creon, their uncle and ruler of the city. Antigone must choose between the good as defined by family custom and the good as defined by political decree, and the choice proves to be deeply tragic for her. If she is loyal to her brother, she must violate her city's laws; if she is loyal to her city, she must betray her family obligations. In Hegel's theory, tragedy is especially likely to occur at the great turning points of history, the transition from one regime to another, when a new way of life comes into opposition with an old. For example, the tragedy of Aeschylus's *Oresteia* trilogy is rooted in the tension between an older, tribal order based on the revenge ethic of the clan and the newly emergent political order in Athens, based on a novel conception of civic justice. As the preeminent philosopher of history, Hegel introduced a historical component into his conception of tragedy. For Hegel tragedy is fundamentally a historical phenomenon; tragedy grows out of the contradictions history keeps generating in its march to higher stages of consciousness.

Hegel's understanding of tragedy originated in his study of Greek drama, and yet Shakespeare's plays figure prominently in his discussion of the subject. And rightly so, because Shakespeare shows, especially in his Roman plays, that he understands the historicity of tragedy. The tragic choices faced by the heroes of *Julius Caesar* and *Antony and Cleopatra* are framed by historical developments. In both plays, the major characters are in effect choosing between the Republic and the Empire, as Rome moves from one regime to the other, largely as a result of the decisions they make. The choice between the republican way of life and the imperial way of life is as fundamental as one can imagine; they represent truly antithetical conceptions of the human good. Juxtaposed as they are in the Roman plays, each regime helps identify the virtues and defects of the other. Memories of the Republic and its civic virtues haunt the Empire and highlight its corruption and loss of a sense of the common good. But the Empire expands the horizons of its subjects and opens up new realms of experience to them, giving them a glimpse of what lies beyond the borders of political life. The Empire thus exposes the narrowness of republican life, the way Rome initially confines its citizens to a very limited range of experience, all bound up with civic existence. But the Republic's focus on political life turns out to be essential to its formation of heroic character and therefore to its military success—the victories that make the city great, the conquests that win it an empire. Yet in the end, the expanded horizons that empire opens up subvert the very Roman virtues that made it possible and leave the imperial Romans bewildered and at sea, no longer possessing the strong sense of political purpose that energized the Republic.

In both the Republic and the Empire, the distinctive virtues of the regime are inextricably and tragically bound up with its defects. By largely absorbing private into public life, the Republic offers its citizens the virtues of widespread and intense participation in politics, but at the price of limiting them to civic existence and cutting them off from any activity that might go beyond or transcend politics. By cordoning off private from public life, the Empire offers its subjects new sources of satisfaction and a wealth of exotic experience, but at the price of losing their grounding in civic existence and perhaps their very sense of purpose and their belief in human agency.

The choice between the Republic and the Empire is thus truly tragic, revealing a fundamental set of human alternatives. The ancient city, such as the Rome of *Coriolanus*, is a tight-knit community with well-defined borders, small enough to exert influence on all aspects of its citizens' lives and also to allow them to participate actively, individually, and directly in its affairs.[195] The Roman Empire of *Antony and Cleopatra* is much larger than the ancient city, and thus its ruler becomes remote from its people, unable to monitor their activities as carefully and also unable to give most of them any role in governing their lives. Many of the regimes with which Shakespeare was familiar in the Europe of his day, including England, either styled themselves as empires or aspired to become empires. Thus, in portraying a republic in *Coriolanus*, Shakespeare was dealing with a kind of regime radically different from what he experienced in Renaissance England. By the time of *Antony and Cleopatra*, Rome has developed into something much closer in political terms to the most prevalent form of government in Shakespeare's Europe. The Rome of Octavius Caesar is based on one-man rule—in that sense, it is a monarchy—and its subjects have developed transpolitical concerns and longings that in principle anticipate Christianity and its contempt for this world and its interest in an afterlife. The Roman Republic represents the form of government that, by calling its citizens to participate in political life, keeps them focused on civic existence and life in this world. The Roman Empire is the prototype of the form of government that, by restricting rule to one person or a very limited number of participants, leaves the rest of the people disenfranchised but therefore free to pursue the nonpolitical dimensions of life, including aspirations to new forms of immortality beyond the borders of conventional civic existence.[196]

We can now see more fully why Shakespeare was drawn to the subject of Rome, and particularly the subject of *republican* Rome. Whatever his practical political concerns may have been, in theoretical terms he was interested in the full range of human possibilities, and that drew him to examine a genuine alternative to the modern monarchical state. The ancient Rome of *Coriolanus*

offered him a well-documented case study of a regime with political principles diametrically opposed to those of Renaissance England. Moreover, in
Shakespeare's reading of Roman history, he saw the Republic transform into
an imperial regime that shared many, although not all, of the characteristics of
the European governments of his day. Read as a trilogy, Shakespeare's Roman
plays in effect trace the process by which the ancient world developed into
the modern.[197] In the movement from *Coriolanus* to *Julius Caesar*, the narrow
focus on life in the polis breaks down. This development leads the Romans
to question their traditional estimation of military and political greatness as
the highest form of human excellence. By the time of *Antony and Cleopatra*,
new forms of excellence—foreign to the traditions of the ancient world—
have begun to emerge, among them romantic love as a new ideal and a new
path to immortality. These new forms of human excellence are related to the
Christian revaluation of pagan values that undermined and transformed the
ancient world. Although the Rome of *Antony and Cleopatra* is not yet Christian, it seems well prepared to accept the coming of Christianity. The ancient
gods are departing, and Rome seems ready to receive a new revelation.

In tracing the dissolution and transformation of the ancient world as the
Roman Republic becomes the Roman Empire, Shakespeare joins company
with some of the most serious thinkers on the subject, including, as we have
seen, Machiavelli and Nietzsche. Like the two philosophers, Shakespeare offers the ancient pagan world exemplified in *Coriolanus* as the fundamental
alternative to the Christian world. But in the way that he develops his Roman
trilogy, Shakespeare differs in his account of the transition from the ancient
to the modern world. For Machiavelli and especially Nietzsche, Christianity plays an active and, indeed, a central role in the subversion of ancient
Rome. With his genius for colorful coinages, Nietzsche called this process
the "slave revolt in morality" ("der Sklavenaufstand in der Moral"), as if the
slaves in Rome rose up on their own and successfully overturned the rule of
their masters.[198] In fact, Nietzsche's account of what happened—developed
aphoristically, not systematically, and scattered throughout several of his
published books as well as his notebooks—is much more complicated than
it may at first seem.[199] For example, renegade priests within the aristocracy
have a crucial role to play in Nietzsche's account of the slave revolt.[200] In that
sense, Nietzsche grants that some kind of weakening of—or at least division
within—the ancient noble castes was necessary to prepare the way for the
subversion of the Roman aristocratic order. Still, the impression that emerges
in Nietzsche's published writings is that Christianity was the culprit in the
dissolution of the ancient world; slavish Christians turned the tables on their
noble Roman masters.

Since Nietzsche defines the masters as strong and the slaves as weak, one might wonder how the slaves found the strength to overcome their masters, if the aristocracy in the ancient world had not already been weakened by the time Christianity appeared on the horizon.[201] Here, *Antony and Cleopatra* fills in a picture that Nietzsche leaves unclear in his published writings. Shakespeare shows that the corruption of the Roman Empire softened it up and made it possible for Christianity to sweep the ancient world. In *Antony and Cleopatra* Shakespeare portrays a nearly moribund Roman aristocracy, corrupted by their wealth and no longer faithful to their traditional virtues. They have lost their way; they are disillusioned, dispirited, and confused by the death of the Republic. Having lost their faith in human agency, they have become indolent, inclined to think that things will happen to them, rather than that they can make things happen. They have come to doubt themselves, their customs, and their beliefs. In their confusion, they are open to all sorts of new possibilities, including the idea that the values they inherited are hollow and should be overturned. They have already begun to wonder whether what they thought of as good might, in fact, be contemptible, and what they thought of as contemptible might be a higher form of good. And all these revaluations are taking place among not just the slaves but the aristocrats in the play, characters such as Antony and Cleopatra, supposedly the highest representatives of the ruling class. Shakespeare shows them mixing with their servants—their slaves—in ways that are unimaginable even in the world of *Julius Caesar*.[202] Indeed, the line dividing masters from slaves is being effaced at the end of *Antony and Cleopatra*. All the paradoxes in the play—defeat is victory, weakness is strength, death is life—show that Rome is already, so to speak, half-Christian. In short, the Rome of *Antony and Cleopatra* is ripe—overripe—for what Nietzsche calls the slave revolt in morality, and the masters have prepared the way for their own overthrow. The undermining of traditional Roman values results partly from the Romans' encounter with alien ways of life in the lands the Republic conquered. Succumbing to the allure of exotic customs, the characters in *Julius Caesar* and *Antony and Cleopatra* become increasingly un-Roman by the standards of the Republic. Adapting to the ways of life of the very peoples they defeated, the Romans come to embrace an ethos of defeat. That is the ultimate tragedy of the Roman Republic.

Polis versus Empire

Coriolanus and *Antony and Cleopatra* are generally regarded as among the last tragedies Shakespeare wrote, and are perhaps an attempt to round out his career as a tragedian. They clearly hark back to *Julius Caesar* and fill in the story Shakespeare was telling in that play of the transition from the Roman Republic to the Roman Empire. *Coriolanus* portrays the Republic at the time of its founding, and *Antony and Cleopatra* portrays the beginnings of the Empire in the wake of the Roman civil wars. But *Antony and Cleopatra* does much more. With its buried allusions to the coming of Christianity, it takes us to the end of the ancient world and the brink of the modern. It shows how the ancient world was transformed as the tight-knit communities that were the original model of Greco-Roman civilization (Sparta, Athens, Rome in its early years) were gradually eclipsed and replaced by burgeoning and sprawling empires (first that of Alexander the Great; then the one the Caesars presided over). This growth in the scale of political communities changed their character as well. In the ancient polis, with its well-defined horizons, politics was the focus of life, and in particular, as Machiavelli noted, there were few if any distractions from earthly glory as the highest form of human aspiration. In the vast expanse of the cosmopolitan Roman Empire, human horizons began to broaden, and, even as old heroic possibilities were foreclosed, new opportunities for striving arose, new aspirations for the infinite.

In dealing with the transition from polis to empire in his Roman plays, Shakespeare is thus exploring a subject larger than the story of the Roman Republic's rise and fall. After all, by the time of *Antony and Cleopatra*, Rome had conquered the Mediterranean world. Thus, *Antony and Cleopatra* portrays the transformation of the entire classical world, the beginning of the end of pagan antiquity and hence one of the great turning points in human history. The movement from polis to empire is one of the most fundamental transformations in the human condition.[203] The roots of this development lie as early as the fifth century BCE in Athens, with all its imperialist ambitions. An Athenian, Alcibiades, may have been the first to conceive the idea of universal empire.[204] Alexander the Great was the ultimate inheritor of these Athenian aspirations and took Greek imperialism to a higher level. In many respects, the Romans merely completed what Alexander set out to do in the East. As Gordon Braden writes, "Roman political history in general recapitulates the Greek experience, from city-state and republic to empire and monarchy."[205] The whole range of social, political, and psychological developments Shakespeare portrays in his Roman plays is related to and grows out of the replacement of polis by empire.

In studying the millennial changes in late antiquity, scholars from a variety of fields converge on the death of the polis as an explanatory principle. We saw the importance Shakespeare places on Stoicism and Epicureanism in the transformation of the Rome of *Julius Caesar*. Here is how the classical scholar Moses Hadas explains the origin of these philosophical sects:

In its origins Stoicism, like its rival Epicureanism, was a response to the new world which came into being after the conquests of Alexander the Great. Geographical and political horizons were enormously expanded, the insulation of the small city-state was stripped away, and individuals had to come to terms with and find a place in an enormously enlarged environment. Epicureans and Stoics alike addressed themselves to the task of redressing the imbalance between little man and huge world.[206]

This passage reads like a description of precisely the challenge confronting the characters in *Antony and Cleopatra*, who are indeed "little men"—and women—trying to find their bearings in a "huge world." Approaching late antiquity from the perspective of political philosophy, Thomas Pangle could also be describing what happens in *Antony and Cleopatra*: "The Roman conquest had largely extinguished independent civic life and had sapped the vitality of civil religion, melting the cities into a polyglot empire whose elite was suffused with the popularized philosophy or theology of a wide variety of Greek sects (Epicureans, Stoics, Skeptics, Peripatetics, Old and New Academics and so forth)."[207] Studies such as these reveal how perceptive Shakespeare was to highlight the spread of Greek philosophy in the Rome of *Julius Caesar*.

T. S. Eliot's famous essay, "Shakespeare and the Stoicism of Seneca," adds an even broader perspective on the death of the polis; he includes Christianity among its consequences:

The original stoicism, and especially the Roman stoicism, was of course a philosophy suited to slaves; hence its absorption into early Christianity. . . . A man does not join himself with the Universe so long as he has anything else to join himself with; men who could take part in the life of a thriving Greek city-state had something better to join themselves to; and Christians have had something better. Stoicism is the refuge for the individual in an indifferent or hostile world too big for him; it is the permanent substratum of a number of versions of cheering oneself up.[208]

Eliot, too, might as well be talking about developments in the Roman plays. What Shakespeare portrays in *Coriolanus* is precisely the story of "men who could take part in the life of a thriving . . . city-state" and thus "had something better to join themselves to" than the vague notion of a cosmopolitan whole that is emerging in *Antony and Cleopatra*. Like Hadas, Eliot dwells on what happens to a man when "the world" has simply "become too big for him." To grasp the relevance of these words to the Roman plays, recall Cassius's vision of "petty men" forced to "walk under" the "huge legs" of Caesar's colossal figure (1.2.136–37) or Cleopatra's dream of a cosmic Antony towering over "the little o' th' earth" (5.2.81).[209]

Although Eliot believes in the superiority of Christianity to Stoicism, he presents both sects as responses to the same phenomenon—the death of the polis—and he thereby correlates philosophical and religious developments in late antiquity. The philosophical developments Shakespeare portrays in the Rome of *Julius Caesar* presage the religious developments he portrays in the Rome of *Antony and Cleopatra*. Apolitical or antipolitical philosophies like Stoicism, Epicureanism, Cynicism, and Skepticism prepare the way for a religion that claims to transcend the whole realm of the political—Christianity coming out of the East.[210] That is the inner connection between the Hellenizing of Rome Shakespeare portrays in *Julius Caesar* and the Egyptianizing of Rome he portrays in *Antony and Cleopatra*. Both processes reflect the dissolution of the classical polis, the first expressed in philosophical terms, the second in wider cultural terms, especially religious. More broadly still, the Egyptianizing of Rome stands for the Orientalizing of Rome, which points ahead to the eventual Christianizing of Rome. From the beginning, *Antony and Cleopatra* is pervaded by a sense of exotic forces coming out of the East and seducing Romans away from their traditional way of life. Cleopatra epitomizes all these forces, and, dressed "in th' abiliments of the goddess Isis" (3.6.17), she represents the triumph of Egyptian gods among the Romans. But the subversion of traditional Roman religion does not involve only the ancestral Egyptian divinities. At the "Alexandrian feast" aboard Pompey's ship, the new hybridization of religion in the Roman Empire culminates in the characters dancing "the Egyptian bacchanals" (2.7.96, 104). Here, the Egyptian and the Greek influences on Rome fuse—Bacchus is the Roman name for the Greek god Dionysus. But Dionysus is not one of the traditional Olympian deities; Shakespeare highlights the eastern origins of the Dionysus cult in the drunken and almost mystical invocation of the deity:

> Come, thou monarch of the vine,
> Plumpy Bacchus with pink eyne!
> In thy fats our cares be drown'd,
> With thy grapes our hairs be crown'd!
> > Cap us till the world go round,
> > Cap us till the world go round! (2.7.113–18)

The cult of Dionysus had much in common with the mystery religions that periodically swept out of the East in the ancient world. The story of Bacchus's death, dismemberment, and resurrection linked the figure with several other Oriental deities, such as Osiris, Thammuz, and Mithras.[211] The biblical references in *Antony and Cleopatra* serve to suggest that the ultimate mystery religion to come out of the East and sweep all before it—making the Roman world "go round"—was Christianity.

The Gulf between Ruler and Ruled: Politics as Theater

The world of *Antony and Cleopatra* is filled with alien gods—gods alien to the traditional Roman civic religions.[212] Both philosophy and religion in late antiquity gave expression to the widespread feeling of alienation the new imperial era produced. In *Coriolanus* Rome is filled with tension and strife, but it is still a homey place. It might come as a surprise "that the word 'home' occurs more frequently in this play than in any other of Shakespeare's."[213] Plebeians and patricians can take comfort in the fact that they live in a community where, as the saying goes, everybody knows your name. Of the three Roman plays, *Coriolanus* is the only one in which Shakespeare shows patricians and plebeians talking to each other on familiar terms (in addition, of course, to shouting at each other). To be sure, the interparty communication mainly takes place between Menenius on the one hand and Sicinius and Brutus on the other. Still, productive communication does take place between these representatives of the opposing parties in the early Roman Republic, whereas in *Julius Caesar* patricians such as Brutus and Antony confine themselves to addressing the plebeians in studied orations, and in *Antony and Cleopatra*, the plebeians never even appear on stage.

In *Julius Caesar*, the tribunes, the representatives of the common people, no longer even seem to know individual plebeians by name. In the opening scene, they are forced to ask the plebeians they meet, "What trade art thou?" (1.1.5). Apparently, they do not know the occupations of the people they represent. By contrast, in *Coriolanus*, the tribunes even speak to individual patricians on what amounts to a first-name basis. Although Menenius disputes the matter with Sicinius and Brutus, the tribunes insist to him: "We know you well enough" (2.1.66), and he feels the same way about them (2.1.21–45). In the small-town environment of *Coriolanus*, Roman politics is personal and largely unmediated. To become consul, Coriolanus must go among the plebeians in the marketplace and meet them by ones and twos. He mocks them, but at least the plebeians have had a chance to talk face to face with the man who is supposedly going to rule them. Roman politics is so intimate that Coriolanus cannot conceal his arrogant nature from the plebeians because they have gotten such a good look at him (in fact, they know all about his pride even before the play's action begins). Roman politics is contentious and even becomes violent in *Coriolanus*, and it does not take place among friends.

But it does occur among people who are at least directly acquainted with each other. Whatever else one might say about republican politics in *Coriolanus*, the Romans on both sides know with whom they are dealing. Patricians and plebeians can put a name and a face on the political forces that directly affect their lives.

All this begins to change in *Julius Caesar* and is totally altered by the time of *Antony and Cleopatra*. In *Julius Caesar*, the rulers of Rome are still forced to take the people into account in their calculations, but politics, as Casca notes almost from the beginning, has become theater (1.2.258–61) and a gap opens up between rulers and citizens. As Coriolanus's hatred of acting reveals, the patricians in the early Republic fail to mask their political intentions with theatrical displays.[214] In modern political terms, we would say that Coriolanus does little if anything to improve his public image. Despite his mother's urging him to "perform a part" (3.2.109), deceive the plebeians, and give them a false impression of his character, Coriolanus refuses to transform politics into theater: "You have put me now to such a part which never / I shall discharge to th' life" (3.2.105–6). Ultimately Coriolanus insists on giving the plebeians an unmediated view of his nature: "I will not do't, / Lest I surcease to honor my own truth" (3.2.120–21). By contrast, thanks to Julius Caesar's genius for theatrical gestures and Antony's grasp of his master's art, the people's relation to their rulers in the late Republic is mediated by theater. Symbolically, in *Julius Caesar* the Senate now meets in "Pompey's theatre" (1.3.152).[215] The plebeians no longer have direct contact with the great patricians. Instead, the patricians appear before the plebeians as if on stage; indeed, they carefully stage manage their appearances in public, as happens when Antony offers the crown to Caesar (in modern political parlance, a classic "trial balloon" maneuver). Like modern politicians, the patricians of the late Republic have learned how to project a public image. Unlike Coriolanus, they are good actors. Even the conspirators conceive of themselves as enacting theatrical roles (3.1.111–13), and Brutus knows how to play the part of the perfect Stoic in public.[216] As a result, the common people in *Julius Caesar* only get to see what public figures such as Caesar choose to reveal of themselves. Images of Caesar are evidently on display all around the city. The tribunes now view their function as to "disrobe the images" to counter the Caesar party's propaganda (1.1.64). Once Caesar is assassinated, his party and the conspirators become engaged in an all-out propaganda war for the hearts and minds of Rome's citizens.[217]

In *Antony and Cleopatra*, the gap between the plebeians and patricians has widened into an unbridgeable gulf. There is no longer anything "homey" about the Rome of the play. The plebeians have lost their place at the center of the action in the city.[218] Both *Coriolanus* and *Julius Caesar* open with scenes set in the heart of Rome, with the plebeians in direct contact with patricians or tribunes, contentiously debating the city's affairs, especially their relation to Rome's great leaders. Strangely for a Roman play, *Antony and Cleopatra* opens in Alexandria, in a lavish imperial court, remote from the everyday concerns of Roman citizens, who in fact have no access to it. One of Rome's supreme leaders, Antony, shows little interest in news from Rome—"Grates me, the sum" (1.1.18)—and dismisses Roman politics with contempt: "Let Rome in Tiber melt, and the wide arch / Of the rang'd empire fall!" (1.1.33–34). In the opening scenes of both *Coriolanus* and *Julius Caesar*, the Roman leaders display at least some acquaintance with the city's ordinary people, but for the imperial Antony and Cleopatra, commoners have become unknown and exotic creatures, to be studied like animal specimens: "To-night we'll wander through the streets and note / The qualities of people" (1.1.53–54). Antony and Cleopatra behave like gods dwelling far above the lives of their ordinary subjects.

With such remote rulers, Roman politics has been completely reduced to theater; the plebeians are now pictured as rude spectators at plays staged for pure propaganda purposes (5.2.55–57, 209–13). The Roman people will not get to see Cleopatra in person; they will see only a representation of the Egyptian queen, carefully staged to create the negative image of her that Octavius wants to project:

> The quick comedians
> Extemporally will stage us, and present
> Our Alexandrian revels: Antony
> Shall be brought drunken forth, and I shall see
> Some squeaking Cleopatra boy my greatness
> I' th' posture of a whore. (5.2.216–21)

Ventidius defines the new imperial world with his phrase: "When him we serve's away" (3.1.15). The Empire is a world of remote commanders. They seem to be inaccessible to ordinary people (the only characters who are shown speaking to the triumvirs are their henchmen, their closest associates, and their soldiers). Subordinates have a hard time getting direct orders from their superiors, and are often forced to guess at their commanders' intentions (as happens with Menas and Pompey in act 2, scene 7). The vast distances that the Empire now encompasses mean that people must communicate through messengers, and all sorts of misunderstandings result. The face-to-face confrontations characteristic of the politics of *Coriolanus* and *Julius Caesar* are no longer the norm in *Antony and Cleopatra*. In the absence of direct contact, characters from Cleopatra to Antony to Octavius to Pompey are reduced to merely imagining what their friends and/or enemies are doing on distant frontiers. They call upon these remote figures in trans-Mediterranean invocations, which have the feeling of prayers to absent gods (1.4.55–70, 1.5.18–34, 2.1.20–27).

Indeed, in the vast world of the Roman Empire, it becomes easier for Rome's rulers to project godlike images of themselves.[219] Already in *Coriolanus*, Shakespeare portrays the disposition of the Roman people to worship their military heroes. After Coriolanus's victory at Corioli, the whole city (including the priests) turns out to welcome him home, paying obeisance to his divine status:

> As if that whatsoever god who leads him
> Were slyly crept into his human powers,
> And gave him graceful posture. (2.1.219–21)

But as soon as Coriolanus returns to the confines of Rome, he loses the divine aura he acquired on the battlefield. Once again able to see him up close, the plebeians recall why they hate him and deny him the consulship to which his military record entitles him. It may at first seem strange that Coriolanus has greater success achieving divine status among the Volsces when he goes over to the other side. As Cominius reports:

> He is their god; he leads them like a thing
> Made by some other deity than Nature,
> That shapes men better. (4.6.90–92)

But the reason Coriolanus has more success in achieving divinity among the Volsces than he does among the Romans is that his own people know him better than these foreigners do. Evidently, when it comes to acquiring divine status, the less people know about you, the more likely they are to worship you as a god. Mystery and divinity go hand in hand.[220]

Accordingly, Julius Caesar is free to become a god in Roman eyes only once his body is dead. While he is alive, sharp-eyed observers like Cassius are alert to Caesar's bodily limitations, which call his divinity into question. In one of the many paradoxes of the imperial era, Caesar's death sets his spirit free to achieve a new divine power. In Decius Brutus's clever reinterpretation of Calphurnia's seemingly ominous dream of Caesar's statue spouting blood, he anticipates the Roman emperors' strategy of setting up monuments to their divinity all around the Empire:

> Your statue spouting blood in many pipes,
> In which so many smiling Romans bath'd,

> Signifies that from you great Rome shall suck
> Reviving blood, and that great men shall press
> For tinctures, stains, relics, and cognizance. (2.2.85–89)

Shakespeare suggests that the weakness of the Roman republican regime was always the possibility that the people might rally behind a single great patrician as a god.[221] For centuries this tendency was counteracted by the small size of the city, which made masquerading as a divinity more difficult. Republican institutions also worked against a patrician achieving divine status. In *Coriolanus*, the tribunes make sure that the plebeians remember why they should hate their triumphant general, rather than worshiping him.

But this kind of skepticism loses its force in the Empire. At the beginning of *Julius Caesar*, the tribunes fail to wean the plebeians away from their newfound devotion to the conqueror of Pompey and his sons. In *Antony and Cleopatra*, the hero and heroine carefully stage manage their appearance in the Alexandria marketplace to surround themselves with an aura of divinity. Ever aware of the power of images, Octavius's associate Maecenas is concerned with this spectacle: "This in the public eye?" (3.6.11) and insists on reporting Antony's impiety to the homeland: "Let Rome be thus / Inform'd" (3.6.19–20). In *Antony and Cleopatra* the remaining contenders for the imperial throne are engaged in a fierce propaganda war with each other, which involves a form of self-mythologizing.[222] For a while, they check each others' claims to divinity. But as soon as Octavius prevails in the military conflict, the way is open for him to establish himself as a god throughout the Roman Empire (which the historical Octavius did in fact do once he was proclaimed Augustus Caesar). With faith in the city and its gods fading fast, the Romans yearn for a new kind of divinity, a god promising a form of universality.[223] This kind of universality makes the particularity of the ancient city's gods look meager by comparison. In the sheer physical extent of the Roman Empire, the ancient cities and their gods dissolve into insignificance and irrelevance.

It is inevitable that in such a world the characters grow disillusioned with civic life, and turn to other sources of satisfaction. As both Moses Hadas and T. S. Eliot suggest, in the post-polis world of *Antony and Cleopatra*, the characters feel dwarfed by the vastness of the imperial realm.[224] The root experience in the Empire is appropriately summed up by a servant: "To be call'd into a huge sphere, and not to be seen to move in't" (2.7.14–15)—to feel lost in the expanse of the Empire and to sense that one is no longer in command over one's own movements. As Shakespeare perceptively shows, a wide variety of phenomena in late antiquity—from Stoicism and Epicureanism to mystery religions and ultimately Christianity—are responses to the pervasive sense of hollowness at the core of the imperial world. The compensation for this emptiness at the center of imperial Rome is that it seems to open up new horizons on its periphery. The world of *Coriolanus* is solid but finite. The world of *Antony and Cleopatra* seems constantly on the verge of dissolving and melting away, precariously hovering between nothingness and infinity. As analysts as varied as Hadas, Pangle, and T. S. Eliot suggest, this is what happened in the ancient world when the polis yielded to empire. It is remarkable that, without the resources available to modern scholars, Shakespeare seems to have grasped the essence of this process and was able to capture it in detail in the movement he portrays from *Coriolanus* to *Antony and Cleopatra*.

From the Ancient to the Modern World

In Shakespeare's Rome, size matters.[225] A large empire is very different from a small polis and shapes human beings differently. As Rome expands externally, the human soul expands inwardly. New depths of interiority open up in response to the closing of traditional political opportunities. In *Antony and Cleopatra* Shakespeare imagines the new infinite yearnings of the ancient world largely in terms of romantic love, but hovering in the background are all the new possibilities for human aspiration opened up by Christianity, among them, the longing for an afterlife. The world of *Antony and Cleopatra* is curiously "modern." Public and private life have been separated; more specifically, the highest good can now be reconceived in private as opposed to public terms.[226] In this new world, one can now "Render to Caesar the things that are Caesar's" (Mark 12:17), and move beyond earthly glory. With the ancient paths to political participation cut off, one can now dismiss politics as contemptible—"'Tis paltry to be Caesar"—and pursue all sorts of alternative paths to greatness, now conceived in more spiritual terms ("I am fire, and air; my other elements / I give to baser life"). By the end of *Antony and Cleopatra* the ancient world has been fundamentally transformed into something entirely new. That is why it makes sense to speak of Rome as dead at the end of *Julius Caesar*. It is dead in principle. What had been regarded in the ancient world as the highest form of nobility—politics—has been demoted to a base way of life, while new avenues of spiritual striving are being explored.

This may sound like an entirely positive development, and Shakespeare certainly exposes the failings and limitations of the Roman Republic. Indeed, he shows how tragic the ancient world could be. The tight-knit, would-be self-contained character of the ancient polis was a formula for tragedy. It meant that the city often came into conflict with the aspirations of its most heroic citizens, as happens in *Coriolanus*, especially when the hero strives to be self-sufficient himself. As the archetypal Roman hero, Coriolanus comes to see how problematic his ideal of self-sufficiency is. He discovers that he cannot live within the bounds Rome insists on setting to his aspirations, but he also discovers that he cannot live without the city. He never finds the "world else-where" (3.3.135) he speaks of when he turns his back on his native city. With Antony's talk of "new heaven, new earth," one might think that the expanded horizons of the Empire would provide the world beyond political life Coriolanus sought in vain in the early days of the Republic. Given its new emphasis on nobility in private life, the Empire seems to offer a refuge from the tragic contradictions of ancient political life. With its window on eternity, does *Antony and Cleopatra* point to a path beyond the world of tragedy? If one accepts the idea of an afterlife, of which both Antony and Cleopatra catch glimpses, then one might interpret their story as a kind of divine comedy. After all, in their own eyes they are in the end married in death and they regard their suicides as a form of triumph over Octavius. Several commentators have claimed that the mood at the end of *Antony and Cleopatra* is unusual for a Shakespearean tragedy, more joyous and triumphal than one would normally expect.[227]

And yet *Antony and Cleopatra* remains a tragedy, if only because the symbolic marriage that unites the hero and heroine at the end is at the same time their death. The infinite horizons that open up to Antony and Cleopatra are deeply problematic and perplexing. For all their claims to victory at the end, a deep sense of loss pervades the closing scenes, including their loss of each other, as well as of their kingdoms. Whatever triumph they experience is profoundly equivocal. Their new experience of infinity may have broadened their horizons, but in the end those horizons have contracted to the narrow confines of a tomb. Moreover, their glimpse of eternity may be an illusion. Cleopatra can only dream of Antony as a new god, and the sober Roman Dolabella refuses to acknowledge the reality of her vision (5.2.93–94). The rustic who brings Cleopatra the asp seems to know a great deal about death, but he gives highly ambiguous and paradoxical answers to her questions about life after death (he speaks, for example, of "a very honest woman—but something given to lie," 5.2.251–52), and he ominously confuses mortality with immortality in his clownish speech. He raises doubts concerning opinions about the afterlife and their relation to salvation: "He that will believe all that they say, shall never be sav'd by half that they do" (5.2.256–57).[228] The price that Antony and Cleopatra pay for their new glimpse of infinity is that they can never be sure that it is real. The visions they see may be remarkable, but they also have an unnerving way of dissolving before their eyes:

That which is now a horse, even with a thought
The rack dislimns, and makes it indistinct
As water is in water. (4.14.9–11)

The sharp outlines and clear guideposts of republican Rome melt away for
Antony and Cleopatra, and they are left to make their way through a world of
flickering shadows, vague prophecies, and ominous omens.

In short, for all the new possibilities offered by the world of the Roman
Empire, Shakespeare does not present it as an unambiguous and unequivo-
cal advance beyond the world of the Roman Republic. In fact, in *Antony and
Cleopatra* he shows that the dissolution of the firmly grounded world of the
ancient city introduces profound new complications into human life, many
of them with tragic implications. In the era of *Coriolanus*, tragedies occur
within the political world, or arise out of clashes between its values and those
of the prepolitical world, institutions such as the family. The world of *Antony and Cleopatra* seems to offer the possibility of transcending politics, but
the hero and heroine never manage fully to extricate themselves from their
political entanglements in an unambiguous way. Tragic conflict now grows
out of the tension between politics and romantic love. Antony finds that he
cannot "live a private man in Athens," and, indeed, neither he nor Cleopatra
ever succeeds in renouncing their public identities.[229] The realms that claim
to transcend politics turn out to be still entangled in it. Insofar as *Antony
and Cleopatra* portrays the passage from the ancient to the modern world, it
suggests that the latter will still be tragic, only in new ways that involve new
sources of tragic conflict.

Antony and Cleopatra thus provides what might be called a genealogy of
the world Shakespeare had already explored in a number of his histories and
tragedies, plays in which he investigates the complexities that Christianity,
with its transpolitical perspective on life, introduced into the postclassical
world.[230] One of the central subjects of his history plays is the way that Christianity becomes a complicating factor in modern politics. The issue comes
up in terms of the conflict between political and ecclesiastical authority that
surfaces in several of the history plays, especially when the great princes of the
Church—the bishops and the archbishops—participate in various forms of
rebellion against the crown. As Shakespeare shows, the transpolitical character of Christianity makes possible divisions in the body politic that were
inconceivable in the days of the classical polis, with its integration of what we
call church and state. At a number of points in the history plays, Shakespeare
examines the way that the otherworldly longings of Christianity can unfit a
king for the active life of politics, for example, in the case of the youthful king,

Henry VI, who is better suited to heading a monastery than a monarchy. Shakespeare's portrait of Henry V is his most complex attempt to show how a monarch might integrate the Church into national politics, and more generally achieve some sort of workable combination of religious and political principles. In particular, his Henry V strives to combine the best of the ancient and the modern worlds, to synthesize classical and Christian values.[231] Shakespeare repeatedly shows his awareness that the central project of the Renaissance age in which he lived was to revive elements of classical antiquity within a Christian culture. The way that *Antony and Cleopatra* reveals the pagan and the Christian worlds to be antithetical exposes how deeply problematic the whole Renaissance project must have seemed to Shakespeare. The Renaissance attempt to synthesize classical and Christian values became for Shakespeare a rich source of tragic conflicts.

Indeed, the tensions between the classical and Christian traditions lie at the heart of several of Shakespeare's tragedies. In both *Othello* and *Macbeth*, he portrays the tragic dilemma of a heroic warrior who basically has his roots in a pagan tradition and is then faced with dealing with the new psychological complexities of the Christian world into which he has been introduced.[232] In *Hamlet*, Shakespeare explores the opposite tragic situation—the dilemma of a sophisticated modern Christian who suddenly finds himself plunged into circumstances straight out of the world of Norse saga, with its cycle of tribal vengeance. The tragedy of Hamlet grows out of the tension between the antithetical responses to the task of revenge dictated by the classical and Christian traditions.[233] Shakespeare's sense of tragedy is deeply rooted in his perception of the way that the Renaissance culture of his day flowed from the confluence of two great ethical traditions—the classical and the Christian—that clash in many fundamental respects. His Roman plays occupy a special place among his works because they trace the way in which the Christian world grew out of the classical, and in the process reveal how truly antithetical the two worlds are. In particular, *Antony and Cleopatra* lays bare the way that the very notion of nobility was redefined at the end of the ancient world, thereby preparing the basis for modern tragedy by supplying new sources of tragic conflict. That is why, in the deepest sense, in the world of Shakespeare's tragedies, all roads eventually lead to Rome.

"The Roman Caesar with Christ's Soul":
Shakespeare and Nietzsche on Rome and Christianity

Nietzsche's Interest in Shakespeare

Sometimes it seems as if everyone in the world studied *Julius Caesar* in high school. In the case of Friedrich Nietzsche, we have documentary proof. In May 1863, he wrote an essay entitled "Charakterschilderung des Cassius aus Julius Caesar" ("Character Portrait of Cassius from *Julius Caesar*").[1] At the time, Nietzsche was enrolled in the famous boarding school Schulpforta, perhaps the best *Gymnasium* in all the German-speaking lands in the nineteenth century.[2] Given the quality of the writing and thought in this essay, it would be too painful to compare it with what the average American high school student writes today. One might console oneself with the consideration that it was the young Nietzsche who wrote this essay, not an average nineteenth-century German high school student (Nietzsche was generally ranked first in his class and regarded as one of the best students Schulpforta had seen in years). Still, it is a sobering experience to see what an eighteen-year-old was capable of writing in a nineteenth-century German high school, even if he was to go on to become one of the greatest philosophers in history, as well as one of the greatest masters of German prose.

Imagine reading a high school essay today and not accusing the student of plagiarism after coming across this characterization of the late scenes between Cassius and Brutus: "These scenes come before me, like the last part of a symphony, in which the same notes, which in the Allegro stormed and flashed, again resound, but almost as a painful sigh in remembrance of the endured woes, almost as transfigured and calmed tones of a breast become silent."[3] The young Nietzsche reads *Julius Caesar* as fundamentally about friendship. That is why he concentrates on the relationship between Brutus and Cassius. Nietzsche concludes, "A friendship of this kind, which burdens both with error and guilt, draws both into destruction, has also something unendingly touching. Such a friendship as that of Brutus and Cassius, it is the soul of the whole piece, that represents, as we otherwise do not find with Shakespeare, the struggle of common human and moral motives with political ones."[4] Only here do we realize that we are dealing with a teenager after all, guilty of that quintessential high-school fault: the wild generalization. If the young Nietzsche had really known his Shakespeare, he would never have said that the conflict between ethical and political principles is restricted to *Julius Caesar* in the playwright's work. In fact, such conflicts are basic to all Shakespeare's history plays and tragedies, and several of his comedies as well.

Nietzsche's interest in Shakespeare seems to have started when, while still in high school, he was "given his complete works as a Christmas present."[5] He also participated in amateur Shakespeare readings at Schulpforta. Years later, his friend Paul Deussen could not recall which role Nietzsche played in *A Midsummer Night's Dream*, but he reported, "I do, however, remember that on the tricentennial anniversary of Shakespeare's birth on April 23, 1864, we gave a public reading of *Henry IV* with assigned roles under Koberstein's direction [a Schulpforta teacher]; Nietzsche had to read the role of the firebrand Percy, which he performed in a mellifluous and pleasant voice, but not without false pathos."[6] Even if Nietzsche overacted, who today would not wish to have been present when the creator of *Zarathustra* read the part of Hotspur on the three-hundredth anniversary of Shakespeare's birth?

Nietzsche's schoolmates may have been entertained by his amateur theatrics, but his family was evidently troubled by his growing interest in Shakespeare. "Aunt Rosalie thought Shakespeare was to blame for making him feel so restless and discontented with everything around him."[7] His sister explained the impact Shakespeare had on him: "Elisabeth, who concluded that Byron and Shakespeare were equally important as catalysts, points out that later, when he wrote to tell her that every form of strength was in itself refreshing and pleasant to watch, he advised her to read Shakespeare: 'He presents you with so many strong men—rough, hard, powerful, iron-willed. It is in men like these that our age is so poor.'"[8] Here we get a glimpse of what really drew Nietzsche to Shakespeare's plays. They opened his eyes to something radically different from the world around him. It was in talking about works by Shakespeare, Byron, and also Friedrich Schiller that Nietzsche first began to use the term *übermenschlich* ("superhuman").[9] What later emerged as a central concept in his philosophy, the *Übermensch* ("overman" or "superman"), grew out of his initial encounter with the tragic heroes of Shakespeare, Byron, and Schiller—larger-than-life characters, transgressive and even law-breaking, living (in Nietzsche's later formulation) "beyond good and evil."

Nietzsche remained fascinated by *Julius Caesar* and returned to the play in section 98 of *Die Fröhliche Wissenschaft (The Gay Science)* in one of the most sustained discussions of an individual Shakespeare play in all his published works. Again Nietzsche is attracted to the theme of friendship, only this time he deals with the bond between Brutus and Caesar:

> Independence of the soul!—that is at stake here. No sacrifice can be too great for that: one must be capable of sacrificing one's dearest friend for it, even if he should also be the most glorious human being, an ornament of the world, a genius without peer—if one loves freedom as the freedom of great souls and he threatens that kind of freedom. That is what Shakespeare must have felt. The height at which he places Caesar is the finest honor that he could bestow on Brutus: that is how he raised beyond measure Brutus' inner problem as well as the spiritual strength that was able to cut *this knot*.[10]

Somewhat surprisingly, Nietzsche calls *Julius Caesar* Shakespeare's "best tragedy,"[11] but perhaps, once again, personal reasons influenced his judgment. As many commentators have suggested, Nietzsche may have seen a parallel between Brutus's willingness to kill his friend Caesar as a matter of principle and Nietzsche's painful break with Richard Wagner, a man in whom he at first recognized the epitome of artistic genius but with whom he eventually decided he had to break to preserve his intellectual independence.[12]

But if these personal considerations were at work in Nietzsche's admiration for *Julius Caesar*, they point to the fact that his experience of the play was deeply bound up with his understanding of himself as a philosopher and his understanding of human greatness. *Julius Caesar* is at the center of Nietzsche's fascination with Shakespeare—from beginning to end—from his high school essay to *The Gay Science* to the very last passage on Shakespeare that appears in Nietzsche's published works, section 4 of "Why I Am So Clever" in his autobiography, *Ecce Homo*. In a final tribute to Shakespeare, Nietzsche writes, "When I seek my ultimate formula for *Shakespeare*, I always find only this: he conceived the type of Caesar."[13]

It is no accident that one of the Roman plays stands at the center of Nietzsche's interest in Shakespeare. The two were united in their fascination with classical antiquity and the great tragic heroes it produced. For Nietzsche, this was a professional matter. At Schulpforta he began the study of Greek and Latin that soon was to propel him to the front ranks of classical philologists in Europe (and a professorship at the University of Basel at the remarkably young age of twenty-four).[14] Evidently, reading Shakespeare was part of Nietzsche's introduction to the classical world and, in particular, to one aspect of it that was to occupy him for the rest of his life—the prevalence of strong individuals among the ancient Greeks and Romans, a heroic spirit celebrated in classical literature from Homer to Plutarch. Above all, Shakespeare and Nietzsche shared an interest in ancient Rome as an alternative to the modern world, which means primarily as an alternative to the Christian world.

Accordingly, I will compare Shakespeare and Nietzsche as two of the most important thinkers who have contemplated the problem of Rome and its relationship to Christianity. This is not a study of intellectual influence. Obviously Nietzsche could not have influenced Shakespeare, and I do not believe that Shakespeare helped to shape Nietzsche's analysis of Rome in its details. To be sure, the evidence shows that Nietzsche was deeply affected by his early encounter with Shakespeare's plays, above all, *Julius Caesar*.[15] But Nietzsche does not appear to have read Shakespeare's plays closely, with a view, for example, to analyzing his understanding of Rome. Nietzsche comments on Shakespeare in passing in his writings, but he never develops a systematic and comprehensive interpretation of one of the plays. The closest he comes is in his discussions of *Hamlet* (in *The Birth of Tragedy*, section 7) and of *Macbeth* (in *Daybreak*, section 240), but even these passages amount to no more than isolated observations.

As for the Roman plays, we know for certain that Nietzsche knew *Julius Caesar*, but I have not been able to find any evidence that he read *Coriolanus* or *Antony and Cleopatra*.[16] The little evidence we have suggests that Nietzsche did not even think of the Roman plays as particularly Roman. He seems to have accepted the common eighteenth-century idea that Shakespeare's Romans are simply Englishmen in disguise. In a notebook entry from 1877, Nietzsche writes, "Shakespeare was correct to let his Romans appear on stage as Englishmen."[17] Given this attitude, Nietzsche was presumably not disposed to search the Roman plays carefully for what they might reveal about the ancient city. But even though Nietzsche failed to see the parallels between his understanding of Rome and Shakespeare's, we can still pursue the enquiry and let the two thinkers illuminate each other. As we saw in chapter 1, Nietzsche's concepts of master morality and slave morality can help in analyzing Shakespeare's Roman plays. Now we will build on that discussion to clarify a central issue in Nietzsche's understanding of Rome: the question of whether ancient Rome was corrupted by Christianity or, on the contrary, prepared the way for it. Using Shakespeare as a guide to Nietzsche will reveal that his understanding of Christianity is considerably more complicated than is usually supposed.

Nietzsche Blames Christianity for Rome's Decline

At first sight, Nietzsche's analysis of ancient Rome and Christianity may seem simple and straightforward. In his view, ancient Rome represents master morality and Christianity represents slave morality, and accordingly he championed Rome and excoriated Christianity, especially as the force that subverted and eventually undermined the glorious Roman Empire.[18] Nietzsche viewed ancient Rome as an aristocratic commonwealth, devoted to military conquest and glorifying the hard virtues that make victory in war possible (just as Shakespeare portrays Rome in *Coriolanus*). Like the Greek heroes in Homer, the Romans set themselves up as masters and define their nobility in contrast to the way of life of their slaves:

> When the ruling group determines what is "good," the exalted, proud states of the soul are experienced as conferring distinction and determining the order of rank. The noble human being separates from himself those in whom the opposite of such exalted, proud states finds expression; he despises them. . . . In this first type of morality the opposition of "good" and "bad" means approximately the same as "noble" and "contemptible." . . . One feels contempt for the cowardly, the anxious, the petty, those intent on narrow utility; also for . . . those who humble themselves, the doglike people who allow themselves to be maltreated, the begging flatterers. . . . The noble human being honors himself as one who is powerful, also as one who has power over himself, . . . who delights in being severe and hard with himself and respects all severity and hardness.[19]

For Nietzsche, slave morality is the revenge of the oppressed against their oppressors. The slaves triumph over their masters by inverting their moral valuations, claiming that their humble way of life is superior to a life of proud nobility:

> It is different with the second type of morality, *slave morality*. Suppose the violated, oppressed, suffering, unfree, who are uncertain of themselves and weary, moralize: what will their moral valuations have in common? . . . The slave's eye is not favorable to the virtues of the powerful: he is skeptical and suspicious, *subtly* suspicious, of all the "good" that is honored there. . . . Conversely, those qualities are brought out and flooded with light which serve to ease existence for those who suffer: here pity, the complaisant and obliging hand, the warm heart, patience, industry, humility, and friendliness are honored.[20]

In Nietzsche's account of what he calls the slave revolt in morality, what is "good" in master morality becomes "evil" in slave morality and what is "bad" in master morality becomes "good" in slave morality:

Here is the place for the origin of that famous opposition of "good" and "evil": into evil one's feelings project power and dangerousness, a certain terribleness, subtlety, and strength that does not permit contempt to develop. According to slave morality, those who are "evil" thus inspire fear; according to master morality it is precisely those who are "good" that inspire, and wish to inspire, fear, while the "bad" are felt to be contemptible.[21]

For Nietzsche, this is the process by which Christian morality grows out of the classical morality of the ancient Greeks and Romans. Frustrated by their lack of power and consumed with envy of their masters' preeminence, the slaves develop a complex of emotions Nietzsche labels with the French word *ressentiment*.[22] Out of spite and a desire for revenge, the slaves try to turn the tables on their masters. Making a virtue out of a necessity, the slaves claim that the weakness and passivity forced upon them by their masters is actually something they have chosen on their own.[23] Their failure to respond to injury is not a sign of cowardice or impotence on their part—they *choose* to turn the other cheek. By the same token, the aggressiveness of the masters is taken as evidence of their weakness—they are unable to control their violent impulses and thus are vicious and villainous. The proud master becomes the model of ethical evil. In the classical world, pride understood as magnanimity or greatness of soul (*megalopsychia* in Greek) was regarded as a virtue (in Aristotle's *Nicomachean Ethics*, for example); in Christianity pride is regarded as the deadliest of sins.

As a characterization of the transformation of classical into Christian morality, Nietzsche's theory of the slave revolt works very well. As we saw in chapter 1, Shakespeare's Roman plays in effect portray this process, beginning with the world of master morality in *Coriolanus* and revealing the genesis of slave morality in *Antony and Cleopatra*. In particular, *Antony and Cleopatra* dramatizes the way that terms are systematically redefined in the early days of the Roman Empire, as weakness becomes strength, defeat becomes victory, and death becomes life. But Nietzsche's account of the slave revolt in morality fails to explain exactly how the slaves manage to pull off this trick.[24] If the masters represent strength and the slaves represent weakness, how can the slaves marshal the power to overcome their masters? One might invoke William Blake's diabolical proverb: "The weak in courage is strong in cunning" and claim that the wily slaves simply outwit their masters.[25] But Nietzsche presents the masters as overwhelmingly secure in their power. How could their slaves ever conquer them? Without some weakening of the masters as a class, it would seem impossible for them to suffer defeat at the hands of mere slaves.

By portraying precisely the progressive weakening, corruption, and dispiriting of the Roman aristocracy, Shakespeare's Roman plays answer the question that Nietzsche initially leaves unanswered in his account of the slave revolt in morality. In Shakespeare, the movement from *Coriolanus* to *Antony and Cleopatra*—and hence from the Republic to the Empire—transforms the Romans from citizens to subjects. What the conspirators hold against Julius Caesar is precisely that he is turning noble Romans into bondsmen. Shakespeare shows that it takes the narrow horizons of a polis like the Rome of *Coriolanus* to enforce the idea that "valor is the chiefest virtue" (2.2.83– 84). In the sprawling, cosmopolitan world of *Antony and Cleopatra*, the Romans lose their ethical and political bearings and as a result even their faith in human agency. They become passive, rather than active, accepting their fate rather than trying to shape their own destinies.[26] As Roman politics becomes more corrupt and self-serving—and all sense of the common good dissolves—the Romans question their old virtues and gravitate to new ones. As we have seen in *Antony and Cleopatra*, "choice of loss" (3.1.23) becomes the keynote of the new Empire.

Thus Shakespeare shows that what Nietzsche calls the "slave revolt" actually began *within* the Roman aristocracy. As we saw in chapter 1, in *Antony and Cleopatra* the line between servant and master begins to break down, and behavior formerly condemned as slavish becomes legitimate among the masters. Shakespeare thus has no difficulty with the problem that shadows Nietzsche's account of the slave revolt in morality. The Roman plays do not juxtapose a solid and unchanging aristocracy with a suddenly rebellious slave class. Instead, they portray an aristocracy that gradually is pacified under an emerging imperial system and becomes slavish itself. Shakespeare shows that much of the ethical transformation that Nietzsche identifies with Christianity—in particular, the inversion of the hierarchy of high and low— could take place before the advent of Jesus Christ and the Christian religion. It is not just that Shakespeare shows a few traitors to their class among the Roman aristocrats. He portrays an entire aristocratic class that destroys itself in internecine struggles, abdicates its traditional role within the republican regime, and embraces a new ethic suitable to losers, rather than the winners celebrated in the republican era.

As we shall see, Nietzsche was aware of the phenomena Shakespeare portrays in his Roman plays, and yet he tended to shy away from dwelling on them in the books he published. Why did Nietzsche not embrace the idea that Roman corruption prepared the way for Christianity? The answer is that his hostility to Christianity was so great that he was reluctant to blame Rome for its own decline. He wanted to make Christianity the sole villain of the story.

That approach would make his calls for overturning the Christian revaluation of classical values more convincing and compelling.

Already in his so-called Middle Period, when Nietzsche began writing his aphoristic books, he had embarked on his campaign against Christianity as the corrupter of ancient Rome. In 1878, in *Human, All Too Human*, Nietzsche writes, "With the decline of Roman culture and its principal cause, the spread of Christianity, a general uglification of man prevailed within the Roman Empire."[27] Nietzsche's crusade against Christianity reached a fever pitch in one of the last books he completed before he went insane, appropriately named *The Antichrist*. In his most sustained and systematic analysis of Christianity in any of his published books, he states unequivocally that Rome was in no way responsible for the rise of Christianity, and he sharply distances himself from contrary views on the subject:

> It is *not*, as is supposed, the corruption of antiquity itself, of *noble* antiquity, that made Christianity possible. The scholarly idiocy which upholds such ideas even today cannot be contradicted loudly enough. At the very time when the sick, corrupt, chandala strata in the whole *imperium* adopted Christianity, the *opposite type*, nobility, was present in its most beautiful and most mature form. The great number became master; the democratism of the Christian instincts *triumphed* . . . . Once more I recall the inestimable words of Paul: "The *weak* things of the world, . . . the *base* and *despised* things of the world hath God chosen." This was the formula; *in hoc signo* decadence triumphed.[28]

In order to condemn Christianity unconditionally, Nietzsche felt that he had to praise the Roman Empire without qualification. Far from representing a decline from the virtues of the Roman Republic (as Shakespeare suggests), the Empire is presented in *The Antichrist* as the peak of Roman civilization, on the verge of unleashing a new and unprecedented era of human flourishing:

> Christianity found its mission in putting an end to precisely such an organization *because life prospered in it*. There the gains of reason, after a long period of experiments and uncertainty, were to be invested for the greatest long-term advantage and the harvest to be brought home as great, as ample, as complete as possible; here, conversely, the harvest was *poisoned* overnight. That which stood there *aere perennius*, the *imperium Romanum*, the most magnificent form of organization under difficult circumstances which has yet been achieved, in comparison with which all before and all afterward are mere botch, patchwork, and dilettantism—these holy anarchists made it a matter of "piety" for themselves to destroy "the world," *that is, the imperium Romanum*, until not one stone remained.[29]

In Nietzsche's hyperbolic rhetoric, Christianity was a purely destructive force in antiquity: "Christianity was the vampire of the *imperium Romanum*: overnight it undid the tremendous deed of the Romans—who had won the ground for a great culture *that would have time.*"[30]

We saw in chapter 1 that Shakespeare bathes the Roman world in *Antony and Cleopatra* in the pale light of the setting sun and views the Empire, even in its early days not as the beginning but the end of an era—indeed, the end of everything that had made Rome great in the days of the Republic. By contrast, Nietzsche views the Empire as the dawn of a new day, which only the corrupting force of Christianity forestalled:

> The *imperium Romanum* . . . this most admirable work of art in the grand style was a beginning; its construction was designed to prove itself through thousands of years: until today nobody has built again like this, nobody has even dreamed of building in such proportions *sub specie aeterni*. This organization was firm enough to withstand bad emperors: the accident of persons may not have anything to do with such matters—*first* principle of all grand architecture. But it was not firm enough against the *most corrupt* kind of corruption, against the *Christians.*[31]

Notice that Nietzsche recognizes that some of the Roman emperors were bad, but here he will not acknowledge that this factor may have played a role in Rome's decline. Instead, he praises the Roman imperial system precisely for the way it was able to maintain its course even in the face of bad rulers at the helm.[32]

Nietzsche's diatribe against Christianity and its impact on ancient Rome builds up to a melancholy and impassioned reflection on all that was lost with the triumph of Christianity:

> The whole labor of the ancient world in vain. . . . And considering that its labor was a preliminary labor, that only the foundation for the labors of thousands of years had just then been laid with granite self-confidence—the whole *meaning* of the ancient world in vain! . . . And not buried overnight by a natural catastrophe, not trampled down by Teutons and other buffaloes, but ruined by cunning, stealthy, invisible, anemic vampires. Not vanquished— merely drained.[33]

Nietzsche no doubt took pleasure in venting his spleen against Christianity in passages such as this, but he was painting himself into an intellectual corner. He only succeeded in heightening the doubts about his theory of the slave revolt in morality.[34] If the Roman Empire was such a rock-solid organization, if it was on course to last for thousands of years, how did a rag-tag gang of Christian outcasts ever succeed in bringing it down?[35]

Renegade Masters

Elsewhere in his writings, Nietzsche does explore the mechanism of the slave revolt—how it actually worked and succeeded. He considers the possibility that only divisions within an aristocratic class could open the way for over-turning its noble ethic. Indeed, one might well argue that as long as aristocrats maintain their solidarity, their political and ethical position is unassailable. But once they break ranks, their hegemony becomes vulnerable. Nietzsche explores this possibility in *On the Genealogy of Morals*, his most extensive analysis of slave morality in his published works. In this book, Nietzsche does not, as some people suppose, present slave morality as an exclusively Christian development but rather as a more pervasive phenomenon, beginning first with the ancient Jews.[36] Nietzsche had already made this point earlier in *Beyond Good and Evil*:

> The Jews—a people "born for slavery," as Tacitus and the whole ancient world say; . . . the Jews have brought off that miraculous feat of an inversion of values, thanks to which life on earth has acquired a novel and dangerous attraction for a couple of millennia: their prophets have fused "rich," "god-less," "evil," "violent," and "sensual" into one and were the first to use the word "world" as an opprobrium. This inversion of things (which includes using the word "poor" as synonymous with "holy" and "friend") constitutes the significance of the Jewish people: they mark the beginning of the slave rebellion in morals.[37]

In *Genealogy of Morals*, Nietzsche analyzes the way the distinctive social organization of ancient Israel made a slave revolt in morality possible. It de-pended on an institutionalized division within the Jewish ruling class, which included a priestly as well as a warrior caste.[38] Nietzsche points out that under such circumstances, the usual master morality conception of the good as the physically powerful can be challenged by a different idea that works more in favor of the priestly caste:

> To this rule that a concept denoting political superiority always resolves itself into a concept denoting superiority of soul it is not necessarily an exception (although it provides occasion for exceptions) when the highest caste is at the same time the *priestly* caste and therefore emphasizes in its total description of itself a predicate that calls to mind its priestly functions. It is then, for example, that "pure" and "impure" confront one another for the first time in descriptions of station; and here too there evolves a "good" and a "bad" in a sense no longer referring to station.[39]

Here Nietzsche comes close to Shakespeare's idea in *Antony and Cleopatra* that a new, more spiritualized, and anti-aristocratic conception of the good might evolve *within* a ruling aristocracy. We saw in chapter 1 that Shakespeare portrays priests gaining in power over time in the Roman plays. In *Coriolanus*, he contradicts his source in Plutarch by all but excluding priests from his portrait of republican Rome; in *Julius Caesar*, he shows priests playing a greater role in the Roman regime but still firmly under political control;[40] finally in *Antony and Cleopatra*, Shakespeare, perhaps aware of the long tradition of priests vying for power with the pharaohs in ancient Egypt, shows Cleopatra's court virtually run by priests, soothsayers, and eunuchs. Shakespeare captures something of what Nietzsche means by a warlike aristocracy subverted from within its ranks when Enobarbus tells Cleopatra that she is not fit to lead in battle:

> 'Tis said in Rome
> That Photinus an eunuch and your maids
> Manage this war. (3.7.13–15)

With a divided ruling class, the interest of the priests and the interests of the warriors may diverge. The warriors will remain loyal to the original form of master morality—a military ethos that celebrates the virtues that make victory in war possible. Unable to match the warriors in feats of strength and martial virtues, the priests will favor more spiritual values that would elevate them to the top of the social hierarchy—above all, the idea that purity of soul, not physical strength, is the highest value: "it is clear from the whole nature of an essentially priestly aristocracy why antithetical valuations could in precisely this instance become dangerously deepened, sharpened, and internalized. . . . There is from the first something *unhealthy* in such priestly aristocracies and in the habits ruling in them which turn them away from action and alternate between brooding and emotional explosions."[41]

For Nietzsche, the term "priestly aristocracy" is almost an oxymoron. Priests do not share the traditional aristocratic values of warriors. In *Genealogy of Morals* Nietzsche traces the slave revolt to what might be called "renegade masters," traitors within the ruling aristocracy who undermine its ethical foundations:

> One will have divined already how easily the priestly mode of valuation can branch off from the knightly–aristocratic and then develop into its opposite; this is particularly likely when the priestly caste and the warrior caste are in jealous opposition to one another and are unwilling to come to terms. The knightly-aristocratic value judgments presupposed a powerful physicality,

a flourishing, abundant, even overflowing health, together with that which serves to preserve it: war, adventure, hunting, dancing, war games, and in general all that involves vigorous, free, joyful activity. The priestly mode of valuation presupposes . . . other things: it is disadvantageous for it when it comes to war![42]

In this account of the slave revolt in morality, the force driving the process is no longer a mystery. In ancient Israel, the priests occupied a position of *power* in the social hierarchy and could thus lead an ethical revolution. Obviously, Shakespeare is dealing with different phenomena in *Antony and Cleopatra*, and yet Shakespeare and Nietzsche share the idea that a revaluation of values is more likely to be the result of leadership *from the top*, rather than a simple case of the lowest strata of society rising up against their masters. As we saw in chapter 1, "renegade masters" are the key to what happens to Rome in *Julius Caesar* and *Antony and Cleopatra*. For the aristocratic regime to be subverted, some members of the patrician party like Julius Caesar and Mark Antony must break ranks and go over to the plebeian party, or at least set themselves up as their champions. In order to gain support when jockeying for control of the city, certain ambitious patricians ignore their traditional class prejudices, and become spokesmen for the plebeians' interests and their view of the world.[43]

For Nietzsche, the military defeats ancient Israel suffered at the hands of foreign conquerors—the Assyrians and the Babylonians at first, but eventually the Romans as well—discredited its warrior class and opened the way for the triumph of its priestly class. In a state that had lost its political but not its religious independence, the priests gained authority and were free to rail against the traditional aristocratic values, associated with military victory, that had evidently failed the Jews in their greatest crisis.[44] It became imperative to find ways of turning military defeat into moral victory, to revalue values so that losing in battle would be regarded as manifesting more virtue than winning.[45] Hence, the Jews took the lead in the slave revolt in morality, as Nietzsche claims in a passage that for the moment minimizes Christianity's role:

All that has been done on earth against "the noble," "the powerful," "the masters," "the rulers," fades into nothing compared with what the *Jews* have done against them; the Jews, that priestly people, who in opposing their enemies and conquerors were ultimately satisfied with nothing less than a radical revaluation of their enemies' values, that is to say, an act of the *most spiritual revenge*. For this alone was appropriate to a priestly people, the people embodying the most deeply repressed priestly vengefulness. It was the Jews who, with awe-inspiring consistency, dared to invert the aristocratic value-equation (good = noble = powerful = beautiful = happy = beloved of God) and to hang on to this inversion with their teeth, the teeth of the most abysmal hatred (the hatred of impotence), saying "the wretched alone are the good; the poor, impotent, lowly alone are the good; the suffering, deprived, sick, ugly alone are pious, alone are blessed by God, blessedness is for them alone—and you, the powerful and noble, are on the contrary the evil, the cruel, the lustful, the insatiable, the godless to all eternity; and you shall be in all eternity the unblessed, accursed, and damned!"[46]

In Nietzsche's discussion of the slave revolt in morality in *Genealogy of Morals*, he gives a plausible account of how it worked, but only because he attributes the motive force to a Jewish priestly caste, not to a mere mob of early Christian rabble-rousers.[47] For Nietzsche, the slave revolt was originally a power play by aristocratic Jewish priests. In a divided ruling class, the priestly caste outmaneuvered a discredited warrior caste by inverting the traditional heroic ethos and reconceiving strength as something spiritual, a quality of soul that only the priests possessed in abundance.[48] All of Nietzsche's other discussions of the slave revolt presuppose the account of Jewish priestly cleverness in *Genealogy of Morals*. Indeed, the passage just quoted continues: "One knows *who* inherited this Jewish revaluation"[49]—meaning of course the Christians. At various points in his writings, Nietzsche acknowledges and insists that whatever Christians did to revalue classical values had its foundation in Jewish predecessors.[50] Having lost their independence as a nation, the Jews turned against politics as such and denied that political success is any measure of moral virtue. Nietzsche views Christianity as growing out of just this attitude: "This was also the case with the earliest Christian community (also Jewish community), whose presupposition is the absolutely unpolitical Jewish society. Christianity could grow only in the soil of Judaism, i.e., amidst a people that had absolutely renounced politics and lived a kind of parasitic existence within the Roman order of things. Christianity is a step further on: one is even more free to 'emasculate' oneself."[51]

In his notebooks of the 1880s, Nietzsche repeatedly wrestled with this subject, trying to work out the exact role of the Jews and the Christians in the slave revolt in morality. In perhaps the most suggestive and fully developed note, Nietzsche views Christianity as a kind of slave revolt within the Jewish slave revolt. The story begins when the priests turn traitor to their class and enlist the common people on their side in their struggle against the warrior class. But then the common people develop *ressentiment* and rebel against their new priestly masters:

The Jews tried to prevail after they had lost two of their castes, that of the warrior and that of the peasant; in this sense they are the "castrated": they have the priests—and then immediately the chandala—

As is only fair, a break develops among them, a revolt of the chandala: the origin of Christianity.

Because they knew the warrior only as their master, they brought into their religion enmity toward the noble, toward the exalted and proud, toward power, toward the ruling orders—: they are pessimists from indignation—

Thus they created an important new posture: the priest at the head of the chandala—against the noble orders—

Christianity drew upon the ultimate conclusion of this movement: even in the Jewish priesthood it still sensed caste, the privileged, the noble—it abolished the priest—

The Christian is the chandala who repudiates the priest—the chandala who redeems himself—

That is why the French Revolution is the daughter and continuation of Christianity—its instincts are against caste, against the noble, against the last privileges—[52]

In a community depoliticized by its repeated military losses to foreign conquerors, Jewish priests assumed the role of spiritual masters, only to become the objects of *ressentiment* and rebellion by the lowest strata of the religious community they led. We will never know how Nietzsche might have developed this material for a published book, but these notes show how complicated his thinking about the slave revolt was and how he kept exploring the subject in many directions. Nietzsche's reflections on the role of the Jews in the slave revolt, in both his published and unpublished writings, show that, like Shakespeare, he was aware that developments *within* an aristocracy could play a crucial role in the overturning of a political hierarchy and the revaluation of its values. Clearly, what Nietzsche says about the Jews in *Genealogy of Morals* and elsewhere contradicts his claim in *The Antichrist* that Christianity was solely responsible for the decadence of the Roman Empire and the slave revolt in morality.[53]

The Corruption of Aristocracies

Nietzsche was interested in the broader subject of how aristocracies in general might become corrupted and decay, and even when he discusses other aristocratic regimes, his thinking is applicable to the Roman situation. In *Beyond Good and Evil*, for example, Nietzsche discusses the eighteenth-century French aristocracy's loss of faith in itself in a way that calls to mind what

Shakespeare shows about the Roman aristocracy in *Julius Caesar* and *Antony and Cleopatra*:

> When, for example, an aristocracy, like that of France at the beginning of the Revolution, throws away its privileges with a sublime disgust and sacrifices itself to an extravagance of its own moral feelings, that is corruption; it was really only the last act of that centuries-old corruption which had led them to surrender, step by step, their governmental prerogatives, demoting themselves to a mere *function* of the monarchy (finally even to a mere ornament and showpiece). The essential characteristic of a good and healthy aristocracy, however, is that it experiences itself *not* as a function (whether of the monarchy or the commonwealth) but as their *meaning* and highest justification—that it therefore accepts with a good conscience the sacrifice of untold human beings who, *for its sake*, must be reduced and lowered to incomplete human beings, to slaves, to instruments.[54]

Here Nietzsche distinguishes between a corrupt aristocracy and a healthy one, and everything hinges on whether the ruling class has faith in itself. Healthy aristocrats, like those in *Coriolanus*, believe firmly in their right to rule. They think of themselves as genuine masters, elevated by nature over a servile class of slaves. Corrupt aristocrats, like those in *Antony and Cleopatra*, have developed a bad conscience about their status as masters—they have begun to doubt their natural superiority—and in a form of self-contempt, they lose their confidence in exercising power. Nietzsche understands that the kings of France worked systematically to break the will of the French nobility, gradually turning them from independent feudal lords, ruling over their own territories and armies, into dependent courtiers, mere appendages of the royal court (where they came to reside). Nietzsche's reference to the French Revolution at the beginning of this passage shows what is at stake. Nietzsche regarded the French Revolution as the continuation (indeed, the culmination) of the slave revolt in morality. In *Beyond Good and Evil*, he suggests that the corruption of the French aristocracy was the precondition of the French Revolution. The lower classes can successfully rebel only against a *weakened* aristocracy, one that has lost its confidence in itself and thus its will to rule.

The parallels to what Shakespeare portrays in *Antony and Cleopatra* should be obvious. Once the imperial system subordinates the Roman aristocrats to the rule of a single Caesar, their behavior becomes increasingly slavish. They are reduced to creatures of the imperial court; Shakespeare hints at this development when he has the younger Pompey refer to Brutus and the other republican conspirators as "courtiers of beauteous freedom" (2.6.17). The one speech in *Antony and Cleopatra* that attempts to revive the rhetoric of the old Republic—"they would / Have one man but a man"

(2.6.18–19)—strikes a hollow note when Pompey aestheticizes the political issue (speaking of "beauteous freedom") and refers to the patricians as mere "courtiers." The noble Romans have lost their sense of playing a genuinely heroic role within the regime, and long to abdicate their positions of power and responsibility. Antony, who begins the play contending for rule of the Roman world, reaches a point where he asks Octavius "to let him breathe between the heavens and earth, a private man in Athens" (3.12.14–15). The depoliticization of the Roman aristocracy follows from their many military losses and their disillusion with imperial politics. The decadence Shakespeare portrays in the Roman aristocracy in *Antony and Cleopatra* is rooted in the same causes Nietzsche sees at work in the French aristocracy on the eve of its surrender to a revaluation of values in the French Revolution.

In part 9 of *Beyond Good and Evil*—entitled "What Is Noble"—Nietzsche continues his discussion of the potential corruption of aristocracies. In section 262, he outlines how an aristocratic commonwealth provides the conditions for developing master morality:

> Now look for once at an aristocratic commonwealth—say, an ancient Greek *polis*, or Venice—as an arrangement, whether voluntary or involuntary, for *breeding*: human beings are together there who are dependent on themselves and want their species to prevail, most often because they *have to* prevail or run the terrible risk of being exterminated. Here that boon, that excess, and that protection which favor variations are lacking; the species needs itself as a species, as something that can prevail and make itself durable by virtue of its very hardness, uniformity, and simplicity of form, in a constant fight with its neighbors or with the oppressed who are rebellious or threaten rebellion. Manifold experience teaches them to which qualities above all they owe the fact that, despite all gods and men, they are still there, that they have always triumphed: these qualities they call virtues, these virtues alone they cultivate. They do this with hardness, indeed they want hardness; every aristocratic morality is intolerant—in the education of youth, in their arrangements for women, in their marriage customs, in the relations of old and young, in their penal laws . . . they consider intolerance itself a virtue, calling it "justice."
>
> In this way a type with few but very strong traits, a species of severe, warlike, prudently taciturn men, close-mouthed and closely linked (and as such possessed of the subtlest feeling for the charms and *nuances* of association), is fixed beyond the changing generations; the continual fight against ever constant *unfavorable* conditions is . . . the cause that fixes and hardens a type.[55]

Although Nietzsche cites the case of a Greek *polis* or Venice, this passage is a remarkably accurate description of the world of Shakespeare's *Coriolanus*.[56]

Nietzsche might just as well have been speaking about the Roman Republic in its early days. Hardness is the keynote of the Roman republican regime as Shakespeare portrays it. As we saw, Coriolanus associates himself with hard things: "He's the rock, the oak not to be wind-shaken" (5.2.110–11). Meanwhile, he associates his enemies, the plebeians, with soft and melting things: "You are no surer, no, / Than is the coal of fire upon the ice, / Or hailstone in the sun" (1.1.172–74). In all the areas Nietzsche mentions—"in the education of youth, in their arrangements for women, in their marriage customs, in the relations of old and young, in their penal laws"—Shakespeare shows how strict the Roman Republic was in imposing a martial way of life on its people.

Nietzsche grounds the toughness of aristocratic regimes in necessity, and Shakespeare makes the same point in *Coriolanus*. Faced with the threat of foreign enemies like the Volsces and the presence of domestic rebellion by the plebeians, the Roman aristocrats cannot afford to let down their guard and must maintain an iron discipline or perish. A conversation among Volscian servants contrasts war and peace—the latter corrupts people, while the former whips them into shape:

2. SERV: This peace is nothing but to rust iron, increase tailors, and breed ballad-makers.

1. SERV: Let me have war, say I, it exceeds peace as far as day does night; it's sprightly walking, audible, and full of vent. Peace is a very apoplexy, lethargy, mull'd, deaf, sleepy, insensible, a getter of more bastard children than war's a destroyer of men.

2. SERV: 'Tis so, and as war, in some sort, may be said to be a ravisher, so it cannot be denied but peace is a great maker of cuckolds.

1. SERV: Ay, and it makes men hate one another.

3. SERV: Reason: because they then less need one another. (4.5.219–32)

If constant warfare with hostile neighbors imposes discipline on the republican Romans, Shakespeare shows in *Antony and Cleopatra* that the imminent arrival of a "time of universal peace" (4.6.4) undermines Rome's traditional martial discipline. Continuing in section 262 of *Beyond Good and Evil*, Nietzsche makes the same point:

> Eventually, however, a day arrives when conditions become more fortunate and the tremendous tension decreases; perhaps there are no longer any enemies among one's neighbors, and the means of life, even for the enjoyment of life, are superabundant. At one stroke the bond and constraint of the old discipline are torn: it no longer seems necessary, a condition of existence—if it persisted it would only be a form of *luxury*, an archaizing *taste*. Variation,

whether as deviation (to something higher, subtler, rarer) or as degeneration and monstrosity, suddenly appears on the scene in the greatest abundance and magnificence; the individual dares to be individual and different.[57]

This passage is actually far more applicable to Rome and the Pax Romana than it is to the history of any Greek polis or Venice. Indeed, this passage reads like an apt description of the world of *Antony and Cleopatra*. No longer faced with the threat of famine with which *Coriolanus* begins, the imperial Romans have the wealth and produce of a vast empire at their command and are free to indulge their appetites in unprecedented ways. As we saw in chapter 1, Shakespeare characterizes the world of *Antony and Cleopatra* precisely by the development of individuality, as the imperial Romans, released from the constraints of the republican martial regime, explore new ways of life.[58]

As section 262 continues, Nietzsche seems more and more to be talking— inadvertently of course—about *Antony and Cleopatra* and the transition from Republic to Empire it portrays:

> At these turning points of history we behold beside one another, and often mutually involved and entangled, a kind of *tropical* tempo in the competition to grow, and a tremendous ruin and self-ruination, as the savage egoisms that have turned, almost exploded, against one another wrestle "for sun and light" and can no longer derive any limit, restraint, or consideration from their previous morality. It was this morality itself that damned up such enormous strength and bent the bow in such a threatening manner; now it is "outlived." The dangerous and uncanny point has been reached where the greater, more manifold, more comprehensive life transcends and *lives beyond* the old morality; the "individual" appears, obliged to give himself laws and develop his own arts and wiles for self-preservation, self-enhancement, self-redemption.[59]

Here Nietzsche captures perfectly the mood of *Antony and Cleopatra*. His mention of a "tropical tempo" seems an apt way to describe Shakespeare's play, given its hothouse atmosphere of temptation, seduction, and over-indulgence, together with all its images of overripeness and overflowing, and its jungle-like growth of liberated individuals. Cleopatra is a potent symbol of the seemingly infinite proliferation of new human possibilities unleashed by the imperial regime and the revaluation of traditional values; as Enobarbus says of her:

> Age cannot wither her, nor custom stale
> Her infinite variety. Other women cloy
> The appetites they feed, but she makes hungry
> Where most she satisfies; for vilest things

> Become themselves in her, that the holy priests
> Bless her when she is riggish. (2.2.234–39)

Cleopatra seduces even the priests into inverting their religious values.

Nietzsche does not say that he is writing about imperial Rome in section 262, but it is hard to think of any period in history that this description fits better. The convergence between what Nietzsche writes and what Shakespeare portrays in *Antony and Cleopatra* only grows deeper as he continues:

> All sorts of new what-fors and wherewithals; no shared formulas any longer; misunderstanding allied with disrespect; decay, corruption, and the highest desires gruesomely entangled; the genius of the race overflowing from all cornucopias of good and bad; a calamitous simultaneity of spring and fall, full of new charms and veils that characterize young, still unexhausted, still unwearied corruption. . . . What may the moral philosophers, emerging in this age have to preach now?
>
> These acute observers and loiterers discover that the end is approaching fast, that everything around them is corrupted and corrupts, that nothing will stand the day after tomorrow, except *one* type of man, the incurably *mediocre*. The mediocre alone have a chance of continuing their type and propagating—they are the men of the future, the only success: "Be like them! Become mediocre!" is now the only morality that still makes sense, that still gets a hearing.[60]

Nietzsche's idea of a world of mediocrity following upon the enervation of an old aristocracy is anticipated by Cleopatra's vision of life after Antony's death:

> The crown o' th' earth doth melt. My lord!
> O, wither'd is the garland of the war.
> The soldier's pole is fall'n! Young boys and girls
> Are level now with men; the odds is gone,
> And there is nothing left remarkable
> Beneath the visiting moon. (4.15.63–68)

I am of course not claiming that Nietzsche was actually commenting on *Antony and Cleopatra* in section 262 of *Beyond Good and Evil*. But again and again Nietzsche seems to capture the essence of what Shakespeare portrays in *Antony and Cleopatra*, especially the play's apocalyptic sense of the aristocratic world coming to an end. Could any phrase describe the mood of the play better than "the calamitous simultaneity of spring and fall, full of new charms and veils"?

Multiple Sources of Rome's Corruption

Far from sticking to the idea he insists on in *The Antichrist* that the Roman Empire was corrupted only by Christianity, Nietzsche kept exploring other possibilities in his notebooks. Evidently he himself was troubled by the question of how the weak could ever manage to overthrow the strong. The question keeps appearing in his notebooks from the 1880s: "What gives authority when one does not have physical power in one's hands (no army, no weapons of any kind—)? How, in fact, does one gain authority over those who possess physical strength and authority?"[61] or "How can one wage war against the manly affects and valuations?"[62] In the most interesting of Nietzsche's notes on Rome (dated 1884), he develops a position remarkably similar to what we have seen in *Antony and Cleopatra*:

> The degeneration of the rulers and the ruling class has been the cause of the greatest mischief in history! Without the Roman Caesars and Roman society, the insanity of Christianity would never have come to power.
>
> When lesser men begin to doubt whether higher men exist, then the danger is great! And one ends by discovering that there is *virtue* among the lowly and subjugated, the poor in spirit, and that *before* God men are equal—which has so far been the *non plus ultra* of nonsense on earth! For ultimately, the higher men measured themselves according to the standard of virtue of slaves—found they were "proud," etc., found all their higher qualities reprehensible.
>
> When Nero and Caracalla sat up there, the paradox arose: "the lowest man is worth more than that man up there!" And the way was prepared for an image of God that was as remote as possible from the image of the most powerful—the god on the cross![63]

In *The Antichrist* Nietzsche insists that the Roman Empire was strong enough to survive even the rule of bad emperors; here in his notebooks he asserts the exact opposite—that moral revulsion against bad emperors like Nero and Caracalla was what made the triumph of Christianity possible. This passage analyzes the experience that Shakespeare encapsulates in Cleopatra's claim: "'Tis paltry to be Caesar." In reaction to the corrupt Caesars, people in Rome—notice that in this passage Nietzsche does not specify Jews or Christians—began to question master morality and the superiority of aristocrats. If the powerful behave so viciously, power cannot be equated with virtue. Rather, virtue will be attributed to the powerless, and the traditional distinction between the high and low will be leveled out or inverted. In the most important parallel to *Antony and Cleopatra*, Nietzsche does not restrict this process to the "lesser men" with whom he begins in the note. He soon says that "the higher men measured themselves according to the standard of virtue of slaves—found they were 'proud,' etc., found all their higher qualities reprehensible." This is exactly the kind of turn within the aristocracy against aristocratic values that Shakespeare portrays, beginning in *Julius Caesar* and culminating in *Antony and Cleopatra*.

In his notebooks, Nietzsche keeps searching for ways in which the Roman aristocrats were involved in and even promoted the process of their own overthrow. At several points, he entertains the familiar idea that misguided Roman rulers actually helped Christianity spread by persecuting Christians and turning them into martyrs, witnesses to the power of their faith: "That one *persecuted* them was a piece of ancient folly in the grand manner: that meant taking them too seriously, that meant making something serious out of them."[64] At one point Nietzsche writes, "When one sees one's dearest sacrificed for one's faith, one becomes aggressive; we owe the triumph of Christianity to its persecution"[65]—that is to say, to actions for which the misguided Roman Caesars, not the Christians themselves, were responsible.

In a note headed "*When the 'masters' could also become Christians,*" Nietzsche speculates on why the Roman rulers did not simply come to tolerate Christianity but actually went on to make it the official state religion of the Empire:

> It lies in the interest of the rulers (be they individuals or classes) to patronize and applaud the virtues that make their subjects useful and submissive. . . .
>
> Submission of the master races to Christianity is essentially the consequence of the insight that Christianity is a herd religion, that it teaches obedience; in short, that Christians are easier to rule than non-Christians. With this hint, the pope recommends Christian propaganda to the emperor of China even today.[66]

Nietzsche develops a conspiratorial view of the triumph of Christianity in the Roman Empire—the emperors came to promote Christianity and its slave morality as a way of keeping their subjects docile. As Nietzsche writes: "The values of the weak prevail because the strong have taken them over as devices of leadership."[67] According to this interpretation of Roman history, the emperor Constantine's conversion to Christianity was not a case of genuine spiritual conviction but a cynical ploy to shore up his throne with a religion well adapted to slaves.[68] As Nietzsche writes in *Daybreak*: "Christianity was made for . . . those weak in will and mind, that is to say for the great mass of slaves."[69]

The more one delves into Nietzsche's notebooks, the more one sees that he had grave doubts about his claim in *The Antichrist* that Christianity was the sole force working to undermine Roman master morality. In addition to Judaism, Christianity had many religious precursors according to Nietzsche:

> Christianity only takes up the fight that had already begun against the *classical* ideal and the *noble* religion.
>
> In fact, this entire transformation is an adaptation to the needs and the level of understanding of the religious masses of the time: those masses which believed in Isis, Mithras, Dionysus, the "Great Mother," and which demanded of religion: (1) hope of a beyond, (2) the bloody phantasmagoria of the sacrificial animal (the mystery), (3) the redemptive deed, the holy legend, (4) asceticism, world-denial, superstitious "purification," (5) a hierarchy, a form of community. In short: Christianity accommodated itself to already existing and established antipaganism, to the cults that had been combatted by Epicurus—more precisely, to the religions of the lower masses, the women, the non-noble classes.[70]

In passages such as this, Nietzsche views Christianity as only one part of a larger pan-Mediterranean movement that had already begun to undermine Roman nobility before Jesus was born.[71] With the references to Isis and Bacchus in *Antony and Cleopatra* and glimpses of enigmatic beliefs among the Egyptians, Shakespeare also links the rise of Christianity to other Mediterranean mystery religions abroad in the final days of the Roman Republic.[72]

In denying that Christianity simply arose out of nowhere to undermine the Roman Empire, Nietzsche also puts some of the blame on Greek philosophy, especially Plato. "Greek moral philosophy had already done everything to prepare the way for and make palatable moral fanaticism even among Greeks and Romans—Plato, the great viaduct of corruption, who first refused to see nature in morality, who had already debased the Greek gods with his concept 'good,' who was already marked by Jewish bigotry (—in Egypt?)."[73] As strange as this passage may sound (Nietzsche was thinking of ancient legends that Plato had visited Egypt), he took seriously the idea that Greek philosophy laid the groundwork for Christianity. He discusses this idea at a number of places in his published books, especially in *Twilight of the Idols*. There Nietzsche connects Greek philosophy, specifically the Socratic critique of traditional Greek ethics, with the decline of the Greek aristocracy: "[Socrates] saw *through* his noble Athenians; he comprehended that his own case, his idiosyncrasy, was no longer exceptional. The same kind of degeneration was quietly developing everywhere: old Athens was coming to an end . . . Everywhere the instincts were in anarchy . . . no one was any longer master of himself, the instincts turned *against* each other."[74]

In Nietzsche's grand historical narrative, the development of Christianity among the ancient Romans was a replay of the development of philosophy among the ancient Greeks (for Nietzsche, Christianity was "Platonism for 'the people'").[75] In both cases, the corruption of an aristocracy that tradition-ally ruled by physical force provoked a spiritual reaction, an attempt to deni-grate the virtues of a decadent master class and redefine "good" as something other than naked political power. Thus for Nietzsche Socratic philosophy was a prototype of Christian moralizing and a symptom of decadence:

> How could one possibly judge the Greeks by their philosophers, as the Ger-mans have done, and use the Philistine moralism of the Socratic schools as a clue to what was basically Hellenic! After all, the philosophers are the deca-dents of Greek culture, the counter-movement to the ancient, noble taste (to the agonistic instinct, to the *polis*, to the value of race, to the authority of de-scent). The Socratic virtues were preached because the Greeks had lost them.[76]

Nietzsche's analysis of Socrates's relation to Greek nobility reinforces what we have seen in his analysis of Christianity's relation to Rome. Only an ar-istocracy already in decline can fall prey to a plebeian assault on master morality.

In a note from 1888, Nietzsche portrays Greek philosophy struggling in late antiquity with the conditions that were soon to give rise to Christianity, and in that respect preparing the way for it:

> The struggle against the "old faith" as undertaken by Epicurus was, in a strict sense, a struggle against pre-existing Christianity—a struggle against the old world grown servile and sick, already gloomy, moralized, soured by feelings of guilt.
>
> Not the "moral corruption" of antiquity, but precisely its *moralization* is the prerequisite through which alone Christianity could become master of it. Moral fanaticism (in short: Plato) destroyed paganism, by revaluing its values and poisoning its innocence.—
>
> We ought finally to understand that what was then destroyed was *higher* than what became master!—
>
> Christianity has grown out of psychological decay, could only take root in decayed soil.[77]

Here Nietzsche argues that Greek philosophy softened up Rome to prepare the way for Christianity, and he clearly states that a healthy paganism would not have yielded to a slave revolt in morality.[78] We saw that Shakespeare sug-gests something similar in *Julius Caesar*. The fact that a variety of Greek phil-osophical sects, including Stoicism and Epicureanism, have become preva-lent in the Rome of the late Republic is, for Shakespeare, one more sign of the city's decadence and the fatal weakening of the republican regime.

Nietzsche's idea that Greek philosophy played a role in preparing Rome to accept Christianity raises the larger issue of the relevance of his thinking about the Greeks to his thinking about the Romans. In his writings about the Greeks, Nietzsche is generally hostile to empire. Unlike most classicists in his day, he preferred the Greek world of the sixth century BCE to that of the fifth (that is, the Periclean Age in Athens). Nietzsche most admired the Greeks when they were divided into small, relatively self-contained cities, competing and even warring with each other. He argues that this kind of competitiveness nurtured the flourishing of Greek literature, music, and art. In Nietzsche's view, the pursuit of empire corrupted the Greek world and eventually destroyed its cultural vitality by the beginning of the fourth century BCE. Far from celebrating Periclean Athens (as his contemporaries tended to do), Nietzsche views it as decadent, eventually requiring the philosophical discipline of Socrates to try to control its degenerating instincts.[79] Once Athens began operating on an imperial scale, it upset the delicate balance among the Greek cities once and for all. In short, Nietzsche's history of the ancient Greeks resembles what we have seen to be Shakespeare's history of the ancient Romans. In Shakespeare, the Roman Republic follows a course very similar to that of the Athenian regime according to Nietzsche's understanding. In both cases, an originally small city undermines what made it great by pursuing a grand imperial design that saps its virtues. In both Athens and Rome, imperial success fundamentally alters the city's very nature and corrupts its nobility.

I raise this issue because it highlights the anomalous status of Nietzsche's praise of the Roman Empire in *The Antichrist* within the whole corpus of his writings. Normally, Nietzsche had a sense of the hollowness of imperial glory and treated the expanded frontiers of an empire as a bloated monstrosity. That was certainly his view of the newly emergent Prussian Empire of his own day. In sharp contrast to many of his German contemporaries, Nietzsche regarded the new German *Reich* as a cultural disaster—not the beginning of a new era of German domination but the end of the great age of Goethe, when the competition of all the petty German states created a vibrant cultural world. As Nietzsche writes in *Twilight of the Idols*:

> Culture and the state . . . are antagonists. . . . All great ages of culture are ages of political decline: what is great culturally has always been unpolitical, even *anti-political* . . . . In the history of European culture the rise of the *"Reich"* means one thing above all: a displacement of the center of gravity. . . . [I]n what matters most—and that always remains culture—the Germans are no longer worthy of consideration. One asks: Can you point to even a single spirit who counts from a European point of view, as your Goethe, your Hegel, your Heinrich Heine, your Schopenhauer counted?[80]

In cultural/political terms for Nietzsche, "small is better." He thought that the smaller the political unit, the more likely it would nourish cultural development.[81] His meditations in the 1870s on empire in the ancient Greek world developed concurrently with his critique of Prussian domination of the German-speaking lands and the attempt to create a large-scale German Empire. All of this is not to deny that Nietzsche praises the Roman Empire extravagantly in *The Antichrist*. But it does suggest that we might be suspicious when we find Nietzsche applauding the Roman Empire, especially as a cultural unit, given the fact that in the cases of the ancient Greeks and the modern Germans Nietzsche is skeptical of empire as the true path to human greatness. In view of Nietzsche's general critique of empire throughout his writings, his praise of the Roman Empire in *The Antichrist* must be taken as the exception, not the rule.[82]

Dumb Masters and Wily Slaves

Nietzsche's understanding of the slave revolt in morality is thus far more complicated than may at first appear. For Nietzsche, there is not simply a single slave revolt, a Christian one. He argues that ancient Jewish priests initiated the slave revolt, and he also discusses Socrates as a clever plebeian who turned the tables on his noble masters in Athens.[83] In both the Jewish and the Greek cases, the slave revolt would have been impossible in the face of a unified, healthy, uncorrupt aristocracy. In both situations, Nietzsche shows that an aristocracy weakened by defeat in war ends up badly divided against itself and/or dispirited, disillusioned, and disheartened. The Jewish and Greek cases supply clues to how Nietzsche interpreted analogous processes in ancient Rome and indeed he insists at various points that the Christian slave revolt drew upon earlier Jewish and Greek developments, as well as other religious movements. *The Antichrist* may be Nietzsche's greatest indictment of Christianity, but in his other writings, he ends up naming many unindicted coconspirators in the Christian crime against Rome.

By piecing together passages from Nietzsche's published works and his notebooks, I have tried to show that he did think carefully about the details of how the slave revolt in morality actually operated; he went beyond a simplistic account of lowly slaves turning the tables on their unsuspecting masters. But I risk giving the impression that Nietzsche had worked out a single (though complex) idea of the mechanism of the slave revolt. Unfortunately, Nietzsche never had the time to tie together his scattered and in many cases undeveloped thoughts on the slave revolt and come up with a unified understanding of the phenomenon. At many points in his published works he continued to

speak simply of what "the slaves" did to their masters, as if he were still working with a simple model of a slave revolt. Aside from obscuring the complexity of Nietzsche's thought on this subject, his use of a simplified terminology
creates confusion as to how he evaluated the slave revolt. If it really was the
work of just a contemptible rabble, then Nietzsche presumably despised it.
But if the slave revolt involved the efforts of a subtle priestly aristocracy and
a philosopher of the stature of Socrates, then it would be more difficult to
dismiss it as a purely debased and debasing phenomenon.[84] In short, if the
mechanism of the slave revolt in Nietzsche's account is much more complex
than at first appears, then we also need to rethink his evaluation of master
morality and slave morality. Perhaps he did not simply prefer the former to
the latter, as is commonly supposed.[85]

To be sure, the way Nietzsche talks about glorious, heroic masters and
wily, scheming slaves may seem to tilt the scales in favor of the masters. But
Nietzsche chooses to complicate matters, especially once he takes into account the contribution of the priestly renegades among the masters: "It is
only fair to add that it was on the soil of this *essentially dangerous* form of human existence, the priestly form, that man first became an *interesting animal,*
that only here did the human soul in a higher sense acquire *depth* and become
evil—and these are two basic respects in which man has hitherto been superior to other beasts!"[86] These are extraordinary claims on behalf of the very
priests whom Nietzsche generally seems to despise. He credits them with in
effect creating humanity as we know it, of first introducing an element of
depth into the human soul, perhaps of creating soul in the first place. The
implication is that originally the masters were superficial; they were not fully
human. Nietzsche is clear on this point: "Human history would be altogether
too stupid a thing without the spirit that the impotent have introduced into
it."[87] Whatever Nietzsche's ultimate judgment may be, clearly he thinks that
the slaves, under the leadership of priestly nobles or other class renegades,
become cleverer than the masters, more developed in the higher, distinctively
human faculties.[88]

However much Nietzsche praises the masters for their warlike qualities—
their courage, their physical strength, their aggressiveness—in the process
he describes them as subhuman: "One cannot fail to see at bottom of all the
noble races the beast of prey, the splendid *blond beast* prowling about avidly
in search of spoil and victory; this hidden core needs to erupt from time to
time, the animal has to get out again and go back to the wilderness: the Roman, Arabian, Germanic, Japanese nobility, the Homeric heroes, the Scandi-
navian Vikings—they all share this need."[89] Many have been quick to assume
that Nietzsche must be glorifying and romanticizing the "blond beast," but

he was merely stating a fact about military aristocracies, that they are brutal and, at their core, brute-like. Nietzsche is, in fact, critical of the masters and dwells specifically upon their intellectual limitations:

> When the noble mode of valuation blunders and sins against reality, it does so in respect to the sphere with which it is *not* sufficiently familiar, against a real knowledge of which it has indeed inflexibly guarded itself: in some circumstances it misunderstands the sphere it despises, that of the common man, of the lower orders. . . . There is indeed too much carelessness, too much taking lightly, too much looking away and impatience involved in contempt.[90]

In short, according to Nietzsche, the masters—for all their nobility—are simply stupid compared to the slaves.[91] Left to themselves, the masters would rest on their laurels and stick to their brute-like ways. Forced to develop their cleverness, the slaves are the motive force of history for Nietzsche, and take humanity out of its original animal state (corresponding roughly to the state of nature in Rousseau).[92] Creativity, the development of the inner world of imagination, is the work of the slaves: "The slave revolt in morality begins when *ressentiment* itself becomes creative and gives birth to values: the *ressentiment* of natures that are denied the true reaction, that of deeds, and compensates itself with an imaginary revenge."[93] Because the masters have the freedom and power to do whatever they wish, they would never turn inward and develop their inner or spiritual resources on their own initiative. By contrast, the slaves, denied external outlets for their impulses, for the first time in history have to evolve a form of psychological richness in their souls: "A race of such men of *ressentiment* is bound to become eventually *cleverer* than any noble race; it will also honor cleverness to a far greater degree: namely, as a condition of existence of the first importance: while with noble men cleverness can easily acquire a subtle flavor of luxury and subtlety—for this it is far less essential than the perfect functioning of the regulating *unconscious* instincts."[94]

For Nietzsche, the virtue of the master is a kind of *unconscious* virtue. It is the slaves who develop human consciousness. Once one grasps this point, one realizes how much Nietzsche has in common with Hegel, despite his many quarrels with Hegel's philosophy of history.[95] *Genealogy of Morals* is a rewriting of Hegel's *Phenomenology of Spirit*—it provides an account of the development of human consciousness out of the struggle between master and slave.[96] Even the structure of Nietzsche's book parallels Hegel's: the first two essays of *Genealogy of Morals* deal with the realm of what Hegel calls "Objective Spirit," especially with the dialectic of the master and the slave, their ethical and political struggles. The third essay deals with the realm of what

Hegel calls "Absolute Spirit"—art, religion, and philosophy. In Hegel too the masters are complacent, content to stand pat in a situation in which they rule comfortably and live off the work of their slaves. In Hegel too the slaves are the motive force of history, doing all the labor and developing consciousness in an effort to turn the tables on their masters and win their freedom. Christianity and the French Revolution play essentially the same role in Hegel's understanding of history as they do in Nietzsche's—they work out the slave ideology in concrete historical terms. Hegel and Nietzsche at first appear to evaluate master and slave differently, but deep down they agree that human consciousness develops out of the struggles of the slaves to liberate themselves from the masters.[97]

Like Hegel, Nietzsche argues that the slaves develop the higher forms of human civilization: "Supposing that . . . the *meaning of all culture* is the reduction of the beast of prey 'man' to a tame and civilized animal, a *domestic animal*, then one would undoubtedly have to regard all those instincts of reaction and *ressentiment* through whose aid the noble races and their ideals were finally confounded and overthrown as the actual *instruments of culture*."[98] Nietzsche grudgingly admits what Hegel celebrates—that left to the masters, the world would remain in a static state; only the slaves propel human progress and develop the higher human functions. The third essay of *Genealogy of Morals* is a sustained study of the sublimation (what Hegel would call the *Aufhebung*) of lower drives into higher.[99] Nietzsche shows that the will to power that fueled the original slave revolt of Jewish priests—sublimated further into the priestly ascetic ideal—went on to energize all the higher cultural developments in religion, art, and philosophy.

Nietzsche identifies as the great turning point in human history the moment when the slaves draw the warlike masters into peaceful civilization, forcing them to move beyond their unconscious existence. Nietzsche describes the evolution of consciousness out of conscience:

> I regard the bad conscience as the serious illness that man was bound to contract under the stress of the most fundamental change he ever experienced— that change which occurred when he found himself finally enclosed within the walls of society and of peace. . . . these semi-animals, well adapted to the wilderness, to war, to prowling, to adventure: suddenly all their instincts were disvalued and "suspended." . . . In this new world they no longer possessed their former guides, their regulating, unconscious and infallible drives: they were reduced to thinking, inferring, reckoning, coordinating cause and effect, these unfortunate creatures; they were reduced to their "consciousness," their weakest and most feeble organ! I believe there has never been such a feeling of misery on earth, such a leaden discomfort.[100]

I introduce Hegel into this discussion to make it clear that the process that Nietzsche seems to be describing in such negative terms is what was normally viewed in positive terms in nineteenth-century thought—the evolution of human consciousness. Nietzsche is describing this development from the point of view of the masters—to whom it looked like the destruction of all that they stood for and a loss of their freedom. But from the point of view of the slaves rather than the masters—that is, the majority of human beings— this movement from the unconscious to the conscious is what is generally regarded as progress, especially the progressive emancipation of humanity from servitude.

Nietzsche understood that frustrating the masters—limiting their free- dom to act on their impulses—was the precondition of any advance in hu- man consciousness: "All instincts that do not discharge themselves outwardly *turn inward*—this is what I call the *internalization* of man: thus it was that man first developed what was later called his 'soul.' The entire inner world, originally as thin as if it were stretched between two membranes, expanded and extended itself, acquired depth, breadth, and height, in the same mea- sure as outward discharge was *inhibited.*"[101] Again, because Nietzsche dis- cusses this process from the point of view of the frustrated and inhibited masters, he makes it sound negative, but he recognizes that this development marked a fundamental advance in the history of humanity: "Let us add at once that . . . the existence on earth of an animal soul turned against itself, taking sides against itself, was something so new, profound, unheard of, enig- matic, contradictory, *and pregnant with a future* that the aspect of this earth was essentially altered."[102] Despite all Nietzsche's efforts to take the side of the masters against the slaves in *Genealogy of Morals*, he is forced to admit Hegel's fundamental point, that the taming of the masters and the slave revolt that engineers it mark the emergence of human consciousness as we know it and all of civilization, including the arts and philosophy (as Nietzsche shows in the third essay).

In sum, the priests, who appear at first to be the villains of *Genealogy of Morals*, on more careful examination turn out to be what Daniel Conway calls "the secret heroes" of Nietzsche's historical narrative.[103] We should never forget that he says that only the priests developed man into an "interesting animal." In an offhand comment in a letter to his friend Franz Overbeck, Nietzsche gives a rare glimpse of the side of him that questioned the Greek masters and admired the slavish Jews: "Incidentally, these Greeks have a great deal on their conscience—falsification was their real trade; the whole of Eu- ropean psychology is sick with Greek *superficialities*, and without the modi- cum of Judaism, and so on, and so on."[104] In the letter, Nietzsche does not spell out fully what he has in mind, but clearly he is referring to what he usually calls the slave revolt in morality and the development of psychological depth as an alternative to ancient Greek and Roman superficiality. In one of his late notebooks, Nietzsche writes, "If Christianity did anything essential in a psychological respect, it was to *raise the temperature of the soul* in the colder and nobler races, who had the upper hand; it was to discover that the most wretched life can become rich and inestimable when its temperature is raised."[105] What seems at first to be a falling-off from the grandeur of the masters is revealed, in mythical terms, to be a Fortunate Fall, the origin of all sophisticated cultural developments. Nietzsche's *Genealogy of Morals* develops a theme common in nineteenth-century thought, epitomized by Hegel's philosophy of history—the positivity of the negative.[106]

What looks at first like a negative development—the triumph of the slaves over the masters and hence a loss of nobility—is ultimately revealed to be a positive development, the enrichment of human consciousness and a necessary stage in creating all higher cultural forms. There can be no question that emotionally Nietzsche takes the side of the masters in *Genealogy of Morals*, but he ends up giving an intellectual defense of the slaves. Nietzsche is constantly juxtaposing the strong and the weak in *Genealogy of Morals*, and he seems to take the side of the former against the latter. And yet in his analysis of the slave revolt, he demonstrates that weakness can turn itself into a new kind of strength, a spiritualized or higher strength.[107] In the course of Nietzsche's attempt to offer the will to power as an explanation for all human phenomena, he must show that the attack on the politically powerful masters is not a negation and renunciation of power-seeking, but a new form of it—a higher, more spiritualized form.

"Master morality" and "slave morality" are no doubt emotionally loaded terms and seem to reflect Nietzsche's preference for the former.[108] Nietzsche thought that slave morality had triumphed in the increasingly democratic Europe of his day and master morality had been all but forgotten. He believed that the time was ripe for an advance beyond slave morality via a new revaluation of all values.[109] He was convinced that only by reminding people of the positive aspects of master morality could he help to break them out of their complacency and spark a new ethical revaluation. But that does not mean that Nietzsche was in favor of a simple return to master morality and the rule of the blond beasts. Just as we saw in *The Antichrist*, in *Genealogy of Morals* Nietzsche's rhetoric obscures the subtlety of his analysis. He felt a need to rail against slave morality, but he nevertheless credited it with creating new depths in human consciousness.[110] The fact that Nietzsche associates the development of Socratic philosophy with the slave revolt in morality shows that he understood that there would be no place for his own activity in the era of the blond beasts. Nietzsche thought of himself as a philosopher of the future; he never advocated turning back to the distant past.[111]

Nietzsche's Praise of Christianity

Nietzsche's grudging acknowledgement of the slave revolt in morality as a necessary stage in human development means that even his evaluation of Christianity is more complicated than at first it appears.[112] Aside from an odd moment when Nietzsche inexplicably refers to Christ as "the noblest human being,"[113] there are several surprisingly positive statements about Christianity in Nietzsche's writings. He occasionally admits that Christians made genuine contributions to history. Consider this remarkably generous account in *Assorted Opinions and Maxims* of the beneficial role that Christianity played in late antiquity:

> This fact can never be sufficiently pondered: Christianity is the religion of antiquity grown old, its presupposition is degenerated ancient cultures; on them it could and can act as a balm. In ages in which ears and eyes are 'filled with mud,' so that they are no longer capable of hearing the voice of reason and philosophy, or of seeing wisdom in bodily form, whether it bear the name of Epictetus or of Epicurus: in such eyes the cross of martyrdom and the 'trumpet of the last judgment' may perhaps still move the peoples to live a *decent* life. If one thinks of the Rome of Juvenal, that poison-toad with the eyes of Venus, one learns what it means to confront the 'world' with a Cross, one comes to respect the quiet Christian community and is grateful that it overran the Graeco-Roman world. When most people were born as though with the souls of slaves and sensuality of old men, what a blessing it must have been to encounter beings who were more soul than body: . . . modest, elusive, benevolent figures living in expectation of a 'better life' and thereby become so undemanding, so silently contemptuous, so proudly patient!—This Christianity as the evening-bell of *good* antiquity, a bell broken and weary yet still sweet-sounding, is a balm to the ears even for him who now wanders through these centuries only as a historian: what must it have been for the men of these centuries themselves![114]

It is difficult to believe that the author of *The Antichrist* wrote this passage. It is a tribute to Nietzsche's open-mindedness as a thinker that he was willing to entertain such antithetical positions. This is not the case of a confused and incoherent thinker who simply does not know that he is contradicting himself or forgets at one moment what he wrote at another. Rather, by exploring different sides of the issue at different times, Nietzsche is trying to be true to the genuine complexities of the underlying phenomena. Although always seeking to systematize his thought, Nietzsche refused to force disparate phenomena prematurely into a single system. It is not easy to determine whether something as complicated as Christianity was a positive or negative force in human history, and it is not illogical to consider the possibility that at different times and in different ways it was both.

Notice that in *Assorted Opinions and Maxims* Nietzsche offers Christianity not as the cause of Roman degeneration but as its cure. In a world that had lost its moral bearings, Christianity provided a new compass and actually served as a moderating and mitigating force in a time of turmoil. Nietzsche can even bring himself—momentarily—to say that he "is grateful that [Christianity] overran the Graeco-Roman world." In his typical complicating fashion, however, Nietzsche goes on to say, "On the other hand, for youthful, vigorous barbarians Christianity is *poison*."[115] In a single aphorism, Christianity goes from balm to poison, once Nietzsche discusses how it enfeebled the northern barbarians of Europe. It unbalanced them in its efforts to "implant the teaching of sinfulness and damnation into the heroic, childish and animal soul of the ancient German."[116] But reversing course yet again, Nietzsche points out that only the weakening of the barbarians prevented the destruction of all the remnants of classical civilization at the hands of marauding hordes: "One must, to be sure, ask what, without this enfeeblement, there would have been left to us of Greek culture! of the entire cultural past of the human race!—for the barbarians races *untouched* by Christianity were capable of doing away with ancient culture altogether; as, for example, was demonstrated with fearful clarity by the pagan conquerors of Romanized Britain."[117]

I dwell on this one aphorism at length because it exemplifies Nietzsche's ability to go back and forth on the issue of whether Christianity was a positive or a negative force in the ancient world and illustrates more generally the complexity of his attitude toward history. On the one hand, Nietzsche often pursued Hegelian arguments in which whatever happened in history is justified because it led to the present. If Christianity served to preserve and transmit the heritage of classical antiquity to modern Europe, then Nietzsche, who was after all a classics professor, can speak in praise of Christianity. On the other hand, in opposition to Hegel, Nietzsche is unwilling to accept the actual course of history as inevitable.[118] He insists on imagining an alternative narrative: "Here too there still remains another counter-question and the possibility of a counter-reckoning: if it had not been enfeebled by the poison referred to, would one or the other of these vigorous peoples, the German possibly, have perhaps been capable of gradually finding a higher culture for themselves, one of their own, a new one?—of which, as things

are, mankind has not now the remotest conception?"[119] Here Nietzsche parts
company with Hegel as a philosopher of history, reminding us that events
could have turned out differently, perhaps with better results, although we
cannot imagine them. Nietzsche kept changing his evaluation of Christianity;
he resisted the idea that the mere fact that Christianity had produced some
positive results is enough to justify its existence, when he could easily think
of many negative results that Christianity had produced.

Despite these reservations, sometimes Nietzsche expressed an outright
preference for Christianity over classical antiquity, or at least he acknowledged the validity of the Christian critique of the pagan world. Normally,
Nietzsche dwells on the meanspiritedness of the Christians who question the
masters' virtues in the ancient world, but in a section entitled "Moral skepticism in Christianity" in *The Gay Science*, Nietzsche treats this antipaganism
as genuinely insightful and even enlightened:

> Christianity, too, has made a great contribution to the enlightenment, and
> taught moral skepticism very trenchantly and effectively, accusing and embit-
> tering men, yet with untiring patience and subtlety; it destroyed the faith in
> his "virtues" in every single individual; it led to the disappearance from the
> face of the earth of all those paragons of virtue of whom there was no dearth
> in antiquity—the popular personalities who, imbued with faith in their own
> perfection, went about with the dignity of a great matador.[120]

As strange as it may at first sound, this passage is entirely consistent with
the way that Nietzsche contrasts the masters with the slaves in *Genealogy of
Morals*. For once, we get a glimpse of Nietzsche's contempt for the masters.
Since the slaves create all psychological depth, the masters must be psychologically superficial. For all Nietzsche's admiration for aristocracy, he sometimes presents it as an act, a show, and even a sham. In their self-assurance
and ingrained sense of superiority, the masters strut around on the stage of
history. Nietzsche's image of the matador is perfect. He must have liked this
image; in a history he titled "My impossible ones" in *Twilight of the Idols*, he
calls Seneca "the toreador of virtue."[121]

We must never forget that for Nietzsche, Christianity invented depth
psychology; it taught humanity to see beneath the surface of mental phenomena.[122] This is the chief respect in which Nietzsche is willing to speak of
modern Europeans as superior to the ancient Greeks and Romans, and in
this sense he acknowledges that Christianity is his teacher: "When we today,
trained in this Christian school of skepticism, read the moral treatises of the
ancients—for example, Seneca and Epictetus—we have a diverting sense of
superiority and feel full of secret insights and over-sights: we feel as embar-

rassed as if a child were talking before an old man, or an over-enthusiastic young beauty before La Rochefoucauld; we know better what virtue is."[123] Here Nietzsche, somewhat surprisingly, finds the ancient world to be childish.[124] This passage shows that, although Nietzsche generally set himself up as a champion of the ancients, he nonetheless thought of himself as a modern and regarded the moderns as superior in psychological insight. Nietzsche hoped to advance beyond slave morality—beyond good and evil—but he did not think that a simple return to master morality would produce this result. Rather, Nietzsche hoped to advance beyond slave morality on the basis of slave morality, to build upon its insights into depth psychology to overcome it. "In the end, however, we have applied this same skepticism also to all *religious* states and processes, such as sin, repentance, grace, sanctification, and we have allowed the worm to dig so deep that now we have the same sense of subtle superiority and insight when we read any Christian book: we also know religious feelings better!"[125]

Being a modern rather than an ancient, Nietzsche searched for ways in which he could regard his age as superior to the past. *Daybreak* contains a section entitled "*We are nobler,*" in which Nietzsche presents modern nobility as preferable to ancient. He expresses admiration for the Christian civilization of the Middle Ages, the world of feudalism and chivalry from which modern Europe inherits its sense of honor: "Loyalty, magnanimity, care for one's reputation: these three united in a single disposition—we call *noble*, and in this quality we excel the Greeks. . . . from the viewpoint of our own aristocracy, which is still chivalrous and feudal in nature, the disposition of even the noblest of Greeks has to seem of a lower sort, and, indeed, hardly decent."[126] By discussing fictional figures such as Odysseus and historical figures such as Themistocles, Nietzsche explains how treacherous ancient Greek nobles could be, contrasting them unfavorably with the more chivalrous heroes of modern Europe. "We excel the Greeks"—Nietzsche has no hesitation making that claim here, which can only mean that Christianity has exerted a genuinely civilizing influence on humanity. To put it bluntly, in the modern world we look back at Homer's heroes and decide that "they don't fight fairly"—especially when we compare them to the chivalric knights in medieval romances.

For someone who is often regarded as simply anti-Christian, Nietzsche can muster a surprising degree of enthusiasm for the Middle Ages, the peak of Christian civilization in Europe, when Christianity developed the interior world of the passions: "The Middle Ages are the era of the greatest passions. Neither antiquity nor our own age possesses this breadth of soul: its *spaciousness* has never been greater and never have men measured on a larger scale."[127] By opening up the depth of the human soul and fueling its passions, Christianity in Nietzsche's view created new subject matter for art and energized the imagination of European artists. Nietzsche normally welcomed the decline of Christian faith in his day, but at times he worried that this development might destroy the religious foundations on which European art had flourished for centuries:

> It is not without profound sorrow that one admits to oneself that in their highest flights the artists of all ages have raised to heavenly transfiguration precisely those concepts which we now recognize as false: they are the glorifiers of the religious and philosophical errors of mankind, and they could not have been so without believing in the absolute truth of these errors. If belief in such truth declines in general, if the rainbow-colours at the extreme limits of human knowledge and supposition grow pale, that species of art can never flourish again, which, like the *Divina Commedia*, the pictures of Raphael, the frescoes of Michelangelo, the Gothic cathedrals, presupposes not only a cosmic but also a metaphysical significance in the objects of art. A moving tale will one day be told how there once existed such an art, such an artistic faith.[128]

However much Nietzsche despised Christianity, he admired the Christian art of the Middle Ages and the Renaissance and viewed it as equal, if not superior, to the art of classical antiquity. In his grand calculus of human development, Nietzsche had to recognize the contribution that Christianity made to European art. He was struck by the way that the combination of Christianity, philosophy, and the arts had deepened the European soul: "We have Christianity, the philosophers, poets, and musicians to thank for the abundance of profound sensations."[129] Watching Nietzsche single out the masterpieces of specifically Christian art—"the *Divina Commedia*, the pictures of Raphael, the frescoes of Michelangelo, the Gothic cathedrals"—we might claim that, for him, Christianity was ultimately justified as an aesthetic phenomenon.[130]

Guilt and Bad Conscience

Without making the absurd claim that Nietzsche was a closet Christian, one can acknowledge that his attitude toward Christianity is not simply hostile, as many have supposed.[131] What we have seen in Shakespeare's Roman plays can help us understand this point. One can no more say that Shakespeare simply preferred the world of *Coriolanus* to the world of *Antony and Cleopatra* than one can say that Nietzsche preferred master morality to slave morality. Indeed the cases are parallel because, as we have seen, *Coriolanus* portrays the world of master morality and *Antony and Cleopatra* portrays the world of slave morality. And Shakespeare presents the same trade-off that Nietzsche analyzes in *Genealogy of Morals*. The characters in *Coriolanus* display the nobility of the old-style masters, but at the expense of psychological depth and intellectual acuity. The characters in *Antony and Cleopatra* can see through the hollowness of the old ideal of martial grandeur and they explore the depths of the human soul in unprecedented ways, but only at the price of abandoning traditional nobility. One cannot simply state that one way of life is superior to the other. The plays are tragic precisely because Shakespeare is able to see the good on either side of the great divide that separates the worlds of *Coriolanus* and *Antony and Cleopatra*.

Shakespeare works out in dramatic terms much of what Nietzsche discusses in *Genealogy of Morals*. The Roman patricians build their sense of self-worth on their contempt for the plebeians. A community directed to victory in war values courage, strength, and aggressiveness. All the customs of Republican Rome—the marital relations, the raising of children, the camaraderie of soldiers—work to subordinate private concerns to public and thus to solidify the people behind the Roman war machine. Consequently, the community is remarkably well organized for war, but it has very limited horizons. Its citizens have a hard time seeing beyond the concerns of the city. Even when Coriolanus leaves Rome and betrays his native land, it turns out that in the end he cannot do anything but think as a Roman. Entire dimensions of life that Shakespeare explores in depth in his other plays are virtually absent from *Coriolanus*. We see almost nothing of erotic love between man and woman in the play and get little or no sense of any religious side of life that might look beyond civic piety and even come into conflict with the city. There is no soul-searching in the Rome of *Coriolanus* because there are no fully developed souls to be searched. We miss the complex soliloquies that for many are the highlights of plays such as *Hamlet*, *Othello*, and *Macbeth*. The Romans in *Coriolanus* are not tormented by doubts or troubled by a bad conscience. As characters, they lack psychological depth.[132] They make up for this lack—at least some of them—by their grandeur, but it is the grandeur of statues. We can look at them and marvel at their courage and fortitude, but we cannot pierce beneath the surface. To see concretely what Nietzsche finds both noble and limited in the masters in *Genealogy of Morals*, one should read *Coriolanus*.

For just the reasons Nietzsche outlines in *Genealogy of Morals* and other writings, the world of Rome is completely transformed in *Antony and Cleopatra*. *Julius Caesar* portrays the transition. Now that Caesar has grabbed the reins of power in Rome for himself, the other patricians find themselves cut off from their traditional ways of fulfilling their ambitions. No longer free to act in the public arena, they feel their frustrations building up, as can be seen most clearly in Cassius. Denied external outlets for their impulses, the patricians turn inward and the interiority of their souls begins to develop. Shakespeare illustrates what Nietzsche calls "the internalization of man" in *Genealogy of Morals*. In *Coriolanus*, the Roman masters can express their aggressive impulses freely, particularly in wartime. In general, they know what they want to do and just do it, and they speak their opinions openly. As Menenius says of Coriolanus, "His heart's his mouth; / What his breast forges, that his tongue must vent" (3.1.256–57). In *Coriolanus* the patricians do not lose any sleep over their decisions. But *Julius Caesar* shows the patricians losing sleep at every turn. The Rome of *Coriolanus* is a daylight world in which people's motives are clear and out in the open for all to see. But a number of scenes in *Julius Caesar* take place at night, and motives and intentions become obscured and hidden. The conspirators slink suspiciously around the city, and Brutus's wife, Portia, complains that he has been concealing his political affairs from her, dealing with men "who did hide their faces / Even from darkness" (2.1.276–77).

At several points in *Julius Caesar*, characters are too worried to sleep or they are suddenly awakened from sleep, sometimes by disturbing dreams. The Roman patricians, so certain of themselves in *Coriolanus*, are no longer sure what course of action to pursue in *Julius Caesar*. Like Brutus, even Caesar seems no longer to know what his next move should be. In a soliloquy, Brutus debates with himself the merits and demerits of assassinating Caesar (2.1.10–38). He internalizes the kind of rhetorical combat that takes place between the warring parties in *Coriolanus*. While paralyzed from acting by this internal debate, Brutus feels a whole new world opening up inside him:

> Since Cassius first did whet me against Caesar,
> I have not slept.
> Between the acting of a dreadful thing
> And the first motion, all the interim is
> Like a phantasm or a hideous dream.
> The Genius and the mortal instruments
> Are then in council; and the state of man,
> Like to a little kingdom, suffers then
> The nature of an insurrection. (2.1.61–69)

Unable to sleep, Brutus internalizes the Roman civil wars; earlier, he speaks of "Brutus, with himself at war" (1.2.46). The Romans used to direct their aggressive impulses outward against their enemies; in the civil wars, they direct these impulses against each other; now Brutus's aggressive impulses are directed inward against himself.[133] He becomes self-divided, and that division opens up an internal world of fantasies and dreams.[134] As Nietzsche writes, "All instincts that do not discharge themselves outwardly *turn inward* . . . . Thus it was that man first developed what was later called his 'soul.' The entire inner world . . . expanded and extended itself . . . in the same measure as outward discharge was inhibited."[135]

The process of internalization begun in *Julius Caesar* accelerates, broadens, and deepens in *Antony and Cleopatra*. With the challenging and energizing presence of external enemies removed, the traditional outlets for ambition closed off in the imperial regime, and the cohesion of the Roman community attenuated by its gigantic size, the Romans in *Antony and Cleopatra* lose interest in political life, turn inward, and develop their psychological richness. In Nietzsche's terms, one could say that in *Antony and Cleopatra* man first becomes an interesting animal—and woman too. With characters like Antony, Cleopatra, and Enobarbus, we see into the soul's depths in ways that are impossible in the Rome of *Coriolanus*. These characters are troubled by doubts (including self-doubts), tormented by regret and remorse, and wracked by guilt. Genuine soliloquies appear in the play, as well as long lyrical passages. In contrast to what occurs in *Coriolanus*, in *Antony and Cleopatra* we feel that we are watching characters grope hesitatingly toward decisions. These characters have genuine psychological depth—that is one reason why viewers and critics have generally preferred *Antony and Cleopatra* to *Coriolanus*. It is more like Shakespeare's other tragedies and allows for more complex character analysis because figures such as Antony, Cleopatra, and Enobarbus are more internally conflicted than the characters in *Coriolanus*.

The fate of Enobarbus epitomizes these new trends; he reveals what it means in Nietzsche's terms in *Genealogy of Morals* to develop a bad conscience. The Romans of *Coriolanus* are like Nietzsche's original masters: they are guided by instinct; they generally act before they think. By contrast, Enobarbus has lost the old Roman confidence, he hesitates before acting, and he begins to experience a gap between his impulses and his reason: "I'll yet follow / The wounded chance of Antony, though my reason / Sit in the wind against me" (3.10.34–36). Enobarbus observes a similar conflict between will and reason in Antony, when he blames his general for the loss at Actium: "Antony only, that would make his will / Lord of his reason" (3.13.3–4). Faced with the widening gap between willfulness and rationality in his commander, Enobarbus concludes that he must follow the dictates of reason and desert Antony:

A diminution in our captain's brain
Restores his heart. When valor preys on reason,
It eats the sword it fights with. I will seek
Some way to leave him. (3.13.197–200)

Unlike a traditional Roman soldier, Enobarbus reasons his way out of his loyalty to his commander. In the Republic, soldiers are simply not supposed to think about such matters, but the Empire forces men like Enobarbus to do so. With the city no longer serving as his guidepost, Enobarbus is thrown back on his own inner resources.

Enobarbus finds, however, that he cannot betray Antony with a good conscience, no matter how rational his decision may have seemed. When Antony pays back Enobarbus's treachery by sending him the treasure he left behind, the deserter is overwhelmed by guilt feelings:

I am alone the villain of the earth,
And feel I am so most. O Antony,
Thou mine of bounty, how wouldst thou have paid
My better service, whose turpitude
Thou dost so crown with gold! (4.6.29–33)

Once personal loyalties take on a new importance in the imperial system, betraying them becomes a sin, the epitome of evil. Ripped apart by the kind of inner insurrection Brutus experienced—Enobarbus speaks of his "life" as "a very rebel to my will" (4.9.14)—he simply expires in a swoon, condemning himself as a "master-leaver and a fugitive" (4.9.22). The case of Enobarbus shows how bewildering political life has become in the imperial world. Torn between his heart and his head, he no longer even wants to live.[136]

The Higher Synthesis of Moralities

With the demotion of political life in imperial Rome, erotic life acquires a new power, and new dimensions of religious life also open up in the world of the play. The new religion is not specifically Christian, but, as we saw in chapter 1, Shakespeare presents it as a religion of love and gives it some of the most important characteristics of Christianity, in particular a focus on the afterlife and the immortality of the soul.[137] In their proto-Christian efforts to redefine moral terms—especially their attempt to reconceive defeat as victory and weakness as strength—the characters create a new moral vocabulary. But judged by the old standards of nobility—which still resonate in the play—several of the characters in *Antony and Cleopatra* behave contemptibly and earn the scorn of their fellow Romans. For all the gains in psychological depth in the world of *Antony and Cleopatra*, a heartbreaking sense of loss pervades the play, as the sun sets on everything that used to make Rome great. The mood of *Antony and Cleopatra* is a peculiar combination of exhilaration and despair, of triumphalism and nihilism. All this parallels Nietzsche's picture of late antiquity and the rise of Christianity. And, like Nietzsche, Shakespeare seems to be fascinated by the strange interweaving and interaction of master morality and slave morality as the old Rome dies and a new Rome struggles to be born.

To understand this point, we must introduce a further complication in Nietzsche's understanding of master morality and slave morality. It is not just that he did not simply prefer the former to the latter. More profoundly, Nietzsche did not think that master morality and slave morality can always be sharply distinguished from each other.[138] In *Beyond Good and Evil*, he writes, "There are *master morality* and *slave morality*—I add immediately that in all the higher and more mixed cultures there also appear attempts at mediating between these two moralities, and yet more often the interpenetration and mutual misunderstanding of both, and at times they occur directly alongside each other—even in the same human being, within a *single* soul."[139] This passage is crucial to a full understanding of Nietzsche's thought.[140] It suggests that master morality and slave morality are not just historical categories for Nietzsche; they do not merely designate two stages of historical development from classical to Christian ethics, and thus a unique sequence of events in history. Rather, Nietzsche offers master morality and slave morality as perennial human possibilities, or at least options that recur in human history.[141] Moreover, Nietzsche reveals that concepts that he originally seems to set up as polar opposites can actually become mixed and mediated in complex, hybrid forms, and perhaps even be synthesized into something entirely new. In one of the earliest books on Nietzsche, his friend and confidante Lou Salomé stressed the personal importance of the master morality/slave morality conflict for Nietzsche: "Whenever he speaks of master and slave natures, one must remember that he speaks about himself, driven by the longing of an inharmonious nature to seek its opposite."[142] In a profound insight into Nietzsche, Salomé argues that he experienced the battle between master morality and slave morality within his own breast, that he was drawn in both directions simultaneously. He experienced the pride and sense of superiority characteristic of the ancient masters, and yet at the same time he could feel the pity characteristic of the modern Christians, as well as their skepticism about heroic virtue.[143] This internal conflict pained Nietzsche, but it also offered him the possibility of achieving an ethical position superior to either master morality or slave morality in isolation.

Salomé works to transform master morality and slave morality from purely historical concepts to broader psychological categories:[144]

> But while Nietzsche allows that one is the precondition for the other, as human nature becomes the arena for these contraries which attempt to subdue each other, he also perceives them as *stages of development within the same creature*; historically considered, they remain contrasts, but psychologically considered they constitute a split within each individual who is capable of development. For that reason, the total significance of Nietzsche's interpretation of the historical battle between master and slave mentalities is nothing less than a radically simplified illustration of what transpires in the superior individual.[145]

Salomé suggests that to understand fully the concepts of master morality and slave morality, we must think about the ways in which the conflict between the two principles might play out within a single soul, with Nietzsche himself being the prime example of the psychological complexity such a battle might produce. Above all, Salomé makes the intriguing suggestion that an individual who managed to combine master morality and slave morality within a single soul would achieve a higher level.[146]

As we saw, despite his professed hatred of Christianity, Nietzsche views slave morality as in some ways an advance beyond master morality.[147] He hoped to move beyond the stage of slave morality by engineering a new revaluation of values. In Hegelian fashion, he looked forward to some kind of grand synthesis, a melding of slave morality and master morality in a higher form of humanity that Nietzsche called the Overman.[148] He speaks of this in *Genealogy of Morals*:

> The two *opposing* values "good and bad," "good and evil" have been engaged in a fearful struggle on earth for thousands of years; and although the latter value has certainly been on top for a long time, there are still places where the struggle is as yet undecided. One might even say that it has risen even higher and thus become more and more profound and spiritual: so that today there is perhaps no more decisive mark of a "*higher nature*," a more spiritual nature, than that of being divided in this sense and a genuine battleground of these opposed values.[149]

Nietzsche saw something positive and something negative in both master morality and slave morality. His ideal is to cancel out the negatives by fusing the positives in one grand Hegelian synthesis—to combine the hardness and grandeur of the master with the cleverness and psychological depth of the slave.[150] In a famous passage in his notebooks, Nietzsche gives an enigmatic and tantalizing formulation of this ideal: "the Roman Caesar with Christ's soul."[151] A fuller sense of what Nietzsche means by this formula emerges elsewhere in his writings. For example, his admiration for the Middle Ages was rooted in the way that the Christians' encounter with barbarians produced a strange mixture of master morality and slave morality: "The jungle physique of the barbarian and the over-soulful, over-wakeful, hectically glittering eyes of the disciple of the Christian mysteries, extreme childishness and youthfulness and likewise extreme over-ripeness and weariness of age, the savagery of the beast of prey and the effeminacy and tenuousness of the spirit of late antiquity—at that time all these not infrequently came together in a single person."[152] Nietzsche does not pursue this matter in literature, but some of the greatest medieval poems, such as *Beowulf* and the *Nibelungenlied*, embody just the kind of mixture of pagan and Christian elements he speaks of in this passage.

Nietzsche looks elsewhere in history for the kind of synthesis of master morality and slave morality he envisioned. He grants that normally the clash of opposing civilizations has a disorienting and debilitating effect: "In an age of disintegration that mixes race indiscriminately, human beings have in their bodies the heritage of multiple origins, that is, opposite, and often not merely opposite, drives and value standards that fight each other and rarely permit each other any rest. Such human beings of late cultures and refracted lights will on the average be weaker human beings: their most profound desire is that the war they *are* should come to an end."[153] But Nietzsche believed that at times the opposing moralities do not battle each other to a standstill, but instead produce a synthesis on a higher level and thus for Nietzsche the highest type of human being:

> But when the opposition and war in such a nature have the effect of one more charm and incentive of life—and if, moreover, in addition to his powerful and irreconcilable drives, a real mastery and subtlety in waging war against oneself, in other words, self-control, self-outwitting, has been inherited or cultivated, too—then those magical, incomprehensible, and unfathomable ones arise, those enigmatic men predestined for victory and seduction, whose most beautiful expression is found in Alcibiades and Caesar.[154]

This passage helps explain Nietzsche's lifelong fascination with Julius Caesar.[155] Perhaps he was most impressed by the fact that Caesar managed to achieve the highest form of aristocratic mastery in an age when slave morality had begun to permeate Rome.[156] Shakespeare points in this direction by showing that Caesar defeated all his patrician rivals precisely by appealing to the plebeians and winning them to his side in his struggle for power in Rome. This achievement was partly intellectual because it required Caesar to rise above his ingrained class prejudices as a patrician. It takes a renegade master to reach out to the slave party and embrace its virtues. Both Alcibiades and Caesar lived in ages when an old aristocracy was degenerating, largely as a result of internecine strife and the corrupting effects of empire. They were products of that degeneration but they took advantage of it to produce a new form of mastery on an imperial scale. In that sense they both ventured beyond the simple mastery of the Homeric age—when the ideology of the master went unchallenged. It was easy to be a master before the slave revolt in morality—when social distinctions were accepted as natural.[157] Nietzsche always conceives of virtue as struggle, and in his view slave morality became the great obstacle for a new generation of masters to overcome. Perhaps Nietzsche's idea is this: the greatest master is the one who—faced with the challenge of slave morality—finds a way to reestablish mastery on a quasi-democratic basis.[158]

Nietzsche's understanding of modern European history lends credence to this view, especially his admiration for Napoleon. He reads European history as a continuing attempt to revive classical values and master morality in the face of the triumph of Christianity and slave morality: "There was to be sure, in the Renaissance an uncanny and glittering reawakening of the classical ideal, of the noble mode of evaluating all things."[159] In Nietzsche's view, this Renaissance achievement was defeated by the plebeian countermovement of the Reformation.[160] He viewed Napoleon as the last nineteenth-century attempt to restore aristocratic greatness in a democratic age:

> With the French Revolution, Judea [slave morality] once again triumphed over the classical ideal, and this time in an even more profound and decisive sense: the last political noblesse in Europe, that of the *French* seventeenth and eighteenth century, collapsed beneath the popular instincts of *ressentiment* . . . . To be sure, in the midst of it there occurred the most tremendous, the most unexpected thing: the ideal of antiquity itself stepped *incarnate* and in unheard-of splendor before the eyes and conscience of mankind—and once again, in opposition to the mendacious slogan of *ressentiment*, "supreme rights of the majority," in opposition to the will to the lowering, the abasement, the leveling and the decline and twilight of mankind, there sounded stronger, simpler, and more insistently than ever the terrible and rapturous counterslogan "supreme rights of the few"! Like a last signpost to the *other* path, Napoleon appeared, the most isolated and late-born man there has ever been, and in him the problem of the *noble ideal as such* made flesh—one might well ponder *what* kind of problem it is: Napoleon, this synthesis of the *inhuman* and *superhuman*.[161]

A Hegelian idea of synthesis seems to shadow Nietzsche's formulation of his ethical ideal, although what exactly he means by "this synthesis of the *inhuman* and *superhuman*" remains unclear. A passage from *The Gay Science* clarifies what Napoleon represents for Nietzsche: the revival of the ancient spirit of the masters against the modern bourgeois world. Nietzsche praises Napoleon for unleashing a new "classical age of war" in Europe:

> He should receive credit some day for the fact that in Europe the *man* [*der Mann*] has again become master [*Herr*] over the businessman [*Kaufmann*] and the philistine. . . . Napoleon, who considered modern ideas and civilization almost as a personal enemy, proved himself one of the greatest continuators of the Renaissance; he brought back a wide slab of antiquity, perhaps even the decisive piece, the piece of granite.[162]

Napoleon seems to be Nietzsche's prime example of recovering ancient aristocratic greatness on the basis of a modern democratic movement (the French Revolution), thereby offering the prospect of some kind of fusion of master morality and slave morality.[163]

Once again, we see that Nietzsche was not a reactionary. He did not advocate a return to some primeval era of Homeric masters. Recognizing that slave morality had introduced a new—and in some respects welcome—spirituality into the world, Nietzsche searched for a new form of aristocracy that could incorporate what was worthwhile in slave morality and still move beyond it, creating a new basis of mastery compatible with the democratic impulses of the modern world. Although necessarily vague about what form this new aristocracy might take, Nietzsche could be eloquent and inspiring on the subject, as he looks forward to the fusion of a new nobility with the old. In *The Gay Science*, he imagines:

> a person whose horizon encompasses thousands of years past and future, being the heir of all the nobility of all past spirit—an heir with a sense of obligation, the most aristocratic of old nobles and at the same time the first of a new nobility—the like of which no age has yet seen or dreamed of; if one could burden one's soul with all of this—the oldest, the newest, losses, hopes, conquests, and the victories of humanity: if one could finally contain all this in one soul and crowd it into a single feeling—this would surely have to result in a happiness that humanity has not known so far: the happiness of a god full of power and love, full of tears and laughter.[164]

"A god full of power and love" seems to be another way of saying "a Roman Caesar with Christ's soul," a higher being (perhaps an Overman) who would combine the toughness of the Homeric hero with the soulfulness of the Christian, a weird combination of Homeric laughter with Christ's tears. If this formulation still leaves Nietzsche's ideal enigmatic, at least we have a few historical examples that caught his eye: Alcibiades, Julius Caesar, and Napoleon. These figures give us a concrete sense of what Nietzsche had in mind when he hoped to find a way to transcend the opposition between master morality and slave morality, no matter how sharply he originally drew the distinction.

Shakespeare's Hybrid Heroes

Nietzsche's quasi-apocalyptic hope for a grand synthesis of antithetical moralities seems far removed from Shakespeare's more sober view of the world. Shakespeare's tragedies seem grounded in his conviction that opposing cultures and clashing civilizations *cannot* be reconciled in some higher synthesis but must remain tragically at odds. In his hopes for an Overman and a higher stage of civilization, Nietzsche betrays his roots in Romanticism and German idealism (despite his many quarrels with both).[165] One can even detect something Wagnerian in Nietzsche's dream of the hero of the future.[166] Whereas Nietzsche hopes to transcend the distinction between master morality and slave morality, Shakespeare dwells on the conflict between them. Nevertheless, Shakespeare shared Nietzsche's interest in the intersection of master morality and slave morality. Nietzsche seems to have divined this possibility; when he talks about the highest human being, who achieves a synthesis of conflicting moralities, he offers Shakespeare as his example:

> In contrast to the animals, man has cultivated an abundance of *contrary* drives and impulses within himself: thanks to this synthesis, he is master of the earth. —Moralities are the expression of locally limited orders of rank in his multifarious world of drives, so man should not perish through their contradictions. . . . The highest man would have the greatest multiplicity of drives, in the relatively greatest strength that can be endured. Indeed, where the plant "man" shows himself strongest one finds instincts that conflict powerfully (e.g., in Shakespeare), but are controlled.[167]

Nietzsche looks for conflicting moral impulses playing out within Shakespeare's soul, but it may be more productive to examine that process within the characters the playwright created. In the case of the Roman plays, ethical hybridity inevitably results from Shakespeare's decision to portray the slave revolt in morality taking place among the Roman nobles, not the lower classes. In Nietzsche's terms, both *Julius Caesar* and *Antony and Cleopatra* offer strange mixtures of an old nobility and a new, and they can help us to understand Nietzsche's vision of a higher and more complex humanity. In these two plays, as in *Genealogy of Morals*, the renegade master is a central theme and the characters experience warring impulses within their souls.

Shakespeare's Julius Caesar is an extraordinary example of ethical hybridity. Sometimes he presents himself on the model of the Homeric hero, when, for example, he insists on going to the Senate despite the unfavorable omens: "Cowards die many times before their deaths, / The valiant never taste of death but once" (2.2.32–33). Just before he is assassinated, Caesar assumes the role of a pagan god, even the unmoved mover of Aristotle, deaf to all human supplications:

> I could be well mov'd, if I were as you;
> If I could pray to move, prayers would move me;
> But I am constant as the northern star,
> Of whose true-fix'd and resting quality
> There is no fellow in the firmament. (3.1.58–62)

Here in the presence of his fellow patricians, Caesar adopts the pose of the hard, unbending classical god-hero (the same image Coriolanus likes to project), but he behaves quite differently in front of the plebeians. With them he is willing to admit to having weaknesses and also to exploit that vulnerability to win their hearts.[168] Casca reports how deftly Caesar handled the incident of his epileptic fit on the occasion of Antony offering him a crown in public: "When he came to himself again, he said, if he had done or said anything amiss, he desir'd their worships to think it was his infirmity. Three or four wenches, where I stood, cried, 'Alas, good soul!' and forgave him with all their hearts" (1.2.269–73). Caesar shows the plebeians that he has "soul." He humbles himself before them, reversing the roles of master and slave by addressing the people as "their worships" and begging for their forgiveness, as if they had power over him. It is very strange to see a Roman patrician advertising his "infirmity" to the plebeians. But this is the renegade patrician in all his new-found plebeianized glory.

It might be too much to speak of a "Roman Caesar with Christ's soul" in this passage, but Shakespeare's Caesar is deliberately projecting a conventionally unheroic image in order to elevate himself in the eyes of the common people and thus to strengthen his control of Rome. His weakness becomes his strength. Cassius cannot understand this strategy. As a conventional patrician, Cassius believes that a true god would never display any form of weakness. Having seen Caesar almost drown and suffer from a fever in Spain— "'tis true, this god did shake" (1.2.121)—Cassius finds it incomprehensible that the Roman people worship this visibly weak creature:

> Ye gods, it doth amaze me
> A man of such a feeble temper should
> So get the start of the majestic world
> And bear the palm alone. (1.2.128–31)

But in contrast to Cassius, Antony, as the true disciple of Caesar, proves that he understands the new basis of Caesar's power when he comes to speak at the great man's funeral. His rhetorical strategy is to deny the central charge that the conspirators made against Caesar—that he was ambitious in the way that a classical hero normally is.[169] Accordingly, Antony stresses the fact that Caesar cared for the common people, and was characterized by his pity, not his toughness:

> He hath brought many captives home to Rome,
> Whose ransoms did the general coffers fill;
> Did this in Caesar seem ambitious?
> When that the poor have cried, Caesar hath wept;
> Ambition should be made of sterner stuff. (3.2.88–92)

When did a traditional Roman patrician ever take pride in weeping? Coriolanus, confronted with an embassy of Roman women, is ashamed to weep in public and says: "Let it be virtuous to be obstinate" (5.3.26). But Antony is willing to deny Caesar the "sterner stuff" that customarily characterized the classical hero in order to make him more attractive to the common people, indeed to make him seem like one of them.

Again, a renegade master goes over to the other side in Rome, as Antony sets himself up as the leader of a slave revolt against the traditional aristocracy in Rome and its values. Antony impresses the plebeians with his own ability to cry; the second plebeian says, "Poor soul, his eyes are red as fire with weeping" (3.2.115). When was a traditional Roman patrician ever pleased to be called a "poor soul" by a plebeian? And yet this moment is the key to Antony's success. It leads the third plebeian to say of him, "There's not a nobler man in Rome than Antony" (3.2.116)—a clear sign that the plebeians are redefining "nobility." Like his master, Caesar, Antony has found a way of turning weakness into strength. Antony plays upon the plebeians' sympathy and pity—"If you have tears, prepare to shed them now" (3.2.169) and convinces them that Caesar was a loving man (3.2.182), above all that he loved the plebeians (3.2.141). Antony manages to turn Caesar's funeral into a veritable orgy of tears and pity:

> O now you weep and I perceive you feel
> The dint of pity. These are gracious drops.

> Kind souls, what weep you when you but behold
> Our Caesar's vesture wounded? (3.2.193–96)

By the time Antony is through, he has remade Caesar's image—from the unmovable god of classical antiquity to something much closer to the Christian conception of deity. Antony has made it possible for the "piteous spectacle" of a wounded corpse to give the plebeians the impression of a "noble Caesar" (3.2.198–99)—in a proto-Christian inversion of values, the "piteous" has become the "noble."[170] Antony's Caesar is moved by the suffering of the people and becomes a sacrifice to their welfare (they will benefit from his death; remember the will). According to Antony, the Roman people should worship Caesar as a fallen god: "they would go and kiss dead Caesar's wounds, / And dip their napkins in his sacred blood; / Yea, beg a hair of him for memory" (3.2.132–34). Caesar will become the object of a cult of worship, complete with sacred relics.[171] The plebeians insist: "We'll burn his body in the holy place" (3.2.254). At the emotional climax of his speech, Antony shamelessly exploits the spectacle of Caesar's mangled corpse to fire up the plebeians' wrath when they see his mortal wounds.[172] Antony's funeral oration results in a peculiar hybridization of heroism, as the conqueror Caesar takes on more and more of the traits of the fallen deity of Christianity.[173]

In *Antony and Cleopatra*, a further hybridization of soul occurs in the Roman Empire. Aristocrats call into question the traditional social hierarchy, proclaiming a leveling of all ranks, and yet paradoxically they expect to maintain their preeminence in the world, precisely for challenging the idea of preeminence. This paradox informs Antony's speech early in the play:

> Let Rome in Tiber melt, and the wide arch
> Of the rang'd empire fall! Here is my space,
> Kingdoms are clay; our dungy earth alike
> Feeds beast as man; the nobleness of life
> Is to do thus [*embracing*]—when such a mutual pair
> And such a twain can do't, in which I bind,
> On pain of punishment, the world to weet
> We stand up peerless. (1.1.33–40)

Nietzsche would recognize the strange interweaving of master morality and slave morality in this speech. A traitor to his class, Antony denies the value of traditional politics in Rome and levels out customary distinctions of rank: "Our dungy earth alike / Feeds beast as man." He redefines nobility so that it becomes a matter of love, not politics.[174] And yet he insists that the whole world still look up to him and honor him for challenging the traditional Roman notion of honor. As Andrew Fichter formulates the paradox: "The love Antony speaks of is both an alternative to empire and an alternative empire."[175] Antony wants the best of both worlds; in effect, he thinks of himself as the master of slave morality. No wonder Cleopatra describes Antony's speech with an oxymoron: "Excellent falsehood!" (1.1.40).

And yet Cleopatra pursues the same paradoxical path to greatness later in the play:

> My desolation does begin to make
> A better life. 'Tis paltry to be Caesar;
> Not being Fortune, he's but Fortune's knave,
> A minister of her will: and it is great
> To do that thing that ends all other deeds,
> Which shackles accidents and bolts up change,
> Which sleeps, and never palates more the dung,
> The beggar's nurse and Caesar's. (5.2.1–8)

Cleopatra uses all the tricks of slave morality to maintain her aristocratic sense of her preeminence (remember that Nietzsche views slave morality as in its own way a manifestation of will to power). Defeat becomes victory and death becomes life for her ("My desolation does begin to make a better life"). Now that she knows for sure that she is defeated militarily, she insists that the imperial rule she had been fighting for is in fact worthless ("'Tis paltry to be Caesar"). She denies any difference between a master and a slave; the dung nurses the beggar and Caesar alike (note the echo of Antony at 1.1.35–36). And yet Cleopatra redefines greatness so that she can still assert her superiority. In a world governed by the arbitrariness of fortune, the only path to genuine greatness is suicide, which allows one to take one's fate into one's own hands and thus to master destiny. Cleopatra's embrace of suicide is another way of turning defeat into victory. Like Antony, Cleopatra is a fascinating example of what Nietzsche means when he talks about master morality and slave morality uneasily coming together in a single soul. In the deeply paradoxical mode of the play, both Antony and Cleopatra find a way to "make defect perfection" (2.2.231).

Tragedy in the Renaissance

Shakespeare's interest in the clash of classical and Christian values extends well beyond the Roman plays—indeed, it is one of the central issues in his works. The question comes up already in some of his earliest plays, the three parts of *Henry VI*. Throughout his history plays, Shakespeare deals with the ways that Christianity complicates politics, and in the *Henry VI* plays he raises the question of whether a king may be too Christian by temperament to rule effectively. Queen Margaret criticizes Henry for the way his Christian attitudes unfit him for the rough world of politics:

> But all his mind is bent to holiness,
> To number Ave-Maries on his beads;
> His champions are the prophets and apostles,
> His weapons holy saws of sacred writ,
> His study is his tilt-yard, and his loves
> Are brazen images of canonized saints.
> I would the college of Cardinals
> Would choose him Pope and carry him to Rome,
> And set the triple crown upon his head—
> That were a state fit for his holiness.[176] (*2 Henry VI*, 1.3.55–64)

When the usurper York challenges Henry's fitness to rule, he turns to the classical world—to the *Iliad*—to draw the contrast between himself and the king:

> That head of thine doth not become a crown:
> Thy hand is made to grasp a palmer's staff
> And not to grace an aweful princely sceptre.
> That gold must round engirt these brows of mine,
> Whose smile and frown, like to Achilles' spear,
> Is able with the change to kill and cure. (*2 Henry VI*, 5.1.96–101)

In the *Henry VI* plays, no one is able to combine classical and Christian values within a single soul, and the ruthless Homeric-style hero prevails over the saintly Christian king. In the fourth play of the first tetralogy, *Richard III*, the anti-Christian attitudes of the evil tyrant produce the most Nietzschean lines in all of Shakespeare:

> Conscience is but a word that cowards use,
> Devis'd at first to keep the strong in awe:
> Our strong arms be our conscience, swords our law!
> March on, join bravely, let us to it pell-mell;
> If not to heaven, then hand in hand to hell. (5.3.309–13)

Richard III attempts to undo the slave revolt in morality; he redefines Christian terms in the direction of master morality. Military strength becomes his new measure of conscience, as he embraces a demonic form of tyranny. But Richard's one-sided commitment to classical heroic values proves no more capable of producing good government than Henry VI's one-sided saintliness. In Shakespeare's plays about King Henry V, he explores the possibility of one man genuinely combining classical and Christian values. In fact, *Henry V* offers perhaps the most extraordinary example of a character, who, in true Nietzschean fashion, contains the two contradictory moralities in a single breast. The Irish captain Macmorris objects violently to the army's decision to retreat: "By Chrish law, 'tish ill done! The work ish give over, the trumpet sound the retreat. . . . I would have blowed up the town, so Chrish save me, law, in an hour!" (3.2.88–92). It takes remarkable hybridity of soul to be able to speak of blowing up a town and being saved by Christ in the same sentence.[177] Macmorris seems to be an example of the kind of medieval barbarian Nietzsche discusses, who combines a patina of Christianity with a core of pagan fierceness.

What Shakespeare treats comically in the figure of Macmorris he takes seriously in the case of Henry V. The challenge Henry faces as a king is precisely to combine the toughness and aggressiveness of a classical hero with the moral decency and sympathetic feelings of a Christian. This is not an easy balancing act, as Henry himself reveals when, in his rousing St. Crispin's Day speech, he admits, "But if it be a sin to covet honor, / I am the most offending soul alive" (4.3.28–29). In Christian terms, it *is* a sin to covet honor, and yet Henry realizes that he needs to call upon his soldiers' sense of honor to get them to fight bravely against overwhelming odds at Agincourt. Henry struggles to navigate between the conflicting demands of classical and Christian values. He hopes to compartmentalize his life, acting like a Christian saint in peacetime and like a classical hero in war:

> In peace there's nothing so becomes a man
> As modest stillness and humility;
> But when the blast of war blows in our ears,
> Then imitate the action of the tiger. (3.1.3–6)

Depending on the differing circumstances, Henry can issue contradictory commands to his troops. At one moment he tells them, "The gates of mercy shall be all shut up" (3.3.10), while at another he insists, "Use mercy to them all" (3.3.54). During the heat of battle, Henry can switch from piteous Christian to ruthless warrior on a moment's notice:

> For hearing this, I must perforce compound
> With mistful eyes, or they will issue too. *Alarum*
> But hark, what new alarum is this same?
> The French have reinforc'd their scatter'd men.
> Then every soldier kill his prisoner. (4.6.33–37)

Henry's decision to execute his battlefield prisoners is the most cold-blooded and merciless choice he ever makes, and he thereby violates the medieval code of chivalry. And yet he was on the verge of tears just before reaching this stern, heartless decision. Henry V seems to encompass antithetical values within a single soul, and comes as close as any character in Shakespeare's plays to embodying Nietzsche's ideal of the "Roman Caesar with Christ's soul." Henry can march in Roman triumph into London to the tune of a *Te Deum*. In *Henry V*, Shakespeare suggests that the ideal king would have to combine classical and Christian virtues, and yet, in practical terms, he shows how difficult it would be to achieve such a synthesis and how remarkable Henry is for even approaching the ideal.[178]

In some of Shakespeare greatest plays—*Hamlet, Othello*, and *Macbeth*—the hoped-for synthesis does not come off, and the conflict between classical and Christian values becomes tragic. Hamlet, Othello, and Macbeth are among the most complicated characters Shakespeare ever created, and they illustrate what Nietzsche means when he talks about the clash of master morality and slave morality in a single soul: "There is perhaps no more decisive mark of a '*higher nature*,' a more spiritual nature, then that of being divided in this sense and a genuine battleground of these opposed values."[179] In the case of Hamlet, Shakespeare takes a sensitive, modern Christian and thrusts him into an ancient pagan situation, straight out of a Norse revenge saga. Hamlet is very much a Christian, obsessed with the afterlife and the immortality of the soul, especially after he encounters his father's ghost. At the same time, Hamlet is fascinated by classical antiquity, and admires the great Roman and Greek heroes, such as Julius Caesar and Alexander the Great. Faced with the task of revenge, Hamlet is deeply divided by the conflicting demands of the classical and Christian principles within his breast. Classical models, beginning with examples from the Trojan War, encourage him to pursue revenge singlemindedly and implacably. But his Christian beliefs run counter to an absolute commitment to revenge and lead him to doubt the efficacy of taking any action in this corrupt and ephemeral world. Making matters even more complicated for Hamlet, when he finally has Claudius at his mercy—alone and defenseless, down on his knees at prayer—Hamlet realizes that if he is to take revenge, it must be something far more gruesome than anything a classical hero ever contemplated—Hamlet must not just kill Claudius's body, he must damn his soul to all eternity.

The ghost of Hamlet's father—drawing him in both pagan and Christian directions at once—puts him in an impossible bind. Hamlet must take absolute revenge on Claudius but in the process he must not harm his mother. In short, Hamlet needs to combine a pagan vengefulness with a Christian tenderness; to achieve the goals the ghost sets for him, he will have to be a "Roman Caesar, with Christ's soul." The division between the pagan and the Christian elements in Hamlet becomes acute when he must contemplate at one and the same time his mandated revenge on Claudius and the ghost's demand that he pity his mother:

> Now could I drink hot blood,
> And do such bitter business as the day
> Would quake to look on. Soft, now to my mother.
> O heart, lose not thy nature! Let not ever
> The soul of Nero enter this firm bosom,
> Let me be cruel, not unnatural;
> I will speak daggers to her but use none. (3.2.390–96)

Here Shakespeare offers a glimpse into the depths of the kind of hybrid soul that fascinated Nietzsche. The division between classical and Christian principles in Hamlet's soul goes a long way toward explaining his paralysis of will. He is tragically divided between antithetical realms of value and they battle to a standstill in his soul.[180]

In *Othello*, Shakespeare inverts the situation in *Hamlet*. Hamlet is a sophisticated and modern European forced into what amounts to a pagan blood feud, and his very sophistication works against his accomplishing his revenge in a straightforward manner. By contrast, it is Othello's lack of this sophistication that leads to his tragedy. Othello has all the simple grandeur and force of a Homeric hero. He is at home only on the battlefield. Once he ends up in the sophisticated and complicated world of Venetian domestic intrigue, all his martial virtues work against him and turn what ought to be a bedroom comedy into a tragedy.[181] Othello is nominally a Christian, but as far as Venice is concerned, he might as well be a Turk. Indeed, the peaceful Venetian merchants have hired him to defend them against the warlike Turks. Othello is a typical master in Nietzsche's terms. He is brave and strong, confident of his physical power. He even speaks in classical Homeric similes:[182]

> Like to the Pontic sea
> Whose icy current and compulsive course
> Nev'r feels retiring ebb, but keeps due on
> To the Propontic and the Hellespont,
> Even so my bloody thoughts, with violent pace,
> Shall nev'r look back. (3.3.453–58)

Secure at first in his heroic self-image, Othello is open and trusting with people. He judges them by their external appearance and never thinks of peering into the depths of their souls.

Tragically, Othello is paired with Iago, the greatest portrait in all literature of what Nietzsche calls *ressentiment*.[183] His triumph over his master, Othello, is an image of the slave revolt in morality in action. In martial combat, Iago could not hope to defeat the warlike Othello. But in mental combat, Iago has the advantage over Othello. Iago is cunning, whereas Othello is guileless.[184] Iago works by introducing the innocent and noble Othello to the slave's notion of psychological depth, teaching him that men—and especially women—are not what they seem to be, but hide an abyss of evil deep in their souls:

> I would not have your free and noble nature
> Out of self-bounty, be abus'd; look to't.
> I know our country disposition well:
> In Venice they do let God see the pranks
> They dare not show their husbands; their best conscience
> Is not to leave't undone, but keep't unknown. (3.3.199–204)

Iago's slavish cynicism infects the noble Othello. Forced for the first time to wonder what evil might be lurking in another's soul—namely, Desdemona's—Othello is profoundly disoriented and unbalanced. He kills Desdemona as a sacrifice to his idea of her purity. By introducing Othello to the notion of moral depravity, Iago is able to destroy his noble captain and prove to himself the superiority of the slave to the master. Anyone familiar with Nietzsche's idea of the slave revolt would not, like Samuel Taylor Coleridge, speak of the "motive hunting of a motiveless malignity" in the case of Iago.[185] Iago is the wily slave who is cleverer than his master, and he resents—and seeks to overturn—a social order that refuses to reward his merit and recognize his superior intelligence.[186]

Macbeth is another tragedy of a noble warrior-type unhinged by his encounter with the complex interior world opened up by Christianity. He begins the play as a heroic and respected warrior, honored for his Homeric deeds—indeed, for mercilessly cleaving an opponent on the battlefield in half.[187] But Macbeth is increasingly forced to grapple with forces, some of them supernatural, that cloud the simple warrior's perspective on the world with which he begins. He is living at a time when a pagan world of warriors has been Christianized. Although like Othello, Macbeth is nominally a Christian, the old pagan warrior in him resists this development. When trying to talk some men into murdering his rival Banquo, Macbeth asks them, "Are you so gospell'd, / To pray for this good man?" (3.1.87–88). Shakespeare gives us a feel for the classical hero's frustration with the new Christian ideal of forbearance.

Like a figure out of the pages of Nietzsche, Macbeth feels that he is living at the wrong moment of history:

> Blood hath been shed ere now, i' th' olden time,
> Ere humane statute purg'd the gentle weal;
> Ay, and since too, murther has been perform'd
> Too terrible for the ear. The time has been,
> That when the brains were out, the man would die,
> And there an end; but now they rise again
> With twenty mortal murthers on their crowns,
> And push us from our stools. This is more strange
> Than such a murther is. (3.4.74–82)

Here Shakespeare captures perfectly the voice of the pagan warrior unhinged by the new Christian dispensation. Macbeth knows the positive effects of Christianity—"humane statute" has "purg'd the gentle weal"—but he prefers the good old days of pagan Scotland when butchery in battle was the order of the day.[188] He recalls the time when murder was a much simpler matter, and, above all, when a man, once dead, stayed dead. Now with the Christian possibility of resurrection ("now they rise again"), Macbeth finds that his life has become a nightmare. His continual wrestling with the antithetical impulses of paganism and Christianity in his breast leads him to destruction.[189] Macbeth is the living embodiment of the barbarian/Christian hybridity Nietzsche speaks of in the Middle Ages. He illustrates what Nietzsche has in mind in the second essay of *Genealogy of Morals* when he analyzes the way that the development of a bad conscience unhinges the hitherto confident mastery of the warrior hero. With their hybrid souls, Hamlet, Othello, and Macbeth have much in common. In varying ways, each is faced with a revelation of evil in his world; each is disoriented by his discovery of and encounter with malignant—and perhaps supernatural—forces lurking behind what they had thought to be benign appearances.[190]

When Nietzsche speaks of master morality and slave morality working at odds in a single soul, we may well wonder, "What exactly is he talking about?" and wish for a concrete illustration of what he has in mind. Shakespeare's plays give us what we are looking for. They offer many examples of classical and Christian values operating at cross purposes within the same character. Shakespeare did not know the term "Renaissance" as historians have come to use it. Yet he was aware of what Jacob Burckhardt, Nietzsche, and others have claimed about the period during which he lived—that it was characterized by an attempt to revive classical values within a Christian civilization. This Renaissance program raised the hope of some kind of higher synthesis of classical and Christian values, a possibility Shakespeare for once explores in *Henry V.*[191] But more often Shakespeare shows that the encounter between classical and Christian values leads to tragedy; indeed it produces the complex tragic heroes of *Hamlet, Othello,* and *Macbeth.* As these cases show, whatever his ultimate judgment on Christianity may have been, Shakespeare agrees with Nietzsche that Christianity makes human beings more interesting.

In sum, comparing Shakespeare and Nietzsche on the subject of Rome and Christianity helps to clarify the thinking of both. Nietzsche's ideas of master morality and slave morality are helpful in understanding Shakespeare's Roman plays; in particular, they elucidate the contrast between the worlds of *Coriolanus* and *Antony and Cleopatra.* By the same token, reading Nietzsche in the light of Shakespeare's Roman plays helps to highlight the complexity of his views on a subject on which he is often thought to have adopted a simple, one-sided position. What we learn from the Roman plays helps us see that Nietzsche's attitude toward Christianity is more complicated than may at first appear, and the intermingling of classical and Christian elements in many of Shakespeare's heroes gives us a concrete sense of what Nietzsche means by ethical hybridity. It may seem odd that two figures as different as Shakespeare and Nietzsche—the Renaissance English playwright and the nineteenth-century German philosopher—should have similar (even if at times divergent) views about Rome and Christianity. As we saw in chapter 1, Machiavelli might be a common source for some of these ideas. In fact their views on the subjects are not that rare; parallels can easily be found in many other thinkers, such as Montesquieu. In the end, the convergence between Shakespeare and Nietzsche is probably best traced to the fact that, when two perceptive minds go to work on the same subject, they may well come to similar conclusions. As a result, Shakespeare and Nietzsche are among our best guides to the classical world and the way it was transformed by Christianity.

Appendix

HEGEL ON ROME AND CHRISTIANITY

We have seen that Hegel's thought can help clarify what is at stake in Nietzsche's concept of the slave revolt in morality. But did Hegel have anything to say on the more specific historical problem of the relation of Rome and Christianity? And, if so, how do his views compare with Shakespeare's and Nietzsche's? Hegel treats the subject of Rome and Christianity at many points in his writings, most famously perhaps in his lectures posthumously published as *The Philosophy of History.* But in terms of the specific issues raised in this chapter, Hegel's most salient comments come in a minor essay called "The Positivity of the Christian Religion" (1795), which he wrote early in his career and left unpublished (it was not in fact published until 1907).[192] The evidence suggests that Hegel never intended this essay for publication; he was using it and other early writings to explore intellectual possibilities that helped him find his way to his mature philosophical positions. In effect, Hegel was writing to himself in this essay; as a result, he may have been more candid in it than he later became in his published writings. In any case, "The Positivity of the Christian Religion" is highly pertinent to our enquiry, and turns out to deal with exactly the question we have been analyzing in Shakespeare and Nietzsche: how did Christianity conquer paganism?

Hegel begins by rather impishly dismissing the explanation most of his contemporaries would have offered, namely that Christianity is the one true religion and superior to any pagan beliefs (and, moreover, vouched for by divine miracles). Instead, Hegel looks for natural causes to explain why Christianity displaced the pagan religions. And that means political causes. He begins his account with the same political circumstances in the early Roman Empire that Shakespeare portrays in *Antony and Cleopatra*:

> Free Rome subjected to her sway a number of states which had lost their freedom, some (those in Asia) earlier, others (those further west) later; a few which had remained free she destroyed altogether, because they refused to bow to the yoke. All that was left to the conqueror of the world was the honor of being the last to lose her freedom. Greek and Roman religion was a religion for free people only, and, with the loss of freedom, its significance and strength, its fitness to men's needs, were also bound to perish. (154)[193]

Again like Shakespeare, Hegel dwells on the way that the ancient aristocracies were corrupted by the wealth they acquired in foreign conquests, a corruption that filtered down to the common people and gradually led to their enslavement:

> Fortunate campaigns, increase of wealth, and acquaintance with luxury and more and more of life's comforts created in Athens and Rome an aristocracy of wealth and military glory. The aristocrats thus acquired a dominion and an influence over the masses and corrupted them by their deeds and still more by the use they made of their riches. The masses then readily and willingly ceded power and preponderance in the state to the aristocrats. (155)

Thus, as Shakespeare dramatizes in *Antony and Cleopatra*, Hegel argues that under the imperial system, people lost faith in human agency and began to feel that they were merely parts in a gigantic machine that could go on running without them:

The picture of the state as a product of his own energies disappeared from the citizen's soul. The care and oversight of the whole rested on the soul of one man or a few. . . . The administration of the state machine was intrusted to a small number of citizens, and these served only as single cogs deriving their worth solely from their connection with others. Each man's allotted part in the congeries which formed the whole was so inconsiderable in relation to the whole that the individual did not need to realize this relation or to keep it in view. (156)

This is precisely the alienation Shakespeare depicts in *Antony and Cleopatra*— human beings dwarfed by the vast expanses of the Empire. In the process, people lost the firm grounding in this world that the Republic used to supply. As Hegel writes:

Freedom to obey self-given laws, to follow self-chosen leaders in peacetime and self-chosen generals in war, to carry out plans in whose formulation one had had one's share—all this vanished. All political freedom vanished also. . . . Death . . . must have become something terrifying. . . . The republican's whole soul was in the republic; the republic survived him, and there hovered before his mind the thought of its immortality. (157; see also 154)

As we saw in Shakespeare's Roman plays, in the Republic, service to the city and the fame it produced could satisfy the human longing for immortality, but under the Empire, new "immortal longings" arose once public life no longer supplied goals adequate to the Romans' ambitions and aspirations. Hegel blames the destruction of the Republic for the awakening in late antiquity of interest in otherworldly realms, a yearning for the soul's survival after death: "Cato turned to Plato's *Phaedo* only when his world, his republic, hitherto the highest order of things in his eyes, had been destroyed; at that point only did he take flight to a higher order still" (155).[194]

For Hegel, Christianity, coming out of the Orient, was the ideal religion for a world in which people had lost their freedom: "In this situation men were offered a religion which . . . was already adapted to the needs of the age (since it had arisen in a people characterized by a similar degeneracy and a similar though differently colored emptiness and deficiency)" (158). Like Nietzsche, Hegel insists that Christianity grew out of Jewish soil.[195] A people who had lost their political independence gave birth to a religion suited to slaves.

The despotism of the Roman princes had hounded the spirit of man from the face of the earth. Deprived of freedom, man was forced to let that in him which was eternal, his absolute, flee into the deity; and the spread of misery forced him to seek and expect blessedness in heaven. The objectification of the deity went hand in hand with the corruption and slavery of man and is really only a revelation and manifestation of this spirit of the age.[196]

Anticipating Nietzsche, Hegel views Christian otherworldliness as a compensatory response to the frustration people experienced living under Roman despotism.[197] Unable to accomplish anything in this world, they could only dream of finding fulfillment in another world, an afterlife.

Even more remarkably, the young Hegel sketches out what was to become Nietzsche's theory of the Christian revaluation of Roman values. Hegel reinterprets Christian humility as a new form of pride. He views the early Christians as deriving compensation for their feeling of powerlessness by disparaging power as a false good: "It satisfied their pride by exculpating them and giving them in the very sense of calamity a reason for pride: it brought disgrace into honor, since it satisfied and perpetuated every incapacity by turning into a sin any possible belief in human potentialities (160)." This is the "'Tis paltry to be Caesar" gambit we saw in *Antony and Cleopatra*, as well as Nietzsche's theory of the slave revolt in morality in embryo.

Hegel fleshes out the theory when analyzing the decline of interest in martial virtue and military service among the imperial Romans:

> With the total extinction of political freedom, all interest in the state has disappeared, because we take an interest in a thing only if we can be active on its behalf. In such a position, when the purpose of life is whittled down to gaining one's daily bread plus a greater or lesser degree of comfort and luxury, and when interest in the state becomes a wholly self-serving one . . . , then among the traits discernible in the spirit of the time there is necessarily present a disinclination for military service. (164)

The loss of confidence in the old republican principle that "valor is the chiefest virtue" paved the way for the triumph of Christianity in the ancient world, as the new religion attracted converts by systematically inverting the meaning of words in the traditional republican vocabulary:

> A nation in this mood must have welcomed a religion which branded the dominant spirit of the age, i. e., moral impotence and the dishonor of being trampled underfoot, with the name of "passive obedience" and then made it an honor and the supreme virtue. This operation gave men a pleasant surprise because it transformed the contempt felt by others and their own sense of disgrace into a glory and a pride. They must have welcomed a religion which preached that to shed human blood was a sin. (165)

Here, almost a century in advance, is the doctrine of *Beyond Good and Evil* and the *Genealogy of Morals*. Hegel claims that what the ancients posited as bad was reinterpreted by the early Christians as good; what the ancients posited as good was reinterpreted by the early Christians as evil. This is how Hegel summarizes his view of the rise of Christianity: "It was cradled in the corruption of the Roman state; it became dominant when that empire was in the throes of its decline, and we cannot see how Christianity could have stayed its downfall. On the contrary, Rome's fall extended the scope of Christianity's domain" (168). This is by now a familiar story. This is exactly the view we have seen in Shakespeare's Roman plays, as well as in Nietzsche's thought (once one takes into account the speculations in his notebooks).

I have dwelled at length on this obscure early essay by Hegel because it deserves to be better known. It reconfirms the fact that Shakespeare and Nietzsche were part of a long and venerable tradition of understanding Rome and its relation to Christianity. Like so many others, Hegel sharply contrasts the Roman Republic with the Empire and views the Empire as a massive falling-off from the Republic in political terms. The Republic represents political virtue for Hegel and the Empire represents political corruption. And like so many others, Hegel sees the imperial corruption of ancient political virtue as the precondition for the rise of Christianity. I am not claiming that "The Positivity of the Christian Religion" was a source for Nietzsche's *Genealogy of Morals*. Hegel's essay was not published until after Nietzsche's death. But it does show that Nietzsche's idea of the slave revolt in morality was less anomalous in nineteenth-century thought than may at first appear. In fact, Hegel's essay, brilliant though it may be, is not all that exceptional. As we have seen, the idea of Christian values as an inversion of classical values goes all the way back to the Renaissance and can be found in writers such as Machiavelli and Rabelais. Hegel is not some kind of missing link between Shakespeare and Nietzsche, but he does provide further evidence of a longstanding way of thinking about Rome and Christianity that stretches from the Renaissance to the present day and includes Shakespeare and Nietzsche as two of its major representatives.

PART TWO

Further Explorations of Shakespeare's Rome

3

Beasts and Gods: Titanic Heroes and the Tragedy of Rome

> After the battle of Marathon the envy of the heavenly powers seized [Miltiades]. And this divine envy is inflamed when it beholds a human being without a rival, unopposed, on a solitary peak of fame. Only the gods are beside him now—and therefore they are against him. They seduce him to a deed of *hybris*, and under it he collapses. Let us note well that, just as Miltiades perishes, the noblest Greek cities perish too, when through merit and good fortune they arrive at the temple of Nike from the racecourse. Athens . . . [and] Sparta . . . have also, after the example of Miltiades, brought their own destruction through deeds of *hybris*, as proof that without envy, jealousy, and ambition in the contest, the Hellenic city, like the Hellenic man, degenerates.
>
> FRIEDRICH NIETZSCHE, "Homer's Contest"

Trying to explain what characterizes the ancient world, Friedrich Nietzsche focuses on the frenzied competitiveness of the classical Greeks, the compulsive need to become the best of the Achaeans that is at the center of the *Iliad*. As pagans, the Greeks regarded the gap between human beings and the gods as great but not unbridgeable.[1] In an ancient city, a hero might strive to become a god in the eyes of his fellow citizens. If he won great victories and surpassed all his contemporaries in his achievements for the city, he could command the worship of the whole community. But Nietzsche views this titanic striving as tragic—in seeking to go beyond the ordinary limits of humanity, the hero commits deeds of hybris and brings on his destruction. Nietzsche goes further and proposes that a whole city might act out a tragedy. Flush with victory and trying to enlarge its dominions, a city might overextend itself and thereby initiate its own destruction. Like a tragic hero, a city might allow the very strengths that made it great tempt it into overreaching. In a tragic reversal, a city might find that the peak of its achievement marked the beginning of its collapse. Referring to Sparta and Athens, Nietzsche has the Peloponnesian War in mind as the greatest of Greek tragedies, the cataclysm that eventually led the Greek cities to lose their independence.

The power that conquered the Greek cities was Rome, specifically the armies of the Republic. Shakespeare's Roman plays—*Coriolanus, Julius Caesar,* and *Antony and Cleopatra*—explore the kind of tragedy Nietzsche views as characteristic of the ancient world. Shakespeare's Romans are extraordinarily competitive, just like Nietzsche's Greeks, to the point of striving to become gods, and they are destroyed in the process. In Shakespeare's portrayal, Rome itself pursues a kind of titanic striving that leads to its self-destruction. To understand Shakespeare's Rome as tragic, one must be aware of the fundamental distinction between the Republic and the Empire and recognize that the death of the Republic was effectively the death of the Roman regime, or at least the death of what Rome traditionally stood for. To be sure, in some sense Rome survives in *Antony and Cleopatra*, but what is left is an empty shell, with the old-style nobility undermined and the possibility of future heroism severely diminished, if not eliminated. As in the case of an individual tragic hero, Rome's greatness is inextricably bound up with its downfall. Its success in conquering the world undermines the character that allowed the city to triumph over all its enemies in the first place. More profoundly, as the course of its history reveals, Rome is tragically torn between its need to maintain its separate identity against the whole world and its longing to make itself into the whole world with the result that the city dissolves into its own empire. To appreciate how *Coriolanus*, *Julius Caesar*, and *Antony and Cleopatra* from a comprehensive trilogy, one must examine the way Shakespeare correlates the tragedies of his individual heroes with the larger tragedy of the Roman Republic.

The thematic unity of the three Roman plays is revealed in the fact that each turns on the issue of the problematic relation of the hero to the city. In each play, the tragedy grows out of the way Rome both nurtures heroic aspiration and tries to contain it. Taught by Rome to strive to be heroes, the greatest of the Romans ultimately refuse to accept the limits the city establishes for them, and they are destroyed in a form of overreaching. Coriolanus, for example, is the perfection of a Roman warrior. No one could fight more valiantly and implacably for his city. But the very virtues that make Coriolanus a hero to the Romans in wartime make him unacceptable to the city in peacetime. The unwavering determination that produces an irresistible foe on the battlefield unfits him for participating in the give-and-take of Roman domestic politics. Rome shapes Coriolanus into a fighting machine and then is appalled when he turns his fury against his fellow citizens. Precisely because Coriolanus takes the demands of the city seriously and struggles to live up to its ideals as fully as possible, he finds himself ultimately in conflict with Rome. As the most Roman of Rome's citizens, Coriolanus must paradoxically be banished from the city.

Mark Antony ends up in a similarly isolated position. In his own fitful way, he tries to remain true to the old Roman ideal of heroic virtue, even as he is among the first to embrace the new possibilities for decadence offered by imperial Rome. Antony is in the end destroyed by Octavius, a man lesser in spirit but more suited to rule in the world of reduced opportunities for heroism that *Antony and Cleopatra* portrays. Ultimately, it is Antony's refusal to compromise with the mediocrity of imperial Rome that allows Octavius to triumph over him. Julius Caesar is the ultimate example of the way that Rome cannot live with the heroic greatness it breeds.[2] Rome encourages its warriors to win great victories for the city by rewarding them with honors and political offices. None of Rome's generals ever won as many great victories as Julius Caesar did or conquered as much territory. But as a result, especially given Caesar's genius for domestic politics, he achieves an unparalleled and unprecedented preeminence in the city. Emerging victorious in the struggle for honors among the Roman nobles, Caesar is struck down by senators who view his preeminent position as incompatible with Rome's republican constitution. With one man towering over them, the Roman nobles come to feel dwarfed by the very greatness they would ordinarily applaud. As Cassius puts it:

> Why, man, he doth bestride the narrow world
> Like a Colossus, and we petty men
> Walk under his huge legs, and peep about
> To find ourselves dishonorable graves. (1.2.135–38)[3]

In Cassius's eyes, and in the eyes of his fellow conspirators, a great Roman can become *too* great—too great to fit into the city as it normally functions. That is why they believe that they must kill Caesar.[4]

The specific charge the conspirators bring against Caesar is that he wishes to become a tyrant. "Tyrant" is the city's name for someone who refuses to accept the limits it tries to set on human aspiration. The tyrant in effect sets himself up as a rival to the city, trying to achieve for himself the self-sufficiency the city claims as its own. Tyranny emerged as the peak of heroic aspiration in the ancient world, at least in political terms. The tyrant tries to become a kind of god in the eyes of the city. The life of tyranny and civic life as conventionally defined are the two poles between which Shakespeare's Roman plays move. The importance of tyranny as an issue is not always as clear in the other plays as it is in *Julius Caesar*, where the question of whether Caesar is a tyrant is explicitly debated. Nevertheless, the problem of tyranny runs throughout the Roman plays and provides a thread of hidden connections among the main characters. One factor that unites Coriolanus, Julius Caesar, and Antony is the way that all three share a tyrannical nature.

In *Shakespeare's Rome*, I analyze at length the tyrannical aspects of Antony's character and the tyrannical nature of his rule.[5] Indeed, tyranny is the concept that supplies the bridge between public and private life in *Antony and Cleopatra*. The common view of the play is that it sets up an opposition between politics and love, but political life and erotic life in the play are actually mirror images of each other. Antony and Cleopatra seek out an imperial form of love that corresponds to the imperial politics of their world. In both love and politics, Antony and Cleopatra display contempt for whatever is conventional and customary. Whether as rulers or as lovers, they consistently refuse to do what is expected of them. Hence their love is characterized by a kind of tyrannical desire. They pursue it against all prudential considerations, allowing their infinite passion to overwhelm all traditional and communal restraints. Similarly, they act tyrannically as rulers, rejecting any limits on their authority and trying to turn their every whim into law.

The blend of the erotic and the political is evident in one of Antony's opening speeches:

> Let Rome in Tiber melt, and the wide arch
> Of the rang'd empire fall! Here is my space,
> Kingdoms are clay; our dungy earth alike
> Feeds beast as man; the nobleness of life
> Is to do thus [*embracing*]—when such a mutual pair
> And such a twain can do't, in which I bind,
> On pain of punishment, the world to weet
> We stand up peerless. (1.1.33–40)

This speech is usually interpreted as expressing Antony's rejection of politics. It does express Antony's contempt for *conventional* politics—politics as usual in imperial Rome—and his indifference to ordinary political concerns and motives. But far from simply rejecting politics, Antony is aspiring to a higher kind of politics, one founded on the grandeur of his love. After all, the speech culminates in Antony laying down a law—"on pain of punishment"—a law that binds not just his ordinary subjects but the whole world to acknowledge the greatness of his love. This speech shows, then, not how love and politics are opposed in Antony's mind but how they have become fused.[6] Antony characteristically thinks of politics in erotic terms; whether his subjects love him is always his chief concern. One reason why the world of *Antony and Cleopatra* is so complex and confusing is that eros and politics have begun to blend together in imperial Rome.[7] In both love and politics Antony and Cleopatra refuse to accept conventional limits and seek out infinite goals instead, such as the eternal embrace of a love-death or the universal rule of the imperial throne.

In many respects, the austere Coriolanus seems to be the diametric opposite of the erotic Antony. But despite all the important differences, Coriolanus displays the same contempt for custom Antony does, the same unwillingness to do what is traditional or expected of him. When asked to solicit the conventional form of approval from the plebeians for his becoming consul, Coriolanus says, "Let me o'erleap that custom" (2.2.136). Forced to endure the humiliation of begging the support of the plebeians, Coriolanus pauses to reflect and heaps scorn upon the power of custom:

> Custom calls me to't.
> What custom wills, in all things should we do't,
> The dust on antique time would lie unswept,
> And mountainous error be too highly heap'd
> For truth to o'erpeer. (2.3.117–21)

Like Antony, Coriolanus refuses to accept the compromises customarily taken for granted in political life. Thus, just like Antony, Coriolanus leaves himself open to the charge of desiring a kind of tyranny as far as conventional political people are concerned. The tribunes claim that "he affects / Tyrannical power" and that he wants "to take / From Rome all season'd office" and "wind" himself "into a power tyrannical" (3.3.1–2, 64–65). Strictly speaking, the tribunes are wrong about Coriolanus's motives. He is not ambitious in the conventional sense and has no secret plans for overturning the Roman regime. But in a deeper sense, the tribunes are right: his contempt for the customary demands of Roman politics masks a more profound contempt for Roman politics as such, and a wish to see a more absolute regime in effect, in which Rome would live up to its claim of forming its citizens rather than allowing the regime to be continually reshaped by the haphazard efforts of would-be legislators.

Coriolanus and Antony thus push politics to its limits by demanding from it more than ordinary politicians do. They both resemble Julius Caesar, who, if anything, surpasses them in his demands upon the city. In their single-minded pursuit of public honors, Shakespeare's Romans are the most fully political of human beings, and in his single-minded pursuit of personal supremacy in Rome, Julius Caesar is the most political of Shakespeare's Romans. Whether or not one chooses to call Caesar a "tyrant," he clearly covets a form of absolute rule in which his will would become sufficient reason in Rome. Early in the play, Antony reveals that Caesar has adopted the role of an Oriental despot: "When Caesar says, 'Do this,' it is perform'd" (1.2.10). Caesar's pompous habit of speaking of himself in the third person—"Caesar shall forth" (2.2.10)—is in keeping with this despotic pose. He speaks with the voice of an absolute monarch whose will is law, when he refuses to explain his decision not to come to the Senate: "The cause is in my will, I will not come: / That is enough to satisfy the Senate" (2.2.71–72). Caesar's tyrannical desire to be able to define right and wrong by his mere will is even clearer in what may well have been the original form of a famous line: "Caesar did never wrong but with just cause."[8] Like Antony and Coriolanus, Caesar ultimately thinks of himself as above existing laws and entitled to lay down new laws solely by virtue of his personal will.

Perhaps this position is what many Roman patricians secretly desired for themselves—to defeat all rivals, put an end to the struggle for preeminence in Rome, and emerge triumphant as the absolute authority in the city. Julius Caesar would then be unique only in his clarity of vision in perceiving both the nature of his own desires and the means to satisfy them, together with his skill and determination in doing whatever is necessary to emerge completely victorious in the struggle for power in the city. Coriolanus, for example, is restrained from becoming master of the city ultimately by the lingering hold that Roman custom has over him. Despite his professed scorn for Roman conventions, in key respects his behavior is governed by what we would call his class prejudices and thus by ingrained, conventional responses. His aristocratic disdain as a patrician for the plebeians is what prevents him from successfully courting their favor. In particular, his aristocratic contempt for the theatrics required by Roman politics (*Coriolanus*, 3.2.99–101) prevents him from winning over the plebeians and coming to power in Rome. Julius Caesar, by contrast, is a master of theatricality and is willing to put on a performance for the Roman mob to win their favor, as Casca notes with patrician disgust: "If the tag-rag people did not clap him and hiss him, according as he please'd and displeas'd them, as they use to do the players in the theatre, I am no true man" (*Julius Caesar*, 1.2.258–61). Ever the politician, Caesar does not let his ingrained notions of nobility stand in the way of his performing in front of the plebeians in ways that other patricians would find base. By seeming to humiliate himself before the plebeians, Caesar wins their support in his struggle against his fellow patricians and thus paradoxically manages to elevate himself above all other Romans by lowering himself in the eyes of his fellow patricians.[9]

In making himself master over Rome, Caesar thus succeeds where all noble Romans before him failed, but he thereby reveals with a new clarity what many patricians before him ultimately desired. As the case of Coriolanus shows, from the beginning of the Republic even the most loyal servant of the city may turn against it at any moment if it crosses his will. The tribune Sicinius seems to see right into the depths of Coriolanus's soul:

> Where is this viper
> That would depopulate the city and
> Be every man himself? (3.1.262–64)

This drive to "be every man himself" is what motivates the Roman heroes in their struggles for preeminence. Confronted by his mother's embassy from Rome, Coriolanus lays claim to being self-sufficient and independent of all ordinary human ties:

> I'll never
> Be such a gosling to obey instinct, but stand
> As if a man were author of himself,
> And knew no other kin. (5.3.34–37)

The choice Shakespeare's Roman heroes face is this: either accept the limits set by the city and accommodate oneself to the regime or seek out some form of tyranny, however subtle or exotic—a way of life independent of and superior to the city's.

Ultimately the tyrannical desire of the Roman heroes takes the form of a will to apotheosis. Spurning any conventional sense of the limits of humanity, these heroes wish to become gods. Coriolanus, Julius Caesar, and Antony all at one point or another are portrayed as divine. Menenius, for example, characterizes the wrathful Coriolanus threatening to destroy Rome in these terms: "What he bids be done is finish'd with his bidding. He wants nothing of a god but eternity and a heaven to throne in" (5.4.22–24).[10] Cominius pictures Coriolanus as achieving divine status among the Volsces:

> He is their god; he leads them like a thing
> Made by some other deity than Nature,
> That shapes men better. (4.6.90–92)

Antony is compared to a number of classical deities, including Mars (1.1.4, 1.2.6, 2.2.5, 2.5.117) and Jupiter (3.2.10) or Jove (4.6.28).[11] Cleopatra's grandiose dream of Antony in act 5, scene 2 provides a vision of him standing above the whole of nature and thus becoming a cosmic deity, not just a civic god. Julius Caesar claims for himself the status of a god, similarly presenting himself as raised above the fickleness of the city, with the constancy of a cosmic god:

> I could be well mov'd, if I were you;
> If I could pray to move, prayers would move me:
> But I am constant as the northern star,
> Of whose true-fix'd and resting quality
> There is no fellow in the firmament.
> The skies are painted with unnumber'd sparks,

> They are all fire, and every one doth shine;
> But there's but one in all doth hold his place.
> So in the world: 'tis furnished well with men,
> And men are flesh and blood, and apprehensive;
> Yet in the number I do know but one
> That unassailable holds on his rank,
> Unshak'd of motion; and that I am he,
> Let me a little show it, even in this—
> That I was constant Cimber should be banish'd,
> And constant do remain to keep him so. (3.1.58–73)

Caesar dies identifying himself with the unshakeable seat of the cosmic gods: "Hence! wilt thou lift up Olympus?" (3.1.74). His attempt at self-apotheosis shows how great the gulf can grow between the Roman hero and the city of Rome. The hero's conception of his absolute virtue is founded on his contempt for the feebleness and mediocrity of other Romans.

The god imagery Shakespeare associates with his Roman heroes is strangely counterpointed by imagery that marks them as beasts. Julius Caesar speaks of himself in such terms: "Caesar should be a beast without a heart" (2.2.42). Although he is assassinated for wanting to become a god, his murder is described in words more appropriate to a beast; it evokes images of butchery (see Brutus at 2.1.166 and Antony at 3.1.255). In an impassioned speech over Caesar's bloody corpse, Antony pictures him in animal terms as a deer brought down by hunters:

> Here wast thou bay'd, brave hart,
> Here didst thou fall, and here thy hunters stand,
> Sign'd in thy spoil, and crimson'd in thy lethe.
> O world! thou wast the forest to this hart,
> And thus indeed, O world, the heart of thee.
> How like a deer, strooken by many princes,
> Dost thou here lie! (3.1.204–10)

In *Antony and Cleopatra*, Antony is compared to a remarkable series of animals, among them a stag (1.4.65), a fish (2.5.10–15), a bird (3.2.12), a horse (3.7.7–9, 5.1.39–40), a duck (3.10.19), a bull (3.13.126–28), and a boar (4.13.2–3). Even in Cleopatra's grand dream of Antony as a god, she compares him to a dolphin (5.2.88–89).

The conjunction of god and beast imagery is prominent in *Coriolanus* as well. In the same passage in which Menenius speaks of Coriolanus as wanting "nothing of a god," he nevertheless compares him to a variety of animals: "he no more remembers his mother now than an eight-year-old horse" (5.4.16–17) and "There is no more mercy in him than there is milk in a male tiger" (5.4.27–28). Indeed, in speaking of Coriolanus's remarkable transformation—his apotheosis among the Volsces—Menenius also evokes images of animal metamorphosis: "There is a difference between a grub and a butterfly, yet your butterfly was a grub. This Martius is grown from man to dragon: he has wings, he's more than a creeping thing" (5.4.11–14).[12] Menenius's images of Coriolanus seem to be at cross-purposes; the great hero appears at one and the same time sublime and subhuman. As paradoxical as the god/beast imagery in the Roman plays may seem at first, it actually illustrates a well-known principle in Aristotle's *Politics*: a man without a city is either a beast or a god.[13] Like Aristotle, Shakespeare shows that radical independence from the city must be either lower or higher than the normal human condition.

Aristotle formulates this principle in the course of developing his definition of the polis in book 1 of the *Politics*. Aristotle understands the city as the unit of human self-sufficiency. Families group together into villages, and villages amalgamate into cities, as human beings try to reach the critical mass of farmers, workers, tradespeople, and other occupations they need to satisfy their basic human needs, such as food, clothing, and shelter. They cannot fulfill their natures as human beings until they band together in cities. Once the city secures what is necessary for mere life, people are finally free to pursue their conception of the good life—the life of a fully developed human being ("while coming into being for the sake of living, [the city] exists for the sake of living well").[14] Thus Aristotle views the city as natural to human beings because only the city allows them to realize their natures. His famous definition—"man is a political animal"—which is usually misunderstood as meaning that human beings are by nature politicians—actually means that man is the living creature whose nature it is to live in the city (*polis*).[15]

To explain this claim, Aristotle points out that human beings are distinguished from other social animals (such as bees) by their ability to speak, specifically to argue about what is just and unjust. And that activity can take place only in the city. Once human beings have secured the means to live, they have the leisure to argue over how best to live. The polis defines and encompasses the normal range of humanity. A being that looked human but could not speak would be an anomaly—either lacking the potential to develop into a human being or raised above human limitations (perhaps some kind of telepathic divinity). As Aristotle writes, "He who is without a city through nature rather than chance is either a mean sort or superior to man."[16] Or in

Aristotle's classic formulation: "One who is incapable of participating or who is in need of nothing through being self-sufficient is no part of the city, and so is either a beast or a god."[17]

Aristotle's understanding of human beings in relation to the city points to a potentially tragic situation, a fundamental tension between the individual and the community. Human beings need the city in order to develop their humanity fully, and yet the city sets limits to that development. This situation is particularly problematic for the warlike heroes prized in the ancient world. As we have seen in the case of Shakespeare's Romans, the city treats its great warriors as heroes—in extreme cases as gods—and yet it wants their warlike nature to be directed solely in the service of Rome. If the hero's aggressive impulses turn against his native city, or if, out of his immoderate desire for preeminence, he wishes to conquer and reign over Rome, then the city must banish him, brand him as a tyrant and kill him, or otherwise treat him like a savage beast that cannot fit into the community. The warrior hero thus exists in a peculiar tension with his native city. He cannot do without the city; if nothing else, he needs its citizens to populate the armies he wishes to command. But the city demands that those armies be used in its service, and not solely for the hero's glory. One might formulate the tragedy of Coriolanus, Julius Caesar, or Antony in these terms: each finds that he cannot live without the city and yet he finds that he cannot live with it either. The city experiences a similarly tragic situation. Rome needs its warlike heroes to defend it and to achieve its goals, but it also finds that these aggressive heroes are difficult to keep under control. They are constantly threatening to turn against the city they serve or to work to enslave it. Rome finds that it cannot live without its heroes, and yet it finds that it cannot live with them either. The deepest root of tragedy in the Roman plays is Shakespeare's understanding of the problematic self-sufficiency of both the ancient hero and the city he belongs to but ultimately does not fit into.

The problematic self-sufficiency of the hero and the city is related to the questionable claim each makes to universality. The quest of Shakespeare's Roman heroes to become gods takes the specific form of a drive to achieve ever-widening recognition of their greatness, an unwillingness to cease their heroic strivings until their preeminence has been acknowledged by the whole world. Only by achieving universal recognition, by getting everyone to admit his superiority, could a hero feel that he had truly attained the status of a god.[18] Caesar perhaps reveals more about himself than he does about Cassius when he says of the "lean and hungry" Roman patrician: "Such men as he be never at heart's ease / Whiles they behold a greater than themselves" (1.2.208–9). Plutarch says that Caesar was motivated by a "senseless covetousness to be the best man in the world."[19] In differing ways, the same passion grips both Coriolanus and Antony as well. Recall that Antony seeks a situation in which "the world" will ratify his claims for Cleopatra and himself: "We stand up peerless" (1.1.39–40).[20]

The problem in achieving universal recognition, particularly in the ancient world with its virtually self-contained cities, is that a man is normally a hero, and hence potentially a god, only to the specific and limited community he serves. Thus the greatest achievement for a hero would be to win the admiration of his enemies, since his fellow citizens are naturally partial to his cause, and only those who have no motives for favoring him can deliver an objective estimation of his worth. The younger Pompey, for example, wrings from a reluctant Enobarbus an acknowledgment of his valor:

> I never lov'd you much, but I ha' prais'd ye
> When you have well deserv'd ten times as much
> As I have said you did. (*Antony and Cleopatra*, 2.6.76–78)

This grudging tribute is all the more powerful because it comes from an enemy. For similar reasons, Coriolanus does not want to feel that he has to serve the plebeians in order to win their admiration, and Antony also worries at times that his soldiers follow him only out of mercenary motives. A god is supposed to be worshiped not for the services he performs but for the sheer fact that he is a god, or, as Cominus tells Coriolanus, his honors are to be: "In sign of what you are, not to reward / What you have done" (1.9.26–27). This is the self-sufficiency of the gods—the admiration they receive comes as a pure tribute to their perfection.[21] Thus to achieve a godlike self-sufficiency, Coriolanus, Julius Caesar, and Antony must find a way to be worshiped by friend and foe alike, to be universally admired, not just praised by a particular community.

Coriolanus at first thinks that the glorious life of a conquering warrior will bring him the universal admiration he seeks, as it forces both domestic and foreign enemies to acknowledge his greatness. This is the prospect Cominius offers him:

> The dull tribunes
> That with the fusty plebeians hate thine honors
> Shall say against their hearts, "We thank the gods
> Our Rome hath such a soldier." (1.9.6–9)

On a grand public occasion, in front of both Roman parties, Cominius proclaims of Coriolanus: "The man I speak of cannot in the world / Be singly counterpos'd" (2.2.86–87). But events in Rome eventually prove Cominius

wrong and call into question Coriolanus's ability to make his enemies within
his own city admire him. His journey to the Volscian city of Antium seems
to be a more satisfactory step in the direction of universality. Apparently his
greatness is so manifest that he can simply walk into an enemy town and be
made commander-in-chief on the spot. His bitterest rival, Aufidius, claims
that he is willing to suppress his "ancient envy" (4.5.103) and follow his long-
time opponent's leadership. Even the common serving people acknowledge
Coriolanus's greatness—"I knew by his face that there was something in
him," "He is simply the rarest man i' th' world" (4.5.154–55, 160–61). They
do not cease in their admiration until they are praising the Roman at the expense of their own Volscian general (4.5.162–66). A Volscian lord proclaims
of Coriolanus: "The man is noble, and his fame folds in / This orb o' th'
earth" (5.6.123–24).

But as Coriolanus's mother finally points out to him, he never truly becomes a citizen of the world; he merely exchanges being a Roman for being
a Volsce (5.3.178–80). To become admired among the Volsces, he must in
fact become despised among the Romans (5.3.140–48). Although Volumnia
assures Coriolanus that he could be honored by both sides (5.3.135–40), in
the end he is honored by neither. It turns out that the Volsces admire him
only for the victories he achieves over the Romans, and when his services fall
below their expectations, they turn against him. He is murdered by a mob
in Antium, just the way he was almost murdered by a mob back in Rome.
Ultimately Coriolanus's quest for universal recognition appears to be in vain.

Antony sees a similar hollowness in Julius Caesar's quest for universal
recognition, above all because his peculiar form of apotheosis required his
death. Only by assassinating Caesar do the conspirators paradoxically set his
spirit free from the limitations of his body, infirmities that had proclaimed
his mortality for all to see. Standing over Caesar's corpse, Antony invokes
his liberated spirit to reign over "all the parts of Italy" (3.1.264) and thus to
achieve a universal revenge on the men who murdered him (3.1.270–75).
Later, Brutus addresses Caesar's spirit and notes his uncanny power to accomplish his revenge no matter where the conspirators flee:

> O Julius Caesar, that art mighty yet!
> Thy spirit walks abroad, and turns our swords
> In our own proper entrails. (5.3.94–96)

Yet for all the manifestations of Caesar's power, at his funeral Antony cannot help noticing that just at the moment when the great man seems to have
achieved a kind of universal power in death, he has lost all his worshipers:

> But yesterday the word of Caesar might
> Have stood against the world; now lies he there,
> And none so poor to do him reverence. (3.2.118–20)

At his first sight of Caesar's mutilated body, Antony is struck not by the way his fame has expanded to encompass the whole world but by the way it has contracted to such a small space:

> O mighty Caesar! Dost thou lie so low?
> Are all thy conquests, triumphs, spoils,
> Shrunk to this little measure? (3.1.148–50)

One ought to bear these passages in mind in analyzing Antony's behavior in *Antony and Cleopatra*. One reason that he pursues conventional political life half-heartedly is that he has seen the depressing results of Julius Caesar's total commitment to Roman politics. Antony's disillusionment with the ultimate fate of Caesar's political ambition, especially the goal of being worshipped by a single city, leads him to take a different approach to the goal of universal recognition, and apparently with greater success if one is to believe Cleopatra's dream of him. She stations him not just above the city gods in scope and stature, but above the cosmic gods as well:

> His face was as the heav'ns, and therein stuck
> A sun and moon, which kept their course, and lighted
> The little o' th' earth.[22] (5.2.79–81)

Cleopatra's grand image of Antony—"His legs bestrid the ocean" (5.2.82) —suggests that his achievement surpasses even Julius Caesar's. Unlike Coriolanus, Caesar succeeds in getting many plebeians as well as many patricians to side with him. He followed a policy of clemency to his patrician opponents so that he could count on even men like Brutus to support him at first. In assessing Caesar when he contemplates the assassination, even Brutus has to admit, "I know no personal cause to spurn at him" (2.1.11). Thus Caesar managed to span the city of Rome and its two parties "like a Colossus" (in Cassius's famous words), but Antony appears to span the entire Mediterranean world. Unlike Caesar, who had to keep his two feet firmly planted in Rome to maintain his control of the city as his first step toward achieving world domination, Antony seems free to take a universal stance. Embracing the emergent cosmopolitanism of his world (partly the result of Julius Caesar's earlier conquests), Antony believes that he can do without a particular city to honor him. In foregoing his chance to rule in a conventional way, he evidently thinks that he can bypass the particularism and exclusiveness of the ancient city and call directly upon the allegiance and devotion of any human being anywhere. He claims that when he possessed Cleopatra's heart, it "had annex'd unto't / A million moe" (4.14.17–18), as if his love alone entitles him to worldwide recognition.

The fact that Antony's cause is purely personal and not bound up with any particular community means that he can have both Romans and Egyptians among his followers. There seems to be no theoretical limit to the number of human beings who might recognize his authority. But unfortunately, the number of those who believe in Antony does not, as he hopes, increase as the play progresses, but rather decreases precipitously. In fact, at the very moment when he lays claim to having had a "million" hearts attached to him, he is thinking of how he has now "lost" them (4.14.18). Without being anchored in a particular community, the recognition Antony achieves is potentially more widespread, but also more fragile and liable to dissolve away at a moment's notice:

> The hearts
> That spanieled me at heels, to whom I gave
> Their wishes, do discandy, melt their sweets
> On blossoming Caesar; and this pine is bark'd
> That overtopp'd them all. (4.12.20–24)

As if afraid of total dissolution, Antony in his final moments tries to reclaim his Roman citizenship as his only secure passport to immortality. He speaks his own epitaph as "a Roman by a Roman / Valiantly vanquish'd" (4.15.57–58). Once again, the hero's desire for universal recognition remains unfulfilled.

Looking at the titanic goals the greatest of Shakespeare's Romans strive for—total self-sufficiency, boundless eros, universal recognition, apotheosis—one might well wonder what ever happened to the early Rome of *Coriolanus*: the city of prudence and moderation, the city where people are merely "ambitious for poor knaves' caps and legs" (2.1.68–69), where they "temp'rately proceed" even to what they would "violently redress" (3.1.218–19), where in general "the word is 'mildly'" (3.2.142). It is at first sight puzzling that the city that tries to channel the aspirations of its citizens into acceptable paths nevertheless gives birth to such heaven-storming spirits as Coriolanus, Julius Caesar, and Antony. Antony's high-aspiring spirit can partly be explained by the moribund status of the republican regime in his time. But Coriolanus pursues his heroic quest early in the days of Rome, and in any case the dissolution of the Republic that apparently frees Antony's spirit results from the limitless ambition of Julius Caesar in the first place. The city of moderation somehow provides lessons in immoderation. In fact Shakespeare's Roman heroes do practice a form of civic piety, but instead of obeying the city, they imitate it; rather than listening to what the city tells them to do, they take their cue from what it does. For Rome as a city does not practice what it preaches; no city could have conquered the world by acting moderately. The most heroic of Shakespeare's Romans learn to aspire as high as they do precisely by observing the most heroic of cities, Shakespeare's Rome.

As we have seen in Aristotle's *Politics*, the city is the origin of the idea and goal of self-sufficiency. Rome claims to be an all-encompassing whole with a total claim on the loyalty of its citizens. The Roman way of life is supposed to be the best way of life, ultimately the only way of life for its citizens. Rome expresses this idea with its implicit claim that the city's gods are identical with the cosmic gods.[23] But Rome's brush with disaster in *Coriolanus* seriously calls into question the self-sufficiency of the city.[24] Rome can hardly call itself untouchable and unmovable when it is threatened with annihilation the moment one of its generals goes over to the enemy side. The sharp division of the world of *Coriolanus* into warring regimes, Roman and Volscian, limits the claims of either. As long as Rome is challenged on the field of battle, it is too insecure to be self-sufficient, and the mere presence of a rival regime may lead its citizens to question the seemingly unquestionable superiority of the Roman way of life. People who travel back and forth between Rome and Antium (4.3) may, for example, have the chance to compare one of the regimes to the other and find it wanting. The proximity of Rome's enemies breaks the city's monopoly on its citizens' devotion, and opens up concrete opportunities for them to find loyalties other than to their native land. This is evident in the case of the spy Nicanor, and also of course in the case of Coriolanus's opportunity to become a traitor.[25] In order to maintain its claim to be a genuine whole, it would seem that Rome would have to make itself into the only city in the world—to become the whole world itself.

Thus, much like its own heroes, Rome, in its will to be self-sufficient and a kind of all-embracing god on earth, is driven to pursue the goal of universality, to attempt to become in Thidias's quaint phrase "the universal landlord" (*Antony and Cleopatra*, 3.13.72). Only by conquering the entire world, by subjecting all regimes to its own, could Rome claim to establish the absolute superiority of its way of life. Thus arises the boundless eros of Rome, its yearning for conquest after conquest and hence the unlimited expansion of its Empire. The fact that the offensive wars Rome conducts are an attempt to satisfy a need the city experiences may explain why at a number of points Shakespeare portrays warfare in erotic terms in the Roman plays.[26] In short, what looks at first un-Roman in Antony and Cleopatra—their boundless desire—actually has its prototype in the city's longing for its empire. Indeed, just as the lovers fear the annihilation of self when they stand on the brink of fulfilling their desires,[27] Rome seems threatened with the loss of its identity as a separate city when it at last conquers all the world. The city dissolves into its own empire the way lovers lose their selves in each other, only Rome has no opportunity to pull back from the consummation of its desire. The Roman world dissolves in *Antony and Cleopatra*, until the city, which in *Coriolanus* "yet distinctly ranges" (3.1.205), becomes "as indistinct as water is in water" (*Antony and Cleopatra*, 4.14.10–11), or as "Rome" is in "Rome"—since by the time of Antony the word can refer either to the concrete city or the much vaguer and abstract notion of the Empire as a whole.

Thus in *Antony and Cleopatra*, Rome, much like a tragic hero, has undergone a *peripeteia*, a reversal. In tragic fashion, the Republic is eventually destroyed by just those qualities that once made it great, and its grandest successes only prepare the way for its utter ruin. Rome wants to establish the superiority of its way of life by conquering the world, but finds that its way of life is corrupted and undermined in the very process of world conquest. By eliminating all its rivals, Rome leaves itself in a situation in which it can no longer maintain its martial discipline. Having attained its goal of world dominion, the city, in Enobarbus's words, "has nothing else to do" (*Antony and Cleopatra*, 2.2.106) and begins to stagnate. The career of Rome as a world conqueror seems prefigured in Valeria's story of Coriolanus's son: "I saw him run after a gilded butterfly, and when he caught it, he let it go again, and after it again, and over and over he comes, and up again; catch'd it again: or whether his fall enrag'd him, or how 'twas, he did so set his teeth and tear it" (1.3.60–65). In Rome's own pursuit of its "gilded butterfly"[28]—the noble but elusive goal of world conquest—the city at first no sooner catches its prey than it lets it go again, as is evident in the treatment of the Volsces in *Coriolanus*.[29] But Rome's cat-and-mouse game with its enemies could not go on forever, and eventually, just as little Martius does, the city destroys what it is playing with, and leaves itself alone and without further purpose in the world.

The transition from the Republic to the Empire in Shakespeare's Roman plays is thus the consummation of the tragedy of Rome, a tragedy in which the city ends up destroying itself. Rome does not fall prey to its enemies; it succumbs to a form of inner degeneration. Moreover, the city's tragic turn threatens to bring an end to the possibility of noble action for its citizens. Antony finds that the only heroic act left him is to reject the world entirely, apparently abandoning it to the common run of humanity. According to Cleopatra, the precondition of universal peace in the Empire is universal mediocrity:

> The soldier's pole is fall'n! Young boys and girls
> Are level now with men; the odds is gone,
> And there is nothing left remarkable
> Beneath the visiting moon. (4.15.65–68)

In *Coriolanus*, Rome manages to survive only at the price of banishing its greatest general. In *Julius Caesar*, Roman senators kill the person Antony describes as "the noblest man / That ever lived in the tide of times" (3.1.256–57).[30] And finally, in *Antony and Cleopatra*, peace is achieved only by eliminating the one man who sees most clearly the hollowness of the new regime's values and has intimations of a world beyond its limits, even if that world seems to lie beyond the limits of the earth itself (1.1.14–17).

With its seemingly universal extent, the Empire may at first appear to be more all-embracing and comprehensive than the Republic. But ultimately the Empire proves to be just as exclusive as the Republic was, and therefore no more of a genuine whole. For all its claims to universality, the Empire turns out to be unable to make room for Antony and Cleopatra and allow them to turn their private vision of love into a new kind of public spectacle. By taking up *Coriolanus*, *Julius Caesar*, and *Antony and Cleopatra* in historical sequence as a trilogy, we can appreciate the deepest level of Shakespeare's originality in the Roman plays, his attempt to go beyond individual tragedies and write the tragedy of a city.[31] In the ancient world, tragedy represented the highest claim of the city—anyone who transgresses the limits the city sets to its citizens will inevitably meet with disaster. But in portraying the tragedy of Rome itself, Shakespeare shows that the city has its limits, too. Like Coriolanus, Rome cannot stand alone against the whole world, and, like Antony and Cleopatra, it cannot make itself into the whole world without losing its separate identity. Ultimately the city's claims to self-sufficiency and universality turn out to be as dubious as those of the heroes who try to become independent of it or to transcend its authority.

What are the larger implications of reading the Roman plays as a trilogy for understanding Shakespeare? In discussing Shakespeare's tragic heroes, many commentators uncritically adopt the perspective of the community in which the hero lives. If the hero and the community are at odds, the critic assumes that Shakespeare takes the side of the community against the hero, as if Hamlet could be adequately judged by the standards of Denmark or Othello by the standards of Venice. This approach loses sight of the genuinely tragic character of Shakespeare's plays, which, as Hegel argued, depend on their being some form of right (and therefore of wrong) on both sides of a dramatic conflict.[32] If the community stands for a legitimate principle, so does the hero, or to put it another way, what the community views as a defect in the hero can be seen from another perspective to be precisely his distinctive virtue.

Studying the Roman plays can help break down the misleading assumption that community as such is a value for Shakespeare, that all communities are essentially the same in his view, and that social order is simply to be preferred to any attempt to go beyond the limits a particular community sets. The Roman plays provide powerful evidence of how richly articulated Shakespeare's sense of the range of human communities was. He was able to portray not only the wide variety of human beings but the wide variety of regimes as well. He could see the distinctive mixture of virtues and vices in individual human beings, and the way virtues and vices can sometimes be inextricably intertwined. But he could do the same for the various kinds of community, such as the contrast between the Republic and the Empire in the Roman plays. Each regime has its positive and negative aspects, and the possibilities one regime denies to human beings are opened up in the other. Thus, although each regime may claim to embody the comprehensive human good, their juxtaposition reveals the limits of both.

Moreover, the Roman plays show that Shakespeare did not have, as many critics have supposed, a static notion of community, but rather a dynamic one. If a regime changes over time, it cannot in itself provide a universal standard. Rome does not stay the same from one play to the next in Shakespeare. The Rome Antony has to deal with is fundamentally different from the Rome that confronts Coriolanus. Thus one cannot analyze the Roman plays in terms of timeless abstractions, such as the community versus the hero, or public versus private life. One must always think in terms of a specific form of community, confronted with the distinctive kind or kinds of hero it breeds. In the Roman plays, public and private life are not opposed but profoundly intertwined, since the different regimes play a crucial role in shaping the human beings who live under them.

Thus, if Shakespeare's plays can lead us to question and pass judgment on a variety of heroes, they can lead us to do the same for a variety of regimes. The conduct of the heroes often provides clues to the limitations of the regimes under which they live. When Shakespeare's heroes chafe under the limits their communities try to impose on them, they are not being merely stubborn or rebellious. To view them that way is to adopt the community's perspective on them, as if its standards were universally valid. But Shakespeare's juxtaposition of different communities reveals the narrowness and exclusiveness of each one's standards. When his tragic heroes try to go beyond the limits of their communities, they are in fact showing their integrity and taking a step in the direction of universality, or at least they catch a glimpse of what lies beyond the borders of political life—think of Coriolanus's statement: "There is a world elsewhere" (3.3.135) or Antony's: "Then must thou needs find out new heaven, new earth" (1.1.17).

The fact that the Roman heroes do not fully achieve a position of universality is rooted in their remaining bound by the conventions of the city, even when they try to transcend them. This is reflected in the fact that each chooses a political means to go beyond politics, even Antony, who will not simply turn his back on his public role but seeks instead to find a new form of public life (or publicity) in love. The inability of the heroes to achieve a stance genuinely beyond politics is what makes their stories tragic. But still they are not simply to be condemned for failing to fit neatly into a particular community. In each case, this failure is also a kind of triumph, for the hero proves his greatness and integrity precisely by refusing to be bound by the exclusive horizons of his community. In short, if the community provides the standards for judging the limits of the hero, the hero at the same time provides the standards for judging the limits of the community. In viewing both Rome and its heroes as tragic, Shakespeare adopts a stance beyond the limited perspective of either the city or its citizens, and thus reveals the genuine path to universality. One can transcend the city, not by trying to transgress its limits in action but only by trying to comprehend them in thought. To return to Nietzsche for the last word: "To live alone one must be a beast or a god, says Aristotle. Leaving out the third case: one must be both—a philosopher."[33]

Shakespeare's Parallel Lives:
Plutarch and the Roman Plays

In Shakespeare's *Henry V*, the Welsh captain Fluellen is obsessed with history. Trying to understand his king, Fluellen views him on the model of a grand historical precedent, Alexander the Great, or, as Fluellen calls him in his Welsh accent, Alexander the Pig (meaning "Big"). This comparison evokes an elaborate set of parallels between the ancient and the modern worlds:

> If you look in the maps of the world, I warrant you shall find, in the comparisons between Macedon and Monmouth, that the situations, look you, is both alike. There is a river in Macedon, and there is also moreover a river at Monmouth. It is call'd Wye at Monmouth; but it is out of my prains what is the name of the other river; but 'tis all one, 'tis alike as my fingers, and there is salmons in both. (4.7.23–31)[1]

Fluellen proceeds to compare the way Alexander killed his "best friend," Cleitus, to the way the newly crowned Henry banished his companion, Falstaff. This comparison seems to redound to the credit of the British king, who behaved more moderately and reasonably than the Greek emperor: "As Alexander kill'd his friend Clytus, being in his ales and his cups; so also Harry Monmouth, being in his right wits and his good judgments, turn'd away the fat knight with the great belly doublet" (4.7.44–48). Here Shakespeare is paying a kind of backhanded compliment to one of his favorite authors by having Fluellen follow the method of Plutarch in his *Parallel Lives*.[2] He even parodies the style of the work as it was available to him in Sir Thomas North's English translation. In the pedantic Fluellen, Shakespeare makes fun of the way anyone who wants to compare heroes from different time periods can stretch a point to come up with parallels, no matter how empty, and force the material to make neat moral observations.

The fact that Shakespeare chose this opportunity to have a little fun at Plutarch's expense is actually evidence of his debt to the Greek author. He read the *Parallel Lives* so carefully that he could slip into the style of North's Plutarch with ease. I will argue that Shakespeare's debt to Plutarch was deeper and more extensive than has often been supposed, and that he penetrated to the core of the Greek author in a profound way, despite having read him in a translation that was twice removed from the original. A good illustration of this point is the scene in *Julius Caesar* in which Brutus and Cassius take leave of each other before the decisive battle of Philippi. This exchange is one of many passages in which Shakespeare follows his source in Plutarch carefully, at times seeming to do little more than versify North's prose. Here is how North's Plutarch describes Brutus's initial attitude toward suicide:

> I trust, (I know not how) a certaine rule of Philosophie, by the which I did greatly blame and reprove Cato for killing of him selfe, as being no lawfull nor godly acte, touching the gods, nor, concerning men, valliant, not to give place and yeld to divine providence, and not constantly and paciently to take whatsoever it pleaseth him to send us, but to drawe backe, and flie.[3]

Here is Brutus's reply in *Julius Caesar* when Cassius asks what he will do if they lose the battle:

> Even by the rule of that philosophy
> By which I did blame Cato for the death
> Which he did give himself—I know not how,
> But I do find it cowardly and vile,
> For fear of what might fall, so to prevent
> The time of life—arming myself with patience
> To stay the providence of some higher powers
> That govern us below. (5.1.100–6)

The way that Shakespeare follows Plutarch so closely here makes it all the more striking when he chooses to depart from his source. In North's Plutarch, Brutus's speech culminates in a vision of his coming reward in the afterlife: "For, I gave up my life for my contry in the Ides of Marche, for the which I shall live in another more glorious worlde."[4] At the corresponding moment in Shakespeare's play, Brutus is also thinking back to the assassination of Julius Caesar, but he lacks such confidence about his survival after death:

> But this same day
> Must end that work the ides of March begun.
> And whether we shall meet again I know not;
> Therefore our everlasting farewell take. (5.1.112–15)

Unlike North's Brutus, Shakespeare's is skeptical about the future and shows no sign of believing in an afterlife.[5]

By dropping the line about the "more glorious world" in North's Plutarch Shakespeare keeps his portrait of Republican Rome in *Julius Caesar* consistent. The Republican Romans in Shakespeare are firmly oriented toward this world, not another. One reason that they are so single-mindedly devoted to political life is that public honor and fame are the only avenues to immortality available to them.[6] Belief in an afterlife might divert them from channeling all their energy and effort into public life in the city. In talking of a world beyond this life, the Brutus of North's Plutarch suddenly sounds strangely Christian, as if Hamlet, with all his concern for "the undiscover'd country, from whose bourn / No traveller returns" (3.1.78–79), had wandered into Republican Rome. Shakespeare evidently sensed something anachronistic in the phrasing in North's Plutarch and decided to change it. Although he probably did not know it, Shakespeare had in fact caught North in a mistranslation of Plutarch. The Greek original of this passage is more properly translated: "On the ides of March I gave my own life to my country, and, since then, for her sake, I have lived another life of liberty and glory."[7] North often introduces errors into his translation of Plutarch, especially since he was not working from the Greek original, but rather from a translation into French by Jacques Amyot.[8] In this case, North evidently became confused about the passage when reading Amyot's French.[9] According to Ben Jonson, Shakespeare may have had "small Latin, and less Greek," but he was able to recognize a discordant note in a portrait of ancient Rome when he heard it.[10]

Shakespeare's "correction" of North's translation shows that he did not follow his text of Plutarch slavishly, but was in fact capable of reading it critically and even willing to depart from it to maintain the consistency of his presentation of ancient Rome. But Shakespeare read not only more carefully in Plutarch than is often supposed; he also read more extensively. Many critics discuss the relation of Shakespeare to Plutarch as if the playwright read only the specific lives of the heroes he portrays in the Roman plays, such as the *Life of Marcus Brutus* or the *Life of Marcus Antonius*. This view may be the result of the way North's Plutarch is generally available today. Most readers get to know the work solely in excerpts printed as appendices in editions of the individual Roman plays, or in anthologies labeled with names such as *Shakespeare's Plutarch*. In these versions, the editors reproduce at most the whole lives that they think are relevant to the Roman plays, and often merely excerpts from those. Thus the editor decides for readers which passages in Plutarch are relevant to understanding the Roman plays, and readers seldom think of looking beyond the borders of a few of the *Lives*. This practice can be misleading about the extent of Plutarch's influence on Shakespeare. For example, Plutarch's normal procedure is to give the life of a Greek hero and then the life of a Roman hero; then he offers a comparison of the two (called a *synkrisis* in Greek), which often contains some of his most significant commentary. But the way North's Plutarch is usually packaged for students of Shakespeare, the comparisons are omitted.

For an example of Shakespeare drawing on one of Plutarch's comparisons, consider act 2, scene 2 of *Coriolanus*, in which two Roman officers are discussing the hero's disdain for the city's common people.[11] One officer views Coriolanus's scorn for the plebeians as genuinely noble, but the other criticizes it:

> If he did not care whether he had their love or no, he wav'd indifferently 'twixt doing them neither good nor harm; but he seeks their hate with greater devotion than they can render it him, and leaves nothing undone that may fully discover him their opposite. Now, to seem to affect the malice and displeasure of the people is as bad as that which he dislikes, to flatter them for their love. (2.2.16–23)

In contrasting flattery of the people with disdain for them, this passage turns out to be based directly on Plutarch's comparison of Coriolanus with his Greek parallel, Alcibiades. Plutarch views the two political leaders as going to opposite extremes in their attitudes toward the common people. Alcibiades does all he can to flatter them and curry their favor, whereas Coriolanus treats them with contempt and earns their hatred. Although he criticizes both approaches, Plutarch, as often happens, prefers the Greek to the Roman:

> Neither the one nor the other was to be commended. Notwithstanding, he is lesse to be blamed, that seeketh to please and gratifie his common people: then he that despiseth and disdaineth them, and therefore offereth them wrong and injurie, bicause he would not seeme to flatter them, to winne the more authoritie. For as it is an evill thing to flatter the common people to winne credit: even so is it besides dishonesty, and injustice also, to atteine credit and authoritie, for one to make him selfe terrible to the people, by offering them wrong and violence.[12]

Clearly, Shakespeare drew upon this passage in creating the officer's comments in *Coriolanus*, and indeed it is remarkable how "Plutarchan" the dialogue at the beginning of act 2, scene 2 sounds. But this is not just a matter of an isolated passage in *Coriolanus* being derived from the wording of North's Plutarch. Rather, Plutarch's basic understanding of Coriolanus's character, especially as developed by contrasting him with Alcibiades, helped to shape Shakespeare's dramatic conception of the Roman hero.

We should beware of underestimating the extent of Shakespeare's reading in North's Plutarch. It seems to have been one of his favorite books and
one which he continually mined for new subject matter. He sometimes took
names for minor characters from lives quite remote from the main stories
on which he was working, suggesting that browsing in North's Plutarch may
have been one of Shakespeare's more productive recreations.[13] As an example
of the way reading widely in Plutarch may have significantly influenced even
the course of Shakespeare's career as a dramatist, I offer the following hypothetical account of how he may have come to write *Coriolanus* and *Antony
and Cleopatra* as the culmination of his exploration of ancient Rome. Shakespeare's *Timon of Athens* is linked with *Antony and Cleopatra* by means of
Plutarch, who tells the story of Timon in his *Life of Marcus Antonius*. Most
critics assume that *Timon of Athens* and *Antony and Cleopatra* were written
at roughly the same time in Shakespeare's career, although they disagree as
to which came first. If Shakespeare wrote *Antony and Cleopatra* first, then
he may have moved on to write *Timon of Athens* because he encountered
the story of the Greek misanthrope while reading Plutarch on Mark Antony.
Alternatively, if Shakespeare wrote *Timon of Athens* first, then he may have
originally come upon the story of Antony in the course of researching the
Greek figure. Having mined Plutarch's *Life of Marcus Antonius* for material
on Timon, he may have concluded that the Roman hero himself would make
an excellent subject for a play.

The other place in Plutarch to which Shakespeare would have turned to
find material for a play about Timon would have been the *Life of Alcibiades*,
since the Greek hero figures in Timon's story. As we noted, Plutarch pairs the
Life of Alcibiades with the *Life of Coriolanus*, comparing and contrasting, as
usual, two successful generals who eventually led armies against their native
cities. Thus, starting from the subject of Timon and attempting to research it
in Plutarch, Shakespeare might have been led to the stories of Mark Antony
and Coriolanus. This account must remain hypothetical, because the exact
chronology of Shakespeare's plays is a matter of conjecture, but that *Timon
of Athens, Antony and Cleopatra*, and *Coriolanus* are linked by Plutarchan
threads cannot be doubted.[14] Perhaps Shakespeare's course of reading in Plutarch might help explain the curious textual state in which *Timon of Athens*
has come down to us. In several respects, the play appears to be rough and
incomplete, leading many scholars to argue that Shakespeare abandoned it
as an unfinished—and unsuccessful—experiment.[15] Geoffrey Bullough suggests that in researching *Timon of Athens*, Shakespeare found in Coriolanus
a more congenial subject, which then led him to abandon the former play:

> *Timon* begins as a study in inordinate friendliness and ends as a study in in-
> sane wrath; and it may be that the play was not completed because the drama-
> tist turned against the double-theme with its "broken-backed" structure, its
> depiction of mere extremities, its hero saved from absurdity only by agonized
> rhetoric and unashamed didacticism. Maybe too he found it difficult to fit
> Alcibiades into the drama by inventing incidents which could be reconciled
> with Plutarch's elaborate *Life* of that benevolent traitor. Alcibiades was Plu-
> tarch's parallel to Coriolanus, and he probably was the final link in the chain
> which brought Shakespeare to discard *Timon* for *Coriolanus*. For Marcius had
> something of Timon in him, but he was a whole man with a life-history, not
> just the personification of ethical excess.[16]

I would carry the speculation further than Bullough, and argue that, while
researching *Timon of Athens*, Shakespeare was led to the stories of both Antony and Coriolanus and concluded that a pair of Roman plays would accomplish his purposes better than the single Greek play. In many ways *Coriolanus*
and *Antony and Cleopatra* develop the thematic material of *Timon of Athens*
and do so more effectively. As a generous and benevolent man eventually
betrayed by his closest allies and hence bitterly disillusioned, Antony recapitulates the story of Timon. As a military victor who suffers ingratitude and
banishment at the hands of the city he serves, Coriolanus recapitulates the
story of Alcibiades. The two Roman plays share many themes with *Timon of
Athens*, centering on the relation of the city and the individual, especially the
question of whether any human being can achieve a godlike self-sufficiency.
Working his way through Plutarch's *Lives*, Shakespeare seems to have come
to conceive of the stories of Coriolanus and Mark Antony as parallel lives,
only instead of serving to contrast the Greek world with the Roman, they
contrast the world of the early Roman Republic with that of the late (which is
at the same time the beginning of the Empire).

In many ways, Antony steps into the role Alcibiades plays in Plutarch as a
contrast to Coriolanus. Whereas Coriolanus manages to alienate even some
of his friends, Antony, just like Alcibiades, is able to win and maintain affection and admiration even from his enemies. Indeed, Plutarch's comparison
of Alcibiades and Coriolanus reads like a description of the contrast Shakespeare develops between Antony and Coriolanus:

> Alcibiades . . . passed all other for winning mens good willes. Whereas all Mar-
> tius' noble actes and vertues, wanting that affabilitie, became hatefull even to
> those that received benefit by them, who could not abide his severitie and selfe
> will. . . . Contrariwise, seeing Alcibiades had a trimme enterteinment and a
> very good grace with him, and could facion him self in all companies: it was

no marvell if his well doing were gloriously commended, and him selfe much honoured and beloved of the people, considering that some faultes he did, were ofetimes taken for matters of sporte, and toyes of pleasure. And this was the cause, that though many times he did great hurte to the common wealth, yet they did ofte make him their general, and trusted him with the charge of the whole citie. Where Martius suing for an office of honour that was due to him, for the sundrie good services he had done to the state, was notwithstanding repulsed, and put by. Thus do we see, that they to whome the one did hurte, had no power to hate him: and thother, that honoured his virtue, had no liking to love his persone.[17]

One could easily substitute the name of Antony for the name of Alcibiades in this passage, especially considering the talk of "trimme entertainment" or "sporte, and toyes of pleasure." Like Alcibiades, and unlike the inflexible Coriolanus, Shakespeare's Antony is mutable and can adapt himself to the manner and mood of the people around him. In contrast to the emotionally cold and austere Coriolanus, Antony in Shakespeare is a warm-hearted and erotic character who, again like Alcibiades, is able to indulge in all sorts of vices without losing his status as a hero.[18] This opposition between austerity and eroticism becomes the focus of Shakespeare's contrast between republican and imperial Rome. Thus for Shakespeare, Coriolanus and Antony become representative figures in the Plutarchan sense, embodying the contrast between two distinct ways of life, two different regimes.[19]

As I argue elsewhere, *Coriolanus* offers a portrait of the early days of the Roman Republic, while *Antony and Cleopatra* offers a portrait of the death of the Republic and the birth of imperial Rome.[20] In *Coriolanus*, Rome is still a virtually self-contained city, living by the austere code of republican and martial virtue (although making concessions to allow for the satisfaction of the bodily appetites of the less noble members of the community). The Rome of *Coriolanus* has its whole future ahead of it, a future of military conquest allowing free rein to the passions for glory of its most ambitious citizens (although the story of Coriolanus shows that the city cannot allow the spiritedness of its heroes to go completely unchecked). The Roman Republic is coming into being in the course of *Coriolanus*, finding the peculiar balance of power between patricians and plebeians that was to energize the country on its long march toward conquering the Mediterranean world.

In *Antony and Cleopatra*, by contrast, we see Rome at a much later stage of its history, a Rome with a long past now behind it, a history that has foreclosed many, if not all, of the heroic possibilities that were open to its citizens in its early days. Above all, we see Rome after the single greatest change in its history, the change from Republic to Empire, brought about by the career of Julius Caesar and the events surrounding his assassination (portrayed in Shakespeare's *Julius Caesar*). From being ruled by a regime that effectively encouraged its citizens' participation in public life, Rome developed a regime that actively discouraged such ambition, if only because the Empire, with its single ruler, did not allow for more than one man at the top at once (the Republic was led by two consuls who served for only one year at a time, thus allowing for rapid turnover in political leaders). In *Antony and Cleopatra*, Rome is no longer a clearly demarcated city walled off from the surrounding territory, but has instead grown to encompass the whole of the Mediterranean world. As a result, Rome loses much of its distinct identity as a community with its own peculiar way of life and begins to take on many of the characteristics of the countries it conquered.

In particular, the contrast between Rome and Egypt that many critics see as central to *Antony and Cleopatra* is in fact blurred within the play, and seems to be in the process of being effaced before our eyes.[21] *Antony and Cleopatra* portrays a highly Egyptianized Rome, a Rome that has been corrupted by its victories and is fast losing its heroic austerity, while learning to indulge in all the luxuries available to a world-conquering imperial power. The most "Egyptian" banquet in the play—indeed, "it ripens towards" "an Alexandrian feast" (2.7.96–97)—turns out to take place squarely within Roman territory on the Italian peninsula, and entirely among Roman citizens, indeed, the whole leadership of Rome.[22] From this perspective, Antony's story should not be viewed as a personal aberration from Roman norms; instead it becomes emblematic of what is happening to Rome as a whole, the Orientalizing of the Empire. The entire Roman community is succumbing to the charms of the Eastern world it subdued militarily but in a sense has surrendered to culturally. Even Octavius Caesar, who seems to represent whatever Roman virtue survives in the world of *Antony and Cleopatra*, gets partially drunk in the "Alexandrian" revel and is threatened with the loss of his famous self-control.

Shakespeare shows in *Antony and Cleopatra* that Roman virtue is fast becoming a thing of the past, if it has not already done so, now that Rome is changing, or has changed, from a republic to an empire. Shakespeare is interested not so much in the contrast between Rome and Egypt (which he shows to be blurring in *Antony and Cleopatra*) as in the contrast between the whole world of Republican Rome in *Coriolanus* and the whole world of imperial Rome in *Antony and Cleopatra* (which now includes Egypt). In Plutarchan fashion, Shakespeare uses the figures of Coriolanus and Antony to represent the two major stages of Roman history. Coriolanus, with his spiritedness and single-minded devotion to the life of the warrior, together with his scorn for all the needs and desires of the body, is emblematic of the republican world, while Antony, indulging in the pleasures of the flesh and companioned by the high priestess of love, Cleopatra, is emblematic of the newly eroticized imperial world.[23]

Thus Shakespeare may have derived more from Plutarch than a few grand passages or even the basic conception of his characters in the Roman plays. In writing *Coriolanus* and *Antony and Cleopatra*, Shakespeare seems to have been thinking in terms of parallel lives, of using the stories of the two heroes to illuminate each other, to highlight by contrast the distinctive mixture of virtues and vices they embodied in their careers, and, moreover, to correlate their distinctive ways of life with the distinctive regimes under which they lived and which they exemplified.[24] The organizing principle of Plutarch's *Parallel Lives* remains a matter of conjecture and dispute. It was long thought that Plutarch, a Greek living in the Roman Empire, wrote the *Lives* to defend Greek honor, to show that Greek heroes could brook comparison with Roman, and indeed in many ways surpass them.[25] But other analysts of Plutarch have argued that, as a citizen of the new Greco-Roman world, he was more interested in the similarities than the differences between his Greek and Roman heroes, and thus was engaged in a cosmopolitan rather than a partisan enterprise, one appropriate to a world in which educated Romans now spoke Greek and Greek cities now lived under Roman rule.[26]

Plutarch was himself the product of the cosmopolitan world Rome created by its conquest of the entire Mediterranean region and in particular its absorption of the Greek cities into its imperial orbit. In his *Lives* of Greek heroes, Plutarch deals with the era when the Greek polis flourished, and he chronicles the high and low points in the histories of the major Greek cities, including Athens, Sparta, and Thebes. Even when writing about Roman heroes, Plutarch deals with the period when Rome could still be thought of as a polis. Indeed, his *Lives* take Roman history up to the time of Julius Caesar, Marcus Brutus, and Mark Antony—that is, the last gasp of the Roman Republic and the first stirrings of the Empire and Caesarean rule.[27]

As a result, Plutarch's *Lives* taken together constitute a sustained reflection on the world of the classical polis in the pre-imperial era. One cannot be certain of Plutarch's intentions, but if one looks at his choice and disposition of his material, one would be justified in concluding that he wrote about the world of the classical polis—especially the flourishing of republican constitutions—from the vantage point of the imperial world that conquered, absorbed, and replaced it. Perhaps he was meditating on the viability of the polis as a form of organization and considering what was gained and lost when republics were replaced by empire. In his *Lives* of the Greeks

and Romans, Plutarch portrayed the way that the organization of civic life
in the ancient world, especially under various forms of republican constitutions, encouraged love of honor and competition for political preeminence.
By thus presenting the ancient polis as a breeding ground of heroic action,
Plutarch became one of the fountainheads of the classical republican tradition in political thought (he was, for example, an important influence on the
American founders, such as James Madison.)[28]

At the same time, however, Plutarch revealed how destructive the conten-
tiousness of the ancient heroes could be; it set polis against polis and sometimes a polis against itself, in an unending series of wars, revolutions, and
violent regime changes. If nothing else, the Roman Empire brought peace to
the ancient world by subduing all the separate cities, and thereby ending their
constant struggles against each other.[29] In this respect, Plutarch seems to welcome the coming of the Roman Empire and to present it as an inevitable
and even providential development.[30] But he also seems to regret the Greek
cities' loss of their independence and to hope that they might recover some
degree of autonomy under Roman rule, at least in terms of local matters. In
the question of polis versus empire, commentators disagree over which side
Plutarch supported, and some say that he tried to mediate between the two.[31]
Whatever Plutarch's position may ultimately have been, merely by posing the
question, his *Lives* provided fertile ground for Shakespeare's reading, given
the interest in the contrast between republic and empire that is at the heart of
his Roman plays, an interest that either drew Shakespeare to Plutarch in the
first place or was sparked by his reading of the *Lives*. The wider Shakespeare
read in Plutarch, the more he would have been struck by the choice between
polis and empire as the fundamental political question of the ancient world.

For all the disputes over Plutarch's intentions, one thing is clear: he links
his stories of individual Greeks and Romans to some kind of larger portrait
of the Greek and Roman worlds that produced them.[32] Plutarch's biographies
thus seem to be informed by the classical concept of the *politeia* as developed
by Plato and Aristotle. The Greek word *politeia* means "regime" in the dual
sense of "form of government" and "way of life." One of the central insights
of the political philosophy of Plato and Aristotle is that forms of government
are formative—they shape the way of life of the people living under them.[33]
It might be going too far to claim that Plutarch's *Parallel Lives* constitute a
systematic examination of the phenomenon of the *politeia* as understood in
classical philosophy, but they do explore the ways in which his heroes' lives
are correlated with the different regimes to which they are subject.

Plutarch regularly uses the word *politeia*, sometimes in its technical sense
of "constitution," especially when he speaks about the legendary founders of

regimes, such as the Spartan Lycurgus. Consider this key passage early in his *Life of Lycurgus*:

> From Crete, Lycurgus sailed to Asia, with the desire, as we are told, of comparing with the Cretan civilization, which was simple and severe, that of the Ionians, which was extravagant and luxurious, just as a physician compares with healthy bodies those which are unsound and sickly; he could then study the difference in their modes of life and forms of government.[34]

The word Perrin here translates as "modes of life" is simply a declension of the Greek word for "life" (*bios*) and the word she translates as "forms of government" is a declension of *politeia*. In short, Plutarch grasps the correlation between *bios* and *politeia*. In his *Life of Lycurgus*, he specifically refers to the contrast between a "simple and severe" way of life and an "extravagant and luxurious" one—exactly the contrast Shakespeare draws between the ways Coriolanus and Antony live. Just as Shakespeare does in *Antony and Cleopatra*, Plutarch associates an "extravagant and luxurious" life with Asia. And, of course, Plutarch dwells on the Asiatic roots of Antony's extravagant way of life throughout his *Life of Marcus Antonius*.[35]

As I argue elsewhere, Shakespeare, like Plutarch, seems to have been fascinated by the phenomenon of the regime, which helps explain the wide range of the political settings of his plays, from ancient pagan republics to modern Christian monarchies.[36] Like Plutarch in his *Parallel Lives*, Shakespeare in his tragedies chooses heroes whose stories have a public and political dimension. Even such seemingly domestic characters as Romeo and Juliet come from prominent aristocratic families in their community and their story turns out to have important implications for their city as a whole (the peace of the entire community is at stake). Shakespeare's Roman plays offer perhaps his most thoroughgoing exploration of the interaction of the public and the private, and thus of the way political life shapes the development of character. Thus Plutarch may have been the source of Shakespeare's Roman plays in a profounder sense than is usually supposed. Reading Plutarch, and noticing the way that the biography of a heroic public figure is a story of at one and the same time a particular way of life and a particular form of government, may have helped Shakespeare toward understanding the phenomenon of the regime and eventually propelled him to the creation of his own parallel lives: the republican Coriolanus and the imperial Mark Antony.

Shakespeare and the Mediterranean: The Centrality of the Classical Tradition in the Renaissance

What might we learn from a map of Shakespeare's imaginative world? What is at its center? As important as England obviously was to Shakespeare, it seems to lie, together with northern Europe in general, on the periphery of a map of the settings of his plays. What seems to be at the center is the Mediterranean, as well it should be in Shakespeare's day. For several centuries, Italian cities such as Florence, Venice, Rome, Genoa, and Naples stood at the forefront of economic, political, intellectual, and artistic developments in Europe. Despite Columbus and the rapidly increasing European presence in the Western hemisphere in the sixteenth century, the Mediterranean was still the commercial and cultural center of the world Shakespeare lived in, and his plays reflect that fact. Of his thirty-seven plays, twenty of them are set either wholly or partially in the Mediterranean world.[1] His Roman plays took him back to the Mediterranean past and the classical world. In his last plays, the romances, Shakespeare seems to be particularly drawn to the Mediterranean. *The Winter's Tale* is partially set in Sicily (as well as a Bohemia that mysteriously has a seacoast, presumably on the Mediterranean), *Pericles* ranges all over the eastern branch of the sea,[2] and *Cymbeline* looks like an attempt to round out Shakespeare's career by linking Britain with the Mediterranean world of Rome and Italy. Although *The Tempest* is set on a nameless and imaginary island, it is located somewhere in the middle of the Mediterranean, poised between Europe and Africa. One might argue that Shakespeare's sources—classical epic and drama, Greek and Roman history, Italian novelle—dictated the Mediterranean settings of his plays. But that still leaves us with the question: why was Shakespeare attracted to just these sources? His choice of sources is in fact the most convincing evidence that the Mediterranean—past and present—stands at the geographic center of Shakespeare's imagination.[3]

Why is it important to remind us of the obvious fact that the settings of Shakespeare's plays are concentrated in the Mediterranean world? For one thing, acknowledging this fact might help to counter, or at least moderate, one of the predominant trends in recent criticism, what might be called the Americanization of Shakespeare studies. Scholars from the United States have increasingly set the agenda for Shakespeare criticism for a variety of reasons—not the least of which is their sheer numbers. U.S. critics have understandably looked for ways to link Shakespeare with their concerns as Americans.[4] The result has been to emphasize the issue of colonialism in Shakespeare, to pursue the connections between Shakespeare and America by foregrounding the subject of the British Empire in his plays.[5] Critics have in effect tried to shift the geographic center of Shakespeare's world from the Mediterranean to the Atlantic.

Nowhere is this trend more evident than in criticism of *The Tempest*. In study after study, the play has been virtually lifted out of the Mediterranean and dropped somewhere in the Caribbean.[6] The mere mention of Bermuda at one point in the play (1.2.229) has been enough to outweigh the repeated Mediterranean references—to Naples, Milan, Tunis, and Algiers, and of course to the Mediterranean itself (1.2.234).[7] To be sure, interpretations of *The Tempest* in terms of the issue of imperialism have a legitimate basis in the text, with its possible connections to Montaigne's essay "Of Cannibals" and reports on the colonization of Virginia.[8] As many critics have pointed out, Shakespeare's portrayal of Caliban is a remarkable anticipation of the problematic position of the colonial subject as it was emerging in the New World in Shakespeare's day.[9] But granted that colonialist interpretations of *The Tempest* have illuminated it in new ways, one may still caution that they risk distorting our understanding of Shakespeare by emphasizing the New World aspects of the play at the expense of the Old. The play is, for example, more indebted to the classical utopian tradition, as begun by Plato's *Republic*, than it is to any account of American colonization.[10] In general, to shift the geographic orientation in Shakespeare studies from the Mediterranean to the Atlantic is to downplay and perhaps even to lose sight of the central importance of the classical tradition in his plays. Critics have become more interested in how Shakespeare looks forward to a world that came to be dominated by Anglo-American traditions and less interested in how he looks back to the Greco-Roman traditions that shaped his own world.

The "Atlantic view" of Shakespeare is, then, rooted in a particular understanding of history, a progressivist view, the same attitude that leads scholars increasingly to call Shakespeare's age the "early modern period," rather than the "Renaissance," as it was traditionally known. To speak of "the early modern period" is to see Shakespeare's age as leading up to our own, and thus to link him with our own concerns. This vocabulary subliminally works to diminish the age in our eyes—as *early* modern, it manifests only the beginnings, perhaps just the bare beginnings, of developments that were to reach their culmination and fruition only in our day—the *fully* modern age. The traditional designation for the age—the Renaissance—was admittedly backward-looking; it pointed to the rebirth of classical antiquity as the hallmark of the period. But this name also was a way of celebrating the period, respecting its integrity and achievement in their own right. Indeed, some of the original developers of the concept of the Renaissance, such as Jacob Burckhardt, regarded it as one of the peaks of human achievement, and were more likely to view later ages as a falling off from its heights. There seems to be something odd about labeling Shakespeare an "early modern dramatist," as if he merely started a process that only the likes of George Bernard Shaw, Eugene O'Neill, and Samuel Beckett were able to bring to fruition. Modernity's belief in scientific and technological progress may not translate so easily into the realm of culture.

What may at first seem to be a mere matter of semantics—what to call Shakespeare's age—thus turns out to have profound implications for how we understand him. The same is true of our geographic orientation in approaching his plays. The Atlantic vision that is widespread today is based on a legitimate historical perception—the fact that in Shakespeare's time the Atlantic was—no puns intended—the wave of the future, and the Mediterranean was becoming a backwater. In a stark formulation, this historical narrative runs something like this: In 1492 Columbus discovered America, while explorers such as Vasco da Gama and Magellan were opening up new trade routes to the Orient; they thereby broke the stranglehold that Mediterranean powers such as Venice had long maintained on the lucrative spice trade; from that point on, Shakespeare, like the rest of Europe, turned his eyes westward and began thinking about English imperial possibilities in the New World. *The Tempest* would then offer his proleptic take on plantation life in the Caribbean.

I have of course caricatured this view by stating it so bluntly. In fact this understanding of sixteenth-century Europe contains a good deal of truth, as well it should, since it has been developed with all the benefits of historical hindsight. Columbus's voyages and other navigational breakthroughs did in fact spell the doom of the Mediterranean as the center of the European world. But the displacement of the Mediterranean by the Atlantic did not happen

overnight, and its full effects and long-term consequences were not immediately apparent to observers at the time. We need to beware of attributing to
Shakespeare and his contemporaries an understanding of historical developments that has emerged only after the events unfolded in their entirety.

As several critics have stressed, just to speak of the British Empire in connection with Shakespeare's plays is to some extent anachronistic and potentially misleading.[11] From our standpoint, we know that Britain was to go on
to build a worldwide empire in the seventeenth and eighteenth centuries. But
Shakespeare witnessed only the first tentative and halting steps in this direction. In his day, the British Empire was still little more than a gleam in the
eyes of visionaries such as Walter Raleigh, Francis Drake, and Francis Bacon.
Shakespeare may have shared this imperial vision, as a play such as *Henry V*
suggests, and he may well have thought about the problem of empire. But
if he did, his primary model was, judging by his plays, the Roman Empire,
and if he looked to any contemporary examples, he would have turned to
the Habsburg and the Ottoman Empires. Note that all three of these empires had strong links to the Mediterranean. Even if we think that empire was
at the center of Shakespeare's concern, in his day the Mediterranean was at
the center of concern with empire.[12] Even the empires in the New World in
Shakespeare's day were being carved out not yet by the British but by Mediterranean peoples, largely from the Iberian Peninsula (sometimes led by Italian navigators).[13] Looking for empire as a subject in Shakespeare only leads us
back to the Mediterranean as the center of his imagination.

Many would say that the greatest scholar of the Mediterranean in the
twentieth century was the French historian Fernand Braudel. His views are
controversial, but no one would question his vast knowledge of the subject,
above all as manifested in his magisterial book, *The Mediterranean and the
Mediterranean World in the Age of Philip II*.[14] Braudel devoted this book to
proving that the Mediterranean world did not undergo a precipitous decline
in its economic power in the sixteenth century. He concentrates on the crucial issue of trade routes: "The circumnavigation of the Cape of Good Hope
did not strike an immediate death-blow to the Mediterranean spice trade,
. . . Germany continued to receive spices and pepper from Venice, and therefore . . . the Portuguese could not have established a permanent monopoly
in this precious traffic."[15] Braudel marshals an impressive array of statistics
to support his claims, especially with regard to the sustained importance of
Venice in the spice trade:

> In 1599, there was a drop in turnover, but Venetian trade was still reaching
> the respectable figure of a million and a half ducats, the total figure for the

whole of Christendom being in the region of 3 million. . . . In 1603 Venetian trade in the city was still worth a million and a half ducats. . . . So in 1600 as far as pepper and spices are concerned the predominance of the ocean route was far from established. With ups and downs, the rivalry between the two routes lasted over a century. . . . The dates and circumstances of the ultimate eclipse of the Mediterranean have yet to be ascertained. It cannot have been very far off as the seventeenth century began, but it was by no means yet accomplished—a hundred years after the date usually suggested as that of the death of the old queen of the world, the Mediterranean, dethroned by the new king, the Atlantic.[16]

Braudel's challenge to the narrative that Columbus and Vasco da Gama put Venice out of business in the sixteenth century helps explain why Shakespeare wrote two plays about the city, whose unusual character seems to have fascinated him. Like many, he may have thought of Venice as a potential model for Britain's future—an island community basing its greatness on its navy and its command of the sea. In addition to its continued economic importance, the Mediterranean maintained its cultural importance in the sixteenth century.

Even more distinctive, to our eyes, is the penetrating influence of western Mediterranean civilization. It spread in fact against the current of world history, reaching out to northern Europe which was soon to become the centre of world power: Mediterranean, Latin culture was to Protestant Europe what Greece was to Rome. It rapidly crossed the Atlantic both in the sixteenth and seventeenth centuries, and with this geographical extension over the ocean, the Mediterranean sphere of influence was finally complete, embracing Hispano-Portuguese America, the most brilliant America of the time.[17]

Braudel reminds us that even if we turn our eyes to the New World in sixteenth-century literary studies, we are looking at a branch of Mediterranean culture. When Braudel is at his most eloquent in speaking of the cultural importance of the Mediterranean, he broadens our sense of the range of that culture:

The Mediterranean remained, for a hundred years after Christopher Columbus and Vasco da Gama, the centre of the world, a strong and brilliant universe. How do we know? Because it was educating others, teaching them its own ways of life. And I would stress that it was the *whole* Mediterranean world, Moslem and Christian, which projected its lights beyond its shores. . . . As for Turkish Islam, it illuminated a cultural area which it owned in part, from the Balkans to the lands of Araby, into the depths of Asia and as far as the Indian Ocean. The art of the Turkish Empire, of which the Sulaimānīye mosque is the crowning achievement, spread far afield, affirming its supremacy, and architecture was only one element in this vast cultural expansion.[18]

Braudel's sixteenth-century Mediterranean is a multicultural world, the point where East met West in a productive exchange that enriched all sides in artistic and intellectual encounters. He is particularly struck by the hybrid character of Mediterranean culture, the way complex cultural syntheses emerged from the clashes of civilizations around its shores: "They merged to produce the extraordinary charivari suggestive of eastern ports as described by romantic poets: a rendezvous for every race, every religion, every kind of man, for everything in the way of hairstyles, fashions, foods and manners to be found in the Mediterranean."[19]

For Braudel to present the Mediterranean as the center of the sixteenth-century world is thus not as Eurocentric as it may at first sound. He may seem to be downgrading the Americas, Africa, and the Far East, but he really is arguing that the Mediterranean was centrally important in the sixteenth century precisely because it was the nodal point at which all the known continents could interact (three of them border on the Mediterranean and the other two were being colonized by Mediterranean peoples). Braudel keeps emphasizing that the Mediterranean constituted the frontier between East and West—specifically between Muslim and Christian civilizations—and in the sixteenth century it was by no means clear that Europe would go on to colonize the rest of the world. In fact, as Braudel repeatedly points out, in the sixteenth century the Ottoman Empire was the equal of, and perhaps even superior to, any European power and was constantly threatening Europe from the East. It crushed Hungarian forces at the Battle of Mohács in 1526 and almost conquered Vienna in 1529. One of the chief advantages of the way Braudel breaks through the normal borders of conventional national histories is that by giving us a picture of the Mediterranean as a whole, he reminds us that Charles V and Süleyman the Magnificent were contemporaries (Charles reigned as Holy Roman Emperor from 1521 to 1557; Süleyman reigned as Ottoman sultan from 1520 to 1566). At the height of their power, they divided the Mediterranean world between them.[20] Later in the century Charles's son, Philip II, saw his forces triumph over the Turks at the Battle of Lepanto in 1571, only to let the forces of Süleyman's son, Selim II, take Cyprus from Christian hands that same year.

Braudel thus shows that we do not need to cross the Atlantic to introduce the concept of multiculturalism into our understanding of the sixteenth century. The Atlantic view of Shakespeare has been part of a larger movement in literary studies to challenge the supremacy of European civilization in the name of multiculturalism. For example, by viewing *The Tempest* as portraying the colonization of the Caribbean, critics have raised the question of how Shakespeare represented the non-European Other in the person of Caliban.

Does the play embody the Eurocentric and racist view of the colonial subject as inferior and perhaps even subhuman, thus anticipating the stereotypes of non-European natives that were to dominate the British imperialist imagination in the nineteenth century? Or does Shakespeare display a secret sympathy for Caliban and question Prospero's title to rule the island, thus undermining the European claims to superiority that underwrote colonialism? In short, was Shakespeare bound by European cultural horizons or was he capable of seeing beyond them and appreciating genuine cultural difference?

These are interesting questions, and worth pursuing, but they are to some extent based on a false dichotomy. Their premise is that sixteenth-century Europe was a monocultural civilization, and thus multiculturalism can be found only outside its borders, perhaps by an Atlantic crossing. But as Braudel reminds us, sixteenth-century Europe was a multicultural civilization precisely because it was still centered on the multicultural Mediterranean. This was true above all in religious terms. When critics think of a culturally monolithic Europe, they particularly have in mind the idea that the continent was uniformly Christian. But in the East, the Ottoman Empire had conquered Greece, the Balkans, and a good deal of Central Europe, spreading Islam in its wake. And in the West, in the Iberian Peninsula, although Granada, the last Moorish (and Islamic) stronghold, had finally fallen in 1492 to the Catholic monarchs Ferdinand and Isabella, Spain in the sixteenth century still had to contend with the Moors who remained in the country (as well as with the Jews).[21] In short, despite the efforts of countries like Spain to establish Christian uniformity, sixteenth-century Europe remained in close contact with "alien" civilizations, especially along its Mediterranean shores. As *The Tempest* shows, in the sixteenth century one did not have to journey to Bermuda to encounter the non-European Other. In religious and other terms, sixteenth-century Europe incorporated the Other within its borders. The way that Shakespeare's plays center on the Mediterranean points to the fact that what we today call multiculturalism was at the center of his concerns as a playwright. In particular, the clash of civilizations turns out to be Shakespeare's fundamental formula for tragedy.

This is especially true in Shakespeare's Venetian plays, *The Merchant of Venice* and *Othello*. Venice seems to have intrigued Shakespeare precisely because of its effort to create a multicultural community, which made it stand out in sixteenth-century Europe.[22] While countries such as Spain were expelling their Moors and Jews, Venice seemed to be opening its doors to them. Venice appeared to be a remarkable experiment, an attempt to found a community not on religious or other cultural grounds but on an economic basis. People were admitted to Venice not because they shared a common culture but because they could contribute to its commercial activity. Venice embraced "aliens" for the sake of commerce and expected to unite them on the basis of commerce. The multicultural and commercial character of Venice is exactly what struck visitors in Shakespeare's day, as is evident in this passage from *Coryats Crudities*, the famous travel book: "Here you may both see all manner of fashions of attire, and heare all the languages of Christendome, besides those that are spoken by the barbarous Ethnickes; the frequencie of people being so great . . . that . . . a man may very properly calle it . . . a market place of the world, not of the citie."[23] As Coryat correctly intuits, the presence of "barbarous Ethnickes," that is, non-Christians, in Venice was somehow related to the city's aspirations to be a world marketplace. Like the stalls of its markets, which took in merchandise from every corner of the globe, Venice seemed to welcome foreigners from all over the world and allow them to participate in the life of the city. Sixteenth-century Venice epitomized the multiculturalism of the Mediterranean world.

But Shakespeare did not accept the multicultural ideal of Venice at face value; rather, he probed its problematic aspects. In the cases of both Shylock and Othello, Shakespeare shows that the integration of aliens into Venetian society is not complete; he thus uncovers the possibility of fundamental conflicts, tragic conflicts, in the city. Shylock does not want to dine with the Christians of Venice, and Brabantio, a Venetian senator, is horrified at the prospect of his daughter marrying the Moor, Othello. Venice admits foreigners into its ranks but it does so precisely for reasons that make it impossible to assimilate them fully. Venice is dominated by commercial interests, and yet it is mainly Christian in its population, and its commerce and its Christianity are at odds. As Christians, the Venetians are forbidden to take interest, but no commercial community can flourish without some kind of money market, which requires a return on loans. Venice's answer to its dilemma as a community at once Christian and commercial is to turn to Jews like Shylock, who can perform the function of moneylenders for the city's merchants. But that means that Shylock is made a citizen of Venice to perform a task that its majority Christians despise, which in turn means that Shylock is regarded as at best a second-class citizen in Venice. Indeed, at the culmination of the trial scene in act 4, Portia confounds Shylock by citing against him a statute that applies to aliens in Venice. Evidently Shylock both is and is not a citizen of Venice. He learns to his sorrow that the multiculturalism of Venice is ultimately a sham. Shakespeare has to labor to create a comic ending to a play that comes very close to turning Shylock into a tragic figure, trapped in the web of contradictions produced by a society that attempts to be both Christian and commercial.[24]

In *Othello*, Shakespeare develops the tragic implications of Venetian multiculturalism to their fullest. Both Venice's Christianity and its commercial character incline the city to peace. But in its efforts to dominate trade in the Mediterranean, Venice keeps running up against hostile neighbors. Chief among them are the Ottoman Turks, a warlike people who were conquering territory in several directions in the sixteenth century. Venice despises the Turks as barbarians, and yet it recognizes its need to enlist a warlike spirit in its own defense. This possibility is foreshadowed in *The Merchant of Venice* when the Prince of Morocco (a kind of comic forerunner of Othello) presents his credentials as a suitor to Portia. He stresses his military prowess, the fact that he "slew the Sophy and a Persian prince" and "won three fields of Sultan Solyman" (2.1.25–26)—that is, Süleyman the Magnificent. This is the kind of warrior Venice can use, and in *Othello* it has hired a barbarian to fight its battles, to fight fire with fire (while hoping not to get burned itself). That is the role Othello comes to play in Venice; as a mercenary soldier, he is the city's paid barbarian.[25] It does not matter to the Venetians that Othello is in fact civilized and a Christian. He has converted to Christianity, and thus his loyalty to his new faith is suspect. As the Jews and the Moors who converted to Christianity in Spain learned throughout the sixteenth century, *conversos* and *Moriscos* were never fully accepted by the orthodox community (this is a central theme in Cervantes's *Don Quixote*, where Sancho Panza prides himself on being an Old Christian, not a New, i.e., a convert). Venice turns to Othello only when it needs him, which is to say, in wartime. In peacetime, it turns to native Christian leaders and dismisses Othello from his post, replacing him with Cassio. As we see in the case of Brabantio, a representative Venetian does not really want his daughter to marry a Moorish foreigner. Only the immediate threat of a Turkish attack convinces the Duke to accept the marriage of Othello and Desdemona. Like Shylock, Othello is revealed to be a second-class citizen in Venice, welcomed and even celebrated when the city needs him to perform a function it cannot handle itself, but ultimately held in contempt because he is suited to that function precisely by an alien quality, what the city in fact regards as barbarism. The way Othello murders Desdemona—despite the fact that he is egged on by the nominally Christian Iago—appears to Venice to confirm its suspicions about his barbarian character; in the eyes of Venice, he reverts to type. Othello is a profoundly tragic figure, caught between the contradictory demands of Christian domesticity and the heroic ethos of a pagan warrior.[26]

The Merchant of Venice and *Othello* reveal what Shakespeare was able to do with a Mediterranean setting. Venice, with its colonial outposts like Cyprus, sat at the crossroads of the Mediterranean, and hence at the center of its great cultural crosscurrents. Above all, it was the point at which Christians, Jews, and Muslims intersected and interacted. Shakespeare portrays this cultural exchange in all its complexity, exploring the hopes it raised but also its potential for tragedy. Accordingly, some of the most interesting work on Shakespeare takes up his plays in a Mediterranean context. I would cite particularly Daniel Vitkus's *Turning Turk: English Theater and the Multicultural Mediterranean, 1570–1630*, which contains an excellent chapter on *Othello*. Vitkus shows that awareness of the Ottoman Turks suffused the drama of Shakespeare's day, in the *Tamburlaine* plays of Marlowe, for example, but also in lesser-known works, such as Thomas Kyd's *The Tragedye of Soliman and Perseda*, Thomas Heywood's *The Fair Maid of the West*, Robert Daborne's *A Christian Turned Turk*, and Philip Massinger's *The Renegado*. Vitkus's book participates in a general reorientation in Renaissance studies that is turning eastward to the Ottoman Empire, rather than westward to the Americas. This movement has been led by Lisa Jardine and Jerry Brotton, for example, in their joint book *Global Interests: Renaissance Art Between East & West* and in Brotton's solo effort, *The Renaissance Bazaar: From the Silk Road to Michelangelo*. Jardine and Brotton argue for a more global conception of the Renaissance, one no longer focused exclusively on Europe, but instead expanded to recognize the contribution of the Ottoman Empire to what has become known as Renaissance culture.[27]

Jardine and Brotton emphasize the economic underpinnings of the Renaissance and see its cultural achievements driven by the new consumer demands of the day and financed by the new wealth generated in the emerging world of capitalist commerce. Since these economic developments were, as Braudel argued, centered on the Mediterranean, it is understandable that this area remained the focus of Renaissance culture even in the sixteenth century, and hence occupied a central place in Shakespeare's imagination. Moreover, like Braudel, Jardine and Brotton emphasize the hybrid character of Renaissance culture. Since they see it as growing out of economic exchange, they go on to conceptualize it as cultural exchange. They stress how trade cuts across political boundaries, even when governments try to inhibit it, and thus the commercial activity of the Mediterranean ran counter to efforts to impose cultural homogeneity.[28] In this economic and cultural exchange, the Ottoman Empire did not play the role of a junior partner, as its later, weakened position vis-à-vis Europe would suggest.[29] On the contrary, in the sixteenth century the Ottoman Empire was an object of envy for Western Europeans, a source of much coveted goods and pictured as a site of unimaginable wealth.

Jardine and Brotton document all the positive contributions the Ottoman Turks made to Renaissance culture in areas as diverse as mathematics and horse breeding, and thereby reconceptualize the Renaissance as a product of East–West hybridity:

> Once it is recognized that for purposes of artistic and other material transaction, the boundaries between what we will refer to here as East and West were thoroughly permeable in the Renaissance, and that even in situations of conflict, mutual recognition of icons and images could be used adversarially with creative verve, fresh possibilities for cultural cross-fertilization and a two-way traffic in influence open up at every turn. With these possibilities and their implications comes the inevitable recognition that cultural histories apparently utterly distinct, and traditionally kept entirely separate, are ripe to be rewritten as shared East/West undertakings.[30]

As interesting as all this sounds for our general understanding of the Renaissance, one might still question its relevance to Shakespeare's England. Today we think of the Ottoman Empire as truly exotic and assume that it must have seemed very remote to the English in Shakespeare's day, at the other end of their world and unrelated to their daily lives. But in fact the Ottoman Empire was much closer to Shakespeare's England than we tend to think today, in many respects closer than the Americas. The Ottoman Empire, especially during the reign of Süleyman the Magnificent, became heavily involved in pan-European politics. In his ongoing struggle against his principal European opponents, the Habsburgs, Süleyman sought alliances with their enemies, such as the French kings, and he also encouraged the rise of Protestantism as a way of weakening the Catholic Habsburgs. Braudel devotes a section of his history of the Mediterranean specifically to Anglo–Turkish relations, as part of his effort to show how important Mediterranean trade was to England in the sixteenth century, far more important than any form of trade in the Atlantic at that moment.

Braudel discusses at length negotiations that took place in 1579 between Queen Elizabeth and the reigning Ottoman sultan, Murad III, noting that the queen "received by way of France, a letter full of promises from the sultan, enjoining her, in order to preserve and make even closer her ties with the king of France, to marry . . . the Duke of Anjou. The letter adds that English merchants whether coming by land or sea would receive a cordial welcome."[31] In trying to ally himself with England, Murad was pursuing Süleyman's strategy of creating a coalition of European forces against the Habsburgs, but he was also interested in developing trade relations with England, especially since the Turks needed English tin to manufacture cannons. The English were similarly interested in cultivating the Ottoman Empire as an ally against the Habsburgs, who from their Spanish stronghold represented by far the greatest military threat to England. The English were drawn to a Turkish alliance out of economic motives as well. The result was a formal treaty between Britain and the Ottoman Empire signed in 1580, which granted the English valuable trading rights in the eastern Mediterranean. Accordingly, in 1581 Elizabeth chartered the Levant Company to exploit the new commercial opportunities, with immediate and great success, as Braudel reports: "By 1595 the Levant Company had fifteen ships and 790 seamen at its disposal. It was trading with Alexandretta, Cyprus, Chios, Zante, and to a lesser extent with Venice and Algiers."[32] Since, as Braudel points out, "the East India Company, founded in 1600, was an offshoot of the Levant company,"[33] Anglo–Turkish relations in the sixteenth century were more important to the ultimate development of the British Empire than anything English merchants were doing in the Atlantic at that time. It was after all India that was the jewel in the crown, not Bermuda.

In short, far from being some remote and shadowy fairyland on the edge of a map, by the 1590s, the Ottoman Empire was an active trading partner of England and a political/military ally. Shakespeare lived before the emergence of modern nation-states in the full sense of the term, and the political boundaries in his day were more fluid than they later were to become. His world was in fact dominated by transnational powers—the Habsburg and the Ottoman Empires—which cut across the borders of the political map of Europe today. Shakespeare's world was more "globalized" than we tend to think, and his contemporaries took a real, not just a fancied, interest in the Ottoman Empire. Actual historical events stand behind Shakespeare's Mediterranean plays. *Othello* points to the eventual conquest of Cyprus by the Turks, and several critics have argued that the destruction of the Turkish fleet in the play calls to mind the Battle of Lepanto.[34] Indeed, the Battle of Lepanto had a great impact on Renaissance literature. It stands behind *Don Quixote* (Cervantes actually fought at Lepanto), and James VI of Scotland (later James I of England) wrote a poem on the subject in 1585. Shakespeare's *Much Ado About Nothing* seems in some strange way to be connected to Lepanto. The play takes place in Messina—the Sicilian port from which the Christian fleet sailed against the Turks at Lepanto—and it contains a Don John, the bastard brother of a Spanish ruler (the Prince of Aragon). The Christian fleet at Lepanto was commanded by Don John of Austria, the bastard brother of King Philip II of Spain (and hence the son of Emperor Charles V and thus linked to the House of Aragon).[35]

References to the Ottoman Turks appear in unlikely places in Shakespeare's plays, even in the English histories. When Prince Hal ascends the throne in *Henry IV, Part II*, he reassures his audience, especially his brothers:

> This is the English, not the Turkish court,
> Not Amurath an Amurath succeeds,
> But Harry Harry. (5.2.47–49)

Henry is referring to the Ottoman sultans' infamous practice—instituted by Süleyman's father Selim I—of having their brothers strangled when they assumed office, and "Amurath" is anachronistically none other than Murad III, the sultan who signed the Anglo-Turkish Treaty of 1580. Shakespeare evidently felt that he could rely on his audience to recognize this reference to recent Turkish history, which was after all a matter of considerable interest to the English people. At the end of *Henry V*, the king introduces another reference to the Ottoman Empire, when he tells Katherine, his hoped-for bride-to-be: "Shall not thou and I, between Saint Denis and Saint George, compound a boy, half French, half English, that shall go to Constantinople and take the Turk by the beard?" (5.2.206–9). This passage involves another anachronism, since Henry died in 1422 and the Turks did not take Constantinople until 1453. This "mistake" therefore offers strong evidence that the Ottoman Empire was on the map of Shakespeare's imagination—he could find no better way of portraying the ultimate imperial ambition than to have Henry speak of reclaiming the empire of the East from the Turks.[36]

Critics are thus right to stress the importance of the Ottoman Empire in Shakespeare's world picture and thereby to recenter it on the Mediterranean. But I would question one aspect of this critical development. Jardine and Brotton believe that by uncovering the importance of the Ottoman contribution to the Renaissance, they have corrected an error that goes back to Burckhardt—an overestimation of the role of classical antiquity in producing the Renaissance. As Brotton argues:

> These stories are just part of a larger body of evidence that confounds an increasingly moribund version of the Renaissance. This account claims that from the late 14th century, European culture rediscovered a lost Graeco-Roman intellectual tradition that allowed scholars and artists based almost exclusively in Italy to develop more cultured and civilized ways of thinking and acting. . . . This book suggests that once we begin to understand the impact of eastern cultures upon mainland Europe c.1400–1600, then this traditional understanding of the European Renaissance collapses.[37]

This traditional understanding may need to be corrected or modified or supplemented, but does it really *collapse*? One may grant Brotton an author's license to trumpet the originality and power of his thesis, but he clearly overstates his case and draws a false conclusion from his evidence. His argument is in fact based on just the kind of sharp dualism between East and West that he and Jardine are elsewhere concerned with deconstructing.

To assert the importance of the Ottoman Empire to the European Renaissance is not to deny the importance of the classical tradition because the Ottoman Empire was itself profoundly influenced by that tradition.[38] One simply has to look at what Braudel called the "crowning achievement" of Ottoman culture, the Süleymaniye Mosque, to see that it was modeled on Hagia Sophia, that is, on a Christian church itself built on Roman models by the Roman emperor Justinian in the sixth century CE. Jardine and Brotton have made a genuine contribution in documenting the fact that the Renaissance in the West incorporated many elements from the East, but, by the same token, the East incorporated many elements from the West. As the representative of the Orient in the East–West nexus of the sixteenth-century Mediterranean, the Ottoman Empire was no more monocultural than Europe: "It was an empire based on an innovative combination of multiple inheritances: Inner Asian, Anatolian, Byzantine, Islamic and European."[39] With its many layers of cultural sedimentation, the Mediterranean is a case of East–West hybridity all the way down to the foundation stones of Troy.[40]

A more careful formulation of the Jardine-Brotton thesis might go this way: the Ottoman Empire made many contributions to the Renaissance, among them the fact that it served as one of the conduits of the classical tradition to Europe. Scholars have long recognized that the Byzantine Empire helped transmit classical ideas and texts to Renaissance Italy. In conquering Constantinople, the Ottoman Empire sought to take the place of the Byzantine, literally occupying the same ground and drawing upon its centuries-old classical heritage. Jardine and Brotton themselves repeatedly show that the Ottoman sultans modeled themselves on classical figures such as Alexander the Great[41] and the Caesars.[42] In discussing the commonalities between East and West, Jardine and Brotton speak of how Western Europe was encouraged "to bond culturally with its Eastern neighbours, as participating in a shared classical heritage, recognized and inhabited by both."[43] Brotton writes at length about Mehmed, the Ottoman conqueror of Constantinople:

> In fact Mehmed was not the barbaric despot often evoked in the western historical imagination. His affinity with the political ambitions and cultural tastes of his Italian counterparts was stronger than is often imagined. While directing the siege of Constantinople, Mehmed employed several Italian humanists who 'read to the Sultan daily from ancient historians such as Laertius, Herodotus, Livy and Quintus Curtius'. . . . Mehmed and his predecessors had spent decades conquering much of the territory of the classical Graeco-Roman world to which 15th-century Italian humanism looked for much of its

inspiration. It is therefore hardly surprising that the cultured Mehmed should share similar cultural and historical influences and aspirations, and that his imperial achievements were "in no way inferior to those of Alexander the Macedonian" (Alexander the Great), as one of Mehmed's Greek chroniclers told him.[44]

If Brotton is correct in this account, then the traditional understanding of the Renaissance as the revival of classical antiquity can hardly be said to collapse.[45] Far from diminishing the importance of classical antiquity, Jardine and Brotton have shown how much broader its sphere of influence was, extending to the Ottoman Empire.[46]

Thus I return to the point with which I began—to understand the centrality of the Mediterranean in Shakespeare's imagination is to understand the centrality of the classical tradition. Just under half his Mediterranean plays are set in classical antiquity, the world of the Greeks and the Romans. For Shakespeare the pull toward the Mediterranean was also a pull toward the past. He evidently wanted to understand the classical roots of European civilization, and devoted a substantial portion of his dramatic career to portraying the world of ancient Rome in particular. For Shakespeare this was a genuinely "archaeological" enterprise. He understood how different the ancient world was from the modern, and he actively explored what it meant to live under radically different customs and institutions, such as a pagan religion or a republican constitution. In many ways, Shakespeare's Romans are as alien to modern Europeans as any figures from the New World. Indeed, in Shakespeare's portrayal, a fierce Roman warrior such as Coriolanus comes across as a kind of savage.[47]

Moreover, Shakespeare views the ancient Mediterranean world as multicultural. In *Antony and Cleopatra*, for example, he stages the encounter between East and West in the form of the meeting of Egypt and Rome, and he traces the Orientalizing of Rome and the Occidentalizing of Egypt.[48] Indeed in *Antony and Cleopatra* we witness the birth of a pan-Mediterranean world as the ultimate legacy of Roman conquests. The result is a whole series of cultural hybrids, including "an Alexandrian feast" and "Egyptian bacchanals" in Italy (2.7.96, 104) and "a Roman thought" in Egypt (1.2.83).[49] The Mediterranean world of *Antony and Cleopatra* is a remarkably fluid world, in which one thing keeps changing into another: "Your serpent of Egypt is bred now of your mud by the operation of your sun. So is your crocodile. . . . It lives by that which nourisheth it, and the elements once out of it, it transmigrates" (2.7.26–27, 44–45). In this mutable and hybrid world, Antony can no longer hold on to a stable identity: "Here I am Antony, / Yet cannot hold this visible shape" (4.14.13–14). The level of hybridity only increases when the ancient Mediterranean meets the modern, as it does in *Cymbeline*, which is set in the time of imperial Rome but seems to look forward to the Italianate treachery of the Renaissance, embodied in Iachimo, the dramatic cousin of Iago in *Othello*.

That Shakespeare mapped the modern Mediterranean on the ancient is evident in a famously enigmatic passage in *The Tempest*, when the ship-wrecked courtiers are discussing the marriage of King Alonso's daughter to the King of Tunis (a pan-Mediterranean union if there ever were one). Somehow the name of Virgil's Dido comes up, provoking this exchange between Adrian and Gonzago:

ADR: "Widow Dido," said you? You make me study of that.
     She was of Carthage, not of Tunis.
GON: This Tunis, sir, was Carthage.
ADR: Carthage?
GON: I assure you, Carthage. (2.1.82–86)

In Shakespeare's imagination, the modern world of the Mediterranean is superimposed on the ancient (even though, as G. Blakemore Evans points out in his note, "Tunis and Carthage were separate cities, though not far apart").[50] In his attraction to the Mediterranean, Shakespeare reveals himself to be a true child of the Renaissance, constantly drawn to classical sources and analogues for modern European civilization.

Thus the importance of the Mediterranean for Shakespeare points not just to East–West hybridity in Renaissance culture, but to ancient-modern hybridity as well, which is to say, classical–Christian hybridity. Shakespeare's plays, especially his tragedies, display a profound awareness of the complex texture of Renaissance culture, as it tried to revive the values of classical antiquity within a largely Christian context. Hamlet is the quintessential Renaissance figure in Shakespeare because he is torn between classical and Christian attitudes toward revenge.[51] Othello's roots in the Ottoman world are important largely because they put him in touch with an ancient, pagan model of the heroic warrior, an ideal in many respects alien to Christian Venice. As if to emphasize the point, Shakespeare has him speak in Homeric similes, filled with classical references as if he had just stepped out of the pages of an ancient epic:[52]

> Like to the Pontic Sea,
> Whose icy current and compulsive course

Nev'r feels retiring ebb, but keeps due on
To the Propontic and the Hellespont,
Even so my bloody thoughts, with violent pace,
Shall nev'r look back. (3.3.453–58)

By evoking the ancient names of the Black Sea, the Sea of Marmara, and the Dardanelles, Shakespeare links the Ottoman world with classical antiquity. For Shakespeare the call of the Mediterranean was the call of the past, and classical culture was an integral part of the multicultural Mediterranean. The importance of the Mediterranean in Shakespeare reminds us that, from the beginning, European culture was multicultural. Thus in addition to drawing upon its fruitful encounters with the exotic East and the wondrous New World, the European Renaissance emerged from a complex clash of antithetical impulses as the classical past met the Christian present. Out of all these encounters, with the Mediterranean past as well as the Mediterranean present, the richness of Shakespeare's imaginative world grew.

Antony and Cleopatra: Empire, Globalization,
and the Clash of Civilizations

Ben Jonson's famous tribute to William Shakespeare—"He was not of an age, but for all time"—has often been taken as a measure of his greatness.[1] Generation after generation has kept coming back to his plays as a font of wisdom. Shakespeare has been praised for the universality of his genius—the fact that even after four centuries his insights remain relevant to our world. But is it really true that Shakespeare has something to say about our problems today? Are there some issues that are uniquely modern, which Shakespeare, as an Elizabethan playwright, could not possibly have comprehended or even been aware of?

Take, for example, the issue of globalization, arguably the central concern of the contemporary world. Many contend that globalization, especially the clash of civilizations it generates, is a phenomenon unique to the late twentieth and early twenty-first centuries. Samuel P. Huntington, for example, writes, "In the post–Cold War world, for the first time in history, global politics has become multipolar *and* multicivilizational. During most of human existence, contacts between civilizations were intermittent or nonexistent."[2] Modern technological advances, above all in high-speed communication and transportation, are often said to explain why the globalization of the modern world constitutes an entirely new and unprecedented development. With no knowledge of jet aircraft or the Internet, how could Shakespeare have anything to say about globalization?

But perhaps contemporary globalization is not entirely without precedent. Globalization in the twentieth century developed out of the era of European imperialist expansion in the nineteenth century. Indeed, many have viewed some aspects of globalization as a form of neocolonialism. If the concept of empire is intertwined with the concept of globalization, then there is at least one historical precedent for the integration of the modern world—the Roman Empire.[3] In its self-understanding, the Roman Empire was a globalizing force. It sought to create one world out of the vast territory that Roman armies had conquered over the centuries. Modern geographers would be quick to point out that even at the peak of its expansion, the Roman Empire never came close to encompassing the whole of the earth. But of course the Romans themselves were aware of this fact. They knew that they traded—and sometimes warred—with people outside the borders of their empire. Nevertheless, in very important ways the Romans chose to regard the Roman world as *the* world simply, and worked to integrate it into a whole in a manner that is very similar to what we now call globalization. For example, in their extensive road-building projects, the Romans understood full well the central importance of rapid transportation in creating an integrated world. Above all, in putting together their empire, the Romans brought about exactly the situation of clashing civilizations that Huntington regards as unique to the contemporary world. Under Roman rule, the Mediterranean world offers fascinating case studies of what happens when widely divergent civilizations come into contact, interact, and transform each other, often in unpredictable and surprising ways.

When people speak of globalization today, they often have in mind the Americanization of the globe, the relentless expansion of American economic and cultural power and influence. For many, the chief form globalization takes is the spread of McDonald's, Coca-Cola, KFC, and other American brands and franchises all around the world. The corresponding phenomenon in antiquity was the Romanization of the Mediterranean world.[4] People from the Iberian Peninsula to the Middle East suddenly found themselves confronted by the strange spectacle of Roman temples, statues, aqueducts, and amphitheaters springing up in their midst. But globalization is not now, and was not then, a one-way street.[5] Even as the globe today is being Americanized, America is being globalized. Its identity is being profoundly transformed by its encounter with alien civilizations, as witness significant changes in its eating habits, clothing fashions, musical taste, and even its religious beliefs, as well as other cultural phenomena subject to foreign influences. Ancient Rome was also profoundly changed by its encounter with alien civilizations and its attempt to bring them within its cultural orbit. The presence of Cestius's pyramid to this day in downtown Rome is a monument to the way Rome was Egyptianized, even as it was Romanizing Egypt.[6] The complex intermixture of cultural forms that the Roman Empire generated is the principal reason why it provides a precedent for contemporary globalization.

From this perspective, Shakespeare did have access to the kind of phenomena we label "globalization," because he was a profound student of Roman history and politics. His interest in Rome is evident throughout his career, from his earliest to his last plays, and can be found even in his poetry (*The Rape of Lucrece*, for example). Shakespeare's Roman plays trace the development of Rome from a republic to an empire, culminating in *Antony and Cleopatra* as his portrait of the nascent imperial regime.[7] The play explores the connections between empire and what we call globalization. It shows that the desire for empire is a drive toward universality, an urge to demolish existing borders and create one world. In Shakespeare's portrayal, the Roman Empire aspires to become "the universal landlord" (3.13.72).[8] The play contains many references to Rome's efforts to defeat the last of its viable enemies on its eastern frontier, the Parthians (see, for example, act 3, scene 1). Once its borders are secure, Rome can go about the task of imposing its rule on the whole Mediterranean world. That is why Octavius Caesar speaks optimistically about the emergence of what came to be known as the *Pax Romana*:

> The time of universal peace is near.
> Prove this a prosp'rous day, the three-nook'd world
> Shall bear the olive freely. (4.6.4–6)

Uniting three continents in peace—Europe, Asia, and Africa—Rome will create a universal community, a unified world.

Roman rhetoric in *Antony and Cleopatra* is emphatically "global." Shakespeare's Romans refer to themselves and to each other in terms that call to mind one world united under their rule. The triumvirs are presented as dividing the whole world among themselves.[9] Antony is called "the triple pillar of the world" (1.1.12); he regards himself as "the greatest prince o' th' world" (4.15.54). Lepidus is referred to as "the third part of the world" (2.7.92). Antony says to Octavius: "The third part o' th' world is yours" (2.2.63). Pompey speaks of the triumvirs as "the senators alone of this great world" (2.6.9), and Menas calls them "these three world-sharers" (2.7.70). Once Octavius triumphs over both Lepidus and Antony, he becomes "sole sir o' th' world" (5.2.120). The Romans are acutely conscious that they are performing on a world stage—that their actions have global consequences and the whole world is watching what they do. Proclaiming the grandeur of his love with Cleopatra, Antony wants "the world to weet / We stand up peerless" (1.1.39–40). Octavius knows that people throughout the Empire will pass judgment on how he treats Cleopatra. Speaking through a subordinate (Proculeius), he calls upon her to act accordingly: "Let the world see / His nobleness well acted" (5.2.44–45). Time and again in *Antony and Cleopatra* words and deeds make it clear that what is at stake in the play is nothing less than the fate of the world as a whole.

When the pirate Menas offers to kill the triumvirs for Pompey, his speech is saturated with language that points to the fact that Rome has brought all the world under one yoke:

MENAS: Wilt thou be lord of all the world?
POMPEY: What say'st thou?
MENAS: Wilt thou be lord of the whole world? That's twice.
POMPEY: How should that be?
MENAS: But entertain it,
And though thou think me poor, I am the man
Will give thee all the world.
POMPEY: Hast thou drunk well?
MENAS: No, Pompey, I have kept me from the cup.
Thou art, if thou dar'st be, the earthly Jove;
Whate'er the ocean pales, or sky inclips,
Is thine, if thou wilt ha't. (2.7.61–69)

Menas understands that in the new era of imperial politics, a truly ambitious man must aim at global hegemony.

Shakespeare draws on his considerable skills as a dramatist to suggest the global dimensions of the new imperial world taking shape in *Antony and Cleopatra*. He took advantage of the fluidity of Elizabethan/Jacobean staging; given the absence of scenery, he is able to change scenes effortlessly to suggest how swiftly things move in the world of *Antony and Cleopatra* and what vast distances can be covered in the blink of an eye. In the divisions editors introduce in modern texts, the play contains an exceptional number of scenes (thirteen in act 3 and fifteen in act 4 alone), as it moves over much of the Mediterranean world with sometimes dizzying speed. The characters themselves remark on how quickly things happen; armies turn up before they are expected and news of their movements arrives even faster. As the crucial battle of Actium develops, Antony is shocked by the speed with which Octavius's forces move:

Is it not strange, Canidius,
That from Tarentum to Brundusium
He could so quickly cut the Ionian Sea
And take in Toryne? (3.7.20–23)

When a messenger arrives with more military bad news, Antony marvels at Octavius's mobility: "Can he be there in person? 'Tis impossible" (3.7.56). We may think of Roman means of transportation as slow, but Shakespeare's Antony is already voicing the typical response to globalizing forces today: "This speed of Caesar's / Carries beyond belief" (3.7.74–75).

Given the size of the Roman Empire portrayed in *Antony and Cleopatra*, communication between its widely dispersed seats of power is remarkably easy and dependable. The Mediterranean world of the play is crisscrossed by apparently tireless messengers. Indeed, "mail delivery" in the Roman Empire seems more frequent than it is in the United States today. Octavius receives messages many times a day from the imperial frontiers:

> Thy biddings have been done, and every hour
> Most noble Caesar, shalt thou have report
> How 'tis abroad. (1.4.34–36)

Cleopatra is just as determined to stay in daily communication with Antony:

> Get me ink and paper.
> He shall have every day a several greeting.
> Or I'll unpeople Egypt. (1.5.76–78)

The imperial messenger service may not be quite as fast as the Internet, but it evidently gets the job done. Rome is technologically primitive by comparison with the contemporary world, but Shakespeare shows it already aspiring to a kind of global integration via rapid transportation and communication.

Having triumphed militarily over all rival regimes and linked up its vast dominions with roads and communication routes, Rome seems poised to impose its way of life on the entire Mediterranean world. With everyone acknowledging the authority of Rome, the Romanization of Egypt seems to be the order of the day. When Cleopatra thinks of committing suicide in the wake of Antony's death, she claims to be following a Roman model: "Let's do't after the high Roman fashion" (4.15.87). Roman religion has evidently begun to permeate Egyptian society at all levels, from the lowest to the highest. The Egyptian eunuch Mardian talks of "what Venus did with Mars" (1.5.18), while Cleopatra's speech is filled with references to Roman deities:

> Though he be painted one way like a Gorgon,
> The other way's a Mars. (2.5.116–17)

> Had I great Juno's power,
> The strong-wing'd Mercury should fetch thee up
> And set thee by Jove's side. (4.15.34–36)

This is exactly what one would expect to see in a *Roman* Empire. The Roman gods begin to take the place of local deities, even in a land as old as Egypt, whose religious traditions predate those of Rome by centuries. A triumphant Empire gets to impose its will and its customs on the people it conquered.

But Shakespeare seems more interested in the Egyptianizing of Rome than in the Romanizing of Egypt.[10] Rome has conquered Egypt militarily, but Egypt seems to be conquering Rome culturally.[11] In postcolonial studies today, this process is often labeled "The Empire Strikes Back," as conquered people pursue subtle strategies of raising doubts about and even subverting the way of life of their ostensible masters.[12] In *Antony and Cleopatra* the Romans are inordinately fascinated by the exotic world of Egypt.[13] They want to hear about its strange customs and listen avidly to tales, no matter how fantastic or improbable, of its pyramids and crocodiles (2.7). Above all, they are entranced by stories of the fabulous Cleopatra, Antony's "Egyptian dish" (2.6.126). Cleopatra symbolizes the many ways that a captive can captivate her conquerors. Repeatedly defeated in battle by Roman armies, she uses her wiles to enchant one Roman ruler after another—from Julius Caesar to Mark Antony to (she hopes) Octavius Caesar. Exploiting her sexual allure, Cleopatra seeks to turn the tables on her masters and bring them under her spell. If she no longer can rule directly as queen of Egypt, she hopes to rule indirectly by mastering her masters. Rumors of her erotic conquests arouse the Romans' senses, and she threatens to overturn their hierarchy of values:

> Other women cloy
> The appetites they feed, but she makes hungry
> Where most she satisfies; for vilest things
> Become themselves in her, that the holy priests
> Bless her when she is riggish. (2.2.235–39)

The breakdown in traditional Roman discipline is evident in their excessive interest in "Egyptian cookery" (2.6.63). A new Roman tendency toward indulgence in food and drink has been inspired by Egyptian models. When the triumvirs banquet with Pompey, their celebration "ripens towards" an "Alexandrian feast" (2.7.96–97). At this feast, the formerly restrained Romans end up abandoning their moderation and dancing "the Egyptian bacchanals" (2.7.104).[14] Even the normally sober and temperate Octavius admits that he grows drunk (2.7.125–26). The Egyptians have begun to talk of Roman deities, but the Romans have undergone a more fundamental transformation: they have begun to behave like Egyptians. Their firm Roman identity is shaken as they become increasingly open to foreign influences. After centuries of martial discipline under the republican regime—the very

source of Rome's ability to triumph over its enemies—imperial Rome becomes decadent, partially as a result of encountering the luxury and idleness
of the Egyptian way of life. Rome's success in militarily defeating its enemies
allows the Romans to relax and rest on their laurels. In the process, they grow
soft and self-indulgent and become the mirror image of the decadent people
they conquered. Shakespeare's Rome illustrates a general principle about
empire—the country that dominates the world is often altered just as much
in the process as the world it tries to dominate.

In *Julius Caesar*, Shakespeare portrays Rome breaking with its longstanding republican traditions and moving toward one-man rule. *Antony
and Cleopatra* portrays the working out of this imperial logic, and Rome's
encounter with Egypt, which had centuries of imperial rule behind it, accelerates the corruption of traditional Roman institutions. Octavius professes
shock at the way Antony blatantly adopts decadent Egyptian customs in his
public behavior with Cleopatra:

> I' th' market-place, on a tribunal silver'd,
> Cleopatra and himself in chains of gold
> Were publicly enthron'd. At their feet sat
> Caesarion, whom they call my father's son,
> And all the unlawful issue that their lust
> Since then hath made between them. Unto her
> He gave the stablishment of Egypt, made her
> Of lower Syria, Cyprus, Lydia,
> Absolute queen.
> . . . .
> His sons he there proclaim'd the kings of kings:
> Great Media, Parthia, and Armenia
> He gave to Alexander; to Ptolemy he assign'd
> Syria, Cilicia, and Phoenicia. She
> In th' abiliments of the goddess Isis
> That day appear'd. (3.6.3–11, 13–18)

When Maecenas chimes in: "Let Rome be thus / Inform'd" (3.6.18–19), he
shows that he is aware of how un-Roman Antony's imperious behavior must
seem to anyone steeped in the city's republican traditions.

In *Julius Caesar*, Antony sees how reluctant his master Julius Caesar is to
adopt the ways of a king in public in Rome (precisely what is at issue when
Antony offers him a crown in act 1, scene 2). Ever the shrewd politician, Caesar knows that the republican Romans loathe the idea of living under a king.
But now in Egypt, Antony embraces kingly grandeur, openly proclaiming his
sons "kings of kings" and displaying an unseemly (and un-Roman) interest

in founding a dynasty. In the Republic, he was the leader of a citizen-army, and at least professed to treat the Roman populace as active participants in the regime. Now Antony elevates himself above the common people, treating them as passive subjects, who must bow down and worship him. He assumes the role not just of a king, but of a god-king, accompanied by Cleopatra in the guise of Isis (an Egyptian goddess, not a Roman one).[15] All the silver and gold are characteristic of Oriental luxury and ostentation, the antithesis of the simplicity and moderation characteristic of republican Rome. Although nominally the conqueror of Egypt, Antony has gone over to the Egyptian side. More generally, in the clash of Roman and Egyptian civilization he has surrendered to the exotic East. In addition to pharaonic models of Oriental despotism, the names Alexander and Ptolemy call to mind the Hellenistic god-kings who came to power in the wake of Alexander the Great and his imperial conquests.[16] Hellenism is one more un-Roman influence on Antony. After his military defeat at Actium, his one request of Octavius is to be allowed to live "a private man in Athens" (3.12.15), where presumably he can indulge his taste for all things Greek.[17]

Octavius sees the propaganda value of making Antony's un-Roman actions known to the Roman public. And yet these actions are un-Roman only by the standards of the now defunct Republic. They are perfectly suited to the new imperial regime. Ironically, Octavius condemns in Antony a public pose that he was soon to adopt himself. As the first established emperor in Rome, Octavius as Augustus Caesar went on to become a god-king himself and founded his own dynasty.[18] Representations of Augustus as a god sprung up throughout the empire, on coins as well as monuments.

Images of Oriental despotism are basic to a broader pattern in *Antony and Cleopatra*, its evocation of stereotypes of the East. Discussions of contemporary globalization and the clash of civilizations are often cast in terms of East versus West, and a frequently debated question is: after centuries of the West dominating the East and the rest of the world, will the positions be reversed, and the East—nations such as China, Japan, and India—come to dominate a globalized world? *Antony and Cleopatra* portrays a world strongly polarized in terms of East versus West, with Egypt representing the former and Rome the latter. The sense of Egypt as the exotic East is emphasized in the play. Of Cleopatra, Alexas reports that Antony says, "All the East, / . . . shall call her mistress" (1.5.46–47). Thinking of Egypt and Cleopatra, Antony says, "I' th' East my pleasure lies" (2.3.41) and later he reiterates the point: "The beds i' th' East are soft" (2.6.50). And as Cleopatra is dying, her maid Charmian thinks of her as the "eastern star" (5.2.308). With all this talk of the East as an exotic, sensuous realm, presided over by the female Cleopatra, *Antony and*

Cleopatra provides a classic example of what is known as Orientalism.[19] The play is constructed in terms of a whole series of binary oppositions that define the West (Rome) by contrast with the East (Egypt).[20] The West is presented as rational, disciplined, active, busy, emotionally restrained, moderate, and masculine, while the East is presented as irrational, undisciplined, passive, idle, emotionally self-indulgent, luxurious, and feminine. Cleopatra's court is a textbook example of an Orientalist fantasy, complete with the eunuchs who help to stamp the Orient as effeminate. Her wild swings of mood and violent outbursts of anger—her inability to control her emotions—identify her as the archetype of the Oriental despot. In terms of another stereotype, she is also the Oriental seductress, who tempts the European hero away from his Western way of life, subverting his allegiance to his homeland and introducing Antony to exotic customs and decadent pleasures that unfit him for command of his armies and himself.[21]

Orientalism is usually thought of as presenting the West as simply superior to and dominant over the East, but Shakespeare complicates the picture in *Antony and Cleopatra* by blurring the lines between East and West, specifically by portraying a heavily Orientalized Rome.[22] The Rome that traditionally represents the West seems to be largely a thing of the past in *Antony and Cleopatra*; it is the Rome of the moribund Republic. Antony provides the best measure of how far the Orientalizing of the Rome of *Antony and Cleopatra* has proceeded. When Octavius speaks of Antony's military discipline—his traditional Roman ability to endure long marches without ordinary nourishment—he is referring to Antony's power in the past, in the waning days of the Republic, when there were still republican consuls to fight (1.4.55–71). As for the present moment in Roman history, as is evident in Antony's initial appearance with Cleopatra in Alexandria, he has become an Oriental despot himself, indulging in the pleasures of the flesh and presiding over a lavish and decadent court.

Above all, in terms of the imagery of the play, Antony has become feminized and thus gone over to the other side in the West–East polarity.[23] From the play's opening lines (1.1.1–10), it emphasizes Antony's transformation. He is always threatening to change places with Cleopatra, as she becomes the more masculine of the two. She makes the point herself:

> Ere the ninth hour, I drank him to his bed;
> There put my tires and mantles on him, whilst
> I wore his sword Philippan. (2.5.21–23)

The blunt soldier Enobarbus dwells on the effeminization of Antony under Cleopatra's influence, telling the queen to her face:

> 'Tis said in Rome
> That Photinus an eunuch and your maids
> Manage this war. (3.7.13–15)

Octavius says of Antony that he

> is not more manlike
> Than Cleopatra; nor the queen of Ptolemy
> More womanly than he. (1.4.5–7)

The spectacle of Antony subordinated to Cleopatra—"the triple pillar of the world transform'd / Into a strumpet's fool" (1.1.12–13)—epitomizes the dissipation of Rome's military power when faced with exotic Egyptian culture and its "infinite variety" (2.2.235). Shakespeare portrays the Roman imperial regime as ultimately hollow. Spiritually empty and having lost its former strong sense of purpose, Rome becomes prey to all sorts of foreign influences, such as soothsayers and other purveyors of mysteries and mystifications who make the claim: "In Nature's infinite book of secrecy / A little I can read" (1.2.9–10).

The Rome of the Republic, especially as Shakespeare portrays its early days in *Coriolanus*, is a self-contained and decidedly finite world, one of fixed horizons with the city narrowly focused on its military affairs. The newly globalized world of *Antony and Cleopatra* has much broader horizons, bordering on the infinite. The opening up of horizons is the keynote of the play, voiced by Antony and Cleopatra in their first exchange:

CLEOPATRA: If it be love indeed, tell me how much.
ANTONY: There's beggary in the love that can be reckon'd.
CLEOPATRA: I'll set a bourn how far to be belov'd.
ANTONY: Then must thou needs find out new heaven, new earth. (1.1.14–17)

Antony's contempt for the bounded and the finite, the local and the particular, is characteristic of the Empire and its drive toward universality. Any boundary is established only to be crossed; any limit is set only to be transcended. This is also the principle of globalization and its aspiration for a borderless world. In their drive to go beyond all boundaries, Antony and Cleopatra become in effect the patron saints of both empire and globalization.

The imperial urge to universality is especially evident in the realm of religion in *Antony and Cleopatra*. The old pagan religions, specific to particular countries such as Rome or Egypt with their local deities, seem inadequate in the new imperial order. Characters repeatedly feel compelled to call on "all the gods" (1.3.99), not just one particular deity. Scarus appeals to "Gods and goddesses, / All the whole synod of them!" (3.10.4–5). As one of the rulers of the imperial world, Antony tries to play the role of a god—perhaps a new universal form of divinity. His servant Eros sees "the worship of the whole world" in Antony's "noble countenance" (4.14.85–86). After Antony's death, Cleopatra's dream of him seems like an attempt to conjure up a universal deity suitable to the global dimensions of the new Roman Empire and its increasingly cosmopolitan culture. Cleopatra's Antony is more like a cosmic god than the city gods of the old pagan religions:

> His face was as the heav'ns, and therein stuck
> A sun and moon, which kept their courses and lighted
> The little o' th' earth.[24]
> . . . .
> His legs bestrid the ocean: his rear'd arm
> Crested the world. (5.2.79–81, 83–84)

Even if only on an imaginary plane, Antony finally provides an image of divinity appropriate to a global empire; as J. L. Simmons writes, "Bestriding the ocean, Antony unites Egypt and Rome into one world."[25] In the Roman Empire only a trans-Mediterranean god is adequate to the religious needs of people who have developed new universal concerns.[26]

Everywhere one looks in *Antony and Cleopatra*, the characters are seeking to break out of the narrow limits of the local and the particular. Cleopatra says of her love with Antony: "Eternity was in our lips and eyes" (1.3.35), and as she contemplates her death—in pagan terms the ultimate instance of human finitude—she refuses to accept it as a limit and insists upon her "immortal longings" (5.2.281). The references to Herod of Jewry in the play (1.2.28, 3.3.3–4, 3.6.73, 4.6.13) together with several biblical allusions, suggest that Shakespeare was aware that the events he portrays in the early days of the Roman Empire were roughly contemporaneous with the birth of Christianity—a transpolitical religion that ultimately aspires to universality.[27] The Orientalizing of the Roman Empire culminated in its being Christianized.[28] As an example of the law of unintended consequences at work in empire and globalization, Rome's imperialist incursions into the East ultimately resulted in this pagan community being transformed into the center of worldwide Christianity.[29]

The way Rome is radically changed by its encounters on the imperial frontier suggests that military power does not simply translate into cultural power, and that the ostensible winner in the contest to dominate the world may end up being the loser in the resulting clash of civilizations.[30] More generally, Shakespeare stresses the sheer unpredictability of what happens when rival civilizations clash. Because no one is fully in control of the process, it

may go in unexpected directions and generate seemingly contradictory responses. Many people today think of globalization as the product of a single
centralizing force, a matter of one government or an international organization imposing order on the whole world. The Roman Empire offers a model
of this conception of globalization. It used its military force to gain control
of the whole Mediterranean world and to exercise hegemony over the many
lands it conquered. This tendency to create a new administrative order becomes evident when Octavius Caesar issues commands to his captains, "Do
not exceed / The prescript of this scroll" (3.8.4–5). Here in a nutshell is the
dream of worldwide Roman rule—a single Roman emperor tells his subjects
exactly what to do, scripting their lives for them down to the smallest details.

Although this vision of the perfectly administered world would seem to
be the new order of the day in *Antony and Cleopatra*, Shakespeare shows
that things do not happen exactly according to the imperial script in Rome,
and Octavius is faced with many surprises. Above all, Antony and Cleopatra
refuse to play the roles that he has in mind for them on the Roman stage.
They kill themselves to thwart Octavius's plans to humiliate them in public.
For a realm that is supposed to be firmly under Roman control, the world
of *Antony and Cleopatra* is strangely chaotic and unpredictable. Things keep
mysteriously transforming into their opposites; as Antony says:

> The present pleasure
> By revolution low'ring, does become
> The opposite of itself. (1.2.124–26)

Even more ominously, the world keeps threatening to dissolve into oblivion
and nothingness. The play is filled with images of instability, of melting and
dissolution, of a world of solid things suddenly losing their clear shape:

> Let Rome in Tiber melt, and the wide arch
> Of the rang'd empire fall! (1.1.33–34)

> Melt Egypt into Nile! (2.5.78)
> Sink Rome! (3.7.15)

This pattern culminates in Antony's haunting vision of the clouds, in which
the whole world dissolves into one vast blur:

> That which is now a horse, even with a thought
> The rack dislimns, and makes it indistinct
> As water is in water. (4.14.9–11)

In passages such as this, Shakespeare conveys a sense of how unnerving and
uncanny globalization can seem. Just at the moment when the world is sup-

posedly being integrated into a whole, it threatens to dissolve. This passage calls to mind the words with which Karl Marx and Friedrich Engels famously characterized the revolutionary disruptions in consciousness created by global capitalism: "All that is solid melts into air, all that is holy is profaned."[31] This sense of global disorientation has been offered as the defining experience of modernity, and yet Shakespeare shows his imperial Romans already in the grip of the same malaise.[32]

Indeed, as imaged in *Antony and Cleopatra*, Roman power seems to dissipate and threatens to dissolve at the moment of what seems to be its greatest triumph. That explains the widely divergent moods that sweep through the play. What is presented by some characters as the beginning of a new world order strikes others as the end of an era:

ANTONY: The long day's task is done,
        And we must sleep. (4.14.35–36)

2. GUARD: The star is fall'n
1. GUARD: And time is at his period.[33] (4.14.106–7)

As is evident today, globalization is both a creative and destructive force; indeed, it creates new orders only by destroying old ones.[34] In particular, as an economic process, globalization sets in motion the force Joseph Schumpeter called "creative destruction."[35] Given a wider range of global options, new forms of production and consumption supplant traditional patterns. Shakespeare does not dwell on the economics of the Roman Empire, but he does show in *Antony and Cleopatra* that one order has to die to bring a new order into life. One of the most pervasive patterns of imagery in the play is the ambivalence of life and death, specifically of dying things coming to life and living things dissolving into death.[36]

That is why empire and globalization produce such contradictory responses. In *Antony and Cleopatra*, Shakespeare captures the blend of millennial hopes and apocalyptic fears generated when a new world order is coming into being and an old one is passing away.[37] As we saw in chapter 1, *Antony and Cleopatra* portrays the dissolution of the civic existence that characterized the ancient world and the emergence of the age of empire, which facilitated many of the developments we associate with the medieval and the modern eras, including the spread of Christianity. The pervasive sense of new possibilities opening up, together with the uncertainty, confusion, and fear they generate, is perhaps the deepest point of contact between the world Shakespeare creates in *Antony and Cleopatra* and our globalizing world today. Thus one might

apply to the play the words of a modern poet confronting a global apocalypse
and the ultimate clash of civilizations:

> Turning and turning in the widening gyre
> The falcon cannot hear the falconer;
> Things fall apart; the centre cannot hold;
> Mere anarchy is loosed upon the world,
> The blood-dimmed tide is loosed, and everywhere
> The ceremony of innocence is drowned;
> The best lack all conviction, while the worst
> Are full of passionate intensity.[38]

In its closing nightmare image of a monstrous sphinx rising from the desert
sands to challenge Western civilization, Yeats's "The Second Coming" turns
to Egypt, just as *Antony and Cleopatra* does, to symbolize the antithesis of
European culture.[39]

Many analysts view globalization as an external force, imposed upon people from above. Indeed, they treat globalization as in effect indistinguishable
from empire, a hegemonic power exercised from a colonizing center on a
colonized periphery. But Shakespeare offers a bottom-up model of globalization as an alternative to the simple top-down model. He dwells on the way
the globalizing impulse wells up from within people because he shows it to be
driven by *desire*.[40] If the Romans in *Antony and Cleopatra* are Egyptianized,
the reason is not that Egyptian armies impose this result on them. Shakespeare shows that the Romans *want* to live like Egyptians. They gaze on Egyptian luxury and crave it for themselves, and exotic Egyptian customs seem to
answer to some new and deep-seated need in their souls. The driving force
behind the Egyptianizing of the Romans as portrayed in *Antony and Cleopatra* is a complex of very human qualities, an amalgam of curiosity, envy,
and desire—all epitomized by the infinitely seductive image of Cleopatra.
When Antony wishes that he had never seen the Egyptian queen, Enobarbus
replies in the spirit of the true global tourist: "O, sir, you had then left unseen
a wonderful piece of work, which not to have been blest withal would have
discredited your travel" (1.2.153–55).[41] Shakespeare's Romans have indeed
become world travelers, actively seeking out the alien and the exotic. Deep
down, they crave to be globalized—they long to merge with what appears
to them to be their antithesis among clashing civilizations. Many critics of
globalization today treat it as a wholly artificial process imposed upon people
against their will by remote and hostile forces. In fact, as Shakespeare suggests, many aspects of globalization—not all—correspond to perfectly human needs and desires. Ever since the first caveman wondered if things might

be better in the cave across the valley, the world has been marching toward globalization. Because globalization is rooted in the "infinite variety" of human desire, it inevitably takes unpredictable and kaleidoscopic forms. Recall Enobarbus's paradoxical image of Cleopatra:

> Other women cloy
> The appetites they feed, but she makes hungry
> Where most she satisfies. (2.2.235–37)

The same might be said of globalization: it constantly awakens new desires in the process of satisfying old ones; it dissolves old orders even as it brings new ones into being.[42]

Antony and Cleopatra thus does offer food for thought about our contemporary issue of globalization. One might turn elsewhere in Shakespeare's plays for more insight into the subject. *The Merchant of Venice*, for example, takes place in the increasingly globalized world of the Italian Renaissance, and its horizons truly stretch across the earth, even as far as the New World. In his portrait of Venice, Shakespeare explores the economic aspects of globalization, specifically the ways that commerce both facilitates and complicates the process. Encompassing a wide range of nationalities and ethnic types, especially the conflict between Christians and Jews, *The Merchant of Venice* is another study of the global clash of civilizations. Perhaps Ben Jonson was right after all—Shakespeare *is* a writer for all ages, even our age of globalization. In fact, Shakespeare can help us to understand that globalization is by no means unique to the contemporary era. As *Antony and Cleopatra* shows, the world was already undergoing globalization in antiquity, and Shakespeare's age continued and extended the process. Shakespeare's own plays are perhaps the greatest fruit of the global expansion of horizons in the Renaissance.

Acknowledgments

As I pointed out in the introduction, I have been working on this book in effect for my whole adult life and thus have incurred many debts over the years. First of all, I would like to reaffirm all the acknowledgments in my first book, *Shakespeare's Rome: Republic and Empire*. Everything I said there to express my gratitude to the people who contributed to my initial work on the Roman plays holds true to this day. Back in 1976, house policy at Cornell University Press did not allow me to mention my editor for *Shakespeare's Rome*, Bernhard Kendler. I welcome this opportunity to correct that omission and to thank him for all that he did to bring my first book into print.

A number of institutions contributed to the genesis of this book. The first chapter—and thus the whole project—grew out of a lecture, "Shakespeare's Roman Trilogy: The Tragedy of the Republic," that I gave on November 23, 2010, at the Carl Friedrich von Siemens Foundation in Munich. I want to thank its director, Heinrich Meier, for this invitation and for his hospitality during my stay, as well as for his ongoing encouragement of my work on Shakespeare. Professor Andreas Höfele of the Ludwig-Maximilians-Universität (München) introduced my lecture with unusual grace and wit.

Thanks to Roger Hertog, his Hertog Political Studies Program in Washington, DC, and the people who have run it (including John Walters, Peter Berkowitz, and Cheryl Miller), I have had the opportunity to teach a week-long seminar on the Roman plays every summer since 2011. The students in these seminars form an all-star team, recruited from across the entire country, and I have benefited greatly from their comments and questions during our sessions. On several occasions, some of the participants turned out to know more about Roman history than I did.

For another valuable teaching opportunity, I am indebted to the Foundation for Constitutional Government, especially to William Kristol, Harvey Mansfield, and Andrew Zwick. Thanks to their support, I was able to teach an undergraduate seminar on Shakespeare's Rome in the Harvard University Government Department during the fall 2007 semester, and then a lecture course, "Shakespeare and Politics," which began with the Roman plays, during the fall 2012 semester. This opportunity to return to the scene where my serious work on the Roman plays began reinvigorated my attempt to rethink and reformulate what they signify.

I have spoken on the Roman plays, sometimes individually, sometimes as a group, at many more institutions, and I wish to thank all the people who sponsored these talks at Boston College; Bowdoin College; Hampden-Sydney College; Tufts University; the University of Alaska, Anchorage; and the Jepson School of Leadership Studies at the University of Richmond. Each occasion gave me a chance to develop and refine my thoughts about the Roman plays.

I have not been as active on the Nietzsche circuit, but I want to thank Steven Lenzner and Peter Thiel for inviting me to a conference on Nietzsche's *Beyond Good and Evil* in Washington, DC, in 2013, which came at a very opportune moment for me—exactly while I was working on chapter 2 of this book.

Among the many individuals who have helped with this book, I want to single out for various forms of assistance along the way Marco Basile, Gordon Braden, Daniel Doneson, Mark Edmundson, Peter Henry, Douglas Hoffman, Michael Valdez Moses, Christopher Oppermann, and Vickie Sullivan. Thanks also to the anonymous readers at the University of Chicago Press for many helpful suggestions for improving this book. My friends Peter Hufnagel and Andrea Dvorak have stood by me through all the ups and downs of working on such a long-term project.

Finally I owe a special debt of gratitude to my editor at the University of Chicago Press, John Tryneski, who has had faith in this project from the beginning and has given me sage advice at all stages. For their help throughout the process of publication, I also thank all the people at the University of Chicago Press who worked with me, especially Margaret Hivnor-Labarbera, Melinda Kennedy, Rodney Powell, and Holly Smith. For an unusually careful, thoughtful, and judicious job of copyediting, I thank Mary Tong.

Portions of chapter 1 were published under the title "'Choice of Loss': The Revaluation of Roman Values in Shakespeare's *Antony and Cleopatra*" in *In Search of Humanity: Essays in Honor of Clifford Orwin*, ed. Andrea Radasanu (Lanham, MD: Lexington, 2015), 187–207. Chapter 4 was published under the same title in *Poetica* 48 (1997): 69–81. Chapter 5 was published online by Blackwell under the title "The Shores of Hybridity: Shakespeare and the Mediterranean," *Literature Compass* 3/4 (2006): 896–913. Chapter 6 was published under the same title in *Shakespeare and Politics*, ed. Bruce E. Altschuler and Michael A. Genovese (Boulder, CO: Paradigm, 2014), 65–83. All these essays have been substantially revised, rewritten, and expanded for this book.

Notes

Introduction

1. Also, to get a fuller sense of my indebtedness to other Shakespeare scholars, readers should consult my earlier book (Paul A. Cantor, *Shakespeare's Rome: Republic and Empire* [Ithaca, NY: Cornell University Press, 1976]). For obvious reasons, I have not repeated in this book all the citations I made in *Shakespeare's Rome* to the vast body of Roman plays criticism.

2. My argument is more about intentionality than intention. As aesthetic objects, *Coriolanus*, *Julius Caesar*, and *Antony and Cleopatra* strike me as fitting together neatly into a trilogy, no matter how that "neatness" may have come about. It is impossible to pin down Shakespeare's intentions in writing these three Roman plays. To be sure, some evidence can be offered that he may have conceived of the three plays as forming a trilogy. We know from his history plays that he did think in terms of units larger than a single play. Critics routinely speak of the first and second tetralogies of the history plays. At the very least, Shakespeare seems to have conceived *Henry VI* in terms of three parts, and *Henry IV Parts I and II* work together with *Henry V* to tell a unified story of the education and reign of Henry V. But my analysis of the Roman trilogy would work even if Shakespeare originally conceived of *Julius Caesar* as a single, stand-alone play and only later came up with the idea of writing *Coriolanus* and *Antony and Cleopatra* to fill out the story of the rise and fall of the Roman Republic—provided, as I intend to show, that he worked to integrate the two later plays with the earlier one. Perhaps the three plays just fell into place as a trilogy as Shakespeare worked on them, given the underlying unities in the historical subject matter. In short, no matter how these three Roman plays came into being, it is still possible to read them as a unified trilogy.

3. By accident, I happened to be reading extensively in Nietzsche's writings at the same time that I was first studying Shakespeare seriously in high school. Walter Kaufmann supplied me with the connection between the two in his *From Shakespeare to Existentialism* (Garden City, NY: Doubleday Anchor, 1960). In the first chapter of this book, Kaufmann introduced me to the value of reading Shakespeare in light of the classical tradition, especially in the way that Kaufmann uses Aristotle's notion of greatness of soul or magnanimity to analyze Shakespeare's sonnet 94 (5–12).

4. See Cantor, *Shakespeare's Rome*, esp. 220–21n18 and 223–24n2.

5. For studies that do provide this kind of analysis, see Clifford Ronan, *"Antike Roman": Power Symbology and the Roman Play in Early Modern England, 1585–1635* (Athens: University of

Georgia Press, 1995) and Warren Chernaik, *The Myth of Rome in Shakespeare and his Contemporaries* (Cambridge: Cambridge University Press, 2011).

6. All quotations from Shakespeare are taken from G. Blakemore Evans, ed., *The Riverside Shakespeare* (Boston: Houghton Mifflin, 1974). Act, scene, and line numbers are incorporated into the text.

7. See Charles Martindale and Michelle Martindale, *Shakespeare and the Uses of Antiquity: An Introductory Essay* (London: Routledge, 1990), 148–50.

8. For serious and productive attempts to integrate *Titus Andronicus*, *The Rape of Lucrece*, and *Cymbeline* into the study of Shakespeare's Rome, see John Alvis, *Shakespeare's Understanding of Honor* (Durham, NC: Carolina Academic Press, 1994); Michael Platt, *Rome and Romans According to Shakespeare*, 2nd ed. (Lanham, MD: University Press of America, 1983); and Robert S. Miola, *Shakespeare's Rome* (Cambridge: Cambridge University Press, 1983). To correct an unfortunate error, I should point out that an essay on *Cymbeline* mistakenly appears under my name in a collection of essays on the Roman plays: Paul A. Cantor, "*Cymbeline*: Beyond Rome," in *Shakespeare: The Roman Plays*, ed. Graham Holderness, Bryan Loughrey, and Andrew Murphy (London: Longman, 1996), 169–84. This essay is in fact by Robert S. Miola and comes from the book cited above. Somehow the editors managed to confuse Miola's *Shakespeare's Rome* with mine. In their analysis of this essay in their introduction, the editors describe me as a "naïve Christian" (14). *Shakespeare's Roman Trilogy* should allow readers to judge the validity of this claim.

9. In an overview of scholarship on the Roman plays, and after surveying developments in the analysis of *Titus Andronicus*, Gordon Braden concludes, "The traditional triptych—Shakespeare's Plutarch plays—still has good claim to being a special phenomenon worth studying on its own" ("Shakespeare's Roman Tragedies," in *A Companion to Shakespeare's Works*, ed. Richard Dutton and Jean E. Howard [Malden MA: Wiley-Blackwell, 2003], vol. 1, 204).

10. On this point, see Martindale and Martindale, *Shakespeare and the Uses of Antiquity*, 125, 129. For their argument against discussing *Titus Andronicus* and *Cymbeline* together with the three "Plutarchan" Roman plays, see 142–44.

11. I am not the only critic to speak of "Shakespeare's Roman Trilogy." In *The Meaning of Shakespeare* (Chicago: University of Chicago Press, 1951), vol. 2, 207, Harold C. Goddard refers to *Coriolanus*, *Julius Caesar*, and *Antony and Cleopatra* as forming "Shakespeare's Roman Trilogy": they "give us a spiritual history of Rome from its austere early days, through the fall of the republic, to the triumph of the empire." But Goddard does not work out this suggestion in his book. In fact, he discusses the three plays in the putative order of their composition: *Julius Caesar*, *Antony and Cleopatra*, *Coriolanus*. When he gets to *Coriolanus*, Goddard restricts himself to saying: "If its author had been historically minded, much of the play might be explained as an attempt to present the spirit of an early austere Rome where war and the struggle for power were the primary concerns" (209). In my view, that is exactly what *Coriolanus* is, but Goddard does not pursue the point. For another conception of Shakespeare's Roman trilogy, see Hugh M. Richmond, "Shakespeare's Roman Trilogy: The Climax in *Cymbeline*," *Studies in the Literary Imagination* 5 (1972): 129–39. For Richmond, Shakespeare's Roman trilogy consists of *Julius Caesar*, *Antony and Cleopatra*, and *Cymbeline*.

12. See, e.g., Martindale and Martindale, *Shakespeare and the Uses of Antiquity*; Charles Martindale and A. B. Taylor, eds., *Shakespeare and the Classics* (Cambridge: Cambridge University Press, 2004); and Robert S. Miola, "Reading the Classics," in *A Companion to Shakespeare*, ed. David Scott Kastan (Oxford, UK: Blackwell, 1999), 172–85.

13. For a prominent Shakespeare scholar who defends the use of the term "Renaissance" because of the centrality of the classical tradition in his work, see Marjorie Garber, *Shakespeare After All* (New York: Anchor, 2005), 724–25.

14. On anachronism in the Roman plays, see Ronan, *"Antike Roman,"* 11–35; and John Sutherland, "The Watch on the Centurion's Wrist," in *Henry V, War Criminal? and Other Shakespeare Puzzles* (Oxford: Oxford University Press, 2000), 7–13.

15. For Shakespeare's understanding of the distinctive Roman attitude toward suicide, see Martindale and Martindale, *Shakespeare and the Uses of Antiquity*, 121–22; A. D. Nuttall, *A New Mimesis: Shakespeare and the Representation of Reality* (London: Methuen, 1983), 101; and Gordon Braden, "Fame, Eternity, and Shakespeare's Romans," in *Shakespeare and Renaissance Ethics*, ed. Patrick Gray and John D. Cox (Cambridge: Cambridge University Press, 2014), 37–55.

16. Paul Hammond, ed., *Selected Prose of Alexander Pope* (Cambridge: Cambridge University Press, 1987), 162. On Pope's view of Shakespeare's Rome, see Martindale and Martindale, *Shakespeare and the Uses of Antiquity*, 148; and Nuttall, *A New Mimesis*, 102, 113.

17. See Chernaik, *Myth of Rome*, 9–10.

18. For an overview of the classical republican tradition and its relation to the United States government, see Paul A. Rahe, *Republics Ancient and Modern* (Chapel Hill: University of North Carolina Press, 1992).

19. Jean Bodin, *Six Books of the Commonwealth*, trans. M. J. Tooley (Oxford: Basil Blackwell, 1967), 112. This book was originally published in French in 1576. It appeared in a Latin translation in 1586. A conflation of the French and Latin versions translated into English by Richard Knolles was published in 1606. For Knolles's translation of this passage (with the ellipsis filled in), see Kenneth Douglas McRae, ed., *Jean Bodin: The Six Bookes of a Commonweale* (Cambridge, MA: Harvard University Press, 1962), 411–12. I have seen no evidence that Shakespeare knew of Bodin's book, but it was widely read in English political and literary circles (even before it was translated into English), and Bodin's ideas were highly influential in England among such figures as Sir Philip Sidney and Sir Walter Raleigh.

20. John Milton, *Paradise Regained, The Minor Poems and Samson Agonistes*, ed. Merritt Y. Hughes (New York: Odyssey, 1937), book 4, lines 131–45.

21. Jonathan Swift, *Gulliver's Travels*, ed. Robert A. Greenberg (New York: W. W. Norton, 1970), book 3, chapter 8, 172.

22. Swift's adherence to the republican tradition is even more evident in his 1701 political tract *A Discourse of the Contests and Dissentions between the Nobles and the Commons in Athens and Rome*, ed. Frank H. Ellis (Oxford: Oxford University Press, 1965). Chapter 3 of this work offers a succinct summary of the standard republican history of Rome, culminating in this comment on Octavius's victory over Mark Antony: "Here ended all Shew or Shadow of Liberty in *Rome*. Here was the Repository of all the wise Contentions and Struggles for Power, between the Nobles and Commons, lapt up safely in the Bosom of a *Nero* and a *Caligula*, a *Tiberius* and a *Domitian*" (111)—again the idea that the reign of Augustus marked the immediate collapse of republican virtue into imperial decadence and tyranny.

23. For the wide range of negative views of the Roman Empire in Roman plays by Shakespeare's contemporaries (hostility derived largely from the Roman historians Tacitus and Sallust), see Chernaik, *Myth of Rome*, 17–25.

24. Our image of the Roman Republic is to some extent an idealization created in the era of the Empire by disaffected members of the patrician class, faced with their loss of power under the imperial regime. See Lidia Storoni Mazzolani, *The Idea of the City in Roman Thought: From*

Walled City to Spiritual Commonwealth, trans. S. O'Donnell, (Bloomington: Indiana University Press, 1970), 26–27.

25. The opposition between republic and empire is so fundamental to political thinking that it has even trickled down to American popular culture. For example, it forms the basis of the *Star Wars* mythology. Even "a long time ago, in a galaxy far, far away," the remnants of a virtuous republic struggled against a corrupt empire.

26. See Mazzolani, *Idea of the City*, who groups the historical Antony with Caligula and Nero as Romans who "had yearnings toward an oriental empire" (95).

27. For examples of this development, see Jonathan Dollimore, *Radical Tragedy: Religion, Ideology and Power in the Dramas of Shakespeare and his Contemporaries* (Chicago: University of Chicago Press, 1984); and Franco Moretti, "The Great Eclipse: Tragic Form as the Deconsecration of Sovereignty," *Signs Taken for Wonders: Essays in the Sociology of Literary Forms*, trans. David Miller (London: Verso, 1988), 42–82.

28. See Andrew Hadfield, *Shakespeare and Republicanism* (Cambridge: Cambridge University Press, 2005). Hadfield summarizes the "historical lesson" available to Shakespeare and his contemporaries from Roman historians this way: "the republic is a far more desirable form of government than the empire" (56).

29. On the importance of Venice as a model of a mixed regime (combining elements of monarchy, aristocracy, and democracy) to republican thinking in Shakespeare's Britain, see Hadfield, *Shakespeare and Republicanism*, 40–43, 214–20.

30. Those who assert that republican thinking was simply unavailable in Shakespeare's day must find a way to explain how it happened that roughly three decades after his death, a civil war erupted in Britain that resulted in the execution of Charles I and the establishment of a republic. Some people in Britain in Shakespeare's day must have known what a republic is, long before it became prudent to speak of such matters openly in print.

31. Hadfield's general remarks on political thinking in Elizabethan and Jacobean England apply to Shakespeare:

> If everyone did believe in the monarchy, there were clearly very different positions taken on its role and purpose, not just on whether it was an institution worth preserving. . . . Worden rightly points out that major writers such as More, Sidney and Bacon did turn to "non-monarchical models of government for guidance," and even if we can agree that "constitutional collapse was the dread, not the hope, of the class of lay intellectuals to which these writers belonged," their exploration of alternative political institutions would appear to indicate that they did not necessarily believe that the monarchy had to remain static, and that a change of the constitution would not make society better. (*Shakespeare and Republicanism*, 51; Hadfield is quoting Blair Worden, "Republicanism, Regicide, and Republic")

32. For the widespread influence of Roman political models in Shakespeare's day (especially the influence of the republican thinking of Polybius and Machiavelli), see Hadfield, *Shakespeare and Republicanism*, 17–32.

33. Again, Hadfield's general remarks on political thinking in Elizabethan and Jacobean England apply to Shakespeare:

> Through the study of Cicero, Aristotle, Plato, Polybius, Thucydides et al. came an interest in the political ideas they espoused, as well as an understanding of the institutions and forms of political organization they advocated. Such study led to a select

group of highly educated men possessing the means and the confidence to distinguish between different constitutions in the ancient world and contemporary Europe and so debate alternative forms of government, including varieties of mixed rule made up of elements of monarchy, oligarchy and democracy, as well as republics such as Rome and Venice. . . . This . . . republicanism seems to have had a particular influence on Shakespeare, who, more than any of his contemporary playwrights, was especially interested in how political institutions functioned, who they represented, and how individuals came to occupy offices of state. (*Shakespeare and Republicanism*, 52–53)

34. This idea is well expressed by the Volscian general Aufidius in *Coriolanus*: "I would I were a Roman, for I cannot / Being a Volsce, be that I am" (1.10.4–5).

35. I am indeed speaking in general terms here. As was argued even in antiquity, Rome differed in important ways from the classical model of the Greek polis, especially in its attitude toward admitting foreigners to the ranks of its citizens. On this complicated subject, see Clifford Ando, "Was Rome a Polis?" *Classical Antiquity* 18 (1999): 5–34.

Chapter One

1. All quotations from Shakespeare are taken from G. Blakemore Evans, ed., *The Riverside Shakespeare* (Boston: Houghton Mifflin, 1974). Act, scene, and line numbers are incorporated into the body of the chapter. For the sake of clarity, I have occasionally altered Evans's text to substitute a more modern form or spelling of a word.

2. The general in question may have been the Earl of Essex or Lord Montjoy. For the controversy surrounding this identification, see Herschel Baker, introduction to *Henry V* in Evans, *Riverside Shakespeare*, 930.

3. On the significance of this passage, see Andrew Hadfield, *Shakespeare and Republicanism* (Cambridge: Cambridge University Press, 2005), 126–28.

4. On the significance of the Roman past for Europe, especially of Roman ruins, see Clifford Ronan, *"Antike Roman": Power Symbology and the Roman Play in Early Modern England, 1585–1635* (Athens, GA: University of Georgia Press, 1995), 36–49, 65–71.

5. See John Alvis, *Shakespeare's Understanding of Honor* (Durham, NC: Carolina Academic Press, 1990), 149–50; and Michael Neill, introduction to *Anthony and Cleopatra* (Oxford: Oxford University Press, 1994), 7.

6. Among critics who emphasize Shakespeare's interest in republican Rome, see Jan Kott, *Shakespeare Our Contemporary*, trans. Boleslaw Taborski (New York: Norton, 1974): "Shakespeare was a far greater innovator in *Julius Caesar* and in *Coriolanus* than in *Antony and Cleopatra*. In the first two plays he introduced into tragedy republican Rome" (185). See also Hadfield, *Shakespeare and Republicanism*: "Shakespeare narrates more of the republican story than any other dramatist working in Elizabethan and Jacobean England" (57). See also Denis Feeney, "Doing the Numbers: The Roman Mathematics of Civil War in Shakespeare's *Antony and Cleopatra*," in *Citizens of Discord: Rome and Its Civil Wars*, ed. Brian W. Reed, Cynthia Damon, and Andreola Rossi (Oxford: Oxford University Press, 2010): "It is a sensibility attuned to republicanism that we see at work in the Roman plays" (286). See also Gordon Braden, "Fame, Eternity, and Shakespeare's Romans," in *Shakespeare and Renaissance Ethics*, ed. Patrick Gray and John D. Cox (Cambridge: Cambridge University Press, 2014), who says of Shakespeare's writing *Coriolanus*: "Shakespeare makes (what is within the general context of Renaissance dramatizations of Roman history) a relatively obscure choice of subject matter from the early Republic,

one that involves understanding and dramatizing some complicated business in the Republic's constitutional history" (42).

7. At the end of his *Life of Marcus Antonius*, Plutarch makes a point of tracing Antony's progeny down through the Claudian dynasty, including Caligula and culminating in Nero. Perhaps Shakespeare was struck by the last sentence of Plutarch's biography of Antony: "This Nero was Emperor in our time, and slew his own mother; had almost destroyed the Empire of Rome through his madness and wicked life, being the fifth Emperor of Rome after Antonius" (T. J. B. Spencer, ed., *Shakespeare's Plutarch* [Harmondsworth, UK: Penguin, 1964], 295). Plutarch notes how quickly the Roman emperors degenerated into monsters. For more on the connection between Antony and Nero, see Patricia Parker, "Barbers, Infidels, and Renegades: *Antony and Cleopatra*," in *Antony and Cleopatra*, ed. Ania Loomba (New York: Norton, 2011), 310–14.

8. See Warren Chernaik, *The Myth of Rome in Shakespeare and his Contemporaries* (Cambridge: Cambridge University Press, 2011), who says of *Julius Caesar*: "To be a Roman is to be a republican" (80). For a similar comment about the historical Rome, see Ronald Syme, *The Roman Revolution* (Oxford: Oxford University Press, 1960): "The men who fell at Philippi fought for a principle, a tradition and a class—narrow, imperfect and outworn, but for all that the soul and spirit of Rome" (205).

9. See, for example, the moment when the younger Pompey harks back to the republican rhetoric of Brutus and Cassius and speaks of their conviction "that they would / Have one man but a man" (*Antony and Cleopatra*, 2.6.18–19). On this point, see Allan Bloom, *Love and Friendship* (New York: Simon & Schuster, 1993), 312. On the decline of political rhetoric and the art of oratory in imperial Rome, see Jan H. Blits, *Rome and the Spirit of Caesar: Shakespeare's Julius Caesar* (Lanham, MD: Lexington, 2015), 104. As Blits points out, Antony's funeral oration for Julius Caesar in act 3 of *Julius Caesar* is the last great political speech given in Shakespeare's Rome. As Blits writes, "While oratory thrives on liberty, it is squelched by monarchy" (104).

10. Images of corruption, specifically of rotting, can be found throughout *Antony and Cleopatra*. Octavius views the Roman people as themselves rotten: "This common body, / Like to a vagabond flag upon the stream, / Goes to and back, lacking the varying tide, / To rot itself with motion" (1.4.44–47). I have restored the Folio reading "lacking" for the standard editorial emendation "lackeying." The original wording—"lacking the varying tide"—creates an effective image of standing water, which is exactly what Shakespeare wishes to convey here and which captures the stagnation of the Roman Empire perfectly. The one editor I have found who agrees with me about restoring the Folio wording here is John F. Andrews, *William Shakespeare: Antony and Cleopatra* (London: J. M. Dent, 1993), 46.

11. The word "consuls" appears only once in *Antony and Cleopatra* (1.4.58), and in this passage Octavius is referring to events in the past, when Antony killed the consuls Hirtius and Pansa in the waning days of the Republic. For a thorough historical treatment of the way republican institutions survived into the era of the Empire (as part of a deliberate imperial strategy), see Syme, *Roman Revolution*. See also Chernaik, *Myth of Rome*, 14–15.

12. The word "plebeians" appears only once in *Antony and Cleopatra* (4.12.34), and in this passage Antony refers to them in their reduced role as mere spectators in imperial Rome.

13. See Pierre Menant, *Metamorphoses of the City: On the Western Dynamic*, trans. Marc Le-Pain (Cambridge, MA: Harvard University Press, 2013): "The city is that ordering of the human world that makes action possible and meaningful. . . . It is in the city that people can deliberate and form projects of action. It is in the city that people discover that they can govern themselves and that they learn to do so. They discover and learn politics, which is the great domain of action" (4).

14. See A. D. Nuttall, *Shakespeare the Thinker* (New Haven, CT: Yale University Press, 2007): "The cultural separateness of the Roman world, its independence of Christianity, makes it a perfect laboratory for free-ranging political hypothesis. . . . Shakespeare, who probably didn't know what a pyramid looked like and believed the Romans wore spectacles . . . is clearly interested in the cultural otherness of the Roman world" (171–72).

15. This possibility may at first seem far-fetched. According to traditional views, Shakespeare in his lifetime witnessed the British monarchy veering toward absolutism under the Tudor and Stuart dynasties and knew nothing of republican thought. But we should remember that by the 1640s, Britain took a turn toward republicanism, culminating in the Commonwealth of Oliver Cromwell. By the end of the seventeenth century, under the leadership of the Whigs, Britain began its long march toward becoming a constitutional monarchy, which today appears to be in most respects indistinguishable from a parliamentary democracy. Perhaps Shakespeare contributed to these developments, helping to introduce republican elements into the British regime. Over the years many observers have chosen to view the British monarchy on the model of the Roman mixed regime. Jonathan Swift, for example, in his analysis of the democratic, aristocratic, and monarchic components of the Roman regime, writes, "This was the utmost Extent of Power pretended by the *Commons* in the time of Romulus; all the rest being divided between the King and the Senate, the whole agreeing very nearly with the Constitution of *England* for some Centuries after the Conquest" (*A Discourse of the Contests and Dissentions Between the Nobles and the Commons in Athens and Rome*, ed. Frank H. Ellis [1701; Oxford: Clarendon Press, 1967], 101). Montesquieu referred obliquely to Britain as "a republic, disguised under the form of monarchy" (*The Spirit of the Laws*, trans. Thomas Nugent [New York: Hafner, 1949], 68 (book 5, chapter 19). Some modern historians have argued that republican thought was available during Shakespeare's lifetime and that the British regime was at times viewed on republican models. Patrick Collinson created a controversy with his essay "The Monarchical Republic of Queen Elizabeth I" (Manchester: John Rylands Library, 1987), in which he points to many republican aspects of the Elizabethan regime, including traditions of local self-government and the influence of Elizabeth's advisors (some of whom came from Parliament) in what amounted to her Cabinet. For discussions of Collinson's thesis, see John F. McDiarmid, ed., *The Monarchical Republic of Early Modern England: Essays in Response to Patrick Collinson* (Aldershot, UK: Ashgate, 2007). For Shakespeare's exposure to republican thinking and the way it is manifested in his plays, see Clifford Chalmers Huffman, *Coriolanus in Context* (Lewisburg, PA: Bucknell University Press, 1971) and Hadfield, *Shakespeare and Republicanism*. Hadfield's book is especially valuable in supplying detailed and convincing evidence that Shakespeare was interested in republican principles and in applying them to Britain. For further evidence that Shakespeare may have been influenced by republican thought, see Martin Dzelzanis, "Shakespeare and Political Thought," in *A Companion to Shakespeare*, ed. David Scott Kastan (Oxford, UK: Blackwell, 1999), 100–16.

16. For an excellent discussion of the importance of ancient Rome in Renaissance thinking, and in Shakespeare's work in particular, see Allan Bloom, *Shakespeare's Politics* (New York: Basic Books, 1964), 76–78.

17. See Jacob Burckhardt, *The Civilization of the Renaissance in Italy*, trans. Ludwig Geiger and Walter Götz (New York: Harper & Row, 1958), esp. part 1, "The State as a Work of Art" and part 3, "The Revival of Antiquity."

18. *The Merchant of Venice* and *Othello* show that Shakespeare was interested in the way the Venetian Republic operated. For more on this subject, see chapter 5 of this volume.

19. On Shakespeare's knowledge of Machiavelli and the *Discourses*, see Andrew Hadfield

and Paul Hammond, eds., *Shakespeare and Renaissance Europe* (London: Thomson Learning, 2005), 61, 63, 81–82, 116–17; and Anne Barton, "Livy, Machiavelli and Shakespeare's *Coriolanus*," *Essays, Mainly Shakespearean* (Cambridge: Cambridge University Press, 1994), 136–60, esp. 148. For a whole book on the subject, see John Roe, *Shakespeare and Machiavelli* (Woodbridge, UK: Boydell & Brewer, 2002). For more on knowledge of Machiavelli among Shakespeare and his contemporaries, see Mario Praz, "The Politic Brain: Machiavelli and the Elizabethans," *The Flaming Heart* (Garden City, NY: Doubleday Anchor, 1958), 90–145, esp. 100 on Elizabethan translations of Machiavelli that, even if not printed, circulated in manuscript.

20. For example, Shakespeare was aware of the role of minor republican officials such as the aediles (*Coriolanus*, 3.1.172), and he even knew that the Romans voted by tribes in the assembly (3.3.11). For a detailed analysis of how the republican regime operates in *Coriolanus*, see Paul A. Cantor, *Shakespeare's Rome: Republic and Empire* (Ithaca, NY: Cornell University Press, 1976), 55–77.

21. See Niccolò Machiavelli, *Discourses on Livy*, trans. Harvey C. Mansfield and Nathan Tarcov (Chicago: University of Chicago Press, 1996): "The ambition of the consuls kept them in the first order, that of making wars brief. Since they had a term of a year to serve, and of that six months were in quarters, they wished to finish the war so as to have a triumph" (141 [book 2, chapter 6]).

22. Note that Sicinius and Brutus get to be called "noble tribunes" at 3.1.325 (by a senator) and at 3.3.143 (by all the plebeians)—no doubt to the tribunes' immense satisfaction.

23. See John Alvis, "Liberty and Responsibility in Shakespeare's Rome," in *The Inner Vision: Liberty and Literature*, ed. Edward R. McLean (Wilmington, DE: ISI, 2006), 26–27.

24. For the classic treatment of the civic religions of antiquity, see Numa Denis Fustel de Coulanges, *The Ancient City: A Study of the Religion, Laws, and Institutions of Greece and Rome* (1864; Baltimore, MD: Johns Hopkins University Press, 1980), esp. book 3, chapter 6 ("The Gods of the City") and chapter 7 ("The Religion of the City").

25. See Michael Platt, *Rome and Romans According to Shakespeare*, 2nd ed. (Lanham, MD: University Press of America, 1983), 169.

26. Machiavelli, *Discourses on Livy*, 131 (book 2, chapter 2).

27. Ibid. On the importance of these passages in the *Discourses*, see Harvey C. Mansfield, *Machiavelli's New Modes and Orders: A Study of the Discourses of Livy* (Ithaca, NY: Cornell University Press, 1979), 194–96; and Vickie B. Sullivan, *Machiavelli's Three Romes: Religion, Human Liberty, and Politics Reformed* (DeKalb: Northern Illinois University Press, 1996), 5–6, 39–40.

28. Machiavelli, *Discourses*, 132 (book 2, chapter 2).

29. See, e.g., Montesquieu, *Considerations on the Causes of the Greatness of the Romans and Their Decline*, trans. David Lowenthal (Ithaca, NY: Cornell University Press, 1968), 91, 103; and Jan H. Blits, *New Heaven, New Earth: Shakespeare's Antony and Cleopatra* (Lanham, MD: Lexington, 2009), 3.

30. See Machiavelli, *Discourses*, 270 (book 3, chapter 24) on the prolongation of military commands:

Although started by the Senate for public utility, that thing was what in time made Rome servile. For the farther the Romans went abroad with arms, the more such extension appeared necessary to them and the more they used it. That thing produced two inconveniences: one, that a lesser number of men were practiced in commands, and because of this they came to restrict reputation to a few; the other, that when a citizen remained commander of an army for a very long time, he would win it over to himself and make it partisan to him, for the army would in time forget the Senate and recognize that head. Because of this, Sulla and Marius could find soldiers who would follow them against the public good; because of this, Caesar could seize the fatherland.

See also Sullivan, *Machiavelli's Three Romes*, 149–50; Chernaik, *Myth of Rome*, 14; and Menant, *Metamorphoses of the City*, 163–64.

31. On this point, see Montesquieu, *Considerations*, 92.

32. For evidence for these claims, see *Coriolanus*, 2.1.205–21, 262–68, and 4.7.28–35.

33. See Alvis, "Liberty and Responsibility," 28.

34. On this point, see Allan Bloom, *Shakespeare's Politics*, 80; and Alvis, *Shakespeare's Understanding of Honor*, 150–51.

35. Spencer, *Shakespeare's Plutarch*, 75.

36. See Allan Bloom, *Shakespeare's Politics*, 82–83. For more on Antony's strategy, see chapter 2 of this volume.

37. See Alvis, *Shakespeare's Understanding of Honor*, 151.

38. See, for example, the Greek historian Polybius on Rome: "When a state, after warding off many great perils, achieves supremacy and uncontested sovereignty, it is evident that under the influence of long-established prosperity life will become more luxurious, and among the citizens themselves rivalry for office and in other spheres of activity will become fiercer than it should" (Polybius, *The Rise of the Roman Empire*, trans. Ian Scott-Kilvert [London: Penguin, 1979], 350 (conclusion to book 6). See also Montesquieu, *Considerations*, 44–45, 74, 98.

39. For concrete details on the wealth of individual patricians in the late days of the Republic, and the way they used it to buy soldiers, see Ernst Badian, *Roman Imperialism in the Late Republic* (Ithaca, NY: Cornell University Press, 1968), 81–90, esp. 81: "Marcus Crassus . . . said that no one was wealthy who could not afford to pay for a legion." In his *Life of Coriolanus*, Plutarch contrasts the political integrity in the early days of the Republic with the corruption in the later days, specifically with regard to the buying of offices:

> For offices of dignity in the city were not then given by favour or corruption. It was but of late time, and long after this, that buying and selling fell out in election of officers, and that the voices of electors were bought for money. But after corruption had once gotten way into the election of offices, it hath run from man to man, even to the very sentence of judges, and also among captains in the wars; so as, in the end, that only turned commonwealths into kingdoms, by making arms subject to money. Therefore methinks he had reason that said: "He that first made banquets and gave money to the common people was the first that took away authority and destroyed commonwealth" (Spencer, *Shakespeare's Plutarch*, 318).

Thus, in his source in Plutarch, Shakespeare was alerted to the theory that the change from republic to empire in Rome was a product of the increasing role of wealth in Roman politics. Plutarch offers Julius Caesar as an example of how the patricians used their wealth to corrupt the Roman political system: "They that made suit for offices at Rome were chosen magistrates by means of Caesar's money which he gave them (with the which, bribing the people, they bought their voices, and when they were in office did all that they could to increase Caesar's power and greatness)" (Spencer, *Shakespeare's Plutarch*, 42).

40. See Platt, *Rome and Romans*, 188–89.

41. Many critics have noted this point. See, e.g., Sigurd Burckhardt, *Shakespearean Meanings* (Princeton, NJ: Princeton University Press, 1968), 9; René Girard, *A Theater of Envy: William Shakespeare* (New York: Oxford University Press, 1991), 194–95; Nuttall, *Shakespeare the Thinker*, 174; and Marjorie Garber, *Shakespeare After All* (New York: Anchor, 2005), 426. H. M. Richmond notes the full irony of this moment; one of the plebeians "proposes to this newest murderer the same triumphal procession that had previously been given to the murderer of Pompey, Caesar himself" (3.2.48–55; *Shakespeare's Political Plays* [Gloucester, MA: Peter Smith, 1977], 209).

42. On the importance of the plebeians in Roman politics, see Allan Bloom, *Shakespeare's Politics*, 82.

43. See Barton, "Livy, Machiavelli," 141; and Adrian Poole, *Coriolanus* (Boston: Twayne, 1988), 1. Whatever may be said against the tribunes in *Coriolanus*, they do succeed in channeling the violent impulses of the plebeians into proceedings that at least have some semblance of legality (on this subject, see Machiavelli, *Discourses on Livy*, book 1, chapter 7, in which he discusses the historical case of Coriolanus). With the tribunes "put to silence" in *Julius Caesar* (1.1.286), Roman politics becomes more irrational. Even though individual tribunes, such as Sicinius and Brutus in *Coriolanus*, may be rabble rousers, the institution of the tribunate introduced an element of rationality into Roman republican politics. In the absence of tribunes, the plebeian mob unleashes its fury on the innocent Cinna the poet. Similarly, a mob in Antium turns on Coriolanus and murders him in its fury. The lack of tribunes among the Volsces may explain why the murderous violence that was avoided in Rome takes place in Antium. Shakespeare appears to connect the murder of Cinna with the murder of Coriolanus. At the end of *Coriolanus* a mob of Volsces says of Coriolanus: "Tear him to pieces!" (5.6.120). The mob of plebeians in *Julius Caesar* says the same of Cinna the poet: "Tear him to pieces" (3.3.28). In both cases, an urban mob kills a lone man who is different from them.

44. Plutarch gives some sense of what Athens meant to Antony in his account of the Roman's first visit to the city: he "gave himself only to hear wise men dispute, to see plays, and also to note the ceremonies and sacrifices of Greece; . . . it pleased him marvelously to hear them call him *Philhellene* (as much as to say, 'a lover of the Grecians')" (Spencer, *Shakespeare's Plutarch*, 197). See also Plutarch's account of Antony's later visit to Athens: "Then he went unto the city of Athens, and there gave himself again to see plays and pastimes and to keep the theatres" (246). On Antony and the Greeks, see Lidia Storoni Mazzolani, *The Idea of the City in Roman Thought: From Walled City to Spiritual Commonwealth*, trans. S. O'Donnell (Bloomington: Indiana University Press, 1970), 147–49. One of the charges Octavius made against Antony was that he planned on moving the capital of the Empire to the Hellenistic city of Alexandria.

45. Evidently the Romans and the Volsces worship the same gods; Aufidius speaks of Jupiter and Mars (*Coriolanus*, 4.5.103, 118; see also 192). The Roman and the Volscian regimes are, of course, not identical. For example, the Volsces do not have tribunes. On this subject, see Jan H. Blits, *Spirit, Soul, and City in Shakespeare's Coriolanus* (Lanham, MD: Lexington, 2006), 232. Barton goes even further in stressing the differences between the Romans and the Volsces ("Livy, Machiavelli," 153–58). For other differences between the two peoples, see Poole, *Coriolanus*, 91. For the contrary view, "that the Volscian state is simply a mirror image of the Roman one," see Barbara L. Parker, *Plato's Republic and Shakespeare's Rome: A Political Study of the Roman Works* (Newark: University of Delaware Press, 2004), 64. For the similarity of the Romans and the Volsces, see also R. B. Parker, introduction to *Coriolanus* (Oxford: Oxford University Press, 1994), 97.

NOTES TO PAGES 36–39

46. On this point, see Montesquieu, *Considerations*, 92–93.

47. Shakespeare invented this moment; it is not found in Plutarch's account. As a matter of fact, in Plutarch's *Life of Caesar*, Casca speaks Greek ("And Casca in Greek to his brother: 'Brother, help me'" [Spencer, *Shakespeare's Plutarch*, 93]). Casca also speaks Greek in Plutarch's *Life of Brutus*: "Casca on the other side cried in Greek" (124). Shakespeare might well have noticed how often Romans speak Greek in Plutarch's accounts. Brutus speaks Greek on several occasions (as a form of esoteric communication)—see Spencer, *Shakespeare's Plutarch*, 153, 170.

48. Cicero, *Tusculan Disputations*, trans. J. E. King (Cambridge, MA: Harvard University Press, 1971), 5 (book 1, sec. 1).

49. For more on this subject, see Miranda Marvin, *The Language of the Muses: The Dialogue between Roman and Greek Sculpture* (Los Angeles: J. Paul Getty Museum, 2008). She gives a good summary of the Romans' sense of their indebtedness to Greek art on 10–15. But her book is devoted to showing that this is largely a myth and that Roman sculpture was far more original than is usually supposed.

50. Ramsey MacMullen, *Romanization in the Time of Augustus* (New Haven, CT: Yale University Press, 2000), 2. As its title indicates, MacMullen's book is fundamentally about Romanization, but it begins with a chapter on the Hellenization of Rome. His quotation from Cicero shows that Shakespeare knew what he was doing when he had the Roman senator speak Greek. MacMullen's book does an excellent job of showing how the currents of cultural influence flowed back and forth between Rome and its conquests in the Mediterranean world, a situation that Shakespeare seems to grasp. For more on the Hellenization of Rome, see Mazzolani, *Idea of the City*, 142–43; Michael Ivanovich Rostovtzeff, *Rome*, trans. J. D. Duff (New York: Oxford University Press, 1960), 91–94; and Fernand Braudel, *Memory and the Mediterranean*, trans. Siân Reynolds (New York: Alfred Knopf, 2001), 303–5.

51. MacMullen, *Romanization in the Time of Augustus*, 29.

52. Rémi Brague, *Eccentric Culture: A Theory of Western Civilization*, trans. Samuel Lester (South Bend, IN: St. Augustine's Press, 2002). For Brague on the Hellenization of Rome, see 35–42.

53. This point was understood already in antiquity, especially with regard to military practices. See, e.g., Polybius, *Rise of the Roman Empire*: "As soon as they made these discoveries the Romans began to copy Greek arms, for this is one of their strong points; no people are more willing to adopt new customs and to emulate what they see is better done by others" (323).

54. Montesquieu, *Considerations*, 24.

55. This is one of the main arguments of Badian, *Roman Imperialism*.

56. This quotation from Cato appears in Pliny the Elder, *Natural History*, trans. W. H. S. Jones (Cambridge, MA: Harvard University Press, 1975), 191–93 (book 29, sec. 7).

57. Many Romans sought ways to push back against the belief in Greek cultural superiority. The *Aeneid* is one of the most obvious cases of the Romans' cultural indebtedness to the Greeks, and yet the cultural myth of the poem is the (entirely manufactured) idea that Rome's heritage was Trojan, not Greek. A famous passage from the *Aeneid* searches for areas in which the Romans might assert their cultural superiority over the Greeks: "Others, I doubt not, shall with softer mould beat out the breathing bronze, coax from the marble features to the life, plead cases with greater eloquence and with a pointer trace heaven's motions and predict the rising of the stars; you, Roman, be sure to rule the world (be these your arts), to crown peace with justice, to spare the vanquished and to crush the proud" (book 6, lines 847–52; Virgil, *Eclogues, Georgics, Aeneid I-VI*, trans. H. Rushton Fairclough, rev. ed. [Cambridge, MA: Harvard University Press,

1999], 593). In short, in the culmination of Anchises's prophecy to his son Aeneas, Virgil has him readily grant Greek superiority in the fine arts and the sciences (sculpture, rhetoric, astronomy), but he insists that the Romans will prevail in the military and political arts. Cicero pursues a similar strategy in the opening of his *Tusculan Disputations*:

> Not that philosophy could not be learnt from Greek writers and teachers, but it has always been my conviction that our countrymen have shown more wisdom everywhere than the Greeks, either in making discoveries for themselves, or else in improving upon what they received from Greece—in such subjects at least as they had judged worthy of the devotion of their efforts. For morality, rules of life, family and household economy are surely maintained by us in a better and more dignified way; and beyond question our ancestors have adopted better regulations and laws than others in directing the policy of government. What shall I say of the art of war? In this sphere our countrymen have proved their superiority by valour as well as in an even greater degree by discipline. When we come to natural gifts apart from book-learning they are above comparison with the Greeks or any other people. Where has such earnestness, where such firmness, greatness of soul, honesty, loyalty, where has such surpassing merit in every field been found in any of mankind to justify comparison with our ancestors? (Cicero, *Tusculan Disputations*, 3–5 [book 1, sec. 1])

Methinks the Roman doth protest too much. This impassioned assertion of Roman superiority in the face of Greek civilization perhaps best reveals the Romans' overwhelming sense of cultural inferiority, or what Harold Bloom would call their anxiety of influence. They are desperate to find areas in which they can claim to surpass the Greeks. See Mazzolani, *Idea of the City*, 143–46: "The [Roman] balance of cultural trade, in fact, was heavily overweighted on the side of imports; but the republic threw into the other scale its traditional piety, the discipline of the legions, the sanctity of the family, the respect for law, the parsimony of the magistrates" (144).

58. The second reference to Greece in Coriolanus's speech appears in Plutarch's account, but the first is Shakespeare's invention (Spencer, *Shakespeare's Plutarch*, 322–23).

59. See David Lowenthal, *Shakespeare and the Good Life: Ethics and Politics in Dramatic Form* (Lanham, MD: Rowman and Littlefield, 1997): "In *Coriolanus*, at the beginning of the Roman republic, life was guided by dominant and unchallenged moral custom. . . . Here there were no philosophers or philosophies" (136).

60. See Platt, *Rome and Romans*, 52–53.

61. See Lowenthal, *Shakespeare and the Good Life*, 137–38.

62. Ibid., 137.

63. I am simply repeating the complaint of the greatest of all Shakespearean nitpickers, Thomas Rymer, who writes of this scene: "Here the Roman Senators, the midnight before *Caesar's* death (met in the Garden of *Brutus*, to settle the matter of their conspiracy) are gazing up at the Stars, and have no more in their heads than to wrangle about which is the East and West" (Thomas Rymer, *A Short View of Tragedy* in *The Critical Works of Thomas Rymer*, ed. Curt A. Zimansky [New Haven, CT: Yale University Press, 1956], 168).

64. For a different and intriguing interpretation of this strange moment, see Burckhardt, *Shakespearean Meanings*, 5–6. Burckhardt relates the dispute over the dawn to controversies surrounding Julius Caesar's introduction of a new calendar in Rome. For further and more detailed discussion of the relevance of Caesar's calendar reform to Shakespeare's play, see Steve Sohmer, *Shakespeare's Mystery Play: The Opening of the Globe Theatre 1599* (Manchester, UK:

Manchester University Press, 1999), esp. 88–95. For yet another interpretation of this daybreak scene, see Harold C. Goddard, *The Meaning of Shakespeare* (Chicago: University of Chicago Press, 1951), vol. 1, 316–17; he interprets this moment as expressing Shakespeare's skepticism about the conspiracy: "These men think they are about to bring a new day to Rome when they cannot agree as to where the geographical east lies."

65. *Julius Caesar* may even contain a kind of quotation from Plato. The dialogue between Brutus and Cassius at 1.2.51–70 deals with the Socratic issue of self-knowledge, and, as several commentators have noted, seems to echo a passage in Plato's dialogue, *Alcibiades I* (132d–133d). I discuss the Brutus–Cassius dialogue in *Shakespeare's Rome*, 108. For an excellent and more detailed discussion of this passage and its link to the *Alcibiades*, see Alvis, *Shakespeare's Understanding of Honor*, 128–32. On the issue of self-knowledge in this passage, see also J. L. Simmons, *Shakespeare's Pagan World: The Roman Tragedies* (Charlottesville: University Press of Virginia, 1973), 78; and Dennis Bathory, "'With Himself at War': Shakespeare's Roman Hero and the Republican Tradition," in *Shakespeare's Political Pageant: Essays in Politics and Literature*, ed. Joseph Alulis and Vickie Sullivan (Lanham, MD: Rowman and Littlefield, 1996), 237–61. Barbara Parker, *Plato's Republic*, suggests another link to Plato in *Julius Caesar*. She notes that its first scene features a carpenter and a cobbler, two of Socrates's favorite professions for illustrating the principle of the division of labor in Plato's *Republic* (see 434a–b, 443c). In the first of these passages, Socrates argues that carpenters and cobblers do not make good warriors. Thus, in the opening scene of *Julius Caesar* Shakespeare may be suggesting a weakness of the late Republic. Once the plebeians have become identified with professions such as carpentry and shoemaking, they will no longer provide the kind of citizen army the republic relied on. Note that in the First Folio, the plebeians are identified as citizens in the opening scene of *Coriolanus*, but they are identified by their professions in the corresponding moment in *Julius Caesar*. The moneymaking professions of the plebeians now mean more to them than their status as citizen-soldiers in the Roman army.

66. See James E. Holton, "Marcus Tullius Cicero," in *History of Political Philosophy*, 3rd ed., ed. Leo Strauss and Joseph Cropsey (Chicago: University of Chicago Press, 1987), 155–56. See also Thomas L. Pangle, "Roman Cosmopolitanism: The Stoics and Cicero," in *Cosmopolitanism in the Age of Globalization*, ed. Lee Trepanier and Khalil M. Habib (Lexington: University Press of Kentucky, 2011), 48; and Gary Wills, *Rome and Rhetoric: Shakespeare's Julius Caesar* (New Haven, CT: Yale University Press, 2011), 9.

67. The subject of philosophy comes up frequently in Plutarch's *Life of Brutus*, but he identifies the Roman as an Academic, not a Stoic: "Now touching the Grecian philosophers, there was no sect nor philosopher of them but he heard and liked it. But above all the rest he loved Plato's sect best, and did not much give himself to the new nor mean Academy, as they call it, but altogether the old Academy" (Spencer, *Shakespeare's Plutarch*, 103). In Plutarch, Brutus actually goes to Athens and studies philosophy there: "He went daily to hear the lectures of Theomnestus, Academic philosopher, and of Cratippus the Peripatetic; and so would he talk with them in philosophy that it seemed he left all other matters and gave himself only unto study. . . . He did also entertain all the young gentlemen of the Romans whom he found in Athens studying philosophy" (133). As for Cassius, Plutarch does identify him specifically as an Epicurean, and in fact gives him a long speech on Epicurean epistemology, which begins: "In our sect, Brutus, we have an opinion that we do not always feel or see that which we suppose we do both see and feel" (149). With all the references to sects of Greek philosophy in Plutarch, it is no wonder that Shakespeare chose to deal with the subject in *Julius Caesar*. One more example of the Greek pen-

etration of Rome is provided by the character Artemidorus, who attempts to warn Julius Caesar of the conspiracy. Plutarch explains how Artemidorus learned of the conspiracy: "One Artemidorus also, born on the isle of Gnidos, a doctor of rhetoric in the Greek tongue, . . . by means of his profession was very familiar with certain of Brutus' confederates and therefore knew the most part of their practices against Caesar" (91). According to Plutarch, Brutus's confederates, by embracing the company of a Greek teacher, nearly betray the conspiracy.

68. For example, *Timon of Athens* contains a character designated as a philosopher, but he is *not* Socrates.

69. On Cicero's role in the play, see Allan Bloom, *Shakespeare's Politics*, 108–10n42; Girard, *Theater of Envy*, 189; Wills, *Rome and Rhetoric*, 2–14; Hadfield, *Shakespeare and Republicanism*, 168–71; and Yasunari Takeda, "Shakespeare's Cicero," *Poetica* 48 (1997): 57–65.

70. Allan Bloom, *Shakespeare's Politics*, 104.

71. On the centrality of anger as an issue in Stoic philosophy, see Gordon Braden, *Renaissance Tragedy and the Senecan Tradition: Anger's Privilege* (New Haven, CT: Yale University Press, 1985), 10–11.

72. One might accuse Brutus of being partly responsible for Portia's death; for the sake of his political purposes, he abandons her and leaves her to deal with her grief alone (*Julius Caesar* 4.3.152–56).

73. Friedrich Nietzsche, *The Gay Science*, trans. Walter Kaufmann (New York: Vintage, 1974), 245 (sec. 306).

74. For good overviews of this complicated controversy, see Warren D. Smith, "The Duplicate Revelation of Portia's Death," *Shakespeare Quarterly* 4 (1953): 153–61; and Brents Stirling, "Brutus and the Death of Portia," *Shakespeare Quarterly* 10 (1959): 211–17. Both Smith and Stirling come up with ingenious interpretations that accept the duplicate revelation of Portia's death as textually authentic, but nevertheless save Brutus's reputation. Among the many critics who agree with my views on this matter, see, e.g., Mungo William MacCallum, *Shakespeare's Roman Plays and Their Background* (London: MacMillan, 1910), 242–43 (MacCallum says that Brutus gives "a demonstration, so to speak, in Clinical Ethics"); Goddard, *Meaning of Shakespeare*, 1:326; Allan Bloom, *Shakespeare's Politics*, 101–2, 110n45; Platt, *Rome and Romans*, 228–29; Wills, *Rome and Rhetoric*, 70–71; Ronan, *"Antike Roman,"* 94–95; Blits, *Rome and the Spirit of Caesar*, 124–25; and Geoffrey Bullough, ed., *Narrative and Dramatic Sources of Shakespeare* (London: Routledge and Kegan Paul, 1964), vol. 5, 48–49.

75. William Shakespeare, *Julius Caesar*, eds. William and Barbara Rosen, 2nd rev. ed. (New York: New American Library, 1998), 105. Here is what the Rosens have to say about the double revelation problem, in their note to Brutus's exchange with Messala: "Some editors suggest that this was the original version of Shakespeare's account of Portia's death and that he later deleted this and wrote [the other account], preferring to demonstrate Brutus's humanity rather than his Stoicism; the Folio printer then set up both versions by mistake" (83).

76. Evans, *Riverside Shakespeare*, 1132.

77. Ibid.

78. Spencer, *Shakespeare's Plutarch*, 155.

79. Ibid.

80. See Allan Bloom, *Shakespeare's Politics*, 102–3; and Alvis, *Shakespeare's Understanding of Honor*, 137–38. Brutus's inconsistent application of his Stoic principles is evident early in the play when he tells Cassius: "Vexed I am / Of late with passions" (*Julius Caesar*, 1.2.39–40).

81. Plutarch describes Brutus as "having framed his manners of life by the rules of virtue and study of philosophy" (Spencer, *Shakespeare's Plutarch*, 102). Shakespeare's Brutus seems

to have reduced the "study of philosophy" to apprehending the "rules of virtue." In *A New Mimesis: Shakespeare and the Representation of Reality* (London: Methuen, 1983), 103–4, A. D. Nuttall views the philosophies of late antiquity as a falling off from the peak of Socrates, Plato, and Aristotle:

> Later philosophers, losing confidence in their ability to achieve true wisdom, reduce philosophy to providing in effect manuals of conduct to promote contentment. They now present themselves as purveyors of mental health. It is as if some immense failure of nerve, a kind of generational neurosis, swept through the ancient world, so that the most serious thinkers found that their urgent task was not to inform or enlighten but to heal. They begin to sound like psychiatrists. This is the period of Stoicism and Epicureanism, in which the philosophers say, again and again, "Come to us and we will give you . . . *freedom from tumult, tranquility*". . . . It has now become natural to expect *solace* from a philosopher—very soon books will appear with such titles as *The Consolation of Philosophy*, which would have seemed strange to Aristotle.

Not to mention Socrates, who thought of himself as a gadfly in the city and sought to provoke the Athenians, not to calm them. Nuttall's view of the philosophy of late antiquity is confirmed by a statement in Epicurus's Letter to Menoeceus: "Prudence is a more valuable thing than philosophy" (*The Epicurus Reader*, trans. and ed. Brad Inwood and L. P. Carson [Indianapolis, IN: Hackett, 1994)], 31).

82. In his discussion "Of the Sect of Stoics," Montesquieu writes: "The several sects of philosophy among the ancients were a species of religion" (*Spirit of the Laws*, 33 [book 24, chapter 10]).

83. The classic essay on this subject is T. S. Eliot, "Shakespeare and the Stoicism of Seneca," *Selected Essays* (New York: Harcourt, Brace, 1950), 107–20. For a comprehensive and incisive discussion of the role of Stoicism in Renaissance drama, see Braden, *Renaissance Tragedy*.

84. Even to call Stoicism a "Greek" movement can be misleading, given the fact that in the Hellenistic age when it arose, the meaning of "Greek" had become attenuated. Franz Cumont, *Astrology and Religion among the Greeks and Romans* (New York: Dover, 1960), writes: "It has often been observed that the masters of the Stoic school are for the most part Orientals. Zeno himself was born at Kition on the island of Cyprus. . . . Diogenes of Babylon, Posidonius of Apamea, Antipater of Tyre—to mention only the leading representatives of these doctrines—were all Syrians. In a certain sense it may be said that Stoicism was a Semitic philosophy" (46–47). Cumont's claim is controversial, but before identifying Stoicism as *the* Roman philosophy, it is worth noting that it was in fact just one more example of the many movements that came out of the East to sweep Rome. Zeno of Kition (or Citium), who lived 334–262 BCE, should not be confused with Zeno of Elea (c.490–c.430 BCE). Zeno of Kition may well have been of Phoenician descent.

85. See Charles Martindale and Michelle Martindale, *Shakespeare and the Uses of Antiquity: An Introductory Essay* (London: Routledge, 1900): "It was in fact only under the Empire that Stoicism became widely popular in Rome" (167).

86. See Mazzolani, *Idea of the City*, 31.

87. Braden, *Renaissance Tragedy*, 16–17. See also Syme, *Roman Revolution*: "As for the tenets of the Stoics, they could support doctrines quite distasteful to Roman Republicans, namely monarchy or the brotherhood of man" (57). For the inner connection between Cynicism and Stoicism, see Moses Hadas, introduction to *Essential Works of Stoicism* (New York: Bantam, 1961), x; Pangle, "Roman Cosmopolitanism," 52–53; Blits, *Rome and the Spirit of*

Caesar, 122; and Leo Strauss, *Natural Right and History* (Chicago: University of Chicago Press, 1953), 146.

88. Stoicism in fact works to efface the distinction between public and private life and thereby the traditional difference between a king and a beggar, or an emperor and a slave. As Moses Hadas writes of the Stoic: "No matter if he possesses none of the 'things indifferent,' the Stoic sage is king and perfectly happy; and the actual king, unless he is a sage, is not happy no matter how much he possesses. The king is not privileged, the pauper under no disabilities; both are equally important in the scheme of nature, which has assigned a necessary role to each" (Hadas, introduction to *Essential Works of Stoicism*, ix). See Cleopatra's remark about the "dung" as "the beggar's nurse and Caesar's" (*Antony and Cleopatra*, 5.2.8).

89. See Lowenthal, *Shakespeare and the Good Life*, 139. On the apolitical character of Stoicism, see Rostovtzeff, *Rome*, 156; Mazzolani, *Idea of the City*, 55–58; and Fustel de Coulanges, *Ancient City*: "The Stoics returned to politics. . . . But their principles were far removed from the old municipal politics" (350). For the apolitical character of Cynicism and Epicureanism, see Fustel de Coulanges, *Ancient City*, 350. For an overview of the ways in which philosophy contributed to the dissolution of civic polity in the ancient world, see Fustel de Coulanges, *Ancient City*, 347–52.

90. The poet/cynic who interrupts Cassius and Brutus in act 4 in effect wants them to be indifferent to politics; they have in fact been arguing over very serious political issues, which they really need to work out. Brutus has contempt for the poet, dismissing him as irrelevant in this charged political situation: "What should the wars do with these jigging fools?" (*Julius Caesar*, 4.3.137). It is interesting that Plutarch presents this figure (named Marcus Faonius) as not a genuine philosopher but only someone masquerading in the role: he "took upon him to counterfeit a philosopher not with wisdom and discretion but with a certain bedlam and frantic motion." Plutarch's Marcus Faonius is clearly indifferent to politics (he "cared for never a Senator of them all"). Plutarch says that Faonius treated Cassius and Brutus "with a certain scoffing and mocking gesture, which he counterfeited of purpose." In Plutarch, it is Brutus, not Cassius, who calls this figure a cynic, specifically a "counterfeit Cynic" (Spencer, *Shakespeare's Plutarch*, 146). Plutarch's emphasis on people who counterfeit being philosophers may have struck Shakespeare. For a very different interpretation of this strange interruption of the quarrel between Cassius and Brutus, see Friedrich Nietzsche, *The Gay Science*, sec. 98. For a critique of Nietzsche's interpretation, see Allan Bloom, *Shakespeare's Politics*, 101 and 110n44. For further interpretation of this scene, see Blits, *Rome and the Spirit of Caesar*, 121–22; and Richard Wilson, *William Shakespeare: Julius Caesar* (London: Penguin, 1992), 114–15.

91. Historically, Cicero did of course become active politically in the events following the assassination of Caesar, championing the republican cause and leading the fight against Mark Antony in his famous orations, the *Philippics*. Shakespeare ignores this part of the story entirely.

92. See Syme, *Roman Revolution*: "Epicureanism, indeed, was heavily frowned upon, being a morally unedifying creed, and likely to inculcate a distaste for public service" (461).

93. Pangle says of the historical Cicero that he "raises the doubt whether the Stoics in fact have any political philosophy worthy of the name" ("Roman Cosmopolitanism," 48).

94. See Lowenthal, *Shakespeare and the Good Life*, 138.

95. Allan Bloom argues, "Brutus' virtue is not an unknown or private virtue, like that of the most authentic Stoics, who took Diogenes as one of their supreme models" (*Shakespeare's Politics*, 95).

96. For an overview of the introduction of philosophy, in particular Stoicism and Epicureanism, into republican Rome and its effect on the Roman regime, see Jan H. Blits, *The Heart of*

Rome: Ancient Rome's Political Culture (Lanham, MD: Lexington, 2014), 93–112. See also Blits, *Rome and the Spirit of Caesar*, xxi.

97. This may be a central theme in *Timon of Athens*. See Paul A. Cantor, "*Timon of Athens*: The Corrupt City and the Origins of Philosophy," *In-between: Essays & Studies in Literary Criticism* 4 (1995): 25–40. For Machiavelli on philosophy as a corrupting force in a political community, see his *Florentine Histories*, trans. Laura F. Banfield and Harvey C. Mansfield (Princeton, NJ: Princeton University Press, 1988), 185 (book 5, chapter 1) and Sullivan, *Machiavelli's Three Romes*, 12–14. Nietzsche writes: "The Romans during their best period lived without philosophy" (*Philosophy in the Tragic Age of the Greeks*, trans. Marianne Cowan [Chicago: Henry Regnery, 1962], 27).

98. Montesquieu, *Considerations*, 97. In *Antony and Cleopatra*, Shakespeare hints at a connection between Epicureanism and imperial Rome's corruption when he has Pompey conjure "epicurean cooks" to "sharpen" Antony's "appetite" and make him lose his "honor" in sexual indulgence (2.1.24–26). This is of course the vulgar meaning of "epicurean," but it is related to the philosophic meaning.

99. G. W. F. Hegel, *Hegel's Philosophy of Right*, trans. T. M. Knox (Oxford: Clarendon Press, 1962), 13.

100. The motif of Antony's serving Cleopatra and un-Roman gods goes back to Virgil's *Aeneid*, where, at the end of book 8, the Roman gods help Octavius defeat Antony and his Egyptian gods at the Battle of Actium. I briefly discuss the relation of *Antony and Cleopatra* to the *Aeneid* in a roundtable in *Poets and Critics Read Vergil*, ed. Sarah Spence (New Haven, CT: Yale University Press, 2001), 188–89. See also Heather James, *Shakespeare's Troy: Drama, Politics, and the Translation of Empire* (Cambridge: Cambridge University Press, 1997), 126n175.

101. See, e.g., Maurice Charney, *Shakespeare's Roman Plays: The Function of Imagery in the Drama* (Cambridge, MA: Harvard University Press, 1961), 109–12; and Janet Adelman, *The Common Liar: An Essay on Antony and Cleopatra* (New Haven, CT: Yale University Press, 1973), 153–54. For a fuller discussion of this topic, see Cantor, *Shakespeare's Rome*, 23–30.

102. See Cantor, *Shakespeare's Rome*, 136–37; and R. B. Parker, introduction to *Coriolanus*: "The play is dense with references to the buildings and fabric of Rome—not only the Capitol, Senate, and marketplace, which are locales for action, but also walls, gates, ports, streets, conduits, temples, storehouses, mills, shops, stalls, windows, leads, roofs, and foundations" (76).

103. As Jan Blits points out, "the Capitol, the only public building in Rome named, is spoken of only in the context of Rome's historic past" (2.1.18; Pompey is speaking of the Rome of Cassius and Brutus); see Blits, *New Heaven*, 4.

104. See, e.g., Charney, *Roman Plays*, 103–5.

105. For the idea that the Romans of *Antony and Cleopatra* are "ill-rooted," see 2.7.2; for the idea that they may "sink" in "quicksands," see 2.7.59–60; for the idea that their world is spinning around in a dizzying fashion, see 2.7.92–94, 117–18. Imagery of sinking and melting runs throughout the play; see, e.g., 1.1.33 and 2.5.78.

106. For the stage history of act 3, scene 1, see Neill, introduction to *Anthony and Cleopatra*, 60–61. Neill states that this scene "is routinely cut from most productions of the play." He himself describes it as a "seemingly unimportant episode."

107. In Plutarch's account, Ventidius eventually gets to celebrate a genuine triumph in Rome (Spencer, *Shakespeare's Plutarch*, 219). For the historical Ventidius, see Syme, *Roman Revolution*, 223–24; and W. W. Tarn and M. P. Charlesworth, *From Republic to Empire: The Roman Civil War 44 B.C.—27 B.C.* (New York: Barnes & Noble, 1996), 63–64, 67. On the historical importance of the Parthians, see Mazzolani, *Idea of the City*, 163–69.

108. See Platt, *Rome and Romans*, 265–67.

109. For this general point, see Montesquieu, *Considerations*, 123–24; he applies it specifically to the historical Ventidius on 126n10. See also Machiavelli, *Discourses*, book 1, chapter 30; this chapter offers good evidence that Shakespeare had read the *Discourses*. See Cantor, *Shakespeare's Rome*, 42–45.

110. On religion in the Roman Republic, specifically the practice of augury, see Machiavelli, *Discourses*, book 1, chapters 11–14.

111. There is one minor reference to an "augurer" in *Coriolanus* at 2.1.1. In one of his trivial mistakes about Rome, Shakespeare substitutes "augurer" for the correct term "augur."

112. See Cantor, *Shakespeare's Rome*, 142–43. In North's Plutarch, when the Roman ambassadors fail to convince Coriolanus to spare Rome, the city turns to religious figures: "For then they appointed all the bishops, priests, ministers of the gods, and keepers of holy things, and all the augurs or soothsayers (which foreshow things to come by observation of the flying of birds, which is an old ancient kind of prophesying and divination among the Romans), to go to Martius appareled as when they do their sacrifices" (Spencer, *Shakespeare's Plutarch*, 349). Earlier in Plutarch's account, just after Coriolanus's banishment, Rome is beset with strange visions: "Moreover the priests, the soothsayers, and private men also, came and declared to the Senate certain sights and wonders in the air" (339). Note that according to North's Plutarch, "soothsayers" were already present in the Rome of Coriolanus.

113. In North's Plutarch, Valeria has the divine vision: "So she suddenly fell into such a fancy . . . and had (by some god, as I think) taken hold of a noble device." Approaching Volumnia and Virgilia with the idea of an embassy to Coriolanus, Valeria stresses the fact that she is operating outside the authority of the Republic: "We ladies are come to visit you, my lady Volumnia and Virgilia, by no direction from the Senate nor commandment of other magistrate, but through the inspiration, as I take it, of some god above" (*Shakespeare's Plutarch*, 351). Poole, *Coriolanus*, points out that Shakespeare "entirely excises the religious aura surrounding this part of the story" (12).

114. For similar conceptions of "fortune" among republican Romans in *Coriolanus*, see Titus Lartius at 1.5.20–24, who basically says that "Fortune" will fall in love with Coriolanus as a "Bold gentleman"; and a Roman patrician at 3.1.253, who says of Coriolanus: "This man has marr'd his fortune" (implying that it was within his power to make his fortune); and Volumnia at 5.3.119–20), who says, "I purpose not to wait on fortune till / These wars determine," meaning that she will take fortune into her own hands. One reason why Machiavelli admired the republican Romans is that they appear to follow his infamous advice about fortune: "Fortune is a woman; and it is necessary, if one wants to hold her down, to beat and strike her down. And one sees that she lets herself be won more by the impetuous than by those who proceed coldly. And so always, like a woman, she is a friend of the young, because they are less cautious, more ferocious, and command her with more audacity" (Niccolò Machiavelli, *The Prince*, trans. Harvey C. Mansfield, 2nd ed. [Chicago: University of Chicago Press, 1998], 101 (chapter 25).

115. In Plutarch's account, Rome builds "a Temple of Fortune of the Women" to celebrate Volumnia's triumph over Coriolanus, and the image of Fortune miraculously says: "Ladies, ye have devoutly offered me up" (Spencer, *Shakespeare's Plutarch*, 359). Shakespeare's omission of this dramatically effective moment once again suggests that he was deliberately downplaying the role of fortune and divine revelation in the Roman Republic.

116. On this point, see Marvin L. Vawter, "'After Their Fashion': Cicero and Brutus in *Julius Caesar*," *Shakespeare Studies* 9 (1976): 207–8.

117. For a contrary view of the extent to which Caesar becomes superstitious, see Allan Bloom, *Shakespeare's Politics*, 107n24.

118. On this point, see ibid., 103; Vawter, "Cicero and Brutus," 212–13; and Richmond, *Shakespeare's Political Plays*, 214–15. On the way that Caesar, Cassius, and Brutus all become superstitious, see Timothy Spiekerman, "The Inevitable Monarchy: Shakespeare's *Julius Caesar*," in *Natural Right and Political Philosophy: Essays in Honor of Catherine Zuckert and Michael Zuckert*, ed. Ann Ward and Lee Ward (Notre Dame, IN: University of Notre Dame Press, 2013), 370–79.

119. Andrews, editor's introduction to *Antony and Cleopatra*, xxiii–xxiv, similarly links Brutus's "tide" speech to the water imagery in *Antony and Cleopatra*.

120. On this point, see Wilson, *Julius Caesar*, 106; Vawter, "Cicero and Brutus," 210; and Goddard, *Meaning of Shakespeare*, 1:328.

121. Spiekerman explores the question of whether or not the conspiracy was doomed to failure from the beginning in "Inevitable Monarchy," 360–82.

122. On this point, see Allan Bloom, *Shakespeare's Politics*, 80.

123. Kott sees this issue playing out in the Roman plays; Shakespeare is "fascinated by history. Where and when is it decided, and who decides it? Does it have a human face, the name and passions of a prince, or is it just a sum total of chance, or mechanism put in motion?" (Kott, *Shakespeare Our Contemporary*, 203).

124. See Derek Traversi, *Shakespeare: The Roman Plays* (Stanford, CA: Stanford University Press, 1963), 127.

125. On this point, see Goddard, *Meaning of Shakespeare*, 2:187. Earlier in the play, Pompey talks about the difficulties of imperial finance: "Caesar gets money where / He loses hearts" (*Antony and Cleopatra*, 2.1.13–14). Note that Ventidius attributes his victory over the Parthians to Antony's "well-paid ranks" (3.1.32). Evidently the Roman army is now dependent on mercenaries. Money is the principal subject of the quarrel between Cassius and Brutus in act 4, scene 3 of *Julius Caesar*. Brutus learns that he cannot conduct his wars "without gold to pay [his] legions" (4.3.76). With an army of citizen-soldiers, Coriolanus never had to worry about paying the Roman army (their share in war booty was enough for them).

126. See Garber, *Shakespeare After All*, 743–45, for the importance of single combat in *Antony and Cleopatra* and in other plays by Shakespeare.

127. See James, *Shakespeare's Troy*: Antony is "an anachronism in the emerging bureaucracy of the Roman empire" (128); and Camille Paglia, *Sexual Personae: Art and Decadence from Nefertiti to Emily Dickinson* (New Haven, CT: Yale University Press, 1990), 214.

128. That is why the Roman Empire was able to maintain order even with incompetent emperors on the throne. The Roman war machine kept functioning even with degenerate madmen such as Nero and Caligula nominally in command. In fact, Roman military commanders periodically intervened to eliminate bad emperors when they became too dysfunctional. Paradoxically, the system of one-man rule in the Roman Empire was actually premised on the idea that a single heroic figure was no longer necessary to preserve Roman order. A military system could take the place of individual heroism in the Empire. This may explain why the Greek historian Polybius devotes so much of his account of the Roman constitution in book 6 of his *Histories* to a detailed description of the Roman military camp and its institutions. Polybius understood that the backbone of the Roman constitution was in fact its military order. Syme, *Roman Revolution*, 352–59, shows that in the imperial era, the Roman military became a much more meritocratic institution and created a new upward social mobility for soldiers, since they were able to rise in social rank by virtue of their service in the army.

129. See Allan Bloom, *Shakespeare's Politics*, 79; Garber, *Shakespeare After All*, 727–28; Neill, introduction to *Anthony and Cleopatra*, 95–96; and Harold Bloom, *Shakespeare: The Invention of the Human* (New York: Riverhead, 1998), 551, 558.

130. On the importance of soothsayers in *Antony and Cleopatra*, see Garber, *Shakespeare After All*, 731; and Blits, *Rome and the Spirit of Caesar*, 11.

131. This fatalism is all-pervasive in the play. Antony speaks of "strong necessity" (1.3.42) and Octavius speaks of "strong necessities" (3.6.83). Cumont in his *Astrology and Religion* writes about the increasing belief in astrological influences in imperial Rome. Shakespeare has Antony speak of "my good stars, that were my former guides" (3.13.145), while Octavius attributes his rival's defeat to astral influences when he refers to "our stars, / Unreconcilable" (5.1.46–47). The widespread belief in astrology in late antiquity may explain why Cassius feels it necessary to say: "The fault, dear Brutus, is not in our stars" (*Julius* Caesar, 1.2.140).

132. This development can be observed in Brutus toward the end of *Julius Caesar*, when he has begun to despair of success: "O, that a man might know / The end of this day's business ere it come!" (5.1.122–23). See Traversi, *Shakespeare: The Roman Plays*, 72.

133. On "idleness" in Egypt, see esp. 1.3.91–93, but "idleness" is also evident in Rome at its heart (1.4.76). This is a good example of how the much-vaunted contrast between Rome and Egypt in *Antony and Cleopatra* is, in fact, being effaced in the era of the Empire. Idleness is a problem in both Rome and Egypt; it is characteristic of a whole empire that has no more worlds to conquer. Antony speaks of the stagnant state of the Empire: "quietness, grown sick of rest, would purge / By any desperate change" (1.3.53–54).

134. In fact, the Roman Empire was to have a long and intermittently glorious history for several centuries after the time of Antony and Cleopatra. It did face many foreign challenges, and up through the reign of the emperor Trajan it continued to add to its territory. Shakespeare, however, seems to suppress this part of Roman history and presents the imperial era as an end for Rome, not a new beginning. For Friedrich Nietzsche's contrary views on this subject, see chapter 2 of this volume.

135. Ventidius's strategy is anticipated earlier in the play when the pirate Mencrates says: "so find we profit / By losing of our prayers" (*Antony and Cleopatra*, 2.1.7–8).

136. Think of Fabius's famous strategy of delay against Hannibal. On the possibility of a tactical retreat in *Coriolanus*, consider Cominius's claim: "We have at disadvantage fought and did / Retire to win our purpose" (1.6.49–50). But notice that Cominius insists that he will still "win our purpose"—even in retreat, he is thinking about winning.

137. The contrast with Coriolanus's attitude toward humility could not be sharper. The tribune Sicinius notes "with what contempt he [Coriolanus] wore the humble weed" (2.3.221). In the world of *Coriolanus*, only the tribunes embrace humility (characteristically as a means of covering up their slavish scheming): "Now we have shown our power, / Let us seem humbler after it is done / Than when it was a-doing" (4.2.3–5).

138. In North's Plutarch, Brutus says at this point: "It rejoiceth my heart that not one of my friends hath failed me at my need, and I do not complain of my fortune, but only for my country's sake" (Spencer, *Shakespeare's Plutarch*, 171). By omitting the phrase "for my country's sake," Shakespeare transforms what in Plutarch is still a political statement into a purely personal statement. See Blits, *Rome and the Spirit of Caesar*, who writes of Brutus's speech: "He is silent about Rome and expresses no lament for its passing. Instead, his last words center on himself, and he judges himself and his life by a standard wholly unconnected and even in conflict with the good of Rome" (149).

139. In *Julius Caesar* Antony learns how "vile" "conquest" is and how "paltry" it is "to be Caesar" when he comes upon the bloody corpse of his friend: "O mighty Caesar! dost thou lie so low? / Are all thy conquests, glories, triumphs, spoils / Shrunk to this little measure?" (3.1.148–50).

140. Andrews, editor's introduction to *Antony and Cleopatra*, xxiv, refers to this speech as "the self-consoling rationalizations of a loser."

141. Antony provides the prototype of following a "fallen lord" in *Julius Caesar* and thereby earns his place in the story.

142. Earlier in the play, Cleopatra reverses this paradox when she speaks of the way that Cneius Pompey would look at her "and die / With looking on his life" (1.5.33–34). See also what she says to Antony at 4.15.38: "Die when thou hast liv'd."

143. On this subject, see Montesquieu, *Considerations*, 203. An extraordinary amount of weeping occurs in *Antony and Cleopatra*; even Octavius has tears in his eyes when he parts from his sister (3.2.50–51); see also his response to news of Antony's death (5.1.27–28). Enobarbus reacts to the tearful parting of Octavius and Octavia with a traditional Roman disdain for weeping (3.2.52–54). In accord with this attitude, very little weeping occurs in *Coriolanus* (and then only among the women; see, e.g., 5.3.156, where Coriolanus "cares not for [Virgilia's] weeping"). Coriolanus can barely be brought to tears: "it is no little thing to make / Mine eyes to sweat compassion" (5.3.195–96). Shakespeare captures Coriolanus's noble contempt for weeping by having him reduce it to a mere physiological reaction ("to sweat compassion").

144. Machiavelli, *Discourses*, 131 (book II, chapter 2).

145. See, e.g., Montesquieu, *Considerations*, 148 and Rostovtzeff, *Rome*, 291–308.

146. Christians claim that Constantine had a divine revelation and converted to Christianity himself before converting the Empire. For the political reading of Constantine's turn to Christianity, see Jacob Burckhardt, *The Age of Constantine the Great*, trans. Moses Hadas (Berkeley: University of California Press, 1983), 292–335; Rostovtzeff, *Rome*, 289–90; and Mazzolani, *Idea of the City*, 212.

147. For the references to Herod in *Antony and Cleopatra*, see 1.2.28–29, 3.3.3–4 (two times), 3.6.73, and 4.6.13—Herod is mentioned a total of five times in the play. Herod is mentioned in Plutarch's account (see Spencer, *Shakespeare's Plutarch*, 250, 269), but Shakespeare has gone out of his way to make Herod more prominent in his play. At one point where North's Plutarch speaks of "Antigonus King of the Jews" (Spencer, *Shakespeare's Plutarch*, 222), Shakespeare changes it to "Herod of Jewry" (3.3.3). For excellent overviews of the Christian references and allusions in *Antony and Cleopatra*, see Andrew Fichter, "'Antony and Cleopatra': 'The Time of Universal Peace,'" *Shakespeare Survey* 33 (1980): 99–111; and Hannibal Hamlin, *The Bible in Shakespeare* (Oxford: Oxford University Press, 2013), 214–30. Hamlin points out that in these references Shakespeare may have either mistakenly or deliberately confused Herod the Great (a contemporary of Antony and Cleopatra) with his son, Herod Antipas (the Herod of the Gospel of Matthew). For more on the importance of these Herod references, see Roy W. Battenhouse, *Shakespearean Tragedy: Its Art and Its Christian Premises* (Bloomington: Indiana University Press, 1969), 173. On the importance of Christianity in *Antony and Cleopatra*, see Allan Bloom, *Love and Friendship*, 299, 303, 317–18. For what may well be an interesting example of Christian iconography in *Antony and Cleopatra*, see Garber, *Shakespeare After All*, 740–41. Northrop Frye comments on *Antony and Cleopatra*: "One cannot read or listen far into this play without being reminded that the action takes place about thirty years before what Shakespeare's audience would have considered the turning point of history, the birth of Christ" (*Northrop Frye*

on Shakespeare, ed. Robert Sandler [New Haven, CT: Yale University Press, 1986], 138). Paglia, *Sexual Personae*, writes: "*Antony and Cleopatra* takes place at a great transition in history, when empire replaces republic, creating the era of international peace in which Christianity would spread" (214). In short, I am by no means the only critic to see a Christian background to *Antony and Cleopatra*. For more general reflections on the importance of Christianity in the play, see Stanley Cavell, *Disowning Knowledge In Six Plays of Shakespeare* (Cambridge: Cambridge University Press, 1987), 18–37; and, derivative from Cavell, Lars Engle, *Shakespearean Pragmatism: Market of His Time* (Chicago: University of Chicago Press, 1993), 220–24.

148. See Platt, *Rome and Romans*, 271–72.

149. See Alvis, *Shakespeare's Understanding of Honor*, 188–89; Hamlin, *Bible in Shakespeare*, 222; Fichter, "Universal Peace," 105; J. A. Bryant, Jr., *Hippolyta's View: Some Christian Aspects of Shakespeare's Plays* (Lexington: University of Kentucky Press, 1961), 179–80; and Robert S. Miola, *Shakespeare's Rome* (Cambridge: Cambridge University Press, 1983), 145.

150. Ethel Seaton, "*Antony and Cleopatra* and the Book of Revelation," *Review of English Studies* 22 (1946): 219–24. See also Kenneth Muir, *Shakespeare's Sources: Comedies and Tragedies* (London: Methuen, 1977), 217–19. For an elaborate attempt to read *Antony and Cleopatra* in light of the Book of Revelation, see Battenhouse, *Shakespearean Tragedy*, 176–81.

151. On these parallels, see Hamlin, *Bible in Shakespeare*, 217.

152. On this scene as a parody of the Last Supper, see Bryant, *Hippolyta's View*, 182–83; Battenhouse, *Shakespearean Tragedy*, 173; Hamlin, *Bible in Shakespeare*, 223; Fichter, "Universal Peace," 105–6; and Ronan, "*Antike Roman,*" 19, 72, 83. See especially Cavell's characterization of this scene: "It is all exactly as mysterious as a last supper in which a death is announced through which hyperbole victory is to be expected in the place of death, and in the expectation of a transformed reappearance" (*Disowning Knowledge*, 151).

153. For Enobarbus as a Judas figure, see Bryant, *Hippolyta's View*, 182; Cavell, *Disowning Knowledge*, 26; Hannibal, *Bible in Shakespeare*, 222–23; and Fichter, "Universal Peace,"105. See also Patricia Parker, "Barbers, Infidels, and Renegades," 309–10, who points out that "Enobarbus" means "red beard" in Latin and in Shakespeare's day, a red beard was associated with Jews and specifically with Judas.

154. For this kind of interpretation, see Simmons, *Shakespeare's Pagan World*, 109–63; Battenhouse, *Shakespearean Tragedy*, 161–83; and Alvis, *Shakespeare's Understanding of Honor*, 191.

155. For an excellent discussion of the spiritual condition of the Mediterranean world in late antiquity, see Hans Jonas, *The Gnostic Religion* (Boston: Beacon, 1963), esp. 3–27.

156. Nietzsche develops these ideas most fully in the first essay of his *On the Genealogy of Morals*. See also sections 260–62 of his *Beyond Good and Evil*. Let me stress that the account I am giving in this chapter of Nietzsche's theory of the slave revolt in morality is preliminary and simplified, although no more simplified than what Nietzsche himself often says in his published writings. I am beginning with "master morality" and "slave morality" as these terms are commonly understood. These terms help clarify what is going on in Shakespeare's Roman plays. Chapter 2 will be largely devoted to showing how complicated the concepts of master morality and slave morality really are in Nietzsche's thought, and the Roman plays will help to reveal that complexity. In particular, we will see that Nietzsche does not simply prefer master morality to slave morality, as is generally supposed. I use these terms with serious reservations because of the emotional charge and sinister associations they carry (especially due to their use in Nazi ideology). For the moment, I am using Nietzsche's terminology purely for its descriptive value. In Chapter 2 I will develop at great length and in great detail a fuller and more nuanced sense of what Nietzsche means by these terms.

157. For the historical basis of Nietzsche's claims, see Fustel de Coulanges, *Ancient City*, 268–69, who, as Nietzsche does, cites the Greek poet Theognis on "good" versus "bad."

158. For the classic study of *ressentiment*, see Max Scheler, *Ressentiment*, trans. William W. Holdheim (New York: Free Press, 1961).

159. François Rabelais, *Gargantua and Pantagruel*, trans. M. A. Screech (London: Penguin, 2006), 345.

160. For similar passages, see *Henry IV, Part I*, 3.1.179–83, where what from one perspective looks like "greatness" and "courage," from another looks like "pride" and "haughtiness," and *Henry IV, Part II*, 2.1.123–25, where Falstaff tells the Lord Chief Justice: "You call honorable boldness impudent sauciness."

161. For more on classical versus Christian elements in *Macbeth*, see chapter 2 of this volume.

162. On this point, see R. B. Parker, introduction to *Coriolanus*, 79; and G. Wilson Knight, *The Imperial Theme* (London: Methuen, 1965), 163.

163. On the importance of the hero's physical strength, see Poole, *Coriolanus*: "No other play of Shakespeare's is dominated to the same extent by the brute physical presence of the central character, the very sight and sound of him. . . . It is necessary to realize the sheer danger of his presence" (xi–xiii). "This is why it is essential for an audience to be physically impressed by the actor playing Martius, to feel his impact, so that we can understand how the other characters come to think of him as superhuman" (19). After a lifetime of searching for a good performance of *Coriolanus* (including a turn at the role by the young Tommy Lee Jones when he was an undergraduate at Harvard), I had given up hope of ever seeing one—until in the spring of 2013 I saw a great one with Patrick Page playing the title role at the Shakespeare Theatre in Washington, DC. Page's volcanic performance—appropriately dominating the stage through the power of his voice—proved that *Coriolanus* works very well when properly produced with the right actor in the title role.

164. This idea is anticipated in *Julius Caesar* when Cassius speaks of suicide as the way the gods "make the weak most strong" (1.3.91). On this passage, see Hamlin, *Bible in Shakespeare*, 185. He cites a number of parallel passages in the New Testament in which "the weak are made strong," such as 2 Cor. 12:10: "For when I am weak, then am I strong" (he also cites 1 Cor. 1:25, 1 Cor. 4:10, 2 Cor. 13:9, and Heb. 11:34).

165. Fichter, "Time of Universal Peace," finds both Stoic and Christian elements in this line: "Antony finds honor in the direction of his downfall, a potential for self-affirmation in self-destruction, and triumph in defeat. Antony expresses it in its Stoic formulation: 'With a wound I must be cur'd' (1. 78); but in this rush of reversals we may also recognize one of Christianity's most fundamental precepts: one must first lose oneself in order to find oneself" (107).

166. In *Julius Caesar*, Calphurnia speaks very differently of beggars and kings, claiming that nature supports political hierarchy: "When beggars die there are no comets seen; / The heavens themselves blaze forth the death of princes" (2.2.30–31).

167. Cleopatra sees the fulfillment of Coriolanus's prophecy to his fellow aristocrats: "You are plebeians, / If they be senators" (3.1.101–2).

168. Cleopatra's lingering aristocratic nature is important to note. Unlike Nietzsche, Shakespeare portrays a revaluation of Roman values *within* the Roman aristocracy. Even as Cleopatra comes to question some aristocratic values, she clings to an aristocratic sense of her own superiority and in fact searches for ways to maintain her preeminence, if necessary in new forms of nobility. Shortly after Cleopatra denies the difference between Caesar and a beggar, she reverses her position and says to death: "Come, come, and take a queen / Worth many babes and beggars!" (5.2.47–48). From the very beginning of the play, she cooperates with Antony in distin-

guishing their love from "beggary" (1.1.15). I want to stress that I am not claiming that characters such as Cleopatra actually become Christians. Although she senses that the difference between nobles and commoners is eroding away, she still has contempt for the results and is not ready to embrace a humbler station in life. However much she is disillusioned with politics, Cleopatra is not about to take a vow of poverty. Although the aristocrats in *Antony and Cleopatra* have developed doubts about traditional Roman notions of nobility, they are only on the verge of re-valuing them as evil. The play contains only hints that the characters have come to think of their actions as evil. See, e.g., 4.5.16–17 (Antony); 4.6.17–19, 29–33 and 4.9.9, 19–22 (Enobarbus); and 4.15.80–82 (Cleopatra). To put the matter in anthropological terms, the Rome of *Antony and Cleopatra* remains a shame culture like the Rome of *Coriolanus* (although the characters are sometimes ashamed for different reasons); it has not yet become a guilt culture (Enobarbus's fate points in that direction; see chapter 2 of this volume). In defeat, Antony reveals his linger-ing Romanness—as a Roman noble, he is ashamed of himself: "Since Cleopatra died / I have liv'd in such dishonor that the gods / Detest my baseness" (4.14.55–57). In Nietzsche's terms, the opposition of good versus evil has not displaced the opposition of good versus bad in *Antony and Cleopatra*. The main characters still think largely in terms of the opposition "noble versus base." In sum, Shakespeare's imperial Romans have come to think that some things traditionally believed to be noble are in fact base; a few are contemplating the idea that some things thought to be base might truly be noble; they have not yet reached the point of thinking that some things thought to be noble are in fact evil. Shakespeare is of course only being true to history by not portraying a fully Christianized Rome in *Antony and Cleopatra*. But he does show a Rome that has taken some of the most important steps toward becoming Christian. For the differences between Shakespeare and Nietzsche in these matters, see chapter 2 of this volume.

169. On the inversion of masters and servants and the effacing of the difference in Christi-anity, see Matthew 23:10–12. Christianity is often credited with developing the idea of human equality, but Shakespeare shows that it might emerge from a disillusioned aristocracy. For the idea that the Roman Empire prepared the way for the Christian idea of equality, see Alexis de Tocqueville, *Democracy in America*, vol. 2, trans. Harvey C. Mansfield and Delba Winthrop (Chicago: University of Chicago Press, 2000), 420 (part 1, chapter 5): "At the moment when the Christian religion appeared on earth, Providence, which was undoubtedly preparing the world for its coming, had united a great part of the human species, like an immense flock, under the scepter of the Caesars. The men who composed this multitude . . . all obeyed the same laws; and each of them was so weak and small in relation to the greatness of the prince that they all ap-peared equal when one came to compare them to him." Tocqueville makes a proto-Nietzschean argument that the Roman Empire turned human beings into a kind of herd, and thus prepared them to accept Christianity. The empire reduces the former Roman citizens to mere subjects and in the process levels the traditional distinction between the patricians and the plebeians. Once one loses faith in the emperor's superiority, as Cleopatra does, one is left with a mass of human beings undifferentiated by rank. For more on the connection between Christianity and the idea of equality, see Fustel de Coulanges, *Ancient City*, 384.

170. Cleopatra's phrase "noble girls" (4.15.84) has a similarly oxymoronic force.

171. This notion of "good will" does appear in *Coriolanus*, but it is articulated by the tribune Sicinius when he is feeling at his weakest; trying to encourage Menenius to save Rome from Co-riolanus's onslaught, Sicinius tells him: "Yet your good will / Must have that thanks from Rome after the measure / As you intended well" (5.1.45–47). Appropriately, slave morality appears in the Republic in the mouth of a plebeian, who believes that all that matters is a person's inten-tions, not his accomplishments.

172. For a full explanation of this point, see chapter 4 of this volume. Belief in an afterlife does begin to surface in *Julius Caesar*, but only in the form of the traditional pagan notion that after death, the soul or spirit might somehow continue to exist separate from the body as a ghost or shade. Antony invokes Julius Caesar's spirit after the assassination: "Caesar's spirit, ranging for revenge, / With Ate by his side come hot from hell" (3.1.270–71). And, of course, Caesar appears as a ghost to Brutus on the eve of the battle of Philippi (4.3). But this apparition tells Brutus, not that he is Caesar's ghost but that he is "thy evil spirit, Brutus" (4.3.282). Thus this seems to be a form not of personal immortality but of haunting. To be sure, at 5.5.17 Brutus speaks of the "ghost of Caesar." The only hint of any kind of personal immortality in *Julius Caesar* can be found when Antony says of Caesar: "If then thy spirit look upon us now" (3.1.195). But even this is an attenuated form of survival after death, not a desirable state.

173. See Alvis, *Shakespeare's Understanding of Honor*, 180.

174. Many commentators have pointed out that Antony gets Virgil's account of the Underworld in the *Aeneid* wrong (see, e.g., Platt, *Rome and Romans*, 280; and Alvis, *Shakespeare's Understanding of Honor*, 180). Dido and Aeneas are not reunited in Virgil's account; Dido spurns the lover who rejected her in this world. Virgil's image of the Underworld as a place of punishment is in keeping with other ancient accounts of the afterlife. He paints a grim picture of life after death, with mere shades leading a shadowy existence. By contrast, Antony's image is more optimistic and what I have been calling proto-Christian; his afterlife is a kind of heaven in which lovers are brought back together triumphantly after death. Plutarch's account contains only the barest hint of belief in an afterlife in Antony's speech; he says nothing about Dido and Aeneas; all he says that implies an afterlife is: "O Cleopatra, it grieveth me not that I have lost thy company, for I will not be long from thee" (Spencer, *Shakespeare's Plutarch*, 277).

175. The Egyptian Charmian characteristically assumes that "the soul and body" separate ("rive") at the time of death (4.13.5).

176. See Franz Cumont, *Oriental Religions in Roman Paganism* (New York: Dover, 1956), who says of Egypt: "Nowhere else was life so completely dominated by preoccupation with life after death" (99).

177. For an overview of Roman suicide in Shakespeare's plays and other works of the time, see Ronan, *"Antike Roman,"* 87–89; and Charney, *Roman Plays*, 209–14.

178. Neill, introduction to *Anthony and Cleopatra*, formulates what happens in *Antony and Cleopatra* in these terms: "self-loss, through an erotic version of a familiar Christian paradox, can finally appear as a more profound kind of self-realization" (103).

179. On this subject, see Cantor, *Shakespeare's Rome*, 166–67.

180. Cleopatra's belief in an afterlife has almost no basis in Plutarch's account; all she says on the subject in Plutarch comes in an address to the dead Antony: "If therefore the gods where thou art now have any power and authority. . . ." (Spencer, *Shakespeare's Plutarch*, 290).

181. See Alvis, *Shakespeare's Understanding of Honor.* Cleopatra "begins to deliver *contemptu mundi* indictments against the earth she leaves to Caesar. . . . Both lovers begin to speak like anchorites as they approach a death which, as Cleopatra observes, has no sting" (187).

182. On the ways the idea of the afterlife transformed the ancient world, see Cumont, *Oriental Religions*, xxii–xxiii.

183. Eternity is precisely what is missing from the world of *Coriolanus*, a fact highlighted by Menenius's characterization of Coriolanus: "He wants nothing of a god but eternity and a heaven to throne in" (5.4.23–24). Antony and Cleopatra hope to discover the eternity denied to the characters in *Coriolanus*.

184. See Hadfield, *Shakespeare and Republicanism*, 221; and James, *Shakespeare's Troy*, 121–23.

185. See James, *Shakespeare's Troy:* "Mythological greatness is Cleopatra's compromise for failing to achieve imperial command" (144).

186. See Cantor, *Shakespeare's Rome,* 190–92. Virgilia is a stay-at-home wife, reluctant to leave the precincts of her household: "I'll not over the threshold till my lord returns from the wars." Volumnia questions this behavior: "You confine yourself most unreasonably" (see *Coriolanus,* 1.3.71–89 for their whole exchange).

187. See Allan Bloom, *Love and Friendship:* "I believe there is no similar example of a love without marriage sympathetically depicted in Shakespeare's plays. . . . The love of Antony and Cleopatra is the perfect example of a love for its own sake, at least on Antony's part, because it can never be good for Antony as anything other than itself, and the possibility of marriage or children is never considered" (304). On marriage in *Antony and Cleopatra,* see Cantor, *Shakespeare's Rome,* 157–59.

188. Only one reference to the East appears in *Coriolanus*—when Volumnia speaks of "Arabia" (4.2.24)—and there it functions as an image of utter remoteness.

189. For Montesquieu's understanding of the Roman Republic as tragic, see Manent, *Metamorphoses of the City:* "Montesquieu pities the republic. The republic, not Cato and even less Brutus and Cassius, is the true tragic hero. Roman history is a tragedy, or more precisely, according to Montesquieu, it is the succession of two tragedies, one that ends with the death of Cato and another that begins . . . with the deaths of Brutus and Cassius (170)."

190. See Blits, *New Heaven, New Earth,* 1. Syme, *Roman Revolution,* speaks of the "Empire of the Roman people, perishing of its own greatness" (9) and also writes, "Therein lay the tragedy—the Empire gave no scope for the display of civic virtue at home and abroad, for it sought to abolish war and politics. There could be no great men anymore: the aristocracy was degraded and persecuted" (508).

191. See Hadfield, *Shakespeare and Republicanism:* "It was a commonplace of Roman history that as Rome expanded and became more powerful, absorbing new peoples, it lost its ancient, republican traditions, partly through the sheer scope of the territories that had to be controlled, which necessitated greater centralization and the concentration of power in one man; partly through the triumph of military men who exercised a greater influence in Roman society; and partly through the absorption into the body politic of barbarians who, hardly surprisingly, had no interest in Roman political traditions" (163–64).

192. For a historical overview of this process, see Fustel de Coulanges, *Ancient City,* book 5, chapter 2 ("The Roman Conquest"). See esp. 359: "The conquests of Rome would not have been so easy if the old municipal spirit had not been everywhere extinct; and . . . the municipal system would not have fallen so soon if the Roman conquest had not dealt it the final blow." See also 380: "Then all the cities gradually disappeared, and the Roman city, the last one left, was itself so transformed that it became the union of a dozen great nations under a single master. Thus fell the municipal system."

193. For more on this subject, see chapter 3 of this volume.

194. For a useful collection of Hegel's writings on tragedy (translated into English), see Anne and Henry Paolucci, eds., *Hegel: On Tragedy* (New York: Anchor Books, 1962). This volume also contains A. C. Bradley's helpful essay "Hegel's Theory of Tragedy." Excellent examples of a Hegelian tragic situation are Volumnia's choice between her son and her country in *Coriolanus* (5.3.106–18) and Octavia's choice between her brother and her husband in *Antony and Cleopatra* (3.4.12–20). Volumnia's words sum up Hegel's definition of tragedy: "We must find / An evident calamity, though we had / Our wish, which side should win" (*Coriolanus,* 5.3.111–13).

195. Martindale and Martindale, *Shakespeare and the Uses of Antiquity* speak of the "claustrophobic atmosphere of a small city state" (151).

196. On the ways that Christianity transformed government in the ancient world, see Fustel de Coulanges, *Ancient City*, book 5, chapter 3, "Christianity Changes the Condition of Government."

197. See Manent, *Metamorphoses of the City*, on the actual historical situation: "a 'passage from the Ancients to the Moderns' already took place at Rome at the end of the republic" (142).

198. See Friedrich Nietzsche, *On the Genealogy of Morals and Ecce Homo*, trans. Walter Kaufmann (New York: Vintage, 1969), 34 (sec. 7) and 36 (sec. 10).

199. For a fuller discussion of this subject, see chapter 2 of this volume.

200. See Nietzsche, *On the Genealogy of Morals*, 33 (sec. 7) and chapter 2 of this volume.

201. In a similar way, Mansfield and Tarcov question whether Machiavelli had a simply negative view of Christianity: "After all, the supposedly strong ancients were spiritually overcome by the supposedly weak moderns [Christians]" (introduction to *Discourses on Livy*, xxxv). See also Sullivan, *Machiavelli's Three Romes*, 58. Mark Hulliung, *Citizen Machiavilli* (Princeton, NJ: Princeton University Press, 1983), writes: "Machiavelli did not explain how the slavish Christians triumphed over the masterful pagans; he did not write the *Genealogy of Morals*" (248). As we shall see in chapter 2 of this volume, Nietzsche may not have fully explained this triumph either in that book.

202. In *Julius Caesar*, Brutus is kind to his servant Lucius and treats him with genuine affection, trying not to overwork him, but there are no signs that he regards Lucius as his equal (see, in particular, 4.3.241, 255–62). That Antony consorts with servants is one of Octavius's chief complaints against his rival: "to sit / And keep the turn of tippling with a slave, / To reel the streets at noon, and stand the buffet / With knaves that smell of sweat" (1.4.18–21). This passage gives a good sense of the traditional aristocratic contempt for working people.

203. See Manent, *Metamorphoses of the City*: "The two great political forms, the two mother forms of the ancient world, are the city and the empire. They are the mother forms, but they are also the polar forms; the city is the narrow framework of a restless life in liberty; the empire is the immense domain of a peaceful life under a master" (105).

204. In his comedy *The Birds*, Aristophanes may well be making fun of Alcibiades's desire for universal empire. In Plato's dialogue *Alcibiades I*, Socrates identifies the young Alcibiades's desire to rule both Greeks and barbarians, and to conquer Asia as well as Europe. For the connection between Alcibiades and Alexander the Great, see Alexandre Kojève, "Tyranny and Wisdom," in Leo Strauss, *On Tyranny* (Chicago: University of Chicago Press, 2000), 170.

205. Braden, *Renaissance Tragedy*, 13. For more on Alexander the Great, especially as a precedent for Julius Caesar's ambition and conquests, see Mazzolani, *Idea of the City*, 82–98. See also Hugh Liebert, "Alexander the Great and the History of Globalization," *Review of Politics* 73 (2011): 533–60; and Vickie B. Sullivan, "Alexander the Great as 'Lord of Asia' and Rome as His Successor in Machiavelli's *Prince*," *Review of Politics* 75 (2013): 515–37.

206. Hadas, introduction to *Essential Works of Stoicism*, vii.

207. Pangle, "Roman Cosmopolitanism," 40. See also Manent, *Metamorphoses of the City*, 135.

208. Eliot, "Shakespeare and the Stoicism of Seneca," 112.

209. See Garber, *Shakespeare After All*: "[Octavius] Caesar's own problem is that he is haunted by the past, haunted by a world too great, a canvas too large, for him fully to dominate or comprehend it" (744).

210. See Martin van Creveld, *The Rise and Decline of the State* (Cambridge: Cambridge University Press, 1999): "The ancient philosophies such as cynicism, epicureanism, and stoicism all grew out of the ruin of the independent city-state and are best understood as reactions to despotism, whether Hellenistic or Roman. . . . In time all these ideologies were overtaken by early Christianity" (39).

211. In a study of what Shakespeare might have known from his sources about ancient Egypt, John Michael Archer points out, "It is significant that their celebration of Bacchus is specifically ascribed to Egypt, for Bacchus or Dionysus . . . was often identified as an Egyptian deity. Herodotus says that the Egyptians think Bacchus is the same as their chief god, Osiris, the consort of Isis or Ceres, and goes on to parallel the Greek worship of Dionysus with Egyptian processions, meetings, and sacrifices to Osiris. . . . In their drunkenness, the Romans on Pompey's galley are honoring Dionysus, or Osiris, through their Egyptian bacchanals in the half-decadent, half-ritual manner that Shakespeare associates with the mysteries of Cleopatra's court" (John Michael Archer, *Old Worlds: Egypt, Southwest Asia, India, and Russia in Early Modern English Writing* [Stanford, CA: Stanford University Press, 2001], 51–52). For Machiavelli on the threat of Bacchanals to Roman integrity, see *Discourses*, book 3, chapter 49; and Sullivan, *Machiavelli's Three Romes*, 97–98. This complex cultural/religious situation is further complicated by the fact that Cleopatra's Egypt was already a hybrid of West and East. Cleopatra was a Ptolemy and thus descended from one of Alexander's Macedonian generals. In a study of Shakespeare's knowledge of Egypt, Geraldo U. de Sousa writes, "Shakespeare's classical and medieval sources represent Cleopatra as a white woman of Macedonian ancestry. . . . Although Plutarch . . . does not mention her race, he seems well aware of her European heritage, tracing her line of descent from Ptolemy I Soter (d. 282 BCE), one of the generals of Alexander the Great. This is especially apparent when he writes that Cleopatra could speak many languages, whereas her Macedonian ancestors could barely master the Egyptian tongue" (*Shakespeare's Cross-Cultural Encounters* [New York: Palgrave, 2002], 140). Given Cleopatra's hybrid heritage, her impact on her Roman conquerors was simultaneously to Hellenize and Orientalize them. In his "Richard Wagner in Bayreuth" (sec. 4), Nietzsche writes that "the twofold task of the great Alexander" was "the Hellenization of the world and, to make this possible, the orientalization of the Hellenic" (*Untimely Meditations*, trans. R. J. Hollingdale [Cambridge: Cambridge University Press, 1983], 208). For more on Orientalism in *Antony and Cleopatra*, see chapter 6 of this volume.

212. On the new remoteness of the gods in *Antony and Cleopatra*, see Cantor, *Shakespeare's Rome*, 139–41.

213. See Poole, *Coriolanus*, 34.

214. Here is another anachronism in Shakespeare: given when Coriolanus lived, he should not know what an actor is or have developed a distaste for theater. Roman drama is generally dated from the third century BCE and in fact is regarded as a good example of the Hellenization of Rome, since it developed only after the Romans encountered Greek civilization.

215. Pompey's theater was, in fact, one of the first permanent theater buildings in Rome; it dates from 55 BCE. We know of no theater buildings that date from Coriolanus's Rome.

216. On theatricality in *Julius Caesar*, see Garber, *Shakespeare After All*, 433.

217. Even before the assassination of Caesar, Brutus worries about how to justify the act in the eyes of the Roman public. He senses that he cannot rely on the truth about Julius Caesar: "the quarrel / Will bear no color for the thing he is" (2.1.28–29). Therefore Brutus knows that he must rely on rhetorical maneuvers—"Fashion it thus" (2.2.30)—to create a negative image of Caesar for the Roman people.

218. What we call public opinion evidently is still important in imperial Rome, and occasionally the ruling figures express concern about what the people may think of their actions, but the plebeians never get to affect the action directly. See *Antony and Cleopatra*, 1.2.185–89, 1.3.49–54, 1.4.36–47.

219. Hugh Liebert, "The Roman Executive," in *Executive Power in Theory and Practice*, ed. Hugh Liebert, Gary L. McDowell, and Terry L. Price (New York: Palgrave Macmillan, 2012), contrasts the classical cities, with their small size, as "visible communities" (in which people can observe their rulers up close) with "vast barbarian nations" as "imaginary communities" (in which people accept "rule by invisible powers," resulting in "one-man quasi-divine rule") (37).

220. The idea that a ruler can acquire a divine aura by keeping his distance from his people is the core of Henry IV's advice to Prince Hal in *Henry IV Part I*. Henry tells his son that he won the allegiance of the English people by withholding himself from frequent public appearances: "By being seldom seen, I could not stir / But like a comet I was wond'red at" (3.2.46–47). I owe this reference to Peter Hufnagel.

221. Sullivan finds a similar idea in Machiavelli's *Discourses* (see *Machiavelli's Three Romes*, 78, 88, 153). On the disposition of the Roman people to gravitate toward one-man rule throughout the history of the Republic, see Blits, *The Heart of Rome*, 113–42.

222. On these propaganda wars, see Mazzolani, *Idea of the City*, 158.

223. After Antony's death, Cleopatra endeavors to create an image of him as a universal deity (5.2.76–100). Like Julius Caesar, Antony becomes more godlike after death—in Harold Bloom's words, "more present by being wholly absent, grander in memory than when we have seen him on stage" (*Shakespeare*, 572). In death, Rome's imperial rulers become even more remote from the people, and it becomes easier to create gods out of them. In the absence of a living Antony, Cleopatra is free to imagine a godlike version of him; she says herself that her project is "t' imagine / An Antony" (5.2.98–99). Note that she attempts to turn Antony's name into a title ("an Antony"), just as had happened with the name "Caesar." Dolabella's refusal to endorse Cleopatra's vision (5.2.94) indicates that her project fails, but if she had been more successful politically, she might have made Antony into a new god. The god she imagined could have formed the basis of a new imaginary community that transcends traditional political boundaries, with the "little o' th' earth" banding together under their Antony.

224. See Mazzolani, *Idea of the City*, 66: "The old, narrow fatherland began to be lost in the vastness of this new world" and 190: "When ethics lays particular stress on loyalty to a vast collective body, there is a change in the psychological nature of the individual. He comes to feel that it is impossible to excel in so vast a community, that his personal worth is ill-recognized, and is in any case ill-adapted to face the difficulties of an existence increasingly dominated by distant, immeasurable forces. . . . Men felt cut off. . . . ; they felt lost, as if no one was interested in them except a secret network of spies."

225. Jacob Burckhardt discusses the proper size of the polis in *The Greeks and Greek Civilization*, trans. Sheila Stern (New York: St. Martin's Griffin, 1998), 54–55. Burckhardt draws heavily on Aristotle for his analysis. In *Politics*, book 7, chapter 4, Aristotle takes up the question of the proper size of a political community and concludes that a typical Greek polis has the right proportions. He argues that maximizing population is not the path to political greatness: "To be a great city and a populous one is not the same thing. . . . It is difficult—perhaps impossible— for a city that is too populous to be well managed" (Aristotle, *The Politics*, trans. Carnes Lord [Chicago: University of Chicago Press, 1984], 204 [1326a25–30]). Aristotle comes up with a Goldilocks model of the proper size of a city—not too large, but not too small. The best city

NOTES TO PAGES 96-97

must be large enough to be self-sufficient (in economic and military terms) but small enough to provide a functioning political system in which "the citizens must necessarily be familiar with one another's qualities" (205 [1326b15–16]). In the best community, the citizens will be in earshot of each other; otherwise they would need "the voice of Stentor" just to hear each other speak (205 [1326b7]). In short, Aristotle argues that politics ideally should be unmediated—the citizens should be in direct contact with each other (thus obviating the need for any kind of vocal amplification, as it were). Aristotle ends up defining the ideal size for a city this way: "the greatest excess of number with a view to self-sufficiency of life that is readily surveyable" (205 [1326b23–25]). In other words, one should be able to take in the whole of the city in one glance. Accordingly, Aristotle regards empires as bloated in size, and therefore incapable of supplying a satisfying political life. Earlier, in book 3, chapter 3, Aristotle makes fun of the unwieldiness of empires—their lack of surveyability—by treating the empire of Babylon as if it were a city: "They say that its capture was not noticed in a certain part of the city for three days" (89 [1276a29–30]). Aristotle laughs at the disunity of a political community that is so large that one part of it cannot readily communicate with the others. In the course of defining the polis in *Politics*, book 1, chapter 2, Aristotle makes the famous statement: "Man is by nature a political animal" (37 [1253a2–3]). This statement is commonly misinterpreted as meaning that human beings are by nature contentious politically. But what Aristotle really means is that human beings are constituted by nature to live in a polis—that is to say, in a community small enough for its citizens to participate actively and directly in its public affairs. If Aristotle is correct, then human beings today are living in artificially large communities, in which their political lives suffer because they lack direct contact with their rulers. I believe that Shakespeare is exploring precisely these issues when he contrasts the small polis world of *Coriolanus* with the immense empire world of *Antony and Cleopatra*. The contrast between the small, organic, virtuous community and the large, artificial, decadent community is a recurrent issue in political philosophy. It resurfaces in the eighteenth century, for example, in the contrast between Geneva and Paris in Rousseau's thought.

226. See Jonas, *Gnostic Religion*: "The classical city-state engaged the citizens in its concerns, and these he could identify with his own, as through the laws of his city he governed himself. The large Hellenistic monarchies neither called for nor permitted such personal identification; and just as they made no moral demands on their subjects, so the individual detached himself in regard to them as a *private* person (a status hardly admitted in the Hellenic world before) found satisfaction of his social needs in voluntarily organized associations based on community of ideas, religion, and occupation" (7).

227. For the most "triumphalist" reading of *Antony and Cleopatra*, see the two essays on the play in Knight, *Imperial Theme*, 199–326. Knight emphasizes the comic elements in the play: "The spirit of the romantic comedies is here blended with tragedy" (254) and concludes, "So Cleopatra and Antony find not death but life" (262). See also Allan Bloom, *Love and Friendship*, 321. For another perspective on the combination of tragedy and comedy at the end of the play, see Anne Barton, "'Nature's Piece 'Gainst Fancy': The Divided Catastrophe in *Antony and Cleopatra*," *Essays, Mainly Shakespearean*, 113–35, esp. 132–35. Harold Bloom, *Shakespeare*, says of Cleopatra, "Her death is triumphal rather than tragic" (547) and says of the whole play, "The comic spirit has a large share in it" (551). He goes on to say, "Extraordinarily, this tragedy is funnier than any of the great Shakespearean comedies" (559). If comedy does prevail at the end of *Antony and Cleopatra*, the reason may be that the Empire has diminished the possibilities for heroism and thus for tragedy. Cleopatra in fact fears that Rome will reduce her story to a cheap comedy: "The quick comedians / Extemporally will stage us" (5.2.216–17).

228. For a more detailed analysis of this moment, see Cantor, *Shakespeare's Rome*, 180–83.

229. On this point, see ibid., 127–28, 184–88.

230. *Antony and Cleopatra* contains hints that Shakespeare thought that medieval civilization had its roots in late antiquity and the complex intermingling of classical and Christian cultures this age produced. The medieval concept of chivalry was an attempt to fuse the martial values of the classical world with Christian values that are in many respects incompatible with them. A Christian knight should be brave in war, but he should also be humble, piteous, charitable, and scrupulously fair in combat (virtues that Homer's heroes tend not to practice). The first stirrings of the world of medieval chivalry may be observed in act 4, scene 8 of *Antony and Cleopatra*. Much like a Roman Lancelot, Antony presents himself as a knight fighting on behalf of his lady fair. He instructs Cleopatra and Scarus to act the roles of a noble lady and her knightly champion: "Commend unto his lips thy favoring hand. / Kiss it, my warrior" (4.8.23–24). Cleopatra responds with a gesture out of courtly romance: "I'll give thee, friend, / Armor all of gold; it was a king's" (4.8.26–27). Earlier, in a scene also reminiscent of courtly romance—the arming of a warrior—Antony refers to Cleopatra as his "squire" (4.4.14). In general, the way Antony combines military and amatory motives in his warfare points beyond the classical world to the medieval world of chivalry. Jonas, *Gnostic Religion*, writes of late antiquity: "Hellenization of the East prevails in the first period, orientalization of the West in the second, the latter process coming to an end by about 300 A.D. The result of both is a synthesis which carried over into the Middle Ages" (18). The key "medieval" aspect of the transformation of heroism that occurs in *Antony and Cleopatra* is the way that it is linked to the love of a noble woman—the result is chivalry. See Ernest L. Fortin, "The Saga of Spiritedness: Christian Saints and Pagan Heroes," in *Ernest Fortin: Collected Essays*, ed. J. Brian Benestad (Lanham, MD: Rowman & Littlefield, 1996). He says of the Crusades: "The long struggle . . . gave rise to a novel form of heroism that goes under the name of chivalry, a complex phenomenon that . . . is distinguished from older forms of heroism by two main features: its expressly religious dimension and the role that it assigns to women in the elaboration of the chivalric ideal" (3:235). For Shakespeare's criticism of chivalry, see my essay "Against Chivalry: The Achievement of Cervantes and Shakespeare," *Weekly Standard* 21 (May 2, 2016): 24–28.

231. On this subject, see chapter 2 of this volume and my essays "'Christian Kings' and 'English Mercuries': *Henry V* and the Classical Tradition of Manliness," in *Educating the Prince: Essays in Honor of Harvey Mansfield*, eds. Mark Blitz and William Kristol (Lanham, MD: Rowman & Littlefield, 2000), 74–87; and "Shakespeare's *Henry V*: From the Medieval to the Modern World," in *Perspectives on Politics in Shakespeare*, ed. John A. Murley and Sean D. Sutton (Lanham, MD: Lexington, 2006), 11–31.

232. On this subject, see chapter 2 of this volume and my essays "*Othello*: The Erring Barbarian among the Supersubtle Venetians," *Southwest Review* 75 (1990): 296–319; and "*Macbeth* and the Gospelling of Scotland," in *Shakespeare as Political Thinker*, ed. John Alvis and Thomas West (Wilmington, DE: ISI, 2000), 315–51.

233. On this subject, see Paul Cantor, *Shakespeare: Hamlet* (Cambridge: Cambridge University Press, 2004). For more on the relation of *Henry V*, *Hamlet*, *Othello*, and *Macbeth* to Shakespeare's Roman plays, see chapter 2 of this volume.

Chapter Two

1. See Hans Joachim Mette, ed., *Friedrich Nietzsche: Frühe Schriften*, vol. 2 (München: C. H. Beck, 1994), 193–200. An English translation of the essay is available in Friedrich Nietzsche, *On*

the Future of Our Educational Institutions, trans. Michael W. Grenke (South Bend, IN: St. Augustine's Press, 2004), appendix C, 168–76.

2. A *Gymnasium* is a kind of German secondary school, one that in Nietzsche's day emphasized humanistic training in Greek and Latin. Walter Kaufmann, *Nietzsche: Philosopher, Psychologist, Antichrist*, 4th ed. (Princeton, NJ: Princeton University Press, 1974), 22, notes that among the distinguished alumni of Schulpforta were Klopstock, Novalis, Fichte, Ranke, and the Schlegel brothers.

3. Nietzsche, *On the Future of Our Educational Institutions*, 174. The passage sounds even better in the original German: "diese Scenen kommen mir vor, wie der letzte Theil einer Sinfonie, in dem die selben Klänge, die in dem Allegro stürmten und zuckten, wieder erklingen, aber bald wie schmerzliche Seufzer in Erinnerung an die durchlebten Wehen, bald wie verklärte und beruhigte Töne einer still gewordnen Brust" (Nietzsche, *Frühe Schriften*, 198–99).

4. Nietzsche, *On the Future of Our Educational Institutions*, 175.

5. Ronald Hayman, *Nietzsche: A Critical Life* (Harmondsworth, UK: Penguin, 1982), 43. For a brief overview of Nietzsche's interest in and acquaintance with Shakespeare and his works, see Thomas H. Brobjer, *Nietzsche and the "English": The Influence of British and American Thinking on His Philosophy* (Amherst, NY: Humanity Books, 2008), 109–15. "William Shakespeare is the English-language writer Nietzsche most frequently refers to and praises. . . . Nietzsche refers to Shakespeare more than a hundred times, and he refers or alludes to more than half of his plays and a number of the sonnets" (109). "Among the authors and thinkers Nietzsche most often referred to and praised in his published writings, only Goethe and Homer are discussed more frequently than Shakespeare" (113). For a deeper and more detailed account of Shakespeare's place in Nietzsche's life and thought, see Duncan Large, "Nietzsche's Shakespearean Figures," in *Why Nietzsche Still? Reflections on Drama, Culture, and Politics*, ed. Alan D. Schrift (Berkeley: University of California Press, 2000), 45–65.

6. Sander L. Gilman, ed., *Conversations with Nietzsche: A Life in the Words of His Contemporaries*, trans. David J. Parent (New York: Oxford University Press, 1991), 14.

7. Hayman, *Nietzsche*, 43.

8. Ibid., 43–44. For the text of this letter (dated November 1883) in English, see Brobjer, *Nietzsche and the "English,"* 114.

9. An entry in Nietzsche's diary, dated August 24, 1859, reads: "The characters seem to me almost superhuman (*übermenschlich*). It is like watching the Titans battling against religion and virtue" (quoted in Hayman, *Nietzsche*, 43). For an overview of the importance of the *Übermensch* in Nietzsche's philosophy, see Michael Allen Gillespie, "'Slouching toward Bethlehem to Be Born': On the Nature and Meaning of Nietzsche's Superman," *Journal of Nietzsche Studies* 30 (2005): 49–69.

10. Friedrich Nietzsche, *The Gay Science*, trans. Walter Kaufmann (New York: Vintage, 1974), 150 (sec. 98) (original emphasis). Where appropriate, I will cite Nietzsche's works by page number and section. Unless otherwise noted, all emphasis in quoted material is original to the source.

11. Nietzsche, *Gay Science*, 150 (sec. 98).

12. For this view, see, e.g., Kaufmann's note 42 in Nietzsche, *Gay Science*, 151–52 and Kaufmann, *Nietzsche*, 35–36.

13. Friedrich Nietzsche, *On the Genealogy of Morals and Ecce Homo*, trans. Walter Kaufmann (New York: Vintage, 1967), 246.

14. Although Nietzsche's teaching duties at Basel chiefly involved Greek literature, his philo-

logical training included Latin as well as Greek. His essay on Diogenes Laertius won the 1867 Leipzig University prize for the best essay written in Latin (see Curtis Cate, *Friedrich Nietzsche* [Woodstock, NY: Overlook, 2005] 75, 79). In the section "What I Owe to the Ancients" in *Twilight of the Idols*, Nietzsche begins by praising Latin authors (Sallust, Horace) for their style, and says of the Greeks, "They *cannot* mean as much to us as the Romans" (Walter Kaufmann, ed. and trans., *The Portable Nietzsche* [New York: Viking, 1954], 557). To be sure, Nietzsche is speaking about learning how to write in this passage, and this praise of Romans at the expense of Greeks is unusual in his works. Still, it is surprising that studies of Nietzsche and classical antiquity focus almost exclusively on his interest in the ancient Greeks. I have consulted three collections of essays dedicated to this subject: James C. O'Flaherty, Timothy F. Sellner, and Robert M. Helm, eds., *Studies in Nietzsche and the Classical Tradition* (Chapel Hill: University of North Carolina Press, 1976); Paul Bishop, ed., *Nietzsche and Antiquity: His Reaction and Response to the Classical Tradition* (Woodbridge, UK: Camden House, 2004); and Anthony K. Jensen and Helmut Heit, eds., *Nietzsche as a Scholar of Antiquity* (London: Bloomsbury, 2014). Of the fifty-nine essays in these three volumes, almost all are devoted solely to Greek subjects and none are devoted solely to Roman subjects. One essay that provides a useful overview of Nietzsche's knowledge of and interest in Rome is Richard Bett, "Nietzsche and the Romans," *Journal of Nietzsche Studies* 42 (2011): 7–31.

15. Evidently the youthful Nietzsche was so caught up in *Julius Caesar* that he concluded a letter (dated February 23, 1887) to his close friend Carl von Gersdorff, with an allusion to Shakespeare's play: "It is agreed when we meet again, we shall smile" (*Selected Letters of Friedrich Nietzsche*, ed. and trans. Christopher Middleton [Chicago: University of Chicago Press, 1969], 13). The allusion is to Brutus's remark: "If we do meet again, why, we shall smile" (5.1.117) and Cassius's response: "If we do meet again, we'll smile indeed" (5.1.120). All quotations from Shakespeare are taken from G. Blakemore Evans, ed., *The Riverside Shakespeare* (Boston: Houghton Mifflin, 1974). Act, scene, and line numbers are given in the body of the chapter.

16. Using the index to the fifteen-volume Nietzsche, *Sämtliche Werke Kritische Studienausgabe*, ed. Giorgio Colli and Mazzino Montinari (Berlin: de Gruyter, 1980), I found references in Nietzsche's writings to the following Shakespeare plays: *Hamlet, Julius Caesar, Richard III, Macbeth, Much Ado About Nothing, Romeo and Juliet, A Midsummer Night's Dream, Timon of Athens, Troilus and Cressida, Othello,* and *Twelfth Night* (vol. 15, 353). Drawing upon Nietzsche's letters and his juvenilia, Large ("Nietzsche's Shakespearean Figures") finds references to a few more plays: *Henry IV Part I, The Merchant of Venice, The Tempest, King Lear,* and *The Taming of the Shrew* (60n1). Obviously, none of this proves that Nietzsche never read *Coriolanus* or *Antony and Cleopatra*, but it does suggest that he did not find either play interesting enough to comment on in writing.

17. *Unpublished Writings from the Period of Unfashionable Observations*, trans. Richard T. Gray (Stanford, CA: Stanford University Press, 1995), 247 (see also 252). Nietzsche derived this understanding of the Roman plays from Goethe. In his second *Untimely Meditation*, "On the Uses and Disadvantages of History for Life," Nietzsche quotes Goethe on the English character of Shakespeare's Romans: "Goethe once said of Shakespeare: 'No one despised outward costume more than he; he knew very well the inner human costume, and here all are alike. They say he hit off the Romans admirably; but I don't find it so, they are all nothing but flesh-and-blood Englishmen, but they are certainly human beings, humans from head to feet, and the Roman toga sits on them perfectly well'" (Friedrich Nietzsche, *Untimely Meditations*, trans. R. J. Hollingdale [Cambridge: Cambridge University Press, 1983], 85). Nietzsche is quoting from

Goethe's 1815 essay "Shakespeare und keine Ende." For an English translation of the entire essay, see Johann Wolfgang von Goethe, *Essays on Art and Literature*, trans. Ellen von Nardroff
and Ernest H. von Nardroff (Princeton, NJ: Princeton University Press, 1994), 166–74 (the passage Nietzsche quotes appears on 168). Goethe makes a similar comment about Shakespeare's
Roman plays in Johann Peter Eckermann, *Conversations with Goethe*, January 31, 1827. In his
famous "Preface to Shakespeare," Samuel Johnson agrees with Goethe: "[Shakespeare's] story
requires Romans . . . , but he thinks only on men" (Samuel Johnson, *Works* [New Haven, CT:
Yale University Press, 1968], vol. 7, 65–66. A form of Enlightenment universalism seems to stand
behind this view of the Roman plays. For a critique of this attitude, see Paul A. Cantor, *Shakespeare's Rome: Republic and Empire* (Ithaca, NY: Cornell University Press, 1976), 7–8.

18. For a concise overview of master morality versus slave morality in Nietzsche, see Daniel Conway, *Nietzsche's* On the Genealogy of Morals: *A Reader's Guide* (London: Continuum,
2008), 40–42; and Michael Allen Gillespie and Keegan F. Callanan, "*On the Genealogy of Morals*," in *A Companion to Friedrich Nietzsche: Life and Works*, ed. Paul Bishop (Woodbridge, UK:
Camden House, 2012), 260–61.

19. Friedrich Nietzsche, *Beyond Good and Evil*, trans. Walter Kaufmann (New York: Vintage,
1966), 204–5 (sec. 260); see also his *Human, All Too Human*, sec. 45.

20. Nietzsche, *Beyond Good and Evil*, 207 (sec. 260).

21. Ibid.

22. For a detailed analysis of this phenomenon, see Max Scheler, *Ressentiment*, trans. William W. Holdheim (New York: Free Press, 1961). Scheler argues that Nietzsche was wrong to view
Christian morality as a product of *ressentiment*; for Scheler it is rather modern bourgeois morality that results from *ressentiment*. For a critique of Scheler on this point, see Kaufmann, editor's
introduction to Nietzsche, *On the Genealogy of Morals*, 7–8. For further analysis of *ressentiment*,
see Bernard Reginster, *The Affirmation of Life: Nietzsche on Overcoming Nihilism* (Cambridge,
MA: Harvard University Press, 2006), 256–60.

23. See Kaufmann, *Nietzsche*, 371–72 and Conway, *Nietzsche's* On the Genealogy of
Morals, 46.

24. See Catherine Zuckert, "Nietzsche on the Origin and Development of the Distinctively
Human," *Polity* 16 (1983): "How could the slaves ever have convinced their lion-like masters to
adopt a pacific, self-effacing morality?" (55).

25. David V. Erdman, ed., *The Complete Poetry and Prose of William Blake* (Berkeley: University of California Press, 1982), 37 (plate 9, *The Marriage of Heaven and Hell*). In Nietzsche's
critique of Darwin in his *Twilight of the Idols*, he sounds like Blake in a statement about biologi-
cal struggle: "The weak prevail over the strong again and again, for they are the great majority—
and they are also more *intelligent*" (Kaufmann, *Portable Nietzsche*, 523). In this context, it is
revealing that Shakespeare has Antony say of Cleopatra: "She is cunning past man's thought"
(*Antony and Cleopatra*, 1.2.145). Like a wily slave, Cleopatra uses her superior intelligence and
guile repeatedly to outwit her ostensible masters and get them to do her bidding.

26. This is the central theme of Mikhail Ivanovich Rostovtzeff's history of Rome. He attributes the decline of Roman civilization to the dispiriting of the Roman aristocracy; see
Rostovtzeff, *Rome*, trans. J. D. Duff (New York: Oxford University Press, 1960), 321–22: "The
creative powers of the aristocracy were finally undermined. The indolent and peaceful content-
ment of the first two centuries [of the Empire] gave place to the apathy of dotage, to indifference
and despair. In their sufferings men sought deliverance not in this life, but beyond it" (324). See
also Ronald Syme, *The Roman Revolution* (Oxford: Oxford University Press, 1960) on the Ro-

man nobility: "The Empire had broken their power and their spirit. . . . The better cause and the best men, the brave and the loyal, had perished. . . . The *nobiles* lost power and wealth, display, dignity and honour. . . . For the *nobiles*, no more triumphs after war, no more roads, temples and towns named after their honour and commemorating the glory of the great houses that were the Republic and Rome" (490–91).

27. Friedrich Nietzsche, *Human, All Too Human: A Book for Free Spirits*, trans. R. J. Hollingdale (Cambridge: Cambridge University Press, 1986), 117 (sec. 247).

28. Kaufmann, *Portable Nietzsche*, 634 (*Antichrist*, sec. 51).

29. Ibid., 647–48 (*Antichrist*, sec. 58). For a different take on the eternity of Rome, see Friedrich Nietzsche, *Daybreak: Thoughts on the Prejudices of Morality*, trans. R. J. Hollingdale (Cambridge: Cambridge University Press, 1982), sec. 71.

30. Kaufmann, *Portable Nietzsche*, 648 (*Antichrist*, sec. 58).

31. Ibid.

32. Support for this view can be found among modern historians. Writing against the Tacitean tradition of Roman history, which focused on the Roman emperors as homicidal maniacs, Gordon Braden says, "A different perspective and respect for different kinds of data have allowed modern historians to write first-century imperial history as one of fairly continuous and intelligible governmental policies in which the aberrant personalities of the individual emperors play only a small role" (Braden, *Renaissance Tragedy and the Senecan Tradition: Anger's Privilege* [New Haven, CT: Yale University Press, 1985], 9).

33. Kaufmann, *Portable Nietzsche*, 650–51 (*Antichrist*, sec. 59).

34. For an expression of these doubts, see R. Lanier Anderson, "On the Nobility of Nietzsche's Priests," in *Nietzsche's On the Genealogy of Morality: A Critical Guide*, ed. Simon May (Cambridge: Cambridge University Press, 2011). He points out that Nietzsche's preliminary discussions of the slave revolt "lack any account of the *transition* from the noble pattern of valuation to slave morality"; Nietzsche fails "to explain *how* the radical transition from a dominant master morality to the slave morality could have taken place" (42).

35. In commenting on Nietzsche's treatment of Christianity in *The Antichrist*, Richard Bett stresses the anomalous status of this book within the body of Nietzsche's writings: "Nietzsche's attitude toward Christianity is one of unmitigated contempt and disgust. Of course, one might think that a movement uniquely capable of undoing something of such extraordinary power and longevity (as Nietzsche sees the Roman Empire) would itself warrant a certain admiration for its strength, its ingeniousness, or something of the kind. But here Nietzsche is in no mood for any such concessions. . . . Instead, the picture seems wholly black and white: Rome good, Christianity bad. But this is just one respect in which *Anitchrist* is perhaps Nietzsche's most uncompromising work (and therefore, arguably, not his most interesting)" ("Nietzsche and the Romans," 13).

36. I am dealing here with a specific issue: Nietzsche's conception of the ancient Jews' role in the development of what he called slave morality. I do not have the space to deal with the larger question of Nietzsche's attitude toward Jews in general, especially the Jews of modern Europe. For a balanced overview of this subject, see Kaufmann, *Nietzsche*, 296–304; and Yirmiyahu Yovel, "Nietzsche and the Jews: The Structure of an Ambivalence," in *Nietzsche's On the Genealogy of Morals: Critical Essays*, ed. Christa Davis Acampora (Lanham, MD: Rowman & Littlefield, 2006), 277–89. Nietzsche's attitude toward the Jews is typically complex and has provoked great controversy, especially in view of the way that many of his ideas have been invoked by anti-Semites, including the Nazis. For the record, both Kaufmann and Yovel emphasize, as

do many scholars, that Nietzsche was a passionate and vocal opponent of anti-Semitism. Among the last words he wrote (at the outbreak of his insanity), in a letter to Franz Overbeck dated January 6, 1889, was this outburst: "I am just having all anti-Semites shot" (Kaufmann, *Portable Nietzsche*, 687).

37. Nietzsche, *Beyond Good and Evil*, 108 (sec. 195).

38. See Conway, *Nietzsche's* On the Genealogy of Morals, 34–39; Zuckert, "Nietzsche on the Origin and Development of the Distinctively Human," 53; Peter Berkowitz, *Nietzsche: The Ethics of an Immoralist* (Cambridge, MA: Harvard University Press, 1995), 76–77; and Mark Migotti, "Slave Morality, Socrates, and the Bushmen: A Critical Introduction to *On the Genealogy of Morality*, Essay I," in Acampora, *Nietzsche's* On the Genealogy of Morals, 114. The best discussion I have found of the role of Jewish priests in Nietzsche's account of the slave revolt in morality is Anderson, "Nietzsche's Priests." Stressing the fact that the priests are nobles, Anderson challenges many common interpretations of Nietzsche's concept of the slave revolt. I agree with much of what Anderson says, but I offer a different historical account of the priest's role in overcoming master morality. See note 45 below.

39. Nietzsche, *On the Genealogy of Morals*, 31. Nietzsche extends this point to the Hindu priesthood on 32 (see also his *Will to Power*, sec. 143).

40. Brutus betrays the old master's contempt for priests when he equates them with cowards (*Julius Caesar*, 2.1.129).

41. Nietzsche, *On the Genealogy of Morals*, 32.

42. Ibid., 33.

43. Shakespeare consistently shows that the plebeians are ineffective without leaders. Even in *Coriolanus*, the plebeians need leadership from the tribunes Sicinius and Brutus, the ambitious members of the plebeian party.

44. See Conway, *Nietzsche's* On the Genealogy of Morals, 112.

45. Nietzsche explains this process more fully in sections 25 and 26 of *The Antichrist*, where he identifies what made the experience of the ancient Jews unusual. All people expect their gods to lead them in battle and grant them victory. Accordingly, faced with military defeat, most people lose faith in their gods and abandon them, usually adopting the gods of their conquerors. This is precisely what the Jews refused to do when they were defeated by the Assyrians and the Babylonians. Rather than abandon their faith in their God, they abandoned their commitment to their original warlike way of life under their kings. Under the leadership of their priests, they turned on their defeated military leaders and reinterpreted their earlier glorious victories as sinful; the warriors' pride and vainglory brought the wrath of God down upon the Jewish people and caused God to punish them with exile from their homeland: "The concept of God becomes a tool in the hands of priestly agitators. . . . In the hands of the Jewish priests the great age in the history of Israel became an age of decay; the Exile, the long misfortune, was transformed into an eternal punishment for the great age—an age in which the priest was still a nobody. . . . They made either wretchedly meek and sleek prigs or 'godless ones' out of the powerful, often very bold figures in the history of Israel" (Kaufmann, *Portable Nietzsche*, 595–97). Thus Nietzsche interprets the account of Jewish history given in the Old Testament as a power play on the part of the priests, who would rather be ascendant among a defeated Jewish people than subordinate to the warrior class in a victorious age. In this revaluation, military defeat became reinterpreted as the means to a spiritual victory. These passages from *The Antichrist* are important for a full understanding of Nietzsche's conception of the slave revolt in morality. Some commentators assume that Nietzsche saw the Jewish priests as at war only with their Roman conquerors. Nietz-

sche did indeed view the priests as turning the tables on their foreign enemies, but he also saw their *ressentiment* directed against their domestic allies—the Jewish warrior class (including warrior kings like David), who, the priests claimed, had failed Israel in its hour of need. As Nietzsche understands the priests' formula, God did not fail Israel, Israel failed God. Thus Nietzsche pushes back the Jewish slave revolt in morality as far as the Babylonian Exile.

46. Nietzsche, *On the Genealogy of Morals*, 33–34.

47. See Reginster, *Affirmation of Life*, 300n19.

48. See Conway, *Nietzsche's* On the Genealogy of Morals, 120.

49. Nietzsche, *On the Genealogy of Morals*, 34.

50. See Conway, *Nietzsche's* On the Genealogy of Morals, 90.

51. Friedrich Nietzsche, *The Will to Power*, trans. Walter Kaufmann and R. J. Hollingdale (New York: Vintage, 1967), 120 (sec. 204; see also sec. 175). I am aware that *The Will to Power* is not a book by Nietzsche, but a sampling of notes from the notebooks he left behind (his so-called *Nachlass*), edited and assembled by his sister, Elisabeth Förster-Nietzsche. Nevertheless, like most commentators on Nietzsche, including Walter Kaufmann (who first vigorously argued against the authority of the *Will to Power* notes), I make use of the Nietzsche *Nachlass* when it can provide a fuller picture of his thinking on some of the central issues of his philosophy, some of which he addressed more thoroughly in his notebooks. See Karl Jaspers, *Nietzsche and Christianity*, trans. E. B. Ashton (Chicago: Henry Regnery, 1961): "Often [Nietzsche's] most essential and original ideas were preserved only in cursory notes" (100).

52. Nietzsche, *Will to Power*, 111 (sec. 184).

53. In *Gay Science*, sec. 538, Nietzsche seems in fact to say just the opposite: "An edifice like Christianity that had been built so carefully over such a long period—it was the last construction of the Romans!—naturally could not be destroyed all at once" (310).

54. Nietzsche, *Beyond Good and Evil*, 202 (sec. 258).

55. Ibid., 210–11 (sec. 262).

56. To show the connection: in section 38 of "Skirmishes of an Untimely Man" in *Twilight of the Idols*, Nietzsche speaks of "aristocratic commonwealths of the type of Rome or Venice" (Kaufmann, *Portable Nietzsche*, 542–43).

57. Nietzsche, *Beyond Good and Evil*, 211 (sec. 262).

58. In *Gay Science*, sec. 23, labeled "The signs of corruption," Nietzsche further outlines what happens in a decaying aristocracy: "The ancient national energy and national passion that became gloriously visible in war and warlike games have now been transmuted into countless private passions that have merely become less visible" (96). In words that could be describing *Antony and Cleopatra*, Nietzsche says, "One lives for today, and this state of the soul makes the game easy for seducers" (97–98). In this discussion of corruption, Nietzsche makes the connection between decadence and tyranny: "When 'morals decay' those men emerge whom we call tyrants.... Once decay has reached its climax along with the infighting of all sorts of tyrants, the Caesar always appears, the final tyrant who puts an end to the weary struggle for solo rule—by putting the weariness to work for himself." This aphorism contains some of Nietzsche's most profound insights into Caesarism, and thus into *Julius Caesar*.

59. Nietzsche, *Beyond Good and Evil*, 211 (sec. 262).

60. Ibid., 211–12.

61. Nietzsche, *Will to Power*, 89 (sec. 140).

62. Ibid., 121 (sec. 204). Coriolanus presciently raises the prospect of the warlike Romans being conquered by forces using something other than martial power. When banished, he tells

his accusers that this will "deliver you as most / Abated captives to some nation / That won you without blows" (3.3.131–33).

63. Nietzsche, *Will to Power*, 467–68 (sec. 874).

64. Ibid., 118 (sec. 202).

65. Ibid., 105 (sec. 174).

66. Ibid., 127 (sec. 216).

67. Ibid., 459 (sec. 863). On the usefulness of Christianity to the Roman Empire, see Ernest L. Fortin, "The Saga of Spiritedness: Christian Saints and Pagan Heroes," *Ernest Fortin: Collected Essays*, vol. 3, ed. J. Brian Benestad (Lanham, MD: Rowman & Littlefield, 1996): "Christianity, whose universality paralleled that of the Roman Empire, had a unique contribution to make. It stressed the virtues of harmony and cooperation among all human beings regardless of ethnic origin, language, or national customs and could thus be pressed into service to counteract the forces of disunity at work within Roman society. . . . Even the disparagement of military valor . . . had suddenly turned into an asset, favoring the ends to which in its self-interest imperial policy was now committed. By the same token, emperors had little to fear from a religion that derived the institution of civil government from the will of God, frowned upon sedition, and discouraged worldly ambition with as much vigor as it extolled the virtue of obedience to one's divinely established rulers. . . . It is no accident that Christianity eventually made its bed in the Roman Empire" (233–34).

68. This interpretation of Constantine's actions was developed by Nietzsche's friend and colleague at the University of Basel, the Swiss historian Jacob Burckhardt. See his *The Age of Constantine the Great*, trans. Moses Hadas (Berkeley: University of California Press, 1983), 292–335.

69. Nietzsche, *Daybreak*, 547 (sec. 546).

70. Nietzsche, *Will to Power*, 115 (sec. 196). See also *Daybreak*, sec. 70–72.

71. See Jaspers, *Nietzsche and Christianity*, 31–32, especially: "Christianity [for Nietzsche] was thus produced by Antiquity itself; it was not something strange to Antiquity, added to it from outside." See also Lawrence J. Hatab, "Why Would Master Morality Surrender Its Power?" in May, *Nietzsche's On the Genealogy of Morals*, 203–4. See also Nietzsche, *Antichrist*, sec. 23: "Christianity wants to become master on soil where some aphrodisiac or Adonis cult has already established the general conception of a cult" (Kaufmann, *Portable Nietzsche*, 591); sec. 37: Christianity "has swallowed doctrines and rites of all the *subterranean* cults of the *imperium Romanum*" (Kaufmann, *Portable Nietzsche*, 610); and sec. 58: Epicurus "fought the *subterranean* cults which were exactly like a latent form of Christianity" (Kaufmann, *Portable Nietzsche*, 649).

72. Nietzsche and Shakespeare thus anticipate the thesis of Franz Cumont's *Oriental Religions in Roman Paganism* (New York: Dover, 1956).

73. Nietzsche, *Will to Power*, 118 (sec. 202).

74. Kaufmann, *Portable Nietzsche*, 477 (*Twilight of the Idols*, "The Problem of Socrates," sec. 9). See Hatab, "Master Morality," 204–7; and Migotti, "Slave Morality, Socrates, and the Bushmen," 115–16. For general discussions of Nietzsche's understanding of Socrates, see Kaufmann, *Nietzsche*, 391–411; and Werner Dannhauser, *Nietzsche's View of Socrates* (Ithaca, NY: Cornell University Press, 1974).

75. Nietzsche, *Beyond Good and Evil*, 3 (preface). See also *Twilight of the Idols*, "How the 'True World' Finally Became a Fable" (Kaufmann, *Portable Nietzsche*, 485–86).

76. Kaufmann, *Portable Nietzsche*, 559–60 (*Twilight of the Idols*, "What I Owe to the Ancients," sec. 3).

77. Nietzsche, *Will to Power*, 242 (sec. 438).

78. See an entry in one of Nietzsche's late notebooks: "The Stoic self-hardening, the Platonic slandering of the senses, the preparation of the ground for Christianity" (Rüdiger Bittner, ed., *Nietzsche: Writings from the Late Notebooks*, trans. Kate Sturge [Cambridge: Cambridge University Press, 2003], 238).

79. See Tracy B. Strong, *Friedrich Nietzsche and the Politics of Transfiguration* (Berkeley: University of California Press, 1975), 198–99.

80. Kaufmann, *Portable Nietzsche*, 509 (*Twilight of the Idols*, "What the Germans Lack," sec. 4).

81. See Strong, *Friedrich Nietzsche and the Politics of Transfiguration*, 216–17. In an early notebook, under the heading "program for contemporary world," Nietzsche writes, "The social crisis can be solved only at the level of the city, not at that of the state" (*Unpublished Writings from the Period of Unfashionable Observations*, 255)

82. For the opposite approach, see Daniel W. Conway, "*Ecce Caesar*: Nietzsche's Imperial Aspirations," in *Nietzsche, Godfather of Fascism? On the Uses and Abuses of a Philosophy*, ed. Jacob Golomb and Robert S. Wistrich (Princeton, NJ: Princeton University Press, 2002), 173–95. Despite admitting that "by the late 1880s, Nietzsche had become extremely critical of European imperialism" (175), Conway sets out "to trace Nietzsche's imperial aspirations to his unabashed admiration for the amoral, self-perpetuating structure of the Roman Empire" (174). As frequently happens, Nietzsche's writings provide evidence for both those who regard him as an imperialist and those who regard him as an anti-imperialist. As suggested by the title of the volume in which Conway's essay appears, the way that the Nazis appropriated Nietzsche's philosophy has led many people to regard him as a champion of fascism and imperialism. Admittedly, there were moments in his youth when he was able to generate enthusiasm for Prussian militarism, but in his maturity he turned passionately against Bismarck and his aggressive policies. On balance, the preponderance of the evidence places Nietzsche in the anti-imperialist camp; he especially had grave misgivings about the impact of imperialism on a nation's culture.

83. On Socrates as plebeian, see "The Problem of Socrates" in *Twilight of the Idols*, sec. 3, 5, and 7. See also *Beyond Good and Evil*, sec. 212, where Nietzsche takes the side of Socrates against the complacent nobility of Athens.

84. See Hatab, "Master Morality": "Slave morality in Nietzsche's analysis did not simply follow from the subordinate conditions of weak types; it was not an expression of the masses, so to speak. Within slave ranks there were *creative* types who fashioned the world view that was able to give meaning to slavish existence and reverse master morality. This is the function of the 'ascetic priest' in the *Genealogy*, the creative type who forms the voice of slave morality. . . . We could insert Socrates into the framework quite easily, as an active, creative individual who serves the inversion and conversion of noble values" (206).

85. See Kaufmann, *Nietzsche*, 297: "In spite of the polemical tone, *it does not follow from Nietzsche's "vivisection" of slave morality that he identifies his own position with that of the masters*"(original emphasis). See also Strong, *Friedrich Nietzsche and the Politics of Transfiguration*, 238; and Gillespie and Callanan, "*On the Genealogy of Morals*": "This genealogical tale also casts doubts upon the sustainability of the noble ideal, which was finally unable to maintain its integrity in the face of the slaves' cleverness and psychic resources" (262).

86. Nietzsche, *On the Genealogy of Morals*, 33. Anderson, "Nietzsche's Priests," 25n2, argues that this passage cannot be used to show that Nietzsche is critical of the noble masters because the priests are nobles themselves. But Nietzsche's main point is that the priests are a different breed of nobles, to be distinguished sharply from the knightly-aristocratic types. Thus the

priests stand for a different kind of nobility, a spiritualized form—from which perspective they in fact criticize the knightly-aristocratic form of nobility.

87. Nietzsche, *On the Genealogy of Morals*, 33. On the importance of this passage, see Gilles Deleuze, *Nietzsche and Philosophy*, trans. Hugh Tomlinson (New York: Columbia University Press, 1983), 66; and Robert B. Pippin, "Lightning and Flash, Agent and Deed," in Acampora, Nietzsche's *On The Genealogy of Morals*, 142.

88. In continuing my analysis of the revaluation of values in the ancient world, I will follow Nietzsche—and his commentators—by speaking simply of "slaves" when a more complex phenomenon is intended. In view of my preceding discussion, "slaves" should be taken as an abbreviation for the much longer phrase "actual low-born slaves and the higher types (priests and philosophers) who lead them in their rebellion against their masters." I realize that it is an oversimplification to speak simply as I do of "masters versus slaves," but it is an oversimplification that Nietzsche himself kept making. The main point to bear in mind is that when Nietzsche speaks of "slaves," he generally assumes that they are being led—by priestly nobles in the case of the ancient Jews. In Nietzsche's account of the rise of Christianity, he assigns a crucial role to Paul as a kind of renegade Jew leading the movement, turning it in a new direction, as Nietzsche explains in *The Antichrist*, sec. 42: "He *invented his own history of earliest Christianity*. Still *further*: he falsified the history of Israel once more. . . . His need was for power once again" (Kaufmann, *Portable Nietzsche*, 617–18; original emphasis).

89. Nietzsche, *On the Genealogy of Morals*, 40–41.

90. Ibid., 37.

91. See Berkowitz, *Ethics of an Immoralist*, 97–98.

92. Although Nietzsche never uses the term "state of nature" to describe presocial existence, he can usefully be viewed as a "state of nature" thinker in the tradition of Hobbes, Locke, and Rousseau. In Nietzsche's reformulation, the stage of master morality corresponds to the state of nature (particularly the way Hobbes conceives it as a state of war). At first, Nietzsche's masters are free to indulge their aggressive impulses, which results in a permanent state of war (like Hobbes, and unlike Rousseau, Nietzsche believes that aggressiveness is natural to human beings). In this warlike condition, human beings cannot develop their civilized qualities and remain in what amounts to a subhuman state. For Nietzsche, then, our true and full humanity emerges only in the stage of slave morality, which corresponds to the state of civil society in Hobbes, Locke, and Rousseau. The masters lose the freedom of their aggressive impulses and are forced to live at peace with other human beings, who are now in a position to create what we think of as civilization and to develop their distinctively human faculties (their "spirituality"). For an extended comparison of Rousseau and Nietzsche, see Keith Ansell-Pearson, *Nietzsche Contra Rousseau: A Study of Nietzsche's Moral and Political Thought* (Cambridge: Cambridge University Press, 1991). Ansell-Pearson discusses Nietzsche as a "state of nature" thinker on 145.

93. Nietzsche, *On the Genealogy of Morals*, 36. In a note headed "One owes to the Christian church," Nietzsche gives a concrete example of the creativity of Christian slavishness: "The intellectualization of *cruelty*: the idea of hell, the tortures and inquisitions, the auto-da-fé, after all, represent great progress over the magnificent but semi-imbecilic butchery in the Roman arenas" (Bittner, *Writings from the Late Notebooks*, 7).

94. Nietzsche, *On the Genealogy of Morals*, 38–39.

95. In the extensive literature comparing Hegel and Nietzsche, perhaps the most famous book is Karl Löwith, *From Hegel to Nietzsche: The Revolution in Nineteenth-Century Thought*, trans. David E. Green (New York: Columbia University Press, 1991). See also Kaufmann, *Nietz-*

sche, 329–31; Strong, *Friedrich Nietzsche and the Politics of Transfiguration*, 237–45, 251–53, 327–29n33; and Francis Fukuyama, *The End of History and the Last Man* (New York: Free Press, 1992), 189, 301, 306, 314.

96. It has become commonplace to compare Hegel and Nietzsche on this subject. It should be noted, however, that their terminology is different in the original German. For "master," both Hegel and Nietzsche use the German word *Herr*, which generally means "lord" (as in the phrase *Herr Gott*, meaning "Lord God"). Nietzsche uses the German word *Sklave*, which does mean "slave," but Hegel uses the German word *Knecht*, which is more properly translated "servant" or "bondsman." Thus in discussions in English of Hegel's views on this subject, one often sees references to "lordship" versus "bondage." Neither Hegel nor Nietzsche ever uses the German word *Meister* in this context (in German, *Meister* has the connotation of superior skill or knowledge—as in Wagner's *Die Meistersinger*—whereas *Herr* has the connotation of superior authority). Nietzsche's infamous phrase "master race" is *Herrenvolk* or *Herrenrasse* in German. One should be aware of the original German in this matter; nevertheless, it is routine to speak of "the dialectic of master and slave" in discussions of Hegel in English and I will follow this convention. For more on this point, see Hatab, "Master Morality": "The master-slave distinction has become a term of art in treatments of Nietzsche" (194n4). For Hegel's analysis of the master/slave dialectic, see the famous section "Lordship and Bondage" (or "Mastery and Slavery"), chapter 4, sec. A of his *Phenomenology of Spirit* (e.g., in the J. B. Baillie English translation, *The Phenomenology of Mind* [New York: Harper & Row, 1967], 229–40). Seldom have so few pages of text generated so many volumes of commentary. I have generally followed the brilliant, albeit controversial, interpretation of this section by Alexandre Kojève, perhaps the person most responsible for placing the master/slave dialectic at the center of Hegel studies. See Alexandre Kojève, *Introduction to the Reading of Hegel*, trans. James H. Nichols (New York: Basic Books, 1969), especially "In Place of an Introduction" (3–30), which consists of a translation of the "Master/Slave" section, interwoven with Kojève's commentary. For further analysis of the master/slave dialectic in Hegel (sometimes developing Kojève's ideas; sometimes criticizing them), see, e.g., Fukuyama, *End of History*, 143–98; Jean Hyppolite, *Genesis and Structure of Hegel's Phenomenology of Spirit*, trans. Samuel Cherniak and John Heckman (Evanston, IL: Northwestern University Press, 1974), 164–77; Hans-Georg Gadamer, *Hegel's Dialectic: Five Hermeneutical Studies*, trans. P. Christope Smith (New Haven, CT: Yale University Press, 1976), 54–74; Stanley Rosen, *G. W. F. Hegel: An Introduction to the Science of Wisdom* (New Haven, CT: Yale, 1974), 151–64; Barry Cooper, *The End of History: An Essay on Modern Hegelianism* (Toronto: University of Toronto Press, 1984), 85–99; Walter Kaufmann, *Hegel: Reinterpretation, Texts, and Commentary* (Garden City, NY: Doubleday, 1965), 152–58; and James H. Nichols, *Alexandre Kojève: Wisdom at the End of History* (Lanham, MD: Rowman and Littefield, 2007), 21–27.

97. But note the important distinction Zuckert draws: the central phenomenon in Hegel's account of masters and slaves is recognition, but "the master does not conquer and enslave from a desire for recognition, according to Nietzsche, and surely not for recognition from slaves. A desire for recognition presupposes an awareness of the importance of others and their opinions and a degree of self-doubt, a degree of rationality and self-reflection, that cannot be attributed to the unself-conscious natural man" ("Nietzsche on the Origin and Development of the Distinctively Human," 54). Zuckert highlights a fundamental distinction between Hegel and Nietzsche. In Hegel, the human condition is initially not differentiated into ranks; only the potentially deadly struggle for recognition produces the distinction between masters and slaves (when the slaves surrender to servitude to save their lives). Nietzsche begins with human beings already

differentiated into conquering master-types and subservient slave-types. In Nietzsche's account, the aristocratic order of rank is thus more natural than it is in Hegel's. Hegel's account of masters and slaves in effect anticipates their eventual equality; the distinction seems to be arbitrary—the result of momentary good fortune in combat. One might say that Hegel writes his account from the perspective of the slaves; Nietzsche writes his from the perspective of the masters. On this difference between Hegel and Nietzsche, see Gillespie and Callanan, *"On the Genealogy of Morals,"* 259–60. Another important difference between Hegel and Nietzsche in their conception of masters and slaves is that Hegel presents only the slaves as creative (in their capacity as workers), whereas for Nietzsche, the masters are also creative—they create the values of master morality.

98. Nietzsche, *On the Genealogy of Morals*, 42.

99. For an extended comparison of *Sublimierung* in Nietzsche with *Aufhebung* in Hegel, see Kaufmann, *Nietzsche*, 236–43.

100. Nietzsche, *On the Genealogy of Morals*, 84. See Conway, *Nietzsche's* On the Genealogy of Morals, 76–77. In "state of nature" thinking, this "most fundamental change" in human experience corresponds to the moment of the social contract, which takes human beings from the state of nature to the state of civil society. For different reasons, Rousseau also describes this transition as a source of great misery.

101. Nietzsche, *On the Genealogy of Morals*, 84.

102. Ibid., 85.

103. Conway, *Nietzsche's* On the Genealogy of Morals, 34.

104. Middleton, *Selected Letters of Friedrich Nietzsche*, February 23, 1887, 261.

105. Bittner, ed., *Writings from the Late Notebooks*, 204.

106. Rousseau was a pioneer in this kind of dialectical thinking. He seems to present the movement from the state of nature to the state of civil society as a catastrophe—in mythical terms, a fall from Eden. Yet, because Rousseau conceives of the state of nature as subhuman (in his account, human beings lack speech and reason in the state of nature), he must acknowledge that the "fall" is "fortunate." Only in civil society do human beings become fully human. For the idea of the "fortunate fall" in Rousseau, see my book *Creature and Creator: Myth-making and English Romanticism* (Cambridge: Cambridge University Press, 1984), 4–19. On "Nietzsche's preeminent concern with the negative," see Kaufmann, *Nietzsche*, 243, and esp. 253, where he speaks of "Nietzsche's dialectic, of his keen emphasis on the negative, and of his ultimate recognition and affirmation of the value of the apparently negative" (see also 254n23). For a contrary view of Nietzsche—that he was *not* a dialectical thinker and was fundamentally opposed to Hegel—see Deleuze, *Nietzsche and Philosophy*, esp. 8—"Anti-Hegelianism runs through Nietzsche's work as its cutting edge"—and 162, 179, and 180, where Deleuze writes, "To the famous positivity of the negative Nietzsche opposes his own discovery: the negativity of the positive" (see also 195–98).

107. As early as *Human, All Too Human*, Nietzsche speaks of a paradoxical *"Ennoblement through degeneration"*: "Degenerate natures are of the highest significance wherever progress is to be effected. Every progress of the whole has to be preceded by a partial weakening. The strongest natures *preserve* the type, the weaker help it to *evolve* . . . . To this extent the celebrated struggle for existence does not seem to me to be the only theory by which progress or strengthening of a man or a race can be explained. . . . It is precisely the weaker nature, as the tender and more refined, that makes any progress possible at all" (107; sec. 224).

108. The wording "master morality" appears less frequently in Nietzsche's published writings than one would guess from reading the critical literature. In fact, as Alexander Nehamas points out, "the notorious expression 'master morality' (*Herren-Moral*) does not appear in the

Genealogy. The term appears only once in Nietzsche's published texts, in *Beyond Good and Evil*, section 260. The expression 'noble morality' (*vornehme Moral*) occurs twice, in *Genealogy of Morals*, First Essay, section 10 and *The Antichrist*, section 24" (*Nietzsche: Life as Literature* [Cambridge: Harvard University Press, 1985], 254n5). It is unfortunate, although hardly surprising, that Nietzsche's most provocative verbal formulation of his concept is the one that has become famous.

109. Here is another fundamental disagreement between Hegel and Nietzsche. Hegel believed that the principle of human freedom had finally triumphed in the French Revolution (and its institutionalization in the modern bourgeois state). This is Hegel's famous "end of history." But what looked like the triumphant "end of history" to Hegel struck Nietzsche as the depressing "last man" of *Thus Spoke Zarathustra*—the empty, tepid, complacent world of the European middle class. In short, what Hegel celebrated, Nietzsche deplored. On this subject, see Fukuyama, *End of History*, esp. 287–339. Thus Nietzsche hoped to move beyond what Hegel calls "the end of history" to a higher stage, which Nietzsche calls the "Overman" in *Thus Spoke Zarathustra*.

110. See Ansell-Pearson, *Nietzsche Contra Rousseau*, 107.

111. See Nietzsche, *Gay Science*: "Alas, my friends, we must overcome even the Greeks" (272 [sec. 340]), and: "We 'conserve' nothing: neither do we want to return to any past periods" (338 [sec. 377]). On this point, see Bruce Detwiler, *Nietzsche and the Politics of Aristocratic Radicalism* (Chicago: University of Chicago Press, 1990), 135–37. Similarly, contrary to popular opinion, Rousseau never advocated a simple return to the state of nature. He realized that such a return would require sacrificing all or most of what we have come to regard as our civilized humanity. See *Second Discourse*, note i, and Cantor, *Creature and Creator*, 8–9, 16.

112. See Jaspers's formulation of this point about Nietzsche: "His thinking had grown out of Christianity, spurred by Christianity's own impulses; and his fight against Christianity did not at all seek merely to discard it, reverse it, or relapse from it. Instead, he wanted to overcome and surpass it, and to do so with the aid of forces evolved by Christianity and by nothing else in the world" (*Nietzsche and Christianity*, 6).

113. Nietzsche, *Human, All Too Human*, 175 (sec. 475). The German is "den edelsten Mensch." *Edel* is the normal German word for "noble" and is used to designate an aristocrat. The context of this surprising statement is a long passage about the contributions the Jews have made to European civilization. Nietzsche says, "We have to thank [them] for the noblest human being (Christ), the purest sage (Spinoza), the mightiest book and the most efficacious moral code in the world." Nietzsche had a higher opinion of Christ than he did of Christianity, and indeed he argues, especially in *The Antichrist*, that institutional Christianity embodies principles very different from those Christ believed and preached. In Nietzsche's famous formulation: "There was only *one* Christian, and he died on the cross" (*Antichrist*, sec. 39; Kaufmann, *Portable Nietzsche*, 612).

114. Nietzsche, *Assorted Opinions and Maxims*, sec. 224 in *Human, All Too Human*, 268–69.

115. Ibid., 269.

116. Ibid.

117. Ibid.

118. For Nietzsche's criticism of Hegel's philosophy of history in some of his early notes (from 1873), see Kaufmann, *Portable Nietzsche*, 39–40.

119. Nietzsche, *Assorted Opinions and Maxims*, sec. 224 in *Human, All Too Human*, 269.

120. Nietzsche, *Gay Science*, 178 (sec. 122). On this section, see Bett, "Nietzsche and the Romans," 21.

121. Kaufmann, *Portable Nietzsche*, 513 (*Twilight of the Idols*, "Skirmishes of an Untimely Man," sec. 1).

122. On this point, see Nietzsche, *Will to Power*: "That species that derived its advantage from depriving man of his self-satisfaction (the representatives of the herd instinct; e.g. the priests and philosophers) became subtle and psychologically astute, so as to demonstrate how nonetheless selfishness ruled everywhere. . . . N.B. Christianity thus demonstrates an advance in the sharpness of psychological insight" (414 [sec. 786]).

123. Nietzsche, *Gay Science*, 178 (sec. 122).

124. See Deleuze, *Nietzsche and Philosophy*: "In comparison with Christianity the Greeks are children" (21).

125. Nietzsche, *Gay Science*, 178 (sec. 122).

126. Nietzsche, *Daybreak*, 118 (sec. 199).

127. Nietzsche, *The Wanderer and His Shadow*, sec. 222 in *Human, All Too Human*, 367. Here is another passage in praise of the Middle Ages from one of Nietzsche's early writings (unpublished during his lifetime), "The Struggle Between Science and Wisdom," sec. 196: "Men became *more clever* during the middle ages. Calculating according to two standards, the sophistry of conscience and the interpretation of texts: these were the means for this development. Antiquity lacked such a method of *sharpening the mind* under the pressure of a hierarchy and theology. On the contrary, the Greeks became credulous and shallow under their great freedom of thought. One commenced or ceased to believe anything as one wished. For this reason they took no pleasure in forced acuteness and thus in the favorite variety of cleverness of modern times. The Greeks were not very *clever*, which is why Socrates's irony created such a sensation among them. In this regard I frequently find Plato to be rather ponderous" (*Philosophy and Truth: Selections from Nietzsche's Notebooks of the Early 1870s*, trans. Daniel Breazeale [Atlantic Highlands, NJ: Harvester, 1979], 136).

128. Nietzsche, *Human, All Too Human*, 102 (sec. 220).

129. Ibid., 116–17 (sec. 244).

130. In Hegel's *Aesthetics*, Christianity similarly supplies the principle of subjectivity by which modern art advances beyond ancient art.

131. Jaspers offers a perceptive analysis of the ambivalence of Nietzsche's attitude toward Christianity. The central claim of his book is "Nietzsche, the pastor's son, knew and admitted the Christian basis of his real motivating forces: his seriousness, truthfulness, and his radically uncompromising approach" (*Nietzsche and Christianity*, vii–viii). For the complexity of Nietzsche's attitude toward Christianity, see also Kaufmann, *Nietzsche*, 270–71; for a concise survey of Nietzsche's views on Christianity, see 337–90.

132. Harold Bloom speaks of Coriolanus's "limited consciousness" in *Shakespeare: The Invention of the Human* (New York: Riverhead, 1998), 105, 577–78.

133. Antony also experiences a kind of "mutiny" within himself (see *Antony and Cleopatra*, 3.11.13).

134. On the discovery of an inner world and increasing self-consciousness among the Romans in *Julius Caesar*, see the "mirror" dialogue between Cassius and Brutus (1.2.48–78). Cassius promises to Brutus to "discover to yourself / That of yourself which you yet know not of" (1.2.69–70).

135. Nietzsche, *On the Genealogy of Morals*, 84. Gordon Braden traces a similar process in the imperial world of Seneca's tragedies: "Conflicts resolved at the periphery replicate themselves at the center. Foreign war is gradually replaced by civil war, internal competition raised to a new

intensity.... Imperial derangement... is in great part the derangement of the classical competitive ethos with nowhere to go" (*Renaissance Tragedy and the Senecan Tradition*, 14).

136. There are strangely Christian overtones to Enobarbus's story. As we saw in chapter 1, he
plays the Judas figure at Antony's "last supper." Enobarbus's conduct also calls to mind Peter's
denial of Jesus. After Enobarbus's desertion, a soldier reports to Antony that Enobarbus will
say: "I am none of thine" "from Caesar's camp" (4.5.7–8). This parallels Peter's response in the
gospels when asked if he is a follower of Jesus: "I do not know the man" (see Matthew 26:72–75).

137. Note Dolabella's words to Cleopatra: "your command / (Which my love makes religion
to obey)" (5.2.198–99).

138. See Hatab, "Master Morality": "The *Genealogy* is sometimes read as a delineation of
two radically different human types, master and slave, strong and weak, where the displacement
of master morality was an unqualified degeneration of life that must in turn be replaced by
something akin to master morality if life is to avoid a collapse into nihilism. One of the hidden
implications of the discussions in this essay, however, is that the typology of master and slave,
strong and weak, is essentially ambiguous, that the boundaries between these tropes are more
porous than we might expect" (207).

139. Nietzsche, *Beyond Good and Evil*, 204 (sec. 260).

140. For the importance of this passage, see Kaufmann's edition of *Beyond Good and Evil*,
204n5; Walter Kaufmann, "How Nietzsche Revolutionized Ethics," *From Shakespeare to Existentialism* (Garden City, NY: Anchor Books, 1960), 207–17; Conway, *Nietzsche's On the Genealogy
of Morals*, 48–49; Strong, *Friedrich Nietzsche and the Politics of Transfiguration*, 239; Hatab,
"Master Morality," 210; and Bett, "Nietzsche and the Romans," 12.

141. See Strong, *Friedrich Nietzsche and the Politics of Transfiguration*, 239.

142. Lou Salomé, *Nietzsche*, trans. Siegfried Mandel (Urbana: University of Illinois Press,
1984), 115. The credibility of Salomé's various accounts of her personal relationship with Nietzsche has been challenged by scholars. See, e.g., Kaufmann, *Nietzsche*, 62–63. This does not
mean, however, that she cannot offer genuine insights into his philosophy.

143. It may seem surprising to speak of a piteous side to Friedrich Nietzsche, but he in fact
identifies his impulse to pity as his great danger in a letter to his friend Malwida von Meysen-
bug: "Schopenhauer's 'pity' has always been the *main* cause of trouble in my life.... For this is
not only a softness which any magnanimous Hellene would have laughed at—it is also a grave,
practical danger. One should *persist* in one's *own* ideal of man; one should impose one's ideal
on one's fellow beings and on oneself overpoweringly.... But to do this, one has to keep a nice
tight rein on one's sympathy" (Middleton, *Selected Letters of Friedrich Nietzsche*, August 1883,
216). This letter describes exactly the conflict in Nietzsche's soul that Salomé outlines—he is
torn between Greek magnanimity and a Christian disposition to pity.

144. This interpretation has become widespread in Nietzsche criticism. See, e.g., Reginster,
Affirmation of Life, who says of "master" and "slave" that "they designate now socio-political
categories, and now character types" (253); and Anderson, "Nietzsche's Priests," who says that
Nietzsche's categories are "not historical and sociological, but rather *moral-psychological*" (30).

145. Salomé, *Nietzsche*, 115.

146. For similar ideas, see Hatab, "Master Morality": "There cannot be rigid delineations
between master, slave, and creative types in Nietzsche's overall analysis.... The internalization
of power in slave morality, while problematic, opens up the capacities of imagination and thus
the more refined forms of culture creation that Nietzsche himself celebrates. Therefore, slavish
tendencies are not only life-enhancing for weaker types, they are also not altogether regret-

table when mixed with creative power. And since Nietzsche claims that such creative power emerges not through the slavish masses but through special individuals (the ascetic priest and its offshoots), then here we notice a possible blending of slavish passivity and masterly activity" (208–9). And see Gillespie and Callanan, "*On the Genealogy of Morals*": "Nietzsche aims not at a straightforward revival of the classical type but rather at a fusion of the master's physiological vigor with the slave's spiritual resources and depth" (263).

147. As Salomé observes: "That which Nietzsche seems to combat most strenuously, is what he fully incorporates into his theories, with extreme consequences and meanings.... Indeed, we can assume with certainty that when Nietzsche denigrates and pursues something with special hatred, he harbors it deep in the heart of his own philosophy or in his own life" (*Nietzsche*, 120).

148. See Ansell-Pearson, *Nietzsche Contra Rousseau*, 133.

149. Nietzsche, *On the Genealogy of Morals*, 52. For comments on this passage, see Gillespie and Callanan, "*On the Genealogy of Morals*," 262; and Bett, "Nietzsche and the Romans," 12: "The Romans' uncomplicated master morality is not, then, the highest thing one could aim for, and Nietzsche is not recommending that we return to it."

150. See Berkowitz, *Ethics of an Immoralist*, 82–83, 254. Again, we see that Nietzsche was a dialectical thinker in a tradition that runs from Rousseau through Hegel to later figures, such as Marx. Like these other thinkers, Nietzsche employs a "three-stage" model of history. In Rousseau, for example, the state of nature is followed by the state of civil society, which exposes a fundamental antinomy in human existence. In the state of nature, human beings are free and happy but subhuman; in the state of civil society, they acquire their distinctively human faculties, but become unhappy and enslaved in the process. Rousseau's quest was for some kind of third stage of history that might combine in a grand synthesis the freedom and happiness of the state of nature with the full development of human faculties in civil society. For more on this subject and its relevance to dialectical thinking in Romantic literature, see Cantor, *Creature and Creator*, 19–23. For Nietzsche, the three stages of history are: 1) master morality, 2) slave morality, 3) his hoped-for synthesis of master and slave morality. Despite Nietzsche's many differences from Hegel, he had a similar dialectical understanding of history. He hoped, as Hegel did, to combine classical and Christian elements in a higher synthesis.

151. Nietzsche, *Will to Power*, 513 (sec. 983; see Kaufmann's note 59). On this paradoxical idea, see Jaspers, *Nietzsche and Christianity*, 93; Ansell-Pearson, *Nietzsche Contra Rousseau*, 49; and Kaufmann, *Nietzsche*, 316.

152. Nietzsche, *The Wanderer and His Shadow*, sec. 222 in *Human, All Too Human*, 367.

153. Nietzsche, *Beyond Good and Evil*, 111 (sec. 200).

154. Ibid., 112.

155. See Bett, "Nietzsche and the Romans": "The only Roman in whom Nietzsche shows any consistent interest—again of a very positive kind—is Julius Caesar" (9). On pp. 15–18, Bett surveys Nietzsche's references to Julius Caesar throughout his writings. See also Gillespie and Callanan, "*On the Genealogy of Morals*," 269.

156. Perhaps relevant to this idea is section 38 of "Skirmishes of an Untimely Man" in *Twilight of the Idols*, where Nietzsche discusses Julius Caesar as the "most beautiful type" of the political man, measured "according to the resistance which must be overcome, according to the exertion required, to remain on top." Nietzsche continues: "The highest type of free man should be sought where the highest resistance is constantly overcome: five steps from tyranny, close to the threshold of the danger of servitude" (Kaufmann, *Portable Nietzsche*, 542). On this passage, see Bett, "Nietzsche and the Romans," 17–18.

157. On this point, Alexis de Tocqueville writes: "All the great writers of antiquity were a part of the aristocracy of masters, or at least they saw that aristocracy established without dispute. . . . It was necessary that Jesus Christ come to earth to make it understood that all members of the human species are naturally alike and equal" (*Democracy in America*, vol. 2, trans. Harvey C. Mansfield and Delba Winthrop [Chicago: University of Chicago Press, 2000], 413 [part 1, chapter 3]).

158. See Detwiler, *Aristocratic Radicalism*, 176–77. In his late notebooks, Nietzsche speculated on ways to reestablish aristocracy on a democratic basis. See, e.g., *Will to Power*: "And would it not be a kind of goal, redemption, and justification for the democratic movement itself if someone arrived who could make use of it—by finally producing beside its new and sublime development of slavery . . . a higher kind of dominating and Caesarean spirits who would stand upon it, maintain themselves by it, and elevate themselves through it?" (501 [sec. 954]). On p. 501 (sec. 955), Nietzsche says that "an audacious ruling race is developing on the basis of an extremely intelligent herd mass." On p. 503 (sec. 957), Nietzsche writes, "The seductive power that antiquity exercises on such well-turned-out, i.e., strong and enterprising, souls is the most subtle and effective of all anti-democratic and anti-Christian influences even today, as at the time of the Renaissance." And on p. 504 (sec. 960), Nietzsche speaks of higher men who will "employ democratic Europe as their most pliant and supple instrument for getting hold of the destinies of the earth." As often happened with Nietzsche's notes, he never fully developed or formulated these ideas, but they do give a sense of the direction in which his thinking was headed at the end of his writing career.

159. Nietzsche, *On the Genealogy of Morals*, 53. Nietzsche's admiration for the Renaissance was no doubt reinforced by his association with Jacob Burckhardt, a great scholar of the Renaissance. For Nietzsche's knowledge of Burckhardt's work on the Renaissance, see Martin A. Ruehl, "*Politeia* 1871: Young Nietzsche on the Greek State," in Bishop, *Nietzsche and Antiquity*, 91–92.

160. As Nietzsche wrote in a letter to Franz Overbeck: "For me, the Renaissance remains the climax of this millennium; and what has happened since then is the grand reaction of all kinds of herd instincts against the 'individualism' of that epoch" (Middleton, *Selected Letters of Friedrich Nietzsche*, October 1882, 195).

161. Nietzsche, *On the Genealogy of Morals*, 54.

162. Nietzsche, *Gay Science*, 318 (sec. 362). For Nietzsche's view of Napoleon, see also section 44 of "Skirmishes of an Untimely Man" in *Twilight of the Idols*: "Napoleon was *different*, the heir of a stronger, older, more ancient civilization than the one which was perishing in France, he became master there, he *was* the only master" (Kaufmann, *Portable Nietzsche*, 547).

163. See Löwith, *From Hegel to Nietzsche*, who says of Nietzsche's "new masters of the earth": "Like Napoleon, they will be men of the people, and at the same time stand above them in absolute self-confidence, as lawgivers and men of violence both" (262). Nietzsche had a longstanding interest in the political phenomenon known as Caesarism or Bonapartism—the coming to power, by extraconstitutional means, of a military leader who presents himself as a man of the people and rules autocratically on the basis of a plebiscite. This interest in Caesarism/Bonapartism is evident already in a paper Nietzsche presented in January 1862 (when he was only seventeen years old) to his Schulpforta classmates Wilhelm Pinder and Gustav Krug. In "Napoleon III als Praesident," Nietzsche celebrates the 1851 *coup d'etat* by means of which Napoleon III overthrew the Second French Republic and became dictator—and later emperor—of France. With youthful enthusiasm, Nietzsche views Napoleon III as standing above the law by virtue of his political genius and his ability to seize the moment (perhaps a prototype of Nietz-

sche's later conception of the Overman). Nietzsche compares Napoleon III specifically to Julius Caesar: "The army's loyalty and confidence in him increased due to his enormous military banquets, which he, like Caesar, defrayed" ("Napoleon III as President," trans. Frank Cameron and Jeff Mitscherling, in *Political Writings of Friedrich Nietzsche*, ed. Frank Cameron and Don Dombowsky [New York: Palgrave Macmillan, 2008], 28). What is most striking in this early essay is Nietzsche's seemingly democratic emphasis on the role of the people in Napoleon III's rule: "The main condition is agreeing to the will of the people; every government that is not to carry within itself the seeds of its own destruction can be traced back to the people. The will of the people makes the ruler; the prototype of a free state is for this reason a presidency determined by the people amidst representatives of the people" ("Napoleon III," 26). But note that the young Nietzsche is not supporting what we would call *liberal democracy*. What he praises in Napoleon III is autocratic rule erected on a democratic basis (plebiscite). This early essay thus sheds light on Nietzsche's later praise of Julius Caesar and Napoleon I. He was always fascinated by the prospect of combining autocracy and democracy in a Caesarist regime, which would mean a fusion of master morality and slave morality. Nietzsche's interest in Caesarism helps explain his continuing fascination with Shakespeare's *Julius Caesar*. (I thank Marco Basile for calling my attention to Nietzsche's Napoleon III essay.)

164. Nietzsche, *Gay Science*, 268 (sec. 337).

165. For the idea of synthesis and a higher stage of human history in Romanticism and German idealism, see Cantor, *Creature and Creator*, 19–23. For Nietzsche's affinities with Romanticism, see Detwiler, *Aristocratic Radicalism*, 190.

166. Nietzsche would hate me for pointing this out, but Wagner's Parsifal embodies the kind of medieval synthesis of Christian and knightly/aristocratic culture that Nietzsche discusses. In general, Wagner's Romantic medievalism leads him to explore in his operas the kind of pagan/Christian hybridity that fascinated Nietzsche. Drawing upon Norse and Germanic sources, Wagner inevitably deals with pagan material, but he keeps infusing it with Christian ideas such as renunciation and redemption.

167. Nietzsche, *Will to Power*, 506–7 (sec. 966). Nietzsche tended to think of Shakespeare in terms of the concept of synthesis. See *Beyond Good and Evil*, 152 (sec. 224), where he refers to Shakespeare as "that amazing Spanish-Moorish-Saxon synthesis of tastes that would have all but killed an ancient Athenian of Aeschylus's circle with laughter or irritation."

168. See Jan H. Blits, *Rome and the Spirit of Caesar: Shakespeare's Julius Caesar* (Lanham, MD: Lexington, 2015), xxiv.

169. There is something peculiar about the way that ambition—the traditional engine of republican politics—is now being questioned by patricians like Brutus. Brutus raises doubts about master morality when he says of Caesar: "Th' abuse of greatness is when it disjoins / Remorse from power" (*Julius Caesar*, 2.1.18–19). Most editors gloss *remorse* as "mercy" or "compassion." The idea that greatness is not simply power but must be joined with compassion would be incomprehensible to Coriolanus. Antony, in his funeral oration, concedes that ambition is a "grievous fault" (3.2.79). Such criticisms of ambition in the late Republic are just one more sign of how Rome is being ethically transformed. Blits, *Rome and the Spirit of Caesar*, writes of this transformation in *Julius Caesar*: "The victory of strength leads to the worship of weakness. Pity supplants courage. Virtue comes to be attached to humility rather than to pride" (xxvi).

170. Without pressing the parallels between Shakespeare and Nietzsche too far, one may note that Antony begins to speak of good versus evil in the funeral oration: "The evil that men do lives after them, / The good is oft interred with their bones" (*Julius Caesar*, 3.2.75–76). An-

tony seems to be saying that Caesar's military conquests were evil—again an un-Roman senti- ment in the traditional meaning of *Roman*. More generally in this speech, Antony makes a mockery of traditional Roman notions of honor, slowly and subtly turning "honorable" into a term of contempt. As a renegade master, Antony appeals to—and unleashes—the plebeians' hatred of the patricians. When Brutus rests his case on time-honored republican principles, the plebeians at first show their old respect for their traditional patrician masters: "Give him a statue with his ancestors" (3.2.50). But Antony turns Brutus's rhetoric on its head and inspires what he himself calls a "mutiny" (3.2.211). In effect, act 3, scene 2 offers Shakespeare's image of the renegade master leading a slave revolt in Rome.

171. Ironically, one of the conspirators, Decius Brutus, foresees this very possibility when he reinterprets Calphurnia's dream of Caesar's statue spouting blood. Decius Brutus predicts that "great men shall press / For tinctures, stains, relics, and cognizance" (2.2.88–89) from Caesar. See Marjorie Garber, *Shakespeare After All* (New York: Anchor, 2005), 417: "Romans of the fu- ture will come to Caesar . . . even for relics, as if he were a Christian saint. And this too will come true in the play, and beyond it, as Antony makes a relic of Caesar's robe with its stab wounds." For more on the association of Caesar with relics, see Derek Traversi, *Shakespeare: The Roman Plays* (Stanford, CA: Stanford University Press, 1963), 49, 56; Gary Wills, *Rome and Rhetoric: Shakespeare's Julius Caesar* (New Haven, CT: Yale University Press, 2011), 30–31; and Clifford Ronan, *"Antike Roman": Power Symbology and the Roman Play in Early Modern England, 1585– 1635* (Athens, GA: University of Georgia Press, 1995), 30. The "Christian" potential of divinity in Rome is evident even in *Coriolanus*. A messenger reports that Coriolanus has been received in the city like a god: "I have seen the dumb men throng to see him, and / The blind to hear him speak" (2.1.262–63). Are these early Romans perhaps already looking for miracle cures from their god-heroes? In *The Bible in Shakespeare* (Oxford: Oxford University Press, 2013), Hanni- bal Hamlin, reading this passage very carefully, notes Coriolanus's limitations as a divinity: "If Coriolanus' 'blind' *listeners* had seen and his 'dumb' *viewers* spoken, his entry into Rome might have seemed more astonishing. As it is, this event, unlike the one recounted in Matthew [15:30], is decidedly unmiraculous" (203; original emphasis).

172. By contrast, Coriolanus would not show his wounds to the Roman people, even when, as candidate for consul, he was bound by tradition to do so. In line with Antony's policy in *Julius Caesar*, in *Antony and Cleopatra*, nearing defeat, he is willing to offer up himself as a "mangled shadow" to his followers (4.2.27). From his experience in *Julius Caesar*, Antony has evidently learned the value of playing the role of "a fall'n lord" to gain the "allegiance" of his soldiers (3.3.44).

173. This scene is further evidence that Shakespeare conceives of the slave revolt in morality as engineered from the top down, not from the bottom up, as Nietzsche often speaks of it. It takes the renegade patrician Antony, turning against members of his own aristocratic caste, to stir up the plebeians. Several critics have noted parallels between Jesus Christ and Julius Caesar in Shakespeare's presentation. See, e.g., Roy W. Battenhouse, *Shakespearean Tragedy: Its Art and Its Christian Premises* (Bloomington: Indiana University Press, 1969): "The holiday of Lupercal, at which Caesar makes his bid for kingship by playing weak and humble, parodies the Christian Passover at which Christ was humble in a different way. And when Antony, after Caesar's death, enlists disciples by displaying the 'wounds' of the dead Caesar, do we not have a counterfeit parallel to the resurrected Christ's offering his wounds to the view of Thomas the doubter?" (92–93). For more elaborate parallels between Julius Caesar and Jesus Christ, see Hamlin, *Bible in Shakespeare*, 184–97; Steve Sohmer, *Shakespeare's Mystery Play: The Opening of the Globe*

Theatre 1599 (Manchester, UK: Manchester University Press, 1999); Nasser Behngar, "Who is Shakespeare's Julius Caesar?" in *Shakespeare and the Body Politic*, ed. Bernard J. Dobski and Dustin Gish (Lanham, MD: Lexington, 2013), 79–93 (Behngar's essay relies heavily on Sohmer's book and contains a convenient summary of its claims); David Kaula, "'Let Us Be Sacrificers': Religious Motifs in *Julius Caesar*," *Shakespeare Studies* 14 (1981): 197–214; and Charles Ross, "Staging the Spirit, Bearing a Corpse, in Shakespeare's *Julius Caesar*," *Literary Imagination*, 73 (Fall 2014), 26–34, 38–41. For more on allusions to Christianity in *Julius Caesar*, see Blits, *Rome and the Spirit of Caesar*, xxv–vi, 50, 100. On connections between Julius Caesar and Jesus Christ in Machiavelli's thought, see Vickie B. Sullivan, *Machiavelli's Three Romes: Religion, Human Liberty, and Politics Reformed* (DeKalb: Northern Illinois University Press, 1996), 61–62, 67, 71–73, 103–4.

174. See Michael Neill, introduction to *Anthony and Cleopatra* (Oxford: Oxford University Press, 1994): "The problem for Anthony is that 'to do thus,' . . . will involve nothing less than an absolute *undoing* of the chivalric military 'doing' that claims his allegiance back in Rome. . . . Two mutually inconsistent ideas of noble doing are expressed" (105–6).

175. Andrew Fichter, "'Antony and Cleopatra': 'The Time of Universal Peace,'" *Shakespeare Survey* 33 (1980): 102.

176. In *Richard II*, the beleaguered king says something similar of himself (3.3.147–54).

177. Shakespeare was not familiar with the Icelandic sagas, but they often display this kind of remarkable combination of Christian sentiments with pagan/heroic attitudes. Consider this passage from *Njal's Saga*, when a bitter woman named Hildigunn goads her uncle Flosi to take vengeance for the murder of her husband Hoskuld: "I call upon God and all good men to witness that I charge you in the name of all the powers of your Christ and in the name of your courage and your manhood, to avenge every one of the wounds that marked his body—or be an object of contempt to all men" (*Njal's Saga*, trans. Magnus Magnusson and Hermann Pállson [Harmondsworth, UK: Penguin, 1960], 240).

178. For a fuller discussion of these issues in *Henry V*, see my essay "'Christian Kings' and 'English Mercuries': *Henry V* and the Classical Tradition of Manliness," in *Educating the Prince: Essays in Honor of Harvey Mansfield*, ed. Mark Blitz and William Kristol (Lanham, MD: Rowman & Littlefield, 2000), 74–87.

179. Nietzsche, *On the Genealogy of Morals*, 52.

180. For a fuller discussion of these issues in *Hamlet*, see my book *Shakespeare: Hamlet* (Cambridge: Cambridge University Press, 2004). Nietzsche's own interpretation of *Hamlet* appears in *The Birth of Tragedy*, sec. 7. In my opinion, Nietzsche's theory of tragedy prevented him from seeing the "Nietzschean" aspects of *Hamlet*. Ironically, it is only Hegel's theory of tragedy that brings out the Nietzschean content of the play.

181. See A. D. Nuttall, *A New Mimesis: Shakespeare and the Representation of Reality* (London: Methuen, 1983), 132–35.

182. On the Homeric dimension of Othello, see Reuben A. Brower, *Hero and Saint: Shakespeare and the Graeco-Roman Heroic Tradition* (New York: Oxford University Press, 1971), 1–28; and Charles Martindale and Michelle Martindale, *Shakespeare and the Uses of Antiquity: An Introductory Essay* (London: Routledge, 1990), 35–36.

183. See Sandra Bonetto, "Coward Conscience and Bad Conscience in Shakespeare and Nietzsche," *Philosophy and Literature* 30 (2006), who refers to Iago as "the man of resentment *par excellence*" (515). For an excellent analysis of Iago as a "man of resentment," see Mark Edmundson, *Self and Soul: A Defense of Ideals* (Cambridge, MA: Harvard University Press, 2015), 146–48.

184. This confrontation between martial prowess and mental cunning comes up in *Coriolanus*. After being repeatedly defeated by Coriolanus on the battlefield, Aufidius realizes that he must change his tactics: "for where / I thought to crush him in an equal force, / True sword to sword, I'll potch at him some way, / Or wrath or craft may get him" (1.10.13–16). Unable to deal with Coriolanus's superior strength, Aufidius must resort to guile, and in acts 4 and 5, he does outwit Coriolanus and ensnare the forthright soldier in the coils of domestic politics. When one of the Volscian soldiers says of Coriolanus, "He's the devil," Aufidius replies, "Bolder, though not so subtle" (1.10.16–17). The opposition between boldness and subtlety is precisely the opposition between master morality and slave morality as Nietzsche formulates it. The way the tribunes Sicinius and Brutus outmaneuver Coriolanus in Roman politics foreshadows what Aufidius does to him at the end of the play and represents another triumph of subtlety over boldness. The tribunes' behavior shows that the potential for a slave revolt in morality already existed in republican Rome. The anachronistic use of "devil" in Aufidius's exchange with the soldier may anticipate the way that the defeated and powerless demonize their opponents in slave morality. Aufidius's case is particularly interesting because it shows that slave morality can arise in an aristocratic warrior if his noble aspirations are frustrated and he no longer feels capable of fulfillment in open combat.

185. Samuel Taylor Coleridge, *Shakespearean Criticism*, vol. 1, ed. Thomas Middleton Raysor (London: Dent, 1960), 94.

186. For a fuller discussion of these issues in *Othello*, see my essay "*Othello*: The Erring Barbarian Among the Supersubtle Venetians," *Southwest Review* 75 (1990): 296–319.

187. See Martindale and Martindale, *Shakespeare and the Uses of Antiquity*, 39.

188. Again, the Icelandic sagas offer parallels to this kind of nostalgia for paganism. In *Grettir's Saga*, a shepherd named Glam angrily rejects the pious suggestion that he must fast on the first day of Christmas: "You have many superstitions which I consider quite pointless. I can't see why people are any better off nowadays than they were before when they didn't bother with such nonsense. I liked the old customs better when people were still heathens" (*Grettir's Saga*, trans. Denton Fox and Hermann Pállson [Toronto: University of Toronto Press, 1974], 71). In general, the Icelandic sagas are a perfect literary reflection of the process Nietzsche analyzes in *On the Genealogy of Morals*. They chronicle what happens when nomadic, marauding warriors (the Vikings) settle on a small island and turn to farming. Forced into relatively close proximity with each other, they have to learn to adapt to civil society. They develop an elaborate and punctilious legal system and even adopt a religion, Christianity, fundamentally opposed to their original warrior ethic. *Grettir's Saga* powerfully portrays the tragedy of a heroic type (whose main virtue is brute strength) torn between the conflicting demands of what Nietzsche calls master morality and slave morality.

189. For a fuller discussion of these issues, see my essay "*Macbeth* and the Gospelling of Scotland," in *Shakespeare as Political Thinker*, ed. John E. Alvis and Thomas G. West (Wilmington, DE: ISI, 2000), 315–51.

190. If one were to classify *Hamlet*, *Othello*, and *Macbeth* as three "Christian" plays, one could contrast them with Shakespeare's three Roman plays in Nietzschean terms—broadly speaking, the three Christian plays dwell on the contrast between good and evil, while the three Roman plays deal with the contrast between good and bad (in the sense of noble versus base). To use anthropological terms, the three Christian plays portray guilt culture; the three Roman plays portray shame culture. On the opposition between Christian and Roman plays, see the excellent essay by John Alvis—"The Coherence of Shakespeare's Roman Plays," *Modern Language Quarterly* 40 (1979): 115–34.

191. One of the most remarkable visual representations of this kind of synthesis is Perugino's Collegio del Cambio in Perugia, in which pagan virtues (Prudence, Justice, Fortitude, and Temperance) are paired with Christian virtues (Faith, Hope, and Charity). See Elvio Lunghi, *The Collegio del Cambio in Perugia* (Assisi, IT: Editrice Minerva, 2003).

192. For discussions of this essay and Hegel's other early writings, see Herbert Marcuse, *Reason and Revolution: Hegel and the Rise of Social Theory* (Boston: Beacon, 1960), 30–42; Kaufmann, *Hegel*, 58–64; and Walter Kaufmann, "The Young Hegel and Religion," *Shakespeare to Existentialism*, 129–61. As Kaufmann points out (130), these essays, which are often misleadingly referred to as "Hegel's Early Theological Writings," are really antitheological. For the record, in his title, Hegel is using "positivity" in a different sense than the one I am using when I speak of the "positivity of the negative" in this chapter. Hegel uses "positivity" to refer to a religion that, in opposition to a pagan or natural religion, is derived from revelation and takes the form of positive regulation of human behavior. See *Early Theological Writings*, trans. T. M. Knox (Philadelphia: University of Pennsylvania Press, 1948: "A positive religion is a contranatural or a supernatural one, containing concepts and information transcending understanding and reason and requiring feelings and actions which would not come naturally to men" (167). All further page references to "The Positivity of the Christian Religion" will be embodied parenthetically in the text.

193. Throughout this essay, Hegel speaks of the Greeks as well as the Romans as examples of pagan religion.

194. The *Phaedo* is famously the dialogue in which Plato has Socrates argue for the immortality of the soul.

195. Like Nietzsche, Hegel argues that the changing political fortunes of the Jews in antiquity changed their religious views: "So long as the Jewish state found spirit and strength enough in itself for the maintenance of its independence, the Jews seldom, or, as many hold, never, had recourse to the expectation of a Messiah. Not until they were subjugated by foreign nations, not until they had a sense of their impotence and weakness, do we find them burrowing in their sacred books for a consolation of that kind" (158–59).

196. When Kaufmann quotes this passage, he offers a better translation of it than Knox does; therefore in this one case I have departed from Knox's wording and used Kaufmann's ("Young Hegel," 148).

197. Kaufmann writes, "Like Nietzsche almost a century later, Hegel considers Christianity a religion adequate for slaves" ("Young Hegel," 148).

Chapter Three

1. See Jacob Burckhardt, *The Greeks and Greek Civilization*, trans. Sheila Stern (New York: St. Martin's Griffin, 1999), 32. Burckhardt's chapter, "The Agonal Age" (160–213), develops a view of Greek competitiveness very similar to Nietzsche's. In light of their close association at the University of Basel, it is often difficult to determine which one influenced the other. On the relation of Burckhardt and Nietzsche, see Walter Kaufmann, *Nietzsche: Philosopher, Psychologist, Antichrist*, 4th ed. (Princeton, NJ: Princeton University Press, 1974), 27–28.

2. For the purposes of this chapter, I am treating Julius Caesar as the hero of *Julius Caesar*. I realize that considerable debate has been devoted to this issue, and that many, if not most, critics regard Brutus as the hero of the play. I treat Brutus at length elsewhere in this book, but want to focus on Julius Caesar at this point to explore the parallels between him and both Coriolanus

and Antony. Shakespeare presents Julius Caesar as a heroic figure, however flawed; the play is after all named after him.

3. All quotations from Shakespeare are taken from G. Blakemore Evans, ed., *The Riverside Shakespeare* (Boston: Houghton Mifflin, 1974), with act, scene, and line numbers incorporated into the body of the chapter.

4. See Nietzsche's discussion of the ancient practice of ostracism in "Homer's Contest" in *The Portable Nietzsche*, ed. and trans. Walter Kaufmann (New York: Viking, 1954), 36-37.

5. See the chapter "Love and Tyranny" in Paul A. Cantor, *Shakespeare's Rome: Republic and Empire* (Ithaca, NY: Cornell University Press, 1976), 184–208.

6. For more on this subject, see Cantor, *Shakespeare's Rome*, 185–86.

7. See W. H. Auden, *Lectures on Shakespeare*, ed. Arthur Kirsch (Princeton, NJ: Princeton University Press, 2000): "In *Antony and Cleopatra* . . . public and private life are entirely interwoven, and the conflict in the play is between two kinds of public life. Antony could not have a relation with Cleopatra if she were just a beautiful slave girl, nor could she with him if he were just a handsome centurion" (233) and: "You cannot imagine Antony and Cleopatra retiring to a cottage" (236).

8. In the text of *Julius Caesar* that has come down to us, Caesar says at this point: "Know, Caesar doth not wrong, nor without cause / Will he be satisfied" (3.1.47–48). But in Ben Jonson's collection of critical pronouncements called *Timber*, he gives as an example of Shakespeare's haste and carelessness in composition the line: "Caesar did never wrong but with just cause." See Ben Jonson, *Timber: Or Discoveries Made Upon Men and Matter* (1641), "De Shakespeare Nostrati," in *Seventeenth-Century Prose and Poetry*, 2nd ed., ed. Alexander M. Witherspoon and Frank J. Warnke (New York: Harcourt, Brace & World, 1963), 119. Jonson may have simply misremembered the line, but several editors have suggested that Jonson gives the original version of the text and that Shakespeare (or someone else) later corrected it in light of Jonson's criticism. For a full discussion of this issue, see Arthur Innes, ed., *Julius Caesar* (Boston: D. C. Heath, 1907), 105–6 (note to 3.1.47–48); S. F. Johnson, ed., *Julius Caesar* in *William Shakespeare: The Complete Works*, ed. Alfred Harbage (Baltimore, MD: Penguin, 1969), 913 (note to 3.1.47–48); and H. M. Richmond, *Shakespeare's Political Plays* (Gloucester, MA: Peter Smith, 1977), 206–7. The version of the line Jonson quotes is entirely consistent with Shakespeare's characterization of Julius Caesar. What seemed like an error to the prosaic Jonson may be just one more example of Shakespeare's poetic genius.

9. On this point, see chapter 1 of this volume, and also Cantor, *Shakespeare's Rome*, 74; and Allan Bloom, *Shakespeare's Politics* (New York: Basic Books, 1964), 80–87.

10. See Seth Benardete, *Achilles and Hector: The Homeric Hero* (South Bend, IN: St. Augustine's Press, 2005): "The play's motif is the transformation of Coriolanus from a man to a god" (72).

11. See G. Wilson Knight, *The Imperial Theme* (London: Methuen, 1965), 246.

12. Coriolanus introduces the image of himself as a dragon at 4.1.30. Roy Battenhouse points out that Shakespeare did not find the beast/god imagery in his principal source for *Coriolanus*: "Shakespeare's paradox, that of a beast-man apotheosized, is distinctly one of his major additions to the Plutarchan narrative. Nowhere in Plutarch was Coriolanus likened either to Mars or to a male tiger" (Roy W. Battenhouse, *Shakespearean Tragedy: Its Art and Its Christian Premises* [Bloomington: Indiana University Press, 1969], 320).

13. For discussions of the relevance of Aristotle's statement to *Coriolanus*, see F. N. Lees, "*Coriolanus*, Aristotle, and Bacon," *Review of English Studies* 1 (1950): 114–25; Maurice Charney,

Shakespeare's Roman Plays: The Function of Imagery in the Drama (Cambridge, MA: Harvard University Press, 1961), 187; and Allan Bloom, *Shakespeare's Politics*, 85–86. Lees points out that Shakespeare could have read Aristotle's *Politics* in an English translation published in London in 1598. For more on beasts and gods in the Roman plays, see Cantor, *Shakespeare's Rome*, 101–5, 205–6.

14. Aristotle, *The Politics*, trans. Carnes Lord (Chicago: University of Chicago Press, 1984), 37 (1253a in the standard numbering).

15. In the 1598 translation of the *Politics*, "man is a political animal" is translated "man is a Ciuill and sociable creature" (Lees, "*Coriolanus*, Aristotle, and Bacon," 118).

16. Aristotle, *Politics*, 37. In the 1598 translation, this passage is rendered: "he which naturally and not by accident or chaunce is cittilesse and unsociable, is to be esteemed either a wicked wretch, or more than a man" (Lees, "*Coriolanus*, Aristotle, and Bacon," 118).

17. Aristotle, *Politics*, 37. In the 1598 translation, this passage is rendered: "But he that can not abide to live in companie, or through sufficiencie hath need of nothing, is not esteemed a part or member of a Cittie, but is either a beast or a God" (Lees, "*Coriolanus*, Aristotle, and Bacon," 119). To show the currency of the "beast/god" phrase in Shakespeare's day, Lees points out that the 1625 version of Francis Bacon's essay "Of Friendship" begins by examining a statement (which he fails to attribute to Aristotle): "Whosoever is delighted in solitude, is either a wild beast or a god" (Lees, "*Coriolanus*, Aristotle, and Bacon," 123–24).

18. For an analysis of the issue of recognition, especially as it was developed by Hegel, see Alexandre Kojève, "Tyranny and Wisdom," in Leo Strauss, *On Tyranny* (Chicago: University of Chicago Press, 2000), particularly 145–47 and also the discussion of Alexander the Great on 169–71.

19. T. J. B. Spencer, ed., *Shakespeare's Plutarch* (Harmondsworth, UK: Penguin, 1964), 180 (in the *Life of Marcus Antonius*).

20. Note that Antony differs from the other two Roman heroes. Coriolanus and Julius Caesar aspire to stand alone—against and above the whole world. Antony pursues a different path to universality, as part of a loving couple with Cleopatra. Antony's "We stand up peerless" contrasts with Coriolanus's "Alone I did it" (5.6.115). But despite this difference, universality is still what is at stake for Antony, as it is for the other two Roman heroes.

21. On this point, see Strauss, *On Tyranny*, 89–90.

22. For an explanation of why I have restored the Folio reading "the little o' th'earth" in place of the usual editorial emendation "the little O, th' earth," see chapter 6, note 24.

23. For a fuller discussion of this issue, see Cantor, *Shakespeare's Rome*, 56–57, 76–77.

24. See ibid., 120–24.

25. For a fuller discussion of Nicanor, see ibid., 117–19.

26. The warriors in *Coriolanus* sometimes speak of their relationship as comrades-in-arms on the model of the relationship of husband and wife. See 1.6.29–32 and 4.5.113–18. The fact that Roman warfare is rooted in a kind of appetite is reflected in the many associations of war with eating in the play. See 1.1.249–50, 1.9.10–11, and 4.5.186–89.

27. See Cantor, *Shakespeare's Rome*, 176–80.

28. For the parallel between the activity of war and "boys pursuing summer butterflies," see *Coriolanus*, 4.6.92–95. On this point, see Benardete, *Achilles and Hector*, 73–74.

29. The Roman patricians appear intent on preserving the Volsces as enemies, perhaps as a way of using foreign wars to divert attention from domestic strife. Notice how certain the Volsces are after their defeat that their town will be "deliver'd back on good condition" (1.10.2).

Menenius calls attention to the frequency of wars with the Volsces within his "age" (4.6.50–52). Plutarch makes this point explicit in his *Life of Coriolanus*; he speaks of the patricians "hoping by the means of foreign war to pacify [the plebeians'] sedition at home" (Spencer, *Shakespeare's Plutarch*, 315).

30. Elsewhere Antony speaks of Caesar possessing "the most noble blood of all this world" (3.1.156). Even Brutus calls Caesar "the foremost man of all this world" (4.3.22)—just the kind of tribute from a political opponent that underwrites a ruler's achievement of universal recognition.

31. For the suggestion that the city is the "truest tragedy," see Plato, *Laws*, 817b. For the idea of the city as tragic, perhaps the closest parallel to Shakespeare's Roman plays is Thucydides's presentation of Athens in his history of the Peloponnesian War. On this subject, see the chapter on Thucydides in Leo Strauss, *The City and Man* (Chicago: Rand McNally, 1964), esp. 226–36, where he discusses "the questionable universalism of the city."

32. For a convenient collection of Hegel's writing on tragedy (translated into English), see Anne and Henry Paolucci, eds., *Hegel on Tragedy* (New York: Anchor Books, 1962).

33. Kaufmann, *Portable Nietzsche*, 467 (*Twilight of the Idols*, "Maxims and Arrows," #3).

Chapter Four

1. All quotations from Shakespeare are taken from G. Blakemore Evans, ed., *The Riverside Shakespeare* (Boston: Houghton Mifflin, 1974). Citations by act, scene, and line number are incorporated into the text.

2. On the reference to Plutarch here, see T. J. B. Spencer, ed., *Shakespeare's Plutarch* (Harmondsworth, UK: Penguin, 1964), 11–12. Critics differ as to whether Fluellen's comparison of Henry to Alexander casts him in a positive or a negative light. For a sampling of the variety of opinions, see Ronald S. Berman, "Shakespeare's Alexander: Henry V," *College English* 23 (1962): 532–39; Robert P. Merrix, "The Alexandrian Allusion in Shakespeare's *Henry V*," *English Literary Renaissance* 2 (1972) 321–33; Stephen Greenblatt, *Shakespearean Negotiations* (Berkeley: University of California Press, 1988), 57; and Judith Mossman, "*Henry V* and Plutarch's Alexander," *Shakespeare Quarterly* 45 (1994): 69–72.

3. From Plutarch's *Life of Brutus*, text from Geoffrey Bullough, ed., *Narrative and Dramatic Sources of Shakespeare*, vol. 5 (London: Routledge and Kegan Paul, 1964), 120.

4. Bullough, *Narrative and Dramatic Sources of Shakespeare*, 5:120.

5. Shakespeare detected another false Christian note in North's translation, and accordingly chose to omit Brutus's Hamlet-like reference to the impiety of suicide in North ("being no lawfull nor godly acte"). For similar analyses of this moment, see Geoffrey Miles, *Shakespeare and the Constant Romans* (Oxford: Clarendon, 1996), 114n13; and Gordon Braden, "Plutarch, Shakespeare and the Alpha Males," in *Shakespeare and the Classics*, ed. Charles Martindale and A. B. Taylor (Cambridge: Cambridge University Press, 2004), 182.

6. For a detailed discussion of this point, see chapter 1 of this volume, and Paul A. Cantor, *Shakespeare's Rome: Republic and Empire* (Ithaca, NY: Cornell University Press, 1976), 139–45.

7. This is the translation of Bernadotte Perrin in the Loeb Classical Library edition of *Plutarch's Lives* (Cambridge, MA: Harvard University Press, 1918), vol. 6, 217.

8. For accounts of the transmission of Plutarch's Greek text through Amyot's French to North's English, see M. W. MacCallum, *Shakespeare's Roman Plays and Their Background* (London: Macmillan, 1910), 95–167; R. H. Barrow, *Plutarch and His Times* (Bloomington: Indiana

University Press, 1967), 162–67; D. A. Russell, *Plutarch* (London: Duckworth, 1973), 143–58; and John Denton, "Plutarch, Shakespeare, Roman Politics, and Renaissance Translation," *Poetica* 48 (1997): 187–209.

9. For an examination of this passage in Amyot and North, see MacCallum, *Shakespeare's Roman Plays*, 184–85.

10. For the Jonson quotation, see his poetic tribute to Shakespeare in the original Shakespeare First Folio (1623).

11. For the importance of this particular scene, see Cantor, *Shakespeare's Rome*, 97. See also David C. Green, *Plutarch Revisited: A Study of Shakespeare's Last Roman Tragedies and Their Source* (Salzburg, Austria: Institut für Anglistik und Americanistik, 1979), 149–51. For an extended treatment of Shakespeare's use of Plutarch's comparisons, see E. A. J. Honigmann, "Shakespeare's Plutarch," *Shakespeare Quarterly* 10 (1959): 25–33.

12. Bullough, *Narrative and Dramatic Sources of Shakespeare*, 5:545.

13. For one example, see my discussion of the character of Nicanor in *Coriolanus* (whose name may have come from Plutarch's *Life of Phocion*) in *Shakespeare's Rome*, 218n24.

14. On this point, see Honigmann, "Shakespeare's Plutarch," 29; and Green, *Plutarch Revisited*, 1.

15. I discuss the unfinished character of the play in my essay "*Timon of Athens*: The Corrupt City and the Origins of Philosophy," *In-between: Essays & Studies in Literary Criticism* 4 (1995): 25–26. Among the signs that *Timon of Athens* may be unfinished are two important points. 1) The Alcibiades subplot is unusually sketchy, especially in act 3, scene 5, in which the principal character being discussed mysteriously goes unnamed. 2) Judging by the wide divergence in some of the financial figures in the play, Shakespeare appears to have been unsure as to the value of the monetary unit called a "talent," and when he keeps writing "so many talents" in act 3, scene 2 (lines 12, 24, and 36), he seems to be making a note to himself to go back and revise the text once he got the economic facts straight. On this point, see Terence Spencer, "Shakespeare Learns the Value of Money: The Dramatist at Work on *Timon of Athens*," *Shakespeare Survey* 6 (1953): 75–78. For more on the unfinished character of *Timon of Athens*, see Maurice Charney, introduction to *Timon of Athens* (New York: New American Library, 1965), xxi–xxii.

16. Bullough, *Narrative and Dramatic Sources of Shakespeare*, 5:455 (see also 6:239).

17. Bullough, *Narrative and Dramatic Sources of Shakespeare*, 5:257.

18. Consider Plutarch's description of Antony: "Things that seeme intolerable in other men, as to boast commonly, to jeast with one or other, to drinke like a good fellow with every body, to sit with the souldiers when they dine, and to eate and drink with them souldierlike: it is incredible what wonderfull love it wane him amongst them" (Bullough, *Narrative and Dramatic Sources of Shakespeare*, 5:257).

19. For an attempt to show that Plutarch's influence goes beyond mere details in Shakespeare and may have helped to shape one of his whole plays, see Mossman, "*Henry V* and Plutarch's Alexander," esp. 73: "In its almost exclusive focus on Henry, *Henry V* is much more like a life in the Plutarch manner than a chronicle history play.... *Henry V* ... has the structure of a classic Plutarch life, revolving around one central figure, with scenes and set pieces so contrived as to reveal the complex features of that dominating character.... [It] is quintessentially Plutarchan." In "Plutarch and Shakespeare's *Henry IV Parts 1 and 2*," *Poetica* 48 (1997): 99–117, Mossman extends her argument about Plutarch's influence on Shakespeare to two more of his history plays.

20. See Cantor, *Shakespeare's Rome*, esp. 21–52.

21. For the classic exposition of the contrast between Rome and Egypt in *Antony and Cleo-*

patra, see Maurice Charney, *Shakespeare's Roman Plays: The Function of Imagery in the Drama* (Cambridge, MA: Harvard University Press, 1961), esp. 93–112.

22. The one critic I have found who attempts to respond to my point about the Egyptianizing of Rome in *Antony and Cleopatra* is Vivian Thomas, who in his *Shakespeare's Roman Worlds* (London: Routledge, 1989), writes of my argument: "This last comment misrepresents the nature of the scene on Pompey's barge (including its essentially masculine nature which contrasts sharply with the deeply feminine associations of Egypt)" (12). Only the most literal-minded reading of act 2, scene 7 can view it as a traditionally Roman scene. Shakespeare goes out of his way to portray a Rome now thoroughly fascinated by, suffused with, and submitting to the erotic, Oriental spirit of Egypt. The Romans even dance "the Egyptian bacchanals" in this scene (2.7.104). The drunken behavior of the triumvirs hardly looks manly to the old-style Roman warriors in the scene (such as Menas and Enobarbus), who observe it with contempt.

23. For the importance of the contrast between spiritedness (Greek: *thumos*) and eros in Plutarch, and its relevance to Shakespeare's Roman plays, see the insightful discussion in Braden, "Plutarch, Shakespeare and the Alpha Males," esp. 194–202. Braden grasps the importance of Plato's tripartite division of the soul to both Plutarch and Shakespeare.

24. On the way that "a hero's faults and virtues are intimately related" in Plutarch in general and in his *Life of Coriolanus* in particular, see Christopher Pelling, "The Shaping of *Coriolanus*: Dionysius, Plutarch, and Shakespeare," *Poetica* 48 (1997): 20, 23, 31. At the beginning of his *Life of Demetrius*, whom he pairs with Antony, Plutarch writes that the two lives "confirm the saying of Plato, that from great minds both great virtues and great vices do proceed" (Roland Baughman, ed., *Plutarch's Lives: Translated by Sir Thomas North*, vol. 2 [New York: Heritage, 1941], 1584). For Shakespeare's plays as Plutarchan parallel lives, see Gary Wills, *Rome and Rhetoric: Shakespeare's Julius Caesar* (New Haven, CT: Yale University Press, 2011): "The technique of balancing strengths and weaknesses is woven through all of Plutarch's biographies, which usually begin with a prologue pointing out similarities between the Greek and Roman figures he is comparing, and then end with a comparison . . . stressing differences between them. This cross-cultural exercise is something Shakespeare was living with all the time he mined Plutarch's lives for his Roman plays" (114–16).

25. For this view, see Russell, *Plutarch*, 109; and John Roe, "'Character' in Plutarch and Shakespeare: Brutus, Julius Caesar, and Mark Antony," in Martindale and Taylor, *Shakespeare and the Classics*, 173–74. For a contrary view, see Barrow, *Plutarch and His Times*, 57–59.

26. For this view, see, e.g., C. P. Jones, *Plutarch and Rome* (Oxford: Clarendon Press, 1971), 103–9, esp. 109: "*The Parallel Lives* do not reveal a cleavage between Greeks and Romans, but rather their unity. They express an age in which Greeks became Roman consuls and commanded Roman armies, when emperors and future emperors could hold the archonship in Athens."

27. Earlier in his career, Plutarch evidently wrote a series of lives of the Roman emperors. Most of these have been lost; lives of Galba and Otho are all that survive of this series (they may be part of a single work). These two lives are sometimes included as a kind of appendix in editions of Plutarch's *Lives*, but everyone agrees that they should not be regarded as part of the *Parallel Lives* project.

28. See Mark Shiffman, "Plutarch among the Postcolonialists," *Perspectives on Political Science* 37 (2008): 223–30, esp. 223: "Plutarch's *Lives* is a massive meditation on noble statesmen of the Greek and Roman past, depicting vividly and attractively the virtues at home in the atmosphere of republican liberty. The collection has inspired generations of enthusiasts of republican, active self-government. . . . Plutarch . . . influenced the political imagination of the Ameri-

can federalists and antifederalists and was probably a principal inspiration of the civic spirit of Benjamin Franklin, whose favorite reading at age twelve was the *Lives*."

29. Shiffman, "Plutarch among the Postcolonialists," quotes one of the characters (Theon) in Plutarch's dialogues (*The Oracles at Delphi No Longer Given in Verse*) speaking on the Pax Romana: "For my part, I am well content with the settled conditions prevailing at present, and I find them very welcome. . . . There is, in fact, profound peace and tranquility; war has ceased, there are no wanderings of peoples, no civil strifes, no despotisms, nor other maladies and ills in Greece requiring many unusual remedial forces" (224).

30. For example, in the comparison of Dion and Brutus, Plutarch writes of Julius Caesar: "It seemed that he was a merciful physician whom God had ordained of special grace to be governor of the empire of Rome, and to set all things again at quiet stay, the which required the counsel and authority of an absolute prince" (Baughman, *Plutarch's Lives*, 2:1911). See also Plutarch's explanation of why Brutus had to lose the battle of Philippi: "Howbeit the state of Rome (in my opinion) being now brought to pass that it could no more abide to be governed by many lords but required one only absolute governor, God, to prevent Brutus that it should not come to his government, kept this victory [at sea] from his knowledge" (Spencer, *Shakespeare's Plutarch*, 165).

31. As Mark Shiffman formulates the question: "Is Plutarch an ardent republican like most of his modern admirers, or is he a provincial accommodationist to Roman dominion?" ("Plutarch among the Postcolonialists," 224). Hugh Liebert, in "Alexander the Great and the History of Globalization," *Review of Politics* 73 (2011): 533–60, initially presents Plutarch as a Greco-Roman syncretist: "Culturally, Plutarch was a native Greek at ease in the larger Roman world; politically, Plutarch was an active citizen of his local polis with excellent connections among the Roman ruling elite. His overlapping political and cultural allegiances surely helped to fashion the literary form of his most famous work, the *Parallel Lives*, in which biographies of Greek and Roman statesmen are presented in tandem and then compared with one another. These *Lives* are often read as though Plutarch's intent were to facilitate a harmonious fusion of Greek and Roman culture. Indeed, on several occasions Plutarch praises statesmen who manage to reconcile alien peoples to political coexistence" (545). But Liebert goes on to challenge this understanding of the *Lives*, wondering whether Plutarch set the Greek world of the polis and the Roman world of empire in opposition: "Plutarch makes Greece vs. Rome . . . the animating opposition of his *Lives*. Given that Plutarch wrote partly as a Greek under Roman hegemony, at a time when he could, on occasion, portray Greece's subjection to Rome as enslavement, penning contests between the leading historical figures of each culture was not an idle decision. . . . Plutarch often selects stories that reveal his interest in the tensions between empire and cities and between different cultural groups" (546). For further development of these ideas, see Hugh Liebert, *Plutarch's Politics: Between City and Empire* (Cambridge: Cambridge University Press, 2016).

32. See Emil Ludwig, introduction to Baughman, *Plutarch's Lives*: "[Plutarch] felt a symbolic quality in the pairing of Greek and Roman, since it enabled him to write, on a deeper level, the history of the two cultures" (xvi).

33. For more on this subject, see my essay "Literature and Politics: Understanding the Regime," *PS: Political Science & Politics* 28 (1995): 192–95. For the classical understanding of the regime, see especially books 8 and 9 of Plato's *Republic* and books 3 and 4 of Aristotle's *Politics*.

34. Perrin, *Plutarch's Lives*, 1:215 (*Life of Lycurgus*, 4.3–4). This important passage was called to my attention in Hugh Liebert, "Plutarch's Critique of Plato's Best Regime," *History of Political*

Thought 30 (2009): 269. Here is Liebert's translation of the concluding sentence (and his transliteration of the Greek): He "puts them alongside one another in order to theorize about the difference in their lives and in their regimes (*paraballōn apotheōresai tēn diaphoran tōn biōn kai tōn politeiōn*)." Here for comparison is North's translation of the whole passage: "At his departing out of Crete, he went into Asia, with intent (as it is said) to compare the manner of life and policy of those of Crete (being then very straight and severe) with the superfluities and vanities of Ionia and thereupon to consider the difference between their two manners and governments, as the physician doth, who to know the whole and healthful the better, doth use to compare them with the sick and diseased" (Baughman, *Plutarch's Lives*, 1:123–24). The notion of *politeia* as a way of life and a constitution is not as clear in North's translation as it is in Perrin's or Liebert's, but if Shakespeare did read this passage in North, he could have noted the link between "manners" and "government."

35. See Simon Swain, "Cultural Exchange in Plutarch's *Antony*," *Quaderni Urbinati di Cultura Classica*, N. S. 34 (1990): 151–57.

36. On this subject, see my essay "Literature and Politics," esp. 194–95. See also Allan Bloom, "Political Philosophy and Poetry," *Shakespeare's Politics* (New York: Basic Books, 1964), 1–12.

Chapter Five

1. Daniel Vitkus comes up with the same number of "Mediterranean" plays in Shakespeare's canon; see his *Turning Turk: English Theater and the Mulitcultural Mediterranean, 1570–1630* (New York: Palgrave, 2003), 39. One could quarrel over whether certain plays belong in the category, but such disputes are as likely to increase the number as reduce it. For example, if one includes *Two Noble Kinsmen* in the Shakespeare canon, then one comes up with a figure of twenty-one Mediterranean plays out of thirty-eight. Gary Taylor has argued that *Measure for Measure* had a Mediterranean setting as Shakespeare originally wrote it (specifically the Italian city of Ferrara) and that Thomas Middleton changed the setting to Vienna for a 1621 revival. See his "Shakespeare's Mediterranean *Measure for Measure*," in *Shakespeare and the Mediterranean*, ed. Tom Clayton, Susan Brock, and Vicente Forés (Newark: University of Delaware Press, 2004), 243–69. If Taylor is correct, we would end up with twenty-two out of thirty-eight Shakespeare plays with Mediterranean settings.

2. See Linda McJannet, "Genre and Geography: The Eastern Mediterranean in *Pericles* and *The Comedy of Errors*," in *Playing the Globe: Genre and Geography in English Renaissance Drama*, ed. John Gillies and Virginia Mason Vaughan (Madison / Teaneck, NJ: Fairleigh Dickinson University Press, 1998), 86–106.

3. Matthew Arnold's "Dover Beach" is a late avatar of an attitude prevalent among Shakespeare's contemporaries—that geographically and culturally, England lay on the periphery of Europe, with the Mediterranean and the classical past at its center.

4. An excellent example of New World criticism in Renaissance studies is Stephen Greenblatt, *Marvelous Possessions: The Wonder of the New World* (Chicago: University of Chicago Press, 1991).

5. For a good overview of this field, see Ania Loomba, *Shakespeare, Race, and Colonialism* (Oxford: Oxford University Press, 2002).

6. A pioneering example of this trend is Leslie A. Fiedler, *The Stranger in Shakespeare* (New York: Stein and Day, 1972), 199–253. See also Paul Brown, "'This thing of darkness I acknowledge mine': *The Tempest* and the Discourse of Colonialism," in *Political Shakespeare: New Essays in*

Cultural Materialism, ed. Jonathan Dollimore and Alan Sinfield (Ithaca, NY: Cornell University Press, 1985), 48–71. As Lawrence Danson writes of this critical trend, it "almost succeeded in transporting Prospero's island to the Caribbean and making Caliban an Amerindian" ("England, Islam, and the Mediterranean Drama: Othello and Others," *Journal for Early Modern Cultural Studies* 2 [2002]: 21).

7. All Shakespeare line references and quotations are taken from G. Blakemore Evans, ed., *The Riverside Shakespeare* (Boston: Houghton Mifflin, 1974). Act, scene, and line numbers are incorporated into the text.

8. For the connection to Montaigne, see Fiedler, *Stranger in Shakespeare*, 231; for the connection to the colonization reports, see Brown, "*The Tempest* and the Discourse of Colonialism," 48–51; and Stephen Greenblatt, *Shakespearean Negotiations* (Berkeley: University of California Press, 1988), 142–58.

9. See, e.g., Fiedler, *Stranger in Shakespeare*, 204–7, 229–30.

10. On the connections to Plato, see my essay "Prospero's Republic: The Politics of Shakespeare's *The Tempest*," in *Shakespeare as Political Thinker*, ed. John E. Alvis and Thomas G. West (Wilmington, DE: ISI, 2000), 241–59.

11. See, e.g., Vitkus, *Turning Turk*, 3–6, 9–10.

12. Ibid., 29: "The nearest and greatest empires of the day, the Spanish and the Turkish, were based in the Mediterranean world (almost dividing it in half)."

13. For a thoroughgoing study of literature and colonialism in the New World from the Spanish perspective, with references to the Ottoman Empire as well, see Barbara Fuchs, *Mimesis and Empire: The New World, Islam, and European Identities* (Cambridge: Cambridge University Press, 2001).

14. I have used the English language abridgment by Richard Ollard: Fernand Braudel, *The Mediterranean and the Mediterranean World in the Age of Philip II*, trans. Siân Reynolds (New York: Harper Collins, 1992). For Braudel's thoughts on the importance of the Mediterranean in the ancient world, see his *Memory and the Mediterranean*, trans. Siân Reynolds (New York: Alfred A. Knopf, 2001).

15. Braudel, *Mediterranean and the Mediterranean World*, 383.

16. Ibid., 403–4.

17. Ibid., 585–86.

18. Ibid., 584.

19. Ibid., 550. On Mediterranean hybridity, see also Vitkus, *Turning Turk*, 7–8, 14–15, 22–24. For a novel that does an excellent job of capturing the cultural hybridity of the Mediterranean world in the sixteenth century, see Amin Maalouf, *Leo the African*, trans. Peter Sluglett (London: Abacus, 1994).

20. Maalouf presents a similar view in his novel: "On the one hand there is Sulaiman, Sultan and Caliph of Islam, young, ambitious, with limitless power. . . . On the other hand there is Charles, King of Spain, even younger and no less ambitious, who has managed, by spending a small fortune, to get himself elected to the throne of the Holy Roman Empire. . . . These two men [are] the most powerful in the world" (*Leo the African*, 238).

21. Moors and Jews were allowed to remain in Spain if they converted to Christianity, but their loyalty to the new religion was suspect, and the religious harmony in sixteenth-century Spain was periodically broken by various forms of strife. See Fuchs, *Mimesis and Empire*, 7. For a concise overview of this subject, see Bernard Lewis, *Cultures in Conflict: Christians, Muslims, and Jews in the Age of Discovery* (New York: Oxford University Press, 1995).

22. For an excellent discussion of the significance of Renaissance Venice to Shakespeare, see Allan Bloom, *Shakespeare's Politics* (New York: Basic Books, 1964), 13–17. See also my essay "Religion and the Limits of Community in *The Merchant of Venice*," *Soundings* 70 (1987): 243–47. See also Danson, "England, Islam, and the Mediterranean Drama," 1–25.

23. As quoted in John Gillies, *Shakespeare and the Geography of Difference* (Cambridge: Cambridge University Press, 1994), 124.

24. I discuss the tension between tragedy and comedy in *The Merchant of Venice* in "Religion and the Limits of Community," 239–42, 255–57.

25. This point is discussed in Geraldo U. de Sousa, *Shakespeare's Cross-Cultural Encounters* (New York: Palgrave, 2002), 116. As another motive for Venice's hiring foreign mercenaries, de Sousa cites its fear of one of its own citizens becoming too powerful. He quotes the English traveler Fynes Moryson: "Besides that this State is not sufficiently furnished with men and more specially with native Commaunders and Generalls . . . to undertake (of their owne power without assistance) a war against the Sultane of Turky. This want of Courage, & especially the feare lest any Citizen becoming a great and popular Commaunder in the Warrs, might thereby have meanes to usurpe upon the liberty of their State, seeme to be the Causes that for their Land forces they seldome have any native Comaunders, and alwayes use a forrayne Generall." On this point, see also Vitkus, *Turning Turk*, 94.

26. I develop this point in my essay "*Othello*: The Erring Barbarian among the Supersubtle Venetians," *Southwest Review* 75 (1990): 296–319.

27. For a detailed discussion of these developments in the fine and the decorative arts, see Rosamond E. Mack, *Bazaar to Piazza: Islamic Trade and Italian Art, 1300–1600* (Berkeley: University of California Press, 2002).

28. See ibid., 179: "Sixteenth-century East-West trade and artistic exchange softened a clash of civilizations, establishing a historical precedent for cultural coexistence and mutual enrichment."

29. See Lisa Jardine and Jerry Brotton, *Global Interests: Renaissance Art Between East & West* (Ithaca, NY: Cornell University Press, 2000), 184. See also Vitkus, *Turning Turk*, 19–20.

30. Jardine and Brotton, *Global Interests*, 8.

31. Braudel, *Mediterranean and the Mediterranean World*, 442.

32. Ibid., 443. Vitkus, *Turning Turk*, quotes one of Queen Elizabeth's officials stating in 1590: "It is well known that the parts of Italy and Turkey will bear a greater trade than all parts of Christendom now in amity with her majesty" (26; see also 32).

33. Braudel, *Mediterranean and the Mediterranean World*, 445.

34. See, e.g., Sousa, *Shakespeare's Cross-Cultural Encounters*, 114–15. See also Vitkus, *Turning Turk*, 80.

35. For these parallels, see Murray J. Levith, *Shakespeare's Italian Settings and Plays* (New York: St. Martin's, 1989), 79–82.

36. Like most people, I used to think of any connection between English kings and Ottoman Turks as purely fanciful. Then in 2013 I visited Bodrum, Turkey (known as Halicarnassus in the ancient world, and thus the site of the ruins of the famous Mausoleum). To this day, Bodrum is dominated by a huge crusader castle in its harbor, the Castle of St. Peter, which contains an English Tower. According to a guidebook, "the top floor, the banqueting hall of the knights, has been restored in medieval style. Over the entrance of the banqueting hall are the arms of Henry IV (1399–1413) during whose reign the tower was built" (Bernard McDonagh, *Blue Guide: Turkey—The Aegean and Mediterranean Coasts* [London: A & C Black, 1989], 343).

In short, as part of the English contribution to crusader efforts in the eastern Mediterranean, Henry IV actually had a tower built in what is now modern Turkey. I do not know if Shakespeare was aware of this fact, but it does suggest that he correctly sensed a connection between the House of Lancaster and the crusader ideal.

37. Jerry Brotton, *The Renaissance Bazaar: From the Silk Road to Michelangelo* (Oxford: Oxford University Press, 2002), 3.

38. See Mack, *Bazaar to Piazza*, 4, 8.

39. Molly Greene, "Resurgent Islam: 1500–1700," in *The Mediterranean in History*, ed. David Abulafia (London: Thames & Hudson, 2003), 234.

40. The discovery of Mycenean pottery at the site of Troy is clear evidence of economic and cultural exchange between the Trojans and mainland Greeks.

41. See Jardine and Brotton, *Global Interests*, 76. See also Mack, *Bazaar to Piazza*, 157, 175.

42. See Brotton, *Renaissance Bazaar*, 115.

43. Jardine and Brotton, *Global Interests*, 62. See also Jerry Brotton, *Trading Territories: Mapping the Early Modern World* (London: Reaktion Books, 1997), 91–93, 98–100.

44. Brotton, *Renaissance Bazaar*, 50.

45. Burckhardt himself did not wish to overestimate the importance of classical antiquity to the Renaissance: "We must insist upon it, as one of the chief propositions of this book, that it was not the revival of classical antiquity alone, but its union with the genius of the Italian people, which achieved the conquest of the Western world" (Jacob Burckhardt, *The Civilization of the Renaissance in Italy*, vol. 1, trans. S. G. C. Middlemore [New York: Harper & Row, 1958], 175). This is only one example of how Jardine and Brotton criticize a caricature of Burckhardt, not what he actually wrote. For example, as if anticipating their argument about the contributions of the East to the West, Burckhardt wrote, "The knowledge and admiration of the remarkable civilization which Islam, particularly before the Mongol inundation, had attained was peculiar to Italy from the time of the crusades. This sympathy was fostered by the half-Mohammedan Government of some Italian princes, by dislike and contempt for the existing Church, and by constant commercial intercourse with the harbours of the Eastern and Southern Mediterranean" (Burckhardt, *Renaissance in Italy*, 2:474–75).

46. To this day, long after the demise of the Ottoman Empire, Turkey continues to pride itself on its classical heritage. It contains, of course, some of the most important sites of classical archaeology, including Ephesus, Pergamum, and the remains of Troy, and the Istanbul Archaeological Museums rank among the greatest repositories of Greek and Roman antiquities. Among the magnificent treasures in Istanbul are the Ephebe of Tralles and the so-called Alexander Sarcophagus, together with the most comprehensive display of Trojan artifacts in the world. See Alpay Pasinli, *Istanbul Archaeological Museums* (Istanbul: A Truizm Yayinlari, 2001). For more on the classical roots of the Ottoman Empire, see Rémi Brague, *Eccentric Culture: A Theory of Western Civilization*, trans. Samuel Lester (South Bend, IN: St. Augustine's Press, 2002), 115: "But what is a Turkish bath if not the ancient thermae forgotten in the Occident, but preserved in the Orient?"

47. *Othello* is Shakespeare's exploration of what an ancient, Achillean hero would look like to the modern Christian world, and indeed Venice eventually comes to view Othello as a savage (as he himself does in his final speech, when he identifies with the kind of "malignant and a turban'd Turk" [5.2.353] he has been fighting much of his life). And in many respects Venice with its modern Christian way of life appears alien to Othello, even though he is a professed Christian and thinks that be belongs in the city. Othello's insecurity about whether he is capable of understanding what may be lurking in the heart of a "supersubtle Venetian" (1.3.356) woman

like Desdemona is the deepest source of his tragedy. I develop this understanding of Othello as an ancient martial hero tragically displaced into a modern Christian community at length in my *Othello* essay.

48. I discuss this subject in chapter 6 of this volume and in my book *Shakespeare's Rome: Republic and Empire* (Ithaca, NY: Cornell University Press, 1976), esp. 23–26.

49. On hybridity in *Antony and Cleopatra*, see Sousa, *Shakespeare's Cross-Cultural Encounters*, 136, 152–55.

50. Evans, *Riverside Shakespeare*, 1619. On this scene, see also Gillies, *Shakespeare and the Geography of Difference*, 49, 201n26, and Jerry Brotton, "'This Tunis, sir, was Carthage': Contesting Colonialism in *The Tempest*," in *Post-Colonial Shakespeares*, ed. Ania Loomba and Martin Orkin (London: Routledge, 1998), 23–42.

51. I develop this point at length in my book *Shakespeare: Hamlet*, 2nd ed. (Cambridge: Cambridge University Press, 2004).

52. For the importance of classical epic language in *Othello*, see Reuben A. Brower, *Hero and Saint: Shakespeare and the Graeco-Roman Heroic Tradition* (Oxford: Oxford University Press, 1971), esp. 12–13.

Chapter Six

1. The line appears in Jonson's poetic tribute to Shakespeare in the original First Folio of his plays (1623).

2. Samuel P. Huntington, *The Clash of Civilizations and the Remaking of World Order* (NY: Simon & Schuster, 2003), 21.

3. The empire of Alexander the Great offers another ancient prototype of globalization. See Hugh Liebert, "Alexander the Great and the History of Globalization," *Review of Politics* 73 (2011): 533–60.

4. For a study of this subject, with wide-ranging geographic reference, see Ramsay Mac-Mullen, *Romanization in the Time of Augustus* (New Haven, CT: Yale University Press, 2000).

5. Looking at Rome and its colonies, MacMullen speaks "of the currents of influence flowing in both directions across the ancient world" (ibid., 16).

6. MacMullen discusses at length a parallel development: the Hellenizing of Rome as it expanded into the eastern Mediterranean; see ibid., 1–29. On the Hellenizing of Rome in *Julius Caesar*, see chapter 1 of this volume.

7. I discuss this subject at length in chapter 1 of this volume and in my book *Shakespeare's Rome: Republic and Empire* (Ithaca, NY: Cornell University Press, 1976).

8. All quotations from *Antony and Cleopatra* and other Shakespeare plays are taken from G. Blakemore Evans, ed., *The Riverside Shakespeare* (Boston: Houghton Mifflin, 1974); citations are incorporated into the body of the chapter, giving act, scene, and line numbers.

9. See G. Wilson Knight, *The Imperial Theme* (London: Methuen, 1965), 208–9.

10. On this subject, see Geraldo U. de Sousa, *Shakespeare's Cross-Cultural Encounters* (New York: Palgrave, 2002), 129–30.

11. MacMullen makes a similar point about Rome's encounter with Greek civilization: "The Romans, to no one's surprise, won out where arms, administration, and practical technology were in question. As to the rest, in familiar words, captive Greece took Rome captive" (*Romanization in the Time of Augustus*, 29). MacMullen is referring to the famous line from Horace's *Epistles*: "Graecia capta ferum victorem cepit" (book 2, lines 156–57).

12. On this subject, see Bill Ashcroft, Gareth Griffiths, and Helen Triffin, *The Empire Writes*

Back: Theory and Practice in Post-Colonial Literatures (London: Routledge, 1989), esp. 78–115. Machiavelli anticipated the "empire strikes back" idea in his *Discourses*: "And truly, similar cities or provinces avenge themselves against their conqueror without fighting and without blood, for by permeating it with their bad customs they expose it to being conquered by whoever assaults it. Juvenal in his *Satires* . . . [says] that through the acquisition of foreign lands, foreign customs entered Roman breasts, and in exchange for thrift and other very excellent virtues, 'gluttony and luxury have made their home and avenge a conquered world'" (2.19; *Discourses on Livy*, trans. Harvey C. Mansfield and Nathan Tarcov [Chicago: University of Chicago Press, 1996], 175). Shakespeare's Coriolanus raises the prospect of the empire striking back when, in his prophecy to the people who banished him, he predicts that their "ignorance" will "deliver you as most / Abated captives to some nation / That won you without blows" (3.3.131–33).

13. See Sousa, *Shakespeare's Cross-Cultural Encounters*, 152–55.

14. For a good analysis of this scene, see John Michael Archer, *Old Worlds: Egypt, Southwest Africa, India, and Russia in Early Modern English Writing* (Stanford, CA: Stanford University Press, 2001), 51–54.

15. On the worship of Isis among Romans, see the chapter on Egypt in Franz Cumont, *Oriental Religions in Roman Paganism*, authorized translation (1921; repr. New York: Dover, 1956), 73–102. One of the most remarkable sights among the ruins of Pompeii is the Temple of Isis. The wall paintings from this temple, housed in the National Archaeological Museum of Naples, are among the most beautiful and haunting (and proto-surrealist) of surviving Roman paintings. As Cumont documents, Isis made a deep impression on the Roman population.

16. On the adopting of the model of Hellenistic god-kings in Rome, see Ronald Syme, *The Roman Revolution* (Oxford: Oxford University Press, 1960), 54.

17. The Hellenic influences on Antony are evident throughout Plutarch's *Life of Marcus Antonius*; see Simon Swain, "Cultural Interchange in Plutarch's *Antony*," *Quaderni Urbinati di Cultura Classica*, N.S. 34 (1990):"Antony moves within three differing cultural systems— Roman, Hellenic, and Egyptian. Hellenic culture and philhellenism are clearly important in the *Life*" (151–52). On Antony's philhellenism, see T. J. B. Spencer, ed., *Shakespeare's Plutarch* (Harmondsworth, UK: Penguin, 1964): "At his first coming into Greece he was not hard nor bitter with the Grecians, but gave himself only to hear wise men dispute, to see plays, and also to note the ceremonies and sacrifices of Greece . . . ; and it pleased him marvelously to hear them call him *Philhellene* (as much as to say, 'a lover of the Grecians'), and specially the Athenians, to whom he did many great pleasures" (197).

18. Archer notes that "Antony is scapegoated for Rome's own covert Egyptianism and current decadence" (*Old Worlds*, 61). On Octavius's conduct as emperor, see Cumont, *Oriental Religions*: "When Rome had become a great cosmopolitan metropolis like Alexandria, Augustus reorganized it in imitation of the capital of the Ptolemies. . . . The absolute monarchy, theocratic and bureaucratic at the same time, that was the form of government of Egypt, Syria and even Asia Minor during the Alexandrine period was the ideal on which the deified Caesars gradually fashioned the Roman empire" (4–5). On Octavius/Augustus as a god, see also Syme, *Roman Revolution*, 473–74.

19. The classic study of this subject is Edward W. Said, *Orientalism* (NY: Vintage, 1979).

20. See Sousa, *Shakespeare's Cross-Cultural Encounters*, 136, 140; and Ania Loomba, *Shakespeare, Race, and Colonialism* (Oxford: Oxford University Press, 2002), 116–18.

21. One archetype of this kind of seductress is Dido in Vergil's *Aeneid*, who tries to prevent Aeneas from completing his divine mission of founding Rome. Shakespeare has Antony refer

to Dido and Aeneas at 4.14.53. For the relevance of the *Aeneid* to *Antony and Cleopatra*, see my comments in the "virtual roundtable" in *Poets and Critics Read Vergil*, ed. Sarah Spence (New Haven, CT: Yale University Press, 2001), 188–89.

22. Thus what I say in this chapter is compatible with what I say elsewhere about the contrast between Rome and Egypt being subordinated in Shakespeare's play to the contrast between the Roman Republic and the Roman Empire. The values of the West are to be found largely in the Republic; already in *Antony and Cleopatra* the Empire shows signs of succumbing to the lure of the East. With the benefit of hindsight, Shakespeare seems to be aware that in Antony's day, the center of gravity in the Roman Empire was moving eastward, a process that, centuries later, culminated in the emperor Constantine's transferring the Empire's capital to Constantinople. Antony anticipated this development in his desire to shift the capital of the Roman Empire to Alexandria.

23. For a good analysis of this process, see Loomba, *Shakespeare, Race, and Colonialism*, 120–27. Loomba is correct to speak of Antony as "going native" (130). The way the Roman general succumbs to the charms of Egypt anticipates a pattern that recurs in nineteenth- and twentieth-century British fiction of empire, story after story of colonial officers and officials on the imperial frontier losing their European discipline through fraternization with the natives (often specifically women). Among the classic "going native" narratives are Rudyard Kipling's "The Man Who Would Be King," Robert Louis Stevenson's *The Beach of Falesá*, Joseph Conrad's *Heart of Darkness* and *Lord Jim*, and Rider Haggard's *She*, perhaps the wildest of Orientalist fantasies. Haggard's exotic queen Ayesha is partly modeled on Cleopatra, and the novel is filled with Egyptian and ancient Greek lore. All these details point to *Antony and Cleopatra* and thus provide a link between Shakespeare's play and fiction of empire—a reminder of the way the British Empire supplies the middle term between the Roman Empire and modern globalization.

24. I have restored the original wording as it appears in the First Folio. Most modern editions accept a far-fetched emendation proposed by the eighteenth-century editor George Steevens, with the line reading "the little O, th'earth." This strange phrase then requires glossing, whereas the original wording makes perfect sense as it is. Indeed, Shakespeare seems to be creating a deliberate contrast between the colossal Antony and the worshipful subjects who now stand beneath him, "the little o' th' earth." The apotheosis of the Roman emperor reduces ordinary human beings to underlings, a point Cassius originally made about Julius Caesar: "Why, man, he doth bestride the narrow world / Like a Colossus, and we petty men / Walk under his huge legs" (*Julius Caesar*, 1.2.135–37). The Steevens emendation has the effect of downplaying the way Cleopatra's dream of Antony as a Colossus echoes Cassius's complaint about Julius Caesar. For the standard editorial position on this phrase, see Michael Neill, ed., *Anthony and Cleopatra* (Oxford: Oxford University Press, 1994), 308n81. Neill says that the Folio's "little o'th' earth" "makes no sense as it stands," even though in note 82, he draws the parallel with the Colossus passage in *Julius Caesar*, in which Cassius explicitly states that Caesar's status as a god makes ordinary Romans feel like little men. The one editor I have found who agrees with me on returning to the Folio Text at this point is John F. Andrews, ed., *William Shakespeare: Antony and Cleopatra* (London: J. M Dent, 1993), 80.

25. J. L. Simmons, *Shakespeare's Pagan World: The Roman Tragedies* (Charlottesville: University Press of Virginia, 1973), 159.

26. Cleopatra's dream of Antony as a single, universal deity illustrates a general principle articulated by Friedrich Nietzsche in his *Genealogy of Morals*: "the advance toward universal empires is always also an advance toward universal divinities; despotism with its triumph over

the independent nobility always prepares the way for some kind of monotheism" (*On the Genealogy of Morals and Ecce Homo*, trans. Walter Kaufmann [New York: Vintage, 1967], 90 [second essay, sec. 20]). As frequently happens, Nietzsche ends up inadvertently describing what occurs in *Antony and Cleopatra*, which shows Octavius Caesar triumphing over all his noble rivals and emerging as a kind of universal god in the newly unified Roman world. As Cumont writes of the actual historical developments: "The change of régime . . . brought about a change of religion. The increasing tendency of Caesarism toward absolute monarchy made it lean more and more upon the Oriental clergy. True to the traditions of the Achemenides and the Pharaohs, those priests preached doctrines tending to elevate the sovereign above humanity, and they supplied the emperors with dogmatic justification for their despotism" (Cumont, *Oriental Religions*, 38).

27. For an overview of the biblical allusions, see chapter 1 of this volume and Cantor, *Shakespeare's Rome*, 220–21n18.

28. This is the central thesis of Cumont's book, which culminates in this sentence: "The religious and mystical spirit of the Orient had slowly prepared all nations to unite in the bosom of a universal church" (Cumont, *Oriental Religions*, 211). See also Mikhail Ivanovich Rostovtzeff, *Rome*, trans. J. D. Duff (New York: Oxford University Press, 1960), 291–308.

29. Many thinkers, from Machiavelli to Nietzsche, have argued that imperial Rome prepared the way for the spread of Christianity, precisely in its role as a "globalizing" force. In material terms, the Roman Empire created the infrastructure—the roads and the trade routes—that made it possible for Christianity to spread as far and as quickly as it did (see Cumont, *Oriental Religions*, 24). But in a deeper, spiritual sense, the Roman Empire undermined the exclusiveness of the ancient cities—especially in religious terms—that stood in the way of any faith with universal aspirations. On this point, see Clifford Ando, "Was Rome a Polis?" *Classical Antiquity* 18 (1999): Rome made "Christian withdrawal from this world. . . . possible by lowering the place such cities held in the hearts of men" (30). For more on this subject, see Vickie Sullivan, "Alexander the Great as 'Lord of Asia' and Rome as His Successor in Machaiavelli's *Prince*," *Review of Politics* 75 (2013): 515–37. This essay helps to explain how "Asia" functions as a concept in Shakespeare's Roman plays. I also owe to this essay the reference to Nietzsche's *Genealogy of Morals* in note 26 of this chapter (see Sullivan, "Alexander the Great as 'Lord of Asia,'" 519).

30. On this point, see Sousa, *Shakespeare's Cross-Cultural Encounters*, 152.

31. From "The Manifesto of the Communist Party," in *Marx and Engels: Basic Writings on Politics and Philosophy*, ed. Lewis S. Feuer (Garden City, NY: Anchor, 1959), 10. Right after these words, Marx and Engels give one of the earliest descriptions of economic globalization: "The bourgeoisie has through its exploitation of the world market given a cosmopolitan character to production and consumption in every country. . . . It has drawn from under the feet of industry the national ground on which it stood. All old-established national industries have been destroyed or are daily being destroyed. They are dislodged by new industries . . . whose products are consumed not only at home, but in every quarter of the globe. . . . In place of the old local and national seclusion and self-sufficiency we have intercourse in every direction, universal interdependence of nations. . . . National one-sidedness and narrow-mindedness become more and more impossible" (10–11). As for the Marx/Engels phrase "all that is holy is profaned," compare Enobarbus's words about Cleopatra: "the holy priests / Bless her when she is riggish" (2.2.38–39).

32. See, e.g., Marshall Berman, *All That Is Solid Melts into Air: The Experience of Modernity* (New York: Penguin, 1988).

33. As a prime example of the way *Antony and Cleopatra* subtly refers to the rise of Chris-

tianity, these lines amount to quotations from the Revelation of John (cf. Rev., viii:10, x:6). The verbal parallels are clearer if one looks at the Geneva translation of the Bible, rather than the King James (the Geneva Bible was evidently the English translation Shakespeare was familiar with). These parallels were first noted in Ethel Seaton, "*Antony and Cleopatra* and the Book of Revelation," *Review of English Studies* 22 (1946): 219–24.

34. On this subject, see Tyler Cowen, *Creative Destruction: How Globalization Is Changing the World's Cultures* (Princeton, NJ: Princeton University Press, 2002).

35. Joseph A. Schumpeter, *Capitalism, Socialism and Democracy* (New York: Harper, 1975), 81–86.

36. Cleopatra, for example, uses the words: "die / With looking on his life" (1.5.33–34) and later says: "My desolation does begin to make / A better life" (5.2.1–2). Her encounter with the rustic clown who brings her the figs in act 5, scene 2 turns on the ambivalence of life and death.

37. On millennial and apocalyptic expectations during the age of Augustus, see Lidia Storoni Mazzolani, *The Idea of the City in Roman Thought: From Walled City to Spiritual Commonwealth*, trans. S. O'Donnell (Bloomington, IN: Indiana University Press, 1970), 218–41.

38. William Butler Yeats, "The Second Coming," *The Collected Poems of W. B. Yeats* (New York: Macmillan, 1956), 184–85. Yeats was fascinated by the theme of apocalyptic violence at the great turning points of history; see also his poems "Leda and the Swan" and "The Mother of God." Yeats saw parallels between the violent events in the twentieth century and those at the time of the founding of the Roman Empire and the birth of Christianity. See especially his play *Resurrection* and book 5 of his *A Vision*. Another modern play that resembles *Antony and Cleopatra* in the way that it portrays eastern decadence, Oriental despotism, apocalyptic fears, and the rise of Christianity is Oscar Wilde's *Salome*.

39. For another literary representation of the clash of civilizations when Europe encounters Egypt, see Bram Stoker's Gothic mummy novel, *The Jewel of Seven Stars* (1903). Throughout modern popular culture, reanimated mummies have embodied Western anxieties about the destructive potential of forces coming out of the East.

40. In similar terms, MacMullen raises the question whether Romanization should be understood as a "push" or a "pull" phenomenon. He contrasts the idea that Roman authorities pushed Roman civilization on conquered people with the idea that the pull (the allure) of Roman civilization is what led people to imitate it. For example, he writes of the unified Roman monetary system: "The fact that at the end of Augustus' reign the whole region had come under a single precious-metal currency system . . . arose out of no central pressure or policy at all. It was a result rather of unhurried market behavior and the realities of power expressed in numberless situations ad hoc" (*Romanization in the Time of Augustus*, 6). Studying multiple examples of Romanization, MacMullen does not find "a Roman will to unify all subjects under a single set of regulations" (11). In the case of the imitation of Roman architecture around the Mediterranean, MacMullen says that we need to resist "the temptation to infer a push from the center in explanation of all the copying, that is, the Romanization, that so plainly went on in the provinces of Augustus' time. For 'push' read 'propaganda,' for 'center' read 'regime,' and the next word out is 'ideology.' No term is more prominent in recent treatments of Augustan art and architecture, importing quite anachronistic assumptions, quite unsupported by evidence, into the discussion. The emperor had no interest at all in how people decorated the walls of their homes. What explains the rapidity of imitation was pull, not push" (113). MacMullen stresses "the intrinsic attractiveness of the Roman way of life seen through the eyes of the indigenous population. . . . Baths and wine and so forth recommended themselves to the senses without

need of an introduction. They felt or they looked good. . . . The natives . . . *pulled* Roman civilization to them—to their homes, their families, their world. It used to be supposed that acculturation was more a matter of push. . . . [But] what determined choice were local tastes, not imperial 'ideology.' . . . It was the eagerness particularly of the urban well-to-do, the pull of that rich class, that so greatly accelerated the process" (134–37). My contention is that Shakespeare develops a similar understanding of the Egyptianizing of Rome. His Romans feel the "pull" of Egyptian civilization; it is not "pushed" on them. In understanding globalization today, we need to bear in mind that it may be more a matter of "pull" than of "push." Much of what we call globalization takes place through channels of trade and other normal forms of interaction between individuals, which do not require governmental apparatus or other forms of central planning. For example, the globalization of the English language is often presented as the result of governments pushing English on their citizens; in fact, the spread of English is more a matter of "pull," of people around the globe spontaneously wanting to learn English for their own personal reasons. On this subject, see David Northrup, *How English Became the Global Language* (New York: Palgrave Macmillan, 2013).

41. Archer perceptively speaks of Antony as "a European sightseer in Egypt" and even "a travel writer" (*Old Worlds,* 54–55).

42. Consider what Marx and Engels say about economic globalization: "In place of the old wants, satisfied by the productions of the country, we find new wants, requiring for their satisfaction the products of distant lands and climes" (Feuer, *Marx and Engels,* 11). It is remarkable how well these words characterize the "globalized" world of *Antony and Cleopatra.*

Index

Lightning Source UK Ltd.
Milton Keynes UK
UKHW012113050422
401139UK00001B/104

9 780226 462516